British Political Facts Since 1979

British Political Facts Since 1979

David Butler

and

Gareth Butler

palgrave
macmillan

First published in 2006 by
PALGRAVE MACMILLAN
Houndmills, Basingstoke, Hampshire RG21 6XS and
175 Fifth Avenue, New York, N.Y. 10010
Companies and representatives throughout the world.

PALGRAVE MACMILLAN is the global academic imprint of the Palgrave Macmillan division of St. Martin's Press, LLC and of Palgrave Macmillan Ltd. Macmillan® is a registered trademark in the United States, United Kingdom and other countries. Palgrave is a registered trademark in the European Union and other countries.

ISBN-13: 978–1–4039–0372–3 hardback
ISBN-10: 1–4039–0372–7 hardback
ISBN-13: 978–1–4039–0373–0 paperback
ISBN-10: 1–4039–0373–5 paperback

This book is printed on paper suitable for recycling and made from fully managed and sustained forest sources.

A catalogue record for this book is available from the British Library.

A catalog record for this book is available from the Library of Congress.

10 9 8 7 6 5 4 3 2 1
15 14 13 12 11 10 09 08 07 06

Printed and bound in Great Britain by
Antony Rowe Ltd, Chippenham and Eastbourne

Contents

Introduction

British Political Facts 1900–2000 was the eighth edition of a work started in 1960. It was an endeavour to set out in compact and accessible form the essential facts and statistics of recent politics. The book grew as more years were covered and as government became more complicated.

The time has come to start again. The twentieth-century volume will, it is hoped, stay in print. But a new approach is needed for the twenty-first century. In the pages that follow all the essential elements of the old work are preserved but often arranged in a new format. However new material and time series, not available to a work that tried to treat 1900 and 1999 equally, are offered here.

Government and Local Authorities now produce much more material about their activities – although some non-government organisations, notably the political parties, produce rather less. But the preparation of reference works has been transformed in recent years by the arrival of the internet. Scholars can now call up from their computers a vast body of data. The great bulk of the information in this book is publicly available on the internet, for those who know where and how to look. We have tried to include appropriate source references.

Because we are starting the book only in 1979, we have been able to include much new information which was not in the old book. The new *British Political Facts* records the share of GDP spent on health, and the percentage of school-leavers going on to university. We now provide information about occupations of politicians in the index of ministers, for example, and much more detailed economic data – the book now sets out the rate of inflation in October 1988, and the growth rate in June 1992.

We have not been rigorously consistent on the starting date for this volume. In many cases we have included names and statistics relating to the period of the 1974–79 Labour Government, even though the rationale for the 1979 start date is of course the election of Mrs Thatcher as Prime Minister on 3 May. We took the view that few readers will be offended if we include a little extra information.

Many of the other rules which applied to previous editions have survived intact. We continue to confine ourselves to *British* material; although there is an expanded chapter on International Relations, our consideration of other countries is seen through the prism of British government policy. There is very limited international comparison in the social and economic statistics.

Equally, we confine ourselves to the *Political*. In the 1979–2005 period, we have taken the view that religious institutions played virtually no part in politics, and we have jettisoned that chapter (influenced, also, by the fact that the statistics on religious affiliations provided by different churches and faiths are extremely suspect, and not really comparable with each other). Monarchy has survived, but in a very limited form, appended to the Parliament chapter.

Facts remain sacrosanct. While we have doubtless made some mistakes, we have done our best throughout to confine ourselves to demonstrable fact. As far as possible we have tried to avoid making subjective judgements (although it is impossible to avoid them in the Allusions chapter). In the 1900–2000 book, some of the statistical time series were creaking with the effort to align the figures on a comparable basis over the whole century. The 1979–2005 statistics are much more robust, drawing as ever on the excellent *Annual Abstract of Statistics* and other Office of National Statistics publications.

In many areas the time frame of the new book allows us to adapt to the changing political agenda. Health and education statistics are improved, while the Commonwealth takes a less prominent place. Finding data on the use of the internet as a news provider has proved difficult, but it takes its place in the new Media chapter. In the Public Sector pages, now part of the Economy chapter, government regulators now take up more space than heads of nationalised industries – another sign of the times.

The old book was organised into four or five very meaty chapters at the front (which we believe were the most heavily used), and a long 'tail' of shorter and shorter chapters with less and less substance. Though very few sections have been lost – apart from Royalty and Religion, mentioned above – we have tried to rationalise the book into a smaller number of weightier chapters, while preserving the early chapters in much the same format. It makes sense to combine local government with devolution, for example, because the London Mayor sits squarely across both; and there is little logic to maintaining a distinction between Britain's relations with Canada or Australia (previously in the Commonweath chapter) and relations with France or Turkey (in the old International Relations).

In previous editions we have included acknowledgements to all the many librarians, scholars and others who have helped and advised us on compiling this book. We are starting again with a clean slate in 2005, so we hope those who have contributed to previous editions will forgive their omission from the acknowledgements this time. The House of Commons Library and the BBC's Political Research Unit remain the most invaluable sources of data. Much of their material already has at least limited public circulation but we are grateful for their help in enabling us to locate what we need. The government departments and political parties have been most helpful. Colleagues at Nuffield College, Oxford and particularly in the Nuffield College library have always been generously supportive. But we should end by thanking the many readers of past editions who have sent in corrigenda. Since error is inevitable in a work of this sort, may we urge them to continue in their friendly monitoring.

I
Ministries

Ministers in the Cabinet are printed in **BOLD TYPE CAPITALS** throughout this section. Ministers outside the Cabinet and Ministers of State are printed in CAPITALS. Junior ministers are in ordinary print. The seven leading offices are placed first in each Ministry; the remainder are arranged alphabetically, except for the Law Officers and the political appointments to the Royal Household which are placed at the end together with the Treasury appointments reserved for whips.

In these lists – and throughout the book – titles are placed in brackets if acquired during the tenure of office or on transfer to the next office. U-S. denotes Under-Secretary; F.S. Financial Secretary; P.S. Parliamentary Secretary.

This section has been sub-divided chronologically at changes of Prime Minister, except when few other offices changed hands.

CONSERVATIVE GOVERNMENT 1979–90

P.M.	**MARGARET**		*F.S.*	N. LAWSON	6 May 79
	THATCHER	4 May 79–		N. RIDLEY	30 Sep 81
		28 Nov 90		J. MOORE	18 Oct 83
Min. of State	P. CHANNON	7 May 79		N. LAMONT	21 May 86
Civil Service	B. HAYHOE	5 Jan 81		P. LILLEY	24 Jul 89
Dept	*(Department abolished 12 Nov 81)*			F. MAUDE	14 Jul 90
Ld Pres.	**Ld SOAMES**	5 May 79	*Econ.*	J. BRUCE-GARDYNE	11 Nov 81
	F. PYM	14 Sep 81	*Sec.*	J. MOORE	13 Jun 83
	J. BIFFEN	7 Apr 82		I. STEWART	18 Oct 83
	Vt WHITELAW	11 Jun 83		P. LILLEY	13 Jun 87
	J. WAKEHAM	10 Jan 88		R. RYDER	24 Jul 89
	Sir G. HOWE	24 Jul 89		J. MAPLES	24 Jul 90
	J. MACGREGOR	2 Nov 90	*Min. of*	P. REES	6 May 79–14 Sep 81
Min. of	E. of GOWRIE	11 Jun 83	*State*	Ld COCKFIELD	6 May 79–6 Apr 82
State, Privy	*(office vacant 11 Sept 84)*			J. BRUCE-GARDYNE	15 Sep 81–
Council	R. LUCE	2 Sep 85			11 Nov 81
Office	D. MELLOR	24 Jul 90		B. HAYHOE	11 Nov 81–2 Sep 85
Ld Chanc.	**Ld HAILSHAM**	5 May 79		J. WAKEHAM	6 Apr 82–13 Jun 83
	Ld HAVERS	13 Jun 87		I. GOW	2 Sep 85–19 Nov 85
	Ld MACKAY			P. BROOKE	19 Nov 85–13 Jun 87
	of CLASHFERN	26 Oct 87		*(office vacant)*	
Privy Seal	**Sir I. GILMOUR**	5 May 79	*For. &*	**Ld CARRINGTON**	5 May 79
	H. ATKINS	14 Sep 81	*Comm. O.*	**F. PYM**	6 Apr 82
	Lady YOUNG	6 Apr 82		**Sir G. HOWE**	11 Jun 83
	J. BIFFEN	11 Jun 83		**J. MAJOR**	24 Jul 89
	J. WAKEHAM	13 Jun 87		**D. HURD**	26 Oct 89
	Ld BELSTEAD	10 Jan 88	*Min. of*	D. HURD	6 May 79–11 Jun 83
Exchequer	**Sir G. HOWE**	5 May 79	*State*	N. RIDLEY	6 May 79–29 Sep 81
	N. LAWSON	11 Jun 83		P. BLAKER	6 May 79–29 May 81
	J. MAJOR	26 Oct 89		R. LUCE	30 Sep 81–5 Apr 82
Chief Sec.	**J. BIFFEN**	5 May 79		Ld BELSTEAD	5 Apr 82–13 Jun 83
	L. BRITTAN	5 Jan 81		C. ONSLOW	5 Apr 82–13 Jun 83
	P. REES	11 Jun 83		R. LUCE	11 Jun 83–2 Sep 85
	J. MACGREGOR	2 Sep 85		Lady YOUNG	13 Jun 83–13 Jun 87
	J. MAJOR	13 Jun 87		M. RIFKIND	13 Jun 83–11 Jan 86
	N. LAMONT	24 Jul 89		T. RENTON	2 Sep 85–13 Jun 87

CONSERVATIVE GOVERNMENT 1979–90 (*contd.*)

	Lynda CHALKER	11 Jan 86–24 Jul 89
	Ld GLENARTHUR	13 Jun 87–24 Jul 89
	D. MELLOR	13 Jun 87–26 Jul 88
	W. WALDEGRAVE	26 Jul 88–2 Nov 90
	Ld BRABAZON of	
	TARA	24 Jul 89–24 Jul 90
	F. MAUDE	24 Jul 89–14 Jul 90
	T. GAREL-JONES	14 Jul 90–28 Nov 90
	E of CAITHNESS	14 Jul 90–28 Nov 90
	D. HOGG	2 Nov 90–28 Nov 90
Min. of	N. MARTEN	8 Oct 79
State	T. RAISON	6 Jan 83
(Overseas	C. PATTEN	10 Sep 86
Dev.)	Lynda CHALKER	24 Jul 89
U-S.	R. Luce	6 May 79
	Ld Trefgarne	14 Sep 81
	M. Rifkind	6 Apr 82
	R. Whitney	13 Jun 83
	T. Renton	11 Sep 84
	T. Eggar	2 Sep 85
	T. Sainsbury	24 Jul 89
	M. Lennox-Boyd	24 Jul 90
Home O.	**W. WHITELAW**	5 May 79
	L. BRITTAN	11 Jun 83
	D. HURD	3 Sep 85
	D. WADDINGTON	26 Oct 89
Min. of	T. RAISON	6 May 79–6 Jan 83
State	L. BRITTAN	6 May 79–5 Jan 81
	P. MAYHEW	5 Jan 81–13 Jun 83
	D. WADDINGTON	6 Jan 83–13 Jun 87
	D. HURD	13 Jun 83–11 Sep 84
	Ld ELTON	11 Sep 84–25 Mar 85
	G. SHAW	11 Sep 84–10 Sep 86
	E of CAITHNESS	10 Sep 86–10 Jan 88
	D. MELLOR	10 Sep 86–13 Jun 87
	J. PATTEN	13 Jun 87–28 Nov 90
	T. RENTON	13 Jun 87–28 Oct 89
	Earl FERRERS	10 Jan 88–28 Nov 90
	D. MELLOR	27 Oct 89–22 Jul 90
	Angela RUMBOLD	23 Jul 90–28 Nov 90
U-S.	Ld Belstead	7 May 79–6 Apr 82
	Ld Elton	6 Apr 82–11 Sep 84
	D. Mellor	6 Jan 83–10 Sep 86
	Ld Glenarthur	27 Mar 85–10 Sep 86
	D. Hogg	10 Sep 86–26 Jul 89
	P. Lloyd	25 Jul 89–28 Nov 90
Ag. Fish.	**P. WALKER**	5 May 79
& Food	**M. JOPLING**	11 Jun 83
	J. MACGREGOR	13 Jun 87
	J. S. GUMMER	24 Jul 89
Min. of	Earl FERRERS	7 May 79–13 Jun 83
State	A. BUCHANAN-SMITH	7 May 79–13 Jun 83

	J. MACGREGOR	13 Jun 83–2 Sep 85
	J. S. GUMMER	2 Sep 85–26 Jul 88
	Ld BELSTEAD	13 Jun 83–13 Jun 87
	Lady TRUMPINGTON	28 Sep 89–28 Nov 90
U-S.	J. Wiggin	7 May 79–29 Sep 81
	Peggy Fenner	14 Sep 81–10 Sep 86
	D. Thompson	10 Sep 86–25 Sep 87
	Lady Trumpington	13 Jun 87–28 Sep 89
	R. Ryder	25 Jul 88–24 Jul 89
	D. Curry	26 Jul 89–28 Nov 90
	D. Maclean	26 Jul 89–28 Nov 90
Min. for	**N. ST JOHN-STEVAS**	5 May 79
the Arts	(*office out of Cabinet*)	
	P. CHANNON	5 Jan 81
	E of GOWRIE	13 Jun 83
	(*D.Lanc. & office in*	
	Cabinet 11 Sep 84)	
	E of GOWRIE	11 Sep 84
	(*office out of Cabinet*)	
	R. LUCE	2 Sep 85
	D. MELLOR	23 Jul 90
Defence	**F. PYM**	5 May 79
	J. NOTT	5 Jan 81
	M. HESELTINE	6 Jan 83
	G. YOUNGER	9 Jan 86
	T. KING	24 Jul 89
Min. of	Ld STRATHCONA	6 May 79
State	Vt TRENCHARD	5 Jan 81–29 May 81
Min. of	P. BLAKER	29 May 81
State	J. STANLEY	13 Jun 83
(Armed	I. STEWART	13 Jun 87
Forces)	A. HAMILTON	25 Jul 88
Min. of	Vt TRENCHARD	29 May 81
State		
Defence	G. PATTIE	6 Jan 83
(Procure-	A. BUTLER	11 Sep 84
ment)	N. LAMONT	2 Sep 85
	Ld TREFGARNE	21 May 86
	A. CLARK	24 Jul 89
Min. of	Ld TREFGARNE	2 Sep 85–21 May 86
State (Defence Support)		
U-S. Army	B. Hayhoe	6 May 79
	P. Goodhart	5 Jan 81–29 May 81
U-S. Navy	K. Speed	6 May 79–18 May 81
U-S. Air	G. Pattie	6 May 79–29 May 81
	(*Defence Dept reorganised May 81*)	
U-S.	P. Goodhart	29 May 81–30 Sep 81
(Armed	J. Wiggin	15 Sep 81–11 Jun 83
Forces)	Ld Trefgarne	13 Jun 83–1 Sep 85
	R. Freeman	21 May 86–15 Dec 88
	M. Neubert	19 Dec 88–23 Jul 90

CONSERVATIVE GOVERNMENT 1979–90 (*contd.*)

U-S.(Def.	G. Pattie	29 May 81		J. Lee	10 Sep 86–26 Jul 89
Procure.)	I. Stewart	6 Jan 83		P. Nicholls	13 Jun 87–28 Jul 90
	J. Lee	18 Oct 83		Ld Strathclyde	26 Jul 89–24 Jul 90
	A. Hamilton	10 Sep 86		R. Jackson	24 Jul 90–28 Nov 90
	T. Sainsbury	13 Jun 87		Vt Ullswater	24 Jul 90–28 Nov 90
	E of Arran	25 Jul 89		E. Forth	24 Jul 90–28 Nov 90
	K. Carlisle	26 Jul 90	Energy	**D. HOWELL**	5 May 79
Educ. &	**M. CARLISLE**	5 May 79		**N. LAWSON**	14 Sep 81
Science	**Sir K. JOSEPH**	14 Sep 81		**P. WALKER**	11 Jun 83
	K. BAKER	21 May 86		**C. PARKINSON**	13 Jun 87
	J. MACGREGOR	24 Jul 89		**J. WAKEHAM**	24 Jul 89
	K. CLARKE	2 Nov 90	Min. of	H. GRAY	7 May 79
Min. of	Lady YOUNG	7 May 79–14 Sep 81	State	A. BUCHANAN-SMITH	13 Jun 83
State	P. CHANNON	5 Jan 81–13 Jun 83		P. MORRISON	13 Jun 87
	C. PATTEN	5 Sep 85–10 Sep 86		(office vacant 26 Jul 90)	
	Angela RUMBOLD	10 Sep 86–24 Jul 90	U-S.	N. Lamont	7 May 79–5 Sep 81
	T. EGGAR	24 Jul 90–28 Nov 90		J. Moore	7 May 79–13 Jun 83
U-S.	R. Boyson	7 May 79–13 Jun 83		D. Mellor	15 Sep 81–6 Jan 83
	N. Macfarlane	7 May 79–15 Sep 81		E of Avon	6 Jan 83–11 Sep 84
	W. Shelton	15 Sep 81–13 Jun 83		G. Shaw	13 Jun 83–11 Sep 84
	W. Waldegrave	15 Sep 81–13 Jun 83		A. Goodlad	11 Sep 84–13 Jun 87
	P. Brooke	13 Jun 83–19 Nov 85		D. Hunt	11 Sep 84–13 Jun 87
	R. Dunn	13 Jun 83–26 Jul 88		M. Spicer	13 Jun 87–3 Jan 90
	G. Walden	19 Nov 85–13 Jun 87		Lady Hooper	26 Jul 88–28 Jul 89
	Lady Hooper	13 Jun 87–26 Jul 88		T. Baldry	3 Jan 90–28 Nov 90
	R. Jackson	13 Jun 87–24 Jul 90		C. Moynihan	24 Jul 90–28 Nov 90
	J. Butcher	26 Jul 88–24 Jul 89	Env.	**M. HESELTINE**	5 May 79
	A. Howarth	24 Jul 89–28 Nov 90		**T. KING**	6 Jan 83
	M. Fallon	24 Jul 90–28 Nov 90		**P. JENKIN**	11 Jun 83
Emp.	**J. PRIOR**	5 May 79		**K. BAKER**	2 Sep 85
	N. TEBBIT	14 Sep 81		**N. RIDLEY**	21 May 86
	T. KING	16 Oct 83		**C. PATTEN**	24 Jul 89
	Ld YOUNG of		Min. of	T. KING	6 May 79
	GRAFFHAM	2 Sep 85	State (Loc.	Ld BELLWIN	6 Jan 83
	N. FOWLER	13 Jun 87	Govt)	K. BAKER	11 Sep 84
	M. HOWARD	3 Jan 90		W. WALDEGRAVE	2 Sep 85
Min. of	E of GOWRIE	7 May 79–15 Sep 81		R. BOYSON	10 Sep 86
State	M. ALISON	15 Sep 81–13 Jun 83		M. HOWARD	13 Jun 87
	P. MORRISON	13 Jun 83–2 Sep 85		J. S. GUMMER	25 Jul 88
	J. S. GUMMER	18 Oct 83–11 Sep 84		D. HUNT	25 Jul 89
	K.CLARKE	2 Sep 85–13 Jun 87		M. PORTILLO	4 May 90
	(Paym.-Gen. and in Cabinet)		Min. of	J. STANLEY	7 May 79
	J. COPE	13 Jun 87–25 Jul 89	State	I. GOW	13 Jun 83
	T. EGGAR	25 Jul 89–23 Jul 90	(Housing)	J. PATTEN	2 Sep 85
	(office vacant)			W. WALDEGRAVE	13 Jun 87
U-S.	J. Lester	7 May 79–5 Jan 81		E of CAITHNESS	25 Jul 88
	P. Mayhew	7 May 79–5 Jan 81		M. HOWARD	25 Jul 89
	D. Waddington	5 Jan 81–6 Jan 83		M. SPICER	3 Jan 90
	P. Morrison	5 Jan 81–13 Jun 83	Min. of	Ld ELTON	27 Mar 85
	J. S. Gummer	6 Jan 83–18 Oct 83	State	W. WALDEGRAVE	10 Sep 86
	A. Clark	13 Jun 83–24 Jan 86		Ld BELSTEAD	13 Jun 87
	P. Bottomley	11 Sep 84–23 Jan 86		E of CAITHNESS	10 Jan 88
	D. Trippier	2 Sep 85–13 Jun 87		M. HOWARD	25 Jul 88
	I. Lang	31 Jan 86–10 Sep 86		D. TRIPPIER	24 Jul 89

CONSERVATIVE GOVERNMENT 1979–90 (*contd.*)

U-S. *(Sport)*	H. Monro	7 May 79–30 Sep 81
	N. MacFarlane	15 Sep 81–2 Sep 85
	R. Tracy	7 Sep 85–13 Jun 87
	C. Moynihan	22 Jun 87–26 Jul 90
	R. Atkins	26 Jul 90–28 Nov 90
U-S.	M. Fox	7 May 79–5 Jan 81
	G. Finsberg	7 May 79–15 Sep 81
	Ld Bellwin	7 May 79–6 Jan 83
	G. Shaw	5 Jan 81–13 Jun 83
	Sir G. Young	15 Sep 81–10 Sep 86
	W. Waldegrave	13 Jun 83–2 Sep 85
	E of Avon	11 Sep 84–27 Mar 85
	Angela Rumbold	2 Sep 85–10 Sep 86
	Ld Skelmersdale	10 Sep 86–13 Jun 87
	C. Chope	10 Sep 86–22 Jul 90
	Marion Roe	13 Jun 87–26 Jul 88
	D. Trippier	13 Jun 87–23 Jul 89
	Virginia Bottomley	25 Jul 88–28 Oct 89
	Ld Hesketh	31 Jan 89–2 Nov 90
	D. Heathcoat-Amory	28 Oct 89–28 Nov 90
	P. Nicholls	26 Jul 90–12 Oct 90
	Ld Strathclyde	26 Jul 90–7 Sep 90
	Lady Blatch	7 Sep 90–28 Nov 90
	R. Key	12 Oct 90–28 Nov 90
Health & *Soc.* *Security* *(Social* *Services)*	**P. JENKIN**	5 May 79
	N. FOWLER	14 Sep 81
	J. MOORE	13 Jun 87
	(Social Security a separate Dept 25 Jul 88)	
Health	**K. CLARKE**	25 Jul 88
	W. WALDEGRAVE	2 Nov 90
Min. of *State* *(Health)*	G. VAUGHAN	7 May 79
	K. CLARKE	5 Mar 82
	B. HAYHOE	2 Sep 85
	A. NEWTON	10 Sep 86
	D. MELLOR	25 Jul 88
	Ld TRAFFORD	25 Jul 89
	Virginia BOTTOMLEY	28 Oct 89
Min. of *State* *(Social* *Security)*	R. PRENTICE	7 May 79
	H. ROSSI	5 Jan 81
	R. BOYSON	12 Jun 83
	A. NEWTON	11 Sep 84
	J. MAJOR	10 Sep 86
	N. SCOTT	13 Jun 87
U-S.	Sir G. Young	7 May 79–15 Sep 81
	Lynda Chalker	7 May 79–5 Mar 82
	G. Finsberg	15 Sep 81–14 Jun 83
	Ld Elton	15 Sep 81–6 Apr 82
	A. Newton	5 Mar 82–11 Sep 84
	Ld Trefgarne	6 Apr 82–14 Jun 83
	J. Patten	14 Jun 83–2 Sep 85
	Ld Glenarthur	14 Jun 83–26 Mar 85
	R. Whitney	11 Sep 84–10 Sep 86
	Lady Trumpington	30 Mar 85–13 Jun 87
	J. Major	2 Sep 85–10 Sep 86
	N. Lyell	10 Sep 86–13 Jun 87
	Edwina Currie	10 Sep 86–16 Dec 88
	M. Portillo	13 Jun 87–25 Jul 88
	Ld Skelmersdale	13 Jun 87–25 Jul 89
	R. Freeman	16 Dec 88–4 May 90
	Lady Hooper	29 Sep 89–28 Nov 90
	S. Dorrell	4 May 90–28 Nov 90
Industry	**Sir K. JOSEPH**	7 May 79
	P. JENKIN	14 Sep 81
	(12 Jun 83 office reorganised as Trade and Industry)	
Min. of *State*	A. BUTLER	6 May 79–5 Jan 81
	Vt TRENCHARD	6 May 79–5 Jan 81
	N. TEBBIT	5 Jan 81–14 Sep 81
	N. LAMONT	14 Sep 81–12 Jun 83
Min. of *State*	K. BAKER	5 Jan 81–12 Jun 83
	(Industry & Info. Tech.)	
U-S.	D. Mitchell	6 May 79–5 Jan 81
	M. Marshall	6 May 79–15 Sep 81
	J. MacGregor	5 Jan 81–14 Jun 83
	J. Wakeham	15 Sep 81–6 Apr 82
	J. Butcher	6 Apr 82–14 Jun 83
D. Lanc.	**N. ST JOHN STEVAS** *(Arts)*	5 May 79
	F. PYM	5 Jan 81
	LADY YOUNG	27 Oct 81
	C. PARKINSON	6 Apr 82
	Ld COCKFIELD	11 Jun 83
	E of GOWRIE *(Arts)*	11 Sep 84
	N. TEBBIT	3 Sep 85
	K. CLARKE	13 Jun 87
	(also Min. Trade)	
	A. NEWTON	25 Jul 88
	K. BAKER	24 Jul 89
Northern *Ireland*	**H. ATKINS**	5 May 79
	J. PRIOR	14 Sep 81
	D. HURD	11 Sep 84
	T. KING	3 Sep 85
	P. BROOKE	24 Jul 89
Min. of *State*	M. ALISON	7 May 79–15 Sep 81
	H. ROSSI	7 May 79–5 Jan 81
	A. BUTLER	5 Jan 81–11 Sep 84
	E of GOWRIE	15 Sep 81–10 Jun 83
	E of MANSFIELD	13 Jun 83–12 Apr 84
	R. BOYSON	11 Sep 84–10 Sep 86
	N. SCOTT	10 Sep 86–13 Jun 87

CONSERVATIVE GOVERNMENT 1979–90 (*contd.*)

	J. STANLEY	13 Jun 87–25 Jul 88
	I. STEWART	25 Jul 88–25 Jul 89
	J. COPE	25 Jul 89–28 Nov 90
U-S.	Ld Elton	7 May 79–15 Sep 81
	P. Goodhart	7 May 79–5 Jan 81
	G. Shaw	7 May 79–5 Jan 81
	D. Mitchell	5 Jan 81–13 Jun 83
	J. Patten	5 Jan 81–13 Jun 83
	N. Scott	15 Sep 81–11 Sep 86
	C. Patten	14 Jun 83–2 Sep 85
	Ld Lyell	12 Apr 84–25 Jul 89
	R. Needham	3 Sep 85–28 Nov 90
	P. Viggers	10 Sep 86–26 Jul 89
	B. Mawhinney	10 Sep 86–28 Nov 90
	P. Bottomley	4 Jul 89–28 Jul 90
	Ld Skelmersdale	24 Jul 89–28 Nov 90
Paym.-	**A. MAUDE**	5 May 79
Gen.	**F. PYM**	5 Jan 81
	C. PARKINSON	14 Sep 81
	(*office vacant 11 Jun 83*)	
	(*office not in Cabinet*)	
	J. GUMMER	11 Sep 84
	(*office in Cabinet*)	
	K. CLARKE (*also Min. Emp.*)	2 Sep 85
	(*office not in Cabinet*)	
	P. BROOKE	13 Jun 87
	E of CAITHNESS	24 Jul 89
	R. RYDER	14 Jul 90
Min.	**Ld YOUNG OF**	
without	**GRAFFHAM**	11 Sep 84–3 Sep 85
Portfolio		
Scot. O.	**G. YOUNGER**	5 May 79
	M. RIFKIND	11 Jan 86
Min. of	E of MANSFIELD	7 May 79–13 Jun 83
State	Ld GRAY of CONTIN	13 Jun 83–11 Sep 86
	Ld GLENARTHUR	10 Sep 86–13 Jun 87
	I. LANG	13 Jun 87–28 Nov 90
	Ld SANDERSON	13 Jun 87–7 Sep 90
	M. FORSYTH	7 Sep 90–28 Nov 90
U-S.	A. Fletcher	7 May 79–14 Jun 83
	R. Fairgrieve	7 May 79–15 Sep 81
	M. Rifkind	7 May 79–6 Apr 82
	A. Stewart	15 Sep 81–10 Sep 86
	J. Mackay	6 Apr 82–14 Jun 87
	M. Ancram	13 June 83–14 Jun 87
	I. Lang	10 Sep 86–13 Jun 87
	Ld J. Douglas-Hamilton[1]	13 Jun 87–28 Nov 90

	M. Forsyth	13 Jun 87–7 Sep 90
	Ld Strathclyde	7 Sep 90–28 Nov 90
Soc.	**J. MOORE**	25 Jul 88
Security	**A. NEWTON**	23 Jul 89
Min. of	N. SCOTT	25 Jul 88
State		
U-S.	Ld Skelmersdale	24 Jul 88–26 Jul 89
	P. Lloyd	25 Jul 88–28 Jul 89
	Ld Henley	25 Jul 89–28 Nov 90
	Gillian Shephard	25 Jul 89–28 Nov 90
Trade	**J. NOTT**	5 May 79
	J. BIFFEN	5 Jan 81
	Ld COCKFIELD	6 Apr 82
	(*office reorganised as Trade and Industry*)	
	C. PARKINSON	12 Jun 83
	N. TEBBIT	16 Oct 83
	L. BRITTAN	2 Sep 85
	P. CHANNON	24 Jan 86
	Ld YOUNG of GRAFFHAM	13 Jun 87
	N. RIDLEY	24 Jul 89
	P. LILLEY	14 Jul 90
Min. for	Sally OPPENHEIM	6 May 79
Consumer	G. VAUGHAN	5 Mar 82
Affairs	(*office abolished 13 Jun 83*)	
Min. of	N. LAMONT	13 Jun 83–2 Sep 85
State	P. MORRISON	2 Sep 85–10 Sep 86
	G. SHAW	10 Sep 86–13 Jun 87
Min. for	C. PARKINSON	7 May 79
Trade	P. REES	14 Sep 81
	P. CHANNON	13 Jun 83
	A. CLARK	24 Jan 86
	Ld TREFGARNE	25 Jul 89
	T. SAINSBURY	23 Jul 90
Min. for	K. BAKER	13 Jun 83
Industry &	G. PATTIE	11 Sep 84
Info. Tech.	(*office vacant 13 Jun 87*)	
Min. for	D. HOGG	24 Jul 89
Industry	Ld HESKETH	2 Nov 90
Min. for	J. REDWOOD	2 Nov 90
Corporate		
Affairs		
U-S.	N. Tebbit	7 May 79–5 Jan 81
	R. Eyre	7 May 79–5 Mar 82
	Ld Trefgarne	5 Jan 81–15 Sep 81
	I. Sproat	15 Sep 81–12 Jun 83
	J. Butcher	14 Jun 83–26 Jul 88
	A. Fletcher	14 Jun 83–2 Sep 85
	D. Trippier	14 Jun 83–2 Sep 85

[1] MP. Not a member of the House of Lords.

CONSERVATIVE GOVERNMENT 1979–90 (*contd.*)

	Ld Lucas of Chilworth	11 Sep 84–13 Jun 87
	M. Howard	2 Sep 85–13 Jun 87
	R. Atkins	13 Jun 87–26 Jul 89
	F. Maude	13 Jun 87–26 Jul 89
	E. Forth	26 Jul 88–24 Jul 90
	J. Redwood	26 Jul 89–2 Nov 90
	E. Leigh	2 Nov 90–28 Nov 90
Transport	N. FOWLER *(Minister)*	11 May 79
	(office in Cabinet 5 Jan 81)	
	N. FOWLER *(Sec. of State)*	5 Jan 81
	D. HOWELL	14 Sep 81
	T. KING	11 Jun 83
	N. RIDLEY	16 Oct 83
	J. MOORE	21 May 86
	P. CHANNON	13 Jun 87
	C. PARKINSON	24 Jul 89
Min. of	Lynda CHALKER	18 Oct 83–10 Jan 86
State	D. MITCHELL	23 Jan 86–25 Jul 88
	M. PORTILLO	25 Jul 88–4 May 90
	R. FREEMAN	4 May 90–28 Nov 90
	Ld BRABAZON of TARA	23 Jul 90–28 Nov 90
P.S.	K. Clarke	7 May 79–5 Jan 81
U-S.	K. Clarke	5 Jan 81–5 Mar 82
	Lynda Chalker	5 Mar 82–18 Oct 83
	R. Eyre	5 Mar 82–11 Jun 83
	D. Mitchell	11 Jun 83–23 Jan 86
	M. Spicer	11 Sep 84–13 Jun 87
	E of Caithness	2 Sep 85–10 Sep 86
	P. Bottomley	23 Jan 86–24 Jul 89
	Ld Brabazon of Tara	10 Sep 86–23 Jul 89
	R. Atkins	25 Jul 89–22 Jul 90
	P. McLoughlin	25 Jul 89–28 Nov 90
	C. Chope	23 Jul 90–28 Nov 90
Wales	**N. EDWARDS**	5 May 79
	P. WALKER	13 Jun 87
	D. HUNT	4 May 90
Min. of	J. S. THOMAS	17 Feb 83
State	*(office vacant 2 Sep 85)*	
	W. ROBERTS	15 Jun 87
U-S.	M. Roberts	7 May 79–6 Jan 83
	W. Roberts	7 May 79–13 Jun 87
	M. Robinson	3 Oct 85–15 Jun 87
	I. Grist	15 Jun 87–28 Nov 90

Law Officers

Att.-Gen.	Sir M. HAVERS	6 May 79
	Sir P. MAYHEW	13 Jun 87

Sol.-Gen.	Sir I. PERCIVAL	6 May 79
	Sir P. MAYHEW	11 Jun 83
	Sir N. LYELL	15 Jun 87
Ld Advoc.	J. MACKAY[1] (Ld)	7 May 79
	Ld CAMERON of LOCHBROOM	16 May 84
	P. (Ld) FRASER	4 Jan 89
Sol.-Gen. Scotland	N. FAIRBAIRN	7 May 79
	P. FRASER[1]	28 Jan 82
	A. RODGER[1]	4 Jan 89

Whips

P.S. to	M. JOPLING	5 May 79
Treasury	J. WAKEHAM	11 Jun 83
	D. WADDINGTON	13 Jun 87
	T. RENTON	28 Oct 89
Lds of	C. Mather	7 May 79–1 Oct 81
Treasury	P. Morrison	7 May 79–5 Jan 81
	Ld J. Douglas-Hamilton[2]	7 May 79–1 Oct 81
	J. MacGregor	7 May 79–5 Jan 81
	D. Waddington	16 May 79–5 Jan 81
	R. Boscawen	9 Jan 81–17 Feb 83
	J. Wakeham	9 Jan 81–15 Sep 81
	J. Cope	9 Jan 81–13 Jun 83
	A. Newton	1 Oct 81–5 Mar 82
	P. Brooke	1 Oct 81–13 Jun 83
	J. S. Gummer	1 Oct 81–6 Jan 83
	A. Goodlad	16 Feb 82–10 Sep 84
	D. Thompson	14 Jan 83–10 Sep 86
	D. Hunt	23 Feb 83–10 Sep 84
	I. Lang	11 Jun 83–1 Feb 86
	T. Garel-Jones	11 Jun 83–16 Oct 86
	J. Major	3 Oct 84–1 Nov 85
	A. Hamilton	3 Oct 84–10 Sep 86
	T. Sainsbury	7 Oct 85–23 Jun 87
	M. Neubert	10 Feb 86–26 Jul 88
	T. Durant	16 Oct 86–19 Dec 88
	M. Lennox-Boyd	16 Oct 86–25 Jul 88
	P. Lloyd	16 Oct 86–24 Jul 88
	D. Lightbown	26 Jun 87–24 Jul 90
	K. Carlisle	27 Jul 88–22 Jul 90
	A. Howarth	27 Jul 88–24 Jul 89
	D. Maclean	27 Jul 88–24 Jul 89
	S. Dorrell	20 Dec 88–3 May 90
	J. Taylor	26 Jul 89–28 Nov 90
	D. Heathcoat-Amory	26 Jul 89–28 Oct 89
	T. Sackville	30 Oct 89–28 Nov 90
	M. Fallon	10 May 90–22 Jul 90

[1] Not a member of the House of Commons.

[2] MP. Not a member of the House of Lords.

CONSERVATIVE GOVERNMENT 1979–90 (*contd.*)

	S. Chapman	25 Jul 90–28 Nov 90
	G. Knight	25 Jul 90–28 Nov 90
	I. Patnick	25 Jul 90–28 Nov 90
Ass.	R. Boscawen	16 May 79–9 Jan 81
Whips	J. Cope	16 May 79–9 Jan 81
	A. Newton	16 May 79–30 Sep 81
	J. Wakeham	16 May 79–9 Jan 81
	P. Brooke	16 May 79–30 Sep 81
	J. S. Gummer	9 Jan 81–30 Sep 81
	A. Goodlad	9 Jan 81–5 Feb 82
	D. Thompson	9 Jan 81–14 Jan 83
	N. Budgen	30 Sep 81–8 May 82
	D. Hunt	30 Sep 81–22 Feb 83
	I. Lang	30 Sep 81–10 Jun 83
	T. Garel-Jones	16 Mar 82–10 Jun 83
	A. Hamilton	11 May 82–3 Oct 84
	J. Major	14 Jan 83–2 Oct 84
	D. Hogg	22 Feb 83–10 Oct 84
	M. Neubert	15 Jun 83–9 Feb 86
	T. Sainsbury	15 Jun 83–7 Oct 85
	T. Durant	3 Oct 84–16 Oct 86
	P. Lloyd	3 Oct 84–16 Oct 86
	M. Lennox-Boyd	3 Oct 84–16 Oct 86
	F. Maude	7 Oct 85–15 Jun 87
	G. Malone	10 Feb 86–15 Jun 87
	M. Portillo	16 Oct 86–15 Jun 87
	D. Lightbown	16 Oct 86–25 Jun 87
	R. Ryder	16 Oct 86–24 Jul 88
	K. Carlisle	18 Jun 87–25 Jul 88
	A. Howarth	18 Jun 87–25 Jul 88
	D. Maclean	18 Jun 87–25 Jul 88
	S. Dorrell	26 Jun 87–19 Dec 88
	J. Taylor	26 Jul 88–25 Jul 89
	D. Heathcoat-Amory	26 Jul 88–25 Jul 89
	T. Sackville	26 Jul 88–29 Oct 89
	M. Fallon	26 Jul 88–10 May 90
	S. Chapman	20 Dec 88–25 Jul 90
	G. Knight	28 Jul 89–25 Jul 90
	I. Patnick	28 Jul 89–25 Jul 90
	N. Baker	2 Nov 89–28 Nov 90
	T. Wood	10 May 90–28 Nov 90
	T. Boswell	25 Jul 90–28 Nov 90
	N. Hamilton	25 Jul 90–28 Nov 90
	T. Kirkhope	25 Jul 90–28 Nov 90

H.M. Household

Treasurer	J. S. THOMAS	6 May 79
	A. BERRY	17 Feb 83
	J. COPE	11 Jun 83
	D. HUNT	15 Jun 87
	T. GAREL-JONES	25 Jul 89
	A. GOODLAD	22 Jul 90

Compt.	S. LE MARCHANT	7 May 79
	A. BERRY	30 Sep 81
	C. MATHER	17 Feb 83
	R. BOSCAWEN	16 Oct 86
	T. GAREL-JONES	26 Jul 88
	A. GOODLAD	25 Jul 89
	Sir G. YOUNG	23 Jul 90
Vice.	A. BERRY	7 May 79
Chamb.	C. MATHER	30 Sep 81
	R. BOSCAWEN	17 Feb 83
	T. GAREL-JONES	16 Oct 86
	M. NEUBERT	26 Jul 88
	T. DURANT	20 Dec 88
	D. LIGHTBOWN	25 Jul 90
Cap. Gent. at Arms	Ld DENHAM	6 May 79
Cap. Yeo. of Guard	Ld SANDYS	6 May 79
	E of SWINTON	20 Oct 82
	Vt DAVIDSON	10 Sep 86
Lords in Waiting	Vt Long	9 May 79–28 Nov 90
	Ld Mowbray and Stourton	9 May 79–22 Sep 80
	Ld Lyell	9 May 79–12 Apr 84
	Ld Cullen of Ashbourne	9 May 79–27 May 82
	Ld Trefgarne	9 May 79–5 Jan 81
	E of Avon	22 Sep 80–6 Jan 83
	Ld Skelmersdale	9 Jan 81–10 Sep 86
	Ld Glenarthur	27 May 82–10 Jun 83
	Ld Lucas of Chilworth	6 Jan 83–9 Sep 84
	Lady Trumpington	11 Jun 83–25 Mar 85
	E of Caithness	8 May 84–2 Sep 85
	Ld Brabazon of Tara	19 Sep 84–10 Sep 86
	Lady Cox	3 Apr 85–2 Aug 85
	Vt Davidson	17 Sep 85–10 Sep 86
	Lady Hooper	17 Sep 85–14 Jun 87
	Ld Hesketh	10 Sep 86–31 Jan 89
	Ld Beaverbrook	10 Sep 86–28 Jul 88
	E of Dundee	3 Oct 86–26 Jul 89
	E of Arran	18 Jun 87–24 Jul 89
	Ld Strathclyde	12 Aug 88–24 Jul 89
	Ld Henley	13 Feb 89–24 Jul 89
	Vt Ullswater	26 Jul 89–22 Jul 90
	Ld Reay	2 Aug 89–28 Nov 90
	E of Strathmore	2 Aug 89–28 Nov 90
	Lady Blatch	15 Jan 90–7 Sep 90
	Ld Cavendish	14 Sep 90–28 Nov 90
	Vt Astor	11 Oct 90–28 Nov 90

CONSERVATIVE GOVERNMENT 1990–97

P.M   **J. MAJOR**   28 Nov 90–2 May 97
First S. of State and Deputy P.M.
      M. HESELTINE   5 Jul 95
Ld Pres.   **J. MACGREGOR**   28 Nov 90
      A. NEWTON   10 Apr 92
U-S.   R. Jackson   28 Nov 90
      (office under Min. for Civil Service
      11 Apr 92)
Ld   **Ld MACKAY of**
Chanc.   **CLASHFERN**   28 Nov 90
U-S.   J. Taylor   14 Apr 92
      J. Evans   29 Nov 95
      G. Streeter   2 Jun 96
Privy   **Ld WADDINGTON**   28 Nov 90
Seal   **Ld WAKEHAM**   10 Apr 92
      Vt CRANBORNE   20 Jul 94
Exchequer **N. LAMONT**   28 Nov 90
      K. CLARKE   27 May 93
Chief   **D. MELLOR**   28 Nov 90
Sec.   **M. PORTILLO**   10 Apr 92
      J. AITKEN   20 Jul 94
      W. WALDEGRAVE   5 Jul 95
F.S.   F. MAUDE   28 Nov 90
      S. DORRELL   14 Apr 92
      Sir G. YOUNG   20 Jul 94
      M. JACK   6 Jul 95
E.S.   J. Maples   28 Nov 90
      A. Nelson
      (Min. of State 20 Jul 94–6 Jul 95)
            14 Apr 92
      Angela Knight   6 Jul 95
Min.   Gillian SHEPHARD   28 Nov 90–
            10 Apr 92
      Sir J. COPE   14 Apr 92–20 Jul 94
      (also Paym.-Gen.)
      A. NELSON   20 Jul 94–6 Jul 95
      D. HEATHCOAT-AMORY
      (also Paym. Gen.)   20 Jul 94–20 Jul 96
Foreign & **D. HURD**   28 Nov 90
Comm. O.   **M. RIFKIND**   5 Jul 95

Min. of   E of CAITHNESS   28 Nov 90–
State   15 Apr 92
      D. HOGG   28 Nov 90–5 Jul 95
      T. GAREL-JONES   28 Nov 90–6 Jun 93
      A. GOODLAD   14 Apr 92–5 Jul 95
      D. HEATHCOAT-AMORY   7 Jun 93–
            20 Jul 94
      D. DAVIS   20 Jul 94–2 May 97
      J. HANLEY   5 Jul 95–2 May 97
      Sir N. BONSOR   6 Jul 95–2 May 97

Min. of   *(Overseas Development)*
State   Lynda (Lady) CHALKER   28 Nov 90
U-S.   M. Lennox-Boyd   28 Nov 90
      A. Baldry   20 Jul 94
      (office vacant 6 Jul 95)
      P. Oppenheim   23 Jul 96–2 May 97
      L. Fox   23 Jul 96–2 May 97
Home O.   **K. BAKER**   28 Nov 90
      K. CLARKE   10 Apr 92
      M. HOWARD   27 May 93
Min. of   J. PATTEN   28 Nov 90–14 Apr 92
State   Earl FERRERS   28 Nov 90–20 Jul 94
      Angela RUMBOLD   28 Nov 90–14 Apr 92
      P. LLOYD   15 Apr 92–20 Jul 94
      M. JACK   15 Apr 92–27 May 93
      D. MACLEAN   27 May 93–2 May 97
      M. FORSYTH   20 Jul 94–5 Jul 95
      Lady BLATCH   20 Jul 94–2 May 97
      Ann WIDDECOMBE   6 Jul 95–2 May 97
U-S.   P. Lloyd   28 Nov 90–15 Apr 92
      C. Wardle   15 Apr 92–20 Jul 94
      N. Baker   20 Jul 94–18 Oct 95
      T. Kirkhope   18 Oct 95–2 May 97
      T. Sackville   29 Nov 95–2 May 97
Ag. Fish. **J. S. GUMMER**   28 Nov 90
& Food   **GILLIAN SHEPHARD**   27 May 93
      W. WALDEGRAVE   20 Jul 94
      D. HOGG   5 Jul 95
Min. of   Lady TRUMPINGTON   28 Nov 90
State   D. CURRY   14 Apr 92
      M. JACK   27 May 93
      A. BALDRY   6 Jul 95
P-S.   D. Curry   28 Nov 90–14 Apr 92
      D. Maclean   28 Nov 90–15 Apr 92
      Earl Howe   14 Apr 92–6 Jul 95
      N. Soames   14 Apr 92–20 Jul 94–
      Angela Browning   20 Jul 94–2 May 97
      T. Boswell   6 Jul 95–2 May 97
Min. for T. RENTON   28 Nov 90–11 Apr 92
the Arts *(11 Apr 92, see National Heritage)*
Defence   **T. KING**   28 Nov 90
      M. RIFKIND   10 Apr 92
      M. PORTILLO   5 Jul 95
Min. of   A. CLARK   28 Nov 90
State   J. AITKEN   14 Apr 92
(Defence R. FREEMAN   20 Jul 94
Procure- J. ARBUTHNOT   6 Jul 95
ment)
Min. of   A. HAMILTON   28 Nov 90
State   J. HANLEY   27 May 93
      (Armed Services)

CONSERVATIVE GOVERNMENT 1990–97 *(contd.)*

	N. SOAMES	20 Jul 94
U-S.	K. Carlisle	28 Nov 90–15 Apr 92
	E of Arran	28 Nov 90–15 Apr 92
	Vt Cranborne	22 Apr 92–20 Jul 94
	Ld Henley	20 Jul 94–6 Jul 95
	Earl Howe	6 Jul 95–2 May 97
Educ. &	**K. CLARKE**	28 Nov 90
Science	*(became Dept for Education*	
	10 Apr 1992)	
	J. PATTEN	10 Apr 92
	GILLIAN SHEPHARD	20 Jul 94
	(became Dept of Education and	
	Employment 5 Jul 95)	
Min. of	T. EGGAR	28 Nov 90
State	Lady BLATCH	14 Apr 92
	E. FORTH	20 Jul 94–2 May 97
	Ld HENLEY	6 Jul 95–2 May 97
U-S.	A. Howarth	28 Nov 90–14 Apr 92
	M. Fallon	28 Nov 90–14 Apr 92
	R. Atkins	28 Nov 90–14 Apr 92
	(Sport)	
	E. Forth	14 Apr 92–20 Jul 94
	N. Forman	14 Apr 92–
		11 Dec 92
	T. Boswell	19 Dec 92–6 Jul 95
	R. Squire	27 May 93–2 May 97
	J. Paice	7 Jul 95–2 May 97
	Cheryl Gillan	6 Jul 95–2 May 97
Employment	**M. HOWARD**	28 Nov 90
	GILLIAN SHEPHARD	11 Apr 92
	D. HUNT	27 May 93
	M. PORTILLO	20 Jul 94
	(office abolished 5 Jul 95)	
Min. of	M. FORSYTH	14 Apr 92
State	Ann WIDDECOMBE	20 Jul 94
U-S.	R.Jackson	28 Nov 90–14 Apr 92
	E. Forth	28 Nov 90–14 Apr 92
	Vt Ullswater	28 Nov 90–16 Sep 93
	P. McLoughlin	14 Apr 92–
		27 May 93
	Ann Widdecombe	27 May 93–
		20 Jul 94
	Ld Henley	16 Sep 93–20 Jul 94
	J. Paice	20 Jul 94–5 Jul 95
	P. Oppenheim	20 Jul 94–6 5 Jul 95
Energy	**J. WAKEHAM**	28 Nov 90
	(office abolished 11 Apr 92)	
U-S.	D. Heathcoat-Amory	28 Nov 90–
		11 Apr 92
	C. Moynihan	28 Nov 90–11 Apr 92
Environment	**M. HESELTINE**	28 Nov 90
	M. HOWARD	11 Apr 92
	J. S. GUMMER	27 May 93

Min. for Local Goverment (and Inner Cities 94)		
	M. PORTILLO	28 Nov 90
	J. REDWOOD	15 Apr 92
	D. CURRY	27 May 93
Min. for Environment (& Countryside)		
	D. TRIPPIER	28 Nov 90
	D. MACLEAN	14 Apr 92
	T. YEO	27 May 93
	R. ATKINS	7 Jan 94
	Earl FERRERS	6 Jul 95
Min. for Housing (Construction 6 Jul 95)		
	Sir G. YOUNG	28 Nov 90
	Vt ULLSWATER	20 Jul 94
	R. JONES	6 Jul 95
Min. of State		
	Lady BLATCH	21 May 91–13 Apr 92
U-S.	Lady Blatch	28 Nov 90–21 May 91
	R. Key	28 Nov 90–15 Apr 92
	T. Yeo	28 Nov 90–15 Apr 92
	T. Baldry	28 Nov 90–20 Jul 94
	Ld Strathclyde	15 Apr 92–16 Sep 34
	R. Squire	15 Apr 92–27 May 93
	Lady Denton	16 Sep 93–11 Jan 94
	E of Arran	11 Jan 94–20 Jul 94
	Sir P. Beresford	20 Jul 94–2 May 97
	R. Jones	20 Jul 94–6 Jul 95
	J. Clappison	6 Jul 95–2 May 97
Health	**W. WALDEGRAVE**	28 Nov 90
	VIRGINIA BOTTOMLEY	10 Apr 92
	S. DORRELL	5 Jul 95
Min. of	Virginia BOTTOMLEY	28 Nov 90
State	B. MAWHINNEY	14 Apr 92
	G. MALONE	20 Jul 94
U-S.	Lady Hooper	28 Nov 90–14 Apr 92
	S. Dorrell	28 Nov 90–14 Apr 92
	T. Sackville	14 Apr 92–29 Nov 95
	T. Yeo	15 Apr 92–27 May 93
	Lady Cumberlege	14 Apr 92–2 May 97
	J. Bowis	27 May 93–23 Jul 96
	J. Horam	29 Nov 95–2 May 97
	S. Burns	23 Jul 96–2 May 97
D. Lanc.	**C. PATTEN**	28 Nov 90
	(from 12 Apr 92 also Min. for Public	
	Service)	
	W. WALDEGRAVE	10 Apr 92
	D. HUNT	20 Jul 94
	R. FREEMAN	5 Jul 95
P.S.	R. Jackson	15 Apr 92
	D. Davis	27 May 93
	R. Hughes	20 Jul 94
	J. Horam	6 Mar 95
	D. Willetts	28 Nov 95
	M. Bates	16 Dec 96

CONSERVATIVE GOVERNMENT 1990–97 (*contd.*)

Min.	**J. HANLEY**	20 Jul 94
without	**B. MAWHINNEY**	5 Jul 95
Portfolio	**D. MELLOR**	11 Apr 92
Nat.	**P. BROOKE**	25 Sep 92
Heritage	**S. DORRELL**	20 Jul 94
	VIRGINIA BOTTOMLEY	5 Jul 95
Min. of	I. SPROAT	6 Jul 95
State		
U-S.	R. Key	14 Apr 92–27 May 93
	I. Sproat	27 May 93–6 Jul 95
	Vt Astor	20 Jul 94–6 Jul 95
	Ld Inglewood	6 Jul 95–2 May 97
Northern	**P. BROOKE**	28 Nov 90
Ireland	**Sir P. MAYHEW**	10 Apr 92
Min. of	B. MAWHINNEY	28 Nov 90–
State		14 Apr 92
	Ld BELSTEAD	28 Nov 90–14 Apr 92
	(*also Paym.-Gen.*)	
	M. MATES	15 Apr 92–24 Jun 93
	R. ATKINS	14 Apr 92–11 Jan 94
	Sir J. WHEELER	25 Jun 93–2 May 97
	M. ANCRAM	11 Jan 94–2 May 97
U-S.	R. Needham	28 Nov 90–15 Apr 92
	J. Hanley	3 Dec 90–27 May 93
	E of Arran	22 Apr 92–11 Jan 94
	M. Ancram	27 May 93–5 Jan 94
	Lady Denton	20 Jul 94–2 May 97
	T. Smith	6 Jan 94–20 Oct 94
	M. Moss	25 Oct 94–2 May 97
Paym.-	Ld BELSTEAD(*see N. Ireland*) 28 Nov 90	
Gen.	Sir J. COPE (*see Treasury*)	14 Apr 92
	D. HEATHCOAT-AMORY (*see Treasury*)	
		20 Jul 94–20 Jul 96
	D. WILLETTS	20 Jul 96
	M. BATES	16 Dec 96
Scot. O.	**I. LANG**	28 Nov 90
	M. FORSYTH	5 Jul 95
Min. of	M. FORSYTH	28 Nov 90
State	Ld FRASER of CARMYLLIE	14 Apr 92
	Ld J.DOUGLAS-HAMILTON[1]	6 Jul 95
U-S.	Ld J.Douglas-Hamilton[1]	28 Nov 90–
		6 Jul 95
	A. Stewart	28 Nov 90–8 Feb 95
	G. Kynoch	8 Feb 95–2 May 97
	Ld Strathclyde	28 Nov 90–14 Apr 92
	Sir H. Munro	14 Apr 92–6 Jul 95
	E of Lindsay	6 Jul 95–2 May 97
	R. Robertson	6 Jul 95–2 May 97
Soc. Sec.	**A. NEWTON**	28 Nov 90
	P. LILLEY	10 Apr 92
Min. of	N. SCOTT	28 Nov 90–20 Jul 94
State	W. HAGUE	20 Jul 94–5 Jul 95

	Ld MACKAY of ARDBRECKNISH	
		20 Jul 94–2 May 97
	A. BURT	6 Jul 95–2 May 97
U-S.	Ld Henley	28 Nov 90–16 Sep 93
	M. Jack	28 Nov 90–14 Apr 92
	Ann Widdecombe	30 Nov 90–
		27 May 93
	A. Burt	14 Apr 92–6 Jul 95
	W. Hague	27 May 93–20 Jul 94
	Vt Astor	16 Sep 93–20 Jul 94
	J. Arbuthnot	20 Jul 94–6 Jul 95
	R. Evans	20 Jul 94–2 May 97
	A. Mitchell	6 Jul 95–2 May 97
	O. Heald	6 Jul 95–2 May 97
Trade	**P. LILLEY**	28 Nov 90
	M. HESELTINE	10 Apr 92
	I. LANG	5 Jul 95
Min. for	T. SAINSBURY	28 Nov 90
Trade	R. NEEDHAM	14 Apr 92
	A. NELSON	6 Jul 95
Min. for	Ld HESKETH	28 Nov 90–21 May 91
Industry	(*office vacant 23 May 91–15 Apr 92*)	
	T. SAINSBURY	15 Apr 92
	(*office vacant 20 Jul 94*)	
Min. for Corporate Affairs		
	J. REDWOOD	28 Nov 90–13 Apr 92
	(*office vacant*)	
Min. for Energy (and Industry 20 Jul 94)		
	T. EGGAR	15 Apr 92
	G. KNIGHT	23 Jul 96
Min. for Consumer Affairs		
	Earl FERRERS	20 Jul 94–6 Jul 95
Min. of	Ld STRATHCLYDE	11 Jan 94–
State		20 Jul 94
	Ld FRASER of	6 Jul 95–2 May 97
	CARMYLLIE	
U-S.	Ld Reay	22 May 91–14 Apr 92
	E. Leigh	28 Nov 90–27 May 93
	N. Hamilton	14 Apr 92–25 Oct 94
	J. Evans	27 Oct 94–29 Nov 95
	Lady Denton	14 Apr 92–16 Sep 93
	P. McLoughlin	27 May 93–20 Jul 94
	Ld Strathclyde	16 Sep 93–11 Jan 94
	C. Wardle	20 Jul 94–11 Feb 95
	I. Taylor	20 Jul 94–2 May 97
	R. Page	14 Feb 95–2 May 97
	P. Oppenheim	7 Jul 95–2 May 97
	J. Taylor	29 Nov 95–2 May 97
Transport	**M. RIFKIND**	28 Nov 90
	J. MACGREGOR	10 Apr 92
	B. MAWHINNEY	20 Jul 94
	Sir G. YOUNG	5 Jul 95

[1] MP. Not a member of the House of Lords.

CONSERVATIVE GOVERNMENT 1990–97 (*contd.*)

Min. of	Ld BRABAZON	28 Nov 90–14 Apr 92		A. Mitchell	20 Jul 94–6 Jul 95
State	of TARA			D. Conway	20 Jul 94–23 Jul 96
(Min. for Public Transport)				B. Wells	8 Jul 95–2 May 97
	R. FREEMAN	28 Nov 90–20 Jul 94		D. Willetts	8 Jul 95–22 Nov 95
(Min. for Railways and Roads)				S. Burns	8 Jul 95–23 Jul 96
	E of CAITHNESS	14 Apr 92–11 Jan 94		M. Bates	18 Oct 95–12 Dec 96
	J. WATTS	20 Jul 94–		P. McLoughlin	23 Jul 96–2 May 97
U-S.	C. Chope	28 Nov 90–14 Apr 92		R. Knapman	23 Jul 96–2 May 97
	P. McLoughlin	28 Nov 90–14 Apr 92		R. Ottaway	23 Jul 96–2 May 97
	S. Norris	14 Apr 92–23 Jul 96		G. Brandreth	12 Dec 96–2 May 97
	K. Carlisle	14 Apr 92–27 May 93	*Ass.*	T. Wood	28 Nov 90–14 Apr 92
	R. Key	27 May 93–20 Jul 94	*Whips*	T. Boswell	28 Nov 90–14 Apr 92
	Ld Mackay of	11 Jan 94–20 Jul 94		N. Hamilton	28 Nov 90–14 Apr 92
	Ardbrecknish			T. Kirkhope	28 Nov 90–11 Jan 93
	Vt Goschen	20 Jul 94–2 May 97		D. Davis	3 Dec 90–27 May 93
	J. Bowis	23 Jul 96–2 May 97		R. Hughes	15 Apr 92–20 Jul 94
Wales	**D. HUNT**	28 Nov 90		J. Arbuthnot	15 Apr 92–20 Jul 94
	J. REDWOOD	27 May 93		A. Mackay	15 Apr 92–27 May 93
	W. HAGUE	5 Jul 95		A. Mitchell	11 Jan 93–20 Jul 94
Min. of	Sir W. ROBERTS	28 Nov 90–20 Jul 94		M. Brown	27 May 93–7 May 94
State				D. Conway	27 May 93–20 Jul 94
U-S.	N. Bennett	3 Dec 90–14 Apr 94		B. Wells	10 May 94–7 Jul 95
	G. Jones	14 Apr 92–2 May 97		M. Bates	20 Jul 94–18 Oct 95
	R. Richards	20 Jul 94–2 Jun 96		S. Burns	20 Jul 94–7 Jul 95
	J. Evans	2 Jun 96–2 May 97		D. Willetts	20 Jul 94–7 Jul 95
				L. Fox	20 Jul 94–28 Nov 95

Law Officers

				P. McLoughlin	7 Jul 95–23 Jul 96
Att.-Gen.	Sir P. MAYHEW	28 Nov 90		R. Knapman	7 Jul 95–23 Jul 96
	Sir N. LYELL	10 Apr 92		G. Streeter	7 Jul 95–2 Jun 96
Sol.-Gen.	Sir N. LYELL	28 Nov 90		R. Ottaway	18 Oct 95–23 Jul 96
	Sir D. SPENCER	14 Apr 92		G. Brandreth	25 Nov 95–12 Dec 96
Ld. Adv.	Ld FRASER of CARMYLLIE	28 Nov 90		L. Fox	12 Nov 95–23 Jul 96
	Ld RODGER	14 Apr 92		S. Coe	2 Jun 96–2 May 97
	Ld MACKAY of	7 Nov 95		A. Coombs	23 Jul 96–2 May 97
	DRUMADOON			Jacqui Lait	23 Jul 96–2 May 97
Sol.-Gen.	A. RODGER[1]	28 Nov 90		P. Ainsworth	23 Jul 96–2 May 97
Scotland	T. DAWSON[1]	14 Apr 92		M. Carrington	12 Dec 96–2 May 97
	D. MACKAY[1]	4 May 95			
	P. CULLEN[1]	7 Nov 95			

H.M. Household

			Treasurer	A. GOODLAD	28 Nov 90
				D. HEATHCOAT-AMORY	15 Apr 92
				G. KNIGHT	7 Jun 93
				A. MACKAY	23 Jul 96

Whips

P.S. to	R. RYDER	28 Nov 90	*Compt.*	D. LIGHTBOWN	28 Nov 90
Treasury	A. GOODLAD	5 Jul 95		T. WOOD	7 Jul 95
Lds of	T. Sackville	28 Nov 90–14 Apr 92	*Vice-*	J. TAYLOR	28 Nov 90
Treasury	S. Chapman	28 Nov 90–14 Apr 92	*Chamb.*	S. CHAPMAN	15 Apr 92
	G. Knight	28 Nov 90–27 May 93		T. KIRKHOPE	7 Jul 95
	I. Patnick	28 Nov 90–20 Jul 94		A. MACKAY	18 Oct 95
	N. Baker	3 Dec 90–20 Jul 94		D. CONWAY	23 Jul 96
	T. Wood	15 Apr 92–6 Jul 95	*Cap. Gent.*	Ld DENHAM	28 Nov 90
	T. Boswell	15 Apr 92–10 Dec 92	*at Arms*	Ld HESKETH	2 May 91
	T. Kirkhope	16 Dec 92–7 Jul 95			
	A. Mackay	27 May 93–18 Oct 95			

[1] Not a member of the House of Commons.

CONSERVATIVE GOVERNMENT 1990–97 (*contd.*)

	Vt ULLSWATER	16 Sep 93	Lady Denton	Jan 92–15 Apr 92
	Ld STRATHCLYDE	20 Jul 94	Vt St. Davids	22 Apr 92–20 Jul 94
Cap. Yeo.	Vt DAVIDSON	28 Nov 90	Vt Goschen	22 Apr 92–20 Jul 94
of Guard	E of STRATHMORE	30 Dec 91	Lady Trumpington	22 Apr 92–2 May 97
	E of ARRAN	20 Jul 94	Ld Mackay of	15 Oct 93–11 Jan 94
	Ld INGLEWOOD	Jan 95	Ardbrecknish	
	Ld CHESHAM	8 Jul 95	Ld Annaly	18 Mar 94–20 Jul 94
Lords in	Vt Long	28 Nov 90–2 May 97	Ld Lucas of	21 Jul 94–2 May 97
Waiting	Ld Reay	28 Nov 90–21 May 91	Crudwell	
	E of Strathmore	28 Nov 90–	Lady Miller of	21 Jul 94–2 May 97
		30 Dec 91	Hendon	
	Ld Cavendish	28 Nov 90–22 Apr 92	Ld Inglewood	21 Jul 94–Jan 95
	Vt Astor	28 Nov 90–16 Sep 93	E of Lindsay	12 Jan 95–6 Jul 95
	Earl Howe	30 May 91–15 Apr 92	E of Courtown	8 Jul 95–2 May 97

LABOUR GOVERNMENT 1997–

P.M.	**T. BLAIR**	2 May 97		S. Twigg	11 Jun 01
Deputy P.M.	**J. PRESCOTT**	2 May 97		B. Bradshaw	29 May 02–12 Jun 03
	(also Sec. of State for the Environment			P. Woolas	12 Jun 03
	2 May 97–8 Jun 01)			J. Murphy	9 May 05
	(also First Sec. of State and Min. for		*Ld Chanc.*	**Ld IRVINE**	2 May 97
	Cabinet Office 8 Jun 01–29 May 02)			**Ld FALCONER**	
	(Deputy P.M.'s Dept responsible for			*(also Min for Const. Aff.)*	11 Jun 03
	the Regions set up 29 May 02)				
	(effectively Deputy to J. Prescott at the		*(Dept for Constitutional Affairs 12 Jun 03)*		
	Office of the Deputy Prime Minister)		*Min. of*	G. HOON	28 Jul 98–17 May 99
Commun-	**D. MILIBAND**	6 May 05	*State*	Harriet HARMAN	9 May 05–
ities and	N. RAYNSFORD	29 May 02	*U-S.*	G. Hoon	6 May 97–28 Jul 98
Local Govt.				K. Vaz	17 May 99–28 Jul 99
Min. for				D. Lock	29 Jul 99–11 Jun 01
Regions				Jane Kennedy	11 Oct 99–11 Jun 01
Min. of	Barbara ROCHE	29 May 02–		Ld Bach	20 Nov 00–11 Jun 01
State		12 Jun 03		Lady Scotland	11 Jun 01–12 Jun 03
	Ld ROOKER	29 May 02–9 May 05		M. Wills	11 Jun 01–29 May 02
	K. HILL	12 Jun 03–9 May 05		Rosie Winterton	11 Jun 01–
	P. WOOLAS	9 May 05–			12 Jun 03
U-S.	C. Leslie	29 May 02–12 Jun 03		Yvette Cooper	29 May 02–12 Jun 03
	T. McNulty	29 May 02–12 Jun 03	*U-S.*	C. Leslie	12 Jun 03–9 May 05
	Yvette Cooper	12 Jun 03–9 May 05		D. Lammy	12 Jun 03–9 May 05
	P. Hope	13 Jun 03–9 May 05		Ld Filkin	12 Jun 03–9 Sep 04
	J. Fitzpatrick	9 May 05–		Lady Ashton	9 Sep 04–
	Lady Andrews	9 May 05–		Bridget Prentice	9 May 05–
Ld Pres.	**Ann TAYLOR**	3 May 97	*U-S.*	Anne McGuire	12 Jun 03–
	Margaret BECKETT	27 Jul 98	*(Scotland)*		
	R. COOK	8 Jun 01	*U-S.*	D. Touhig	12 Jun 03–
	J. REID	12 May 03	*(Wales)*		
	Ld WILLIAMS of	8 Jun 01	*Privy Seal*	**Ld RICHARD**	3 May 97
	MOSTYN			**Lady JAY** *(Min. for Women)*	27 Jul 98
	Lady AMOS	7 Oct 03		**P. HAIN** *(also S. of S. Wales)*	11 Jun 03
P.S.	P. Tipping	16 Dec 99		**G. HOON**	6 May 05

LABOUR GOVERNMENT 1997– (*contd.*)

U-S.	P. Woolas	12 Jun 03		**D. BLUNKETT**	8 Jun 01
	N. Griffiths	9 May 05		**C. CLARKE**	15 Dec 04
Exchequer	**G. BROWN**	2 May 97	*Min. of*	A. MICHAEL	6 May 97–27 Oct 98
Chief Sec.	**A. DARLING**	3 May 97	*State*	Joyce QUIN	6 May 97–28 Jul 98
	S. BYERS	27 Jul 98		Ld WILLIAMS of MOSTYN	28 Jul 98–29 Jul 99
	A. MILBURN	23 Dec 98		P. BOATENG	28 Oct 98–11 Jun 01
	A. SMITH	11 Oct 99		C. CLARKE	29 Jul 99–11 Jun 01
	P. BOATENG	29 May 02		Barbara ROCHE	29 Jul 99–11 Jun 01
	D. BROWNE	6 May 05		J. DENHAM	11 Jun 01–13 May 03
F.S.	Dawn PRIMAROLO	6 May 97		K. BRADLEY	11 Jun 01–29 May 02
	Barbara ROCHE	4 Jan 99		Ld ROOKER	11 Jun 01–29 May 02
	S. TIMMS	29 Jul 99		Ld FALCONER	29 May 02–11 Jun 03
	P. BOATENG	9 Jun 01		Beverley HUGHES	29 May 02– 1 Apr 04
	Ruth KELLY	29 May 02		D. BROWNE	1 Apr 04–6 May 05
	S.TIMMS	7 Sep 04		H. BENN	29 May 02–13 May 03
	J. HEALEY	9 May 05		Hazel BLEARS	12 Jun 03–
E.S.	Helen LIDDELL	6 May 97		Lady SCOTLAND	12 Jun 03–
	Patricia HEWITT	28 Jul 98		T. McNULTY	9 May 05–
	Melanie JOHNSON	29 Jul 99	*U-S.*	Ld Williams of Mostyn	6 May 97–28 Jul 98
	Ruth KELLY	9 Jun 01		G. Howarth	6 May 97–29 Jul 99
	J. HEALEY	29 May 02		M. O'Brien	6 May 97–11 Jun 01
	I. LEWIS	9 May 05		Kate Hoey	28 Jul 98–29 Jul 99
Paym.-	G. ROBINSON	3 May 97		Ld Bassam	29 Jul 99–11 Jun 01
Gen.	Dawn PRIMAROLO	4 Jan 99		Beverley Hughes	11 Jun 01– 29 May 02
Foreign. &	**R. COOK**	2 May 97		R. Ainsworth	11 Jun 01–12 Jun 03
Comm. O.	**J. STRAW**	8 Jun 01		Angela Eagle	11 Jun 01–29 May 02
Min. of	D. HENDERSON 3 May 97–27 Jul 98			Ld Filkin	29 May 02–12 Jun 03
State	D. FATCHETT 6 May 97–10 May 99			M. Wills	1 Jun 02–11 Jul 03
	T. LLOYD 6 May 97–29 Jul 99			P. Goggins	13 May 03–9 May 05
	Joyce QUIN 28 Jul 98–29 Jul 99			Caroline Flint	12 Jun 03–
	G. HOON 17 May 99–11 Oct 99			Fiona MacTaggart	12 Jun 03–
	J. BATTLE 29 Jul 99–9 Jun 01			A. Burnham	9 May 05–
	P. HAIN 29 Jul 99–24 Oct 02		*Ag. Fish.*	**J. CUNNINGHAM**	3 May 97
	K.VAZ 11 Oct 99–9 Jun 01		*& Food*	**N. BROWN**	27 Jul 98
	B. WILSON 24 Jan 01–9 Jun 01			*(renamed Environment Food and*	
	Lady SYMONS 9 Jun 01–			*Rural Affairs 8 Jun 01)*	
	(also in Trade to 12 Jun 03)			**Margaret BECKETT**	8 Jun 01
	P. HAIN 9 Jun 01–24 Oct 02		*Min. of*	J. ROOKER	6 May 97–29 Jul 99
	D. MACSHANE 27 Oct 02–9 May 05		*State*	Joyce QUIN	29 Jul 99–9 Jun 01
	M. O'BRIEN *(also in Trade)* 12 Jun 03–			Lady HAYMAN	29 Jul 99–9 Jun 01
	D. ALEXANDER 9 Sep 04–6 May 05			M. MEACHER	9 Jun 01–12 Jun 03
	(also in Trade)			A. MICHAEL	9 Jun 01–9 Jun 05
	K. HOWELLS	9 May 05–		E. MORLEY	12 Jun 03–
	I. PEARSON	9 May 05–	*P.S.*	E. Morley	6 May 97–12 Jun 03
U-S.	Lady Symons	6 May 97–29 Jul 99		Ld Donoughue	6 May 97–29 Jul 99
	Lady Scotland	29 Jul 99–11 Jun 01		Ld Whitty	11 Jun 01–9 May 05
	B. Bradshaw	11 Jun 01–20 May 02		B. Bradshaw	12 Jun 03–
	Lady Amos	11 Jun 01–13 May 03		J. Knight	9 May 05–
	D. MacShane	29 May 02–27 Oct 02		Ld Bach	9 May 05–
	M. O'Brien	29 May 02–12 Jun 03			
	B. Rammell	27 Oct 02–9 May 05			
	C. Mullin	12 Jun 03–			
	Ld Triesman	9 May 05–			
Home O.	**J. STRAW**	2 May 97	*Defence*	**G. ROBERTSON (*Ld*)**	3 May 97

LABOUR GOVERNMENT 1997– *(contd.)*

	G. HOON	11 Oct 99
	J. REID	6 May 05
Min.of	J. REID	6 May 97–28 Jul 98
State	D. HENDERSON	28 Jul 98–29 Jun 99
(Armed	J. SPELLAR	29 Jul 99–9 Jun 01
Forces)		
State	Ld GILBERT	6 May 97–29 Jul 99
(Def. Proc.)	Lady SYMONS	29 Jul 99–9 Jun 01
Min. of	A. INGRAM	9 Jun 01–
State		
U-S.	J. Spellar	6 May 97–29 Jul 99
	P. Kilfoyle	29 Jul 99–29 Jan 01
	L. Moonie	29 Jan 00–12 Jun 03
	Ld Bach	11 Jun 01–9 May 05
	I. Caplin	12 Jun 03–9 May 05
	D. Touhig	9 May 05–
	Ld Drayson	9 May 05–
Educ. &	**D. BLUNKETT**	2 May 97
Employ-	*(renamed Education and Skills 8 Jun 01)*	
ment	**Estelle MORRIS**	8 Jun 01
	C. CLARKE	24 Oct 02
	Ruth KELLY	16 Dec 04
Min. of	A. SMITH	3 May 97–11 Oct 99
State	S. BYERS	6 May 97–27 Jul 98
	Lady BLACKSTONE	6 May 97–
		9 Jun 01
	Estelle MORRIS	28 Jul 98–8 Jun 01
	Tessa JOWELL	11 Oct 99–8 Jun 01
	S.TIMMS	9 Jun 01–29 May 02
	Margaret HODGE	9 Jun 01–9 May 05
	(also Min. for Children 12 Jun 03)	
	D. MILIBAND	20 May 02–
		15 Dec 04
	A. JOHNSON	12 Jun 03–7 Sep 04
	S. TWIGG	16 Dec 04–9 May 05
	K. HOWELLS	9 Sep 04–9 May 05
	Jacqui SMITH	9 May 05–
	B. RAMMELL	9 May 05–
	Beverley HUGHES	9 May 05–
U-S.	A. Howarth	6 May 97–28 Jul 98
	Estelle Morris	6 May 97–28 Jul 98
	K. Howells	6 May 97–28 Jul 98
	Margaret Hodge	28 Jul 98–9 Jun 01
	G. Mudie	28 Jul 98–29 Jul 99
	C. Clarke	28 Jul 98–29 Jul 99
	Jacqui Smith	29 Jul 99–11 Jun 01
	M. Wicks	29 Jul 99–11 Jun 01
	M. Wills	29 Jul 99–11 Jun 01
	Lady Ashton	11 Jun 01–9 Sep 04
	I. Lewis	11 Jun 01–9 May 05
	J. Healey	11 Jun 01–29 May 02
	S. Twigg	29 May 02–16 Dec 04
	Ld Filkin	9 Sep 04–9 May 05
	D. Twigg	16 Dec 04–9 May 05

	Ld Adonis	9 May 05–
	P. Hope	9 May 05–
	Maria Eagle	9 May 05–
Environ-	**J. PRESCOTT**	2 May 97
ment	*(also Deputy P.M.)*	
	(office redistributed 8 Jun 01;	
	see Transport; see also	
	Environment Food and	
	Rural Affairs under Agriculture)	
Min. for	**G. STRANG**	3 May 97
Transport	*(office not in Cabinet 29 May 02)*	
	J. REID	27 Jul 98–17 May 99
	Helen LIDDELL	17 May 99–29 Jul 99
	Ld MACDONALD	29 Jul 99–9 Jun 01
	of TRADESTON	
Min. for	M. MEACHER	3 May 97–9 Jun 01
Environment		
Min. for	Hilary ARMSTRONG	6 May 97–
Local Govt		9 Jun 01
Min. for	R. CABORN	6 May 97–9 Jun 01
Regions	N. RAYNSFORD	29 Jul 99–9 Jun 01
U-S.	N. Raynsford	6 May 97–29 Jul 99
	Glenda Jackson	6 May 97–29 Jul 99
	Angela Eagle	6 May 97–28 Jul 98
	Lady Hayman	6 May 97–28 Jul 98
	A. Meale	28 Jul 98–29 Jul 99
	Ld Whitty	28 Jul 98–11 Jun 01
	Beverley Hughes	29 Jul 99–11 Jun 01
	K. Hill	29 Jul 99–11 Jun 01
	C. Mullin	29 Jul 99–25 Jan 01
	R. Ainsworth	25 Jan 01–11 Jun 01
Health	**F. DOBSON**	3 May 97
	A. MILBURN	11 Oct 99
	J. REID	11 Jun 03
	Patricia HEWITT	6 May 05
Min. of	Tessa JOWELL	6 May 97–11 Oct 99
State	A. MILBURN	6 May 97–23 Dec 98
	Lady JAY	6 May 97–27 Jul 98
	J. DENHAM	30 Dec 98–9 Jun 01
	J. HUTTON	11 Oct 99–6 May 05
	Jacqui SMITH	9 Jun 01–12 Jun 03
	Rosie WINTERTON	12 Jun 03–
	Jane KENNEDY	9 May 05–
	Ld WARNER	9 May 05–
U-S.	P. Boateng	6 May 97–28 Oct 98
	Lady Hayman	28 Jul 98–29 Jul 99
	J. Hutton	29 Oct 98–11 Oct 99
	Ld Hunt of	29 Jul 99–10 May 03
	King's Heath	
	Gisela Stuart	29 Jul 99–11 Jun 01
	Yvette Cooper	11 Oct 99–29 May 02
	Hazel Blears	11 Jan 01–12 Jun 03
	D. Lammy	29 May 02–12 Jun 03
	Melanie Johnson	12 Jun 03–9 May 05

LABOUR GOVERNMENT 1997– *(contd.)*

	S. Ladyman	12 Jun 03–9 May 05
	Ld Warner	12 Jun 03–9 May 05
	Caroline Flint	9 May 05–
	L. Byrne	9 May 05–
Internat.	**Clare SHORT**	3 May 97
Dev.	**Lady AMOS**	13 May 03
	H. BENN	7 Oct 03
Min. of	H. BENN	13 May 03–7 Oct 03
State		
U-S.	G. Foulkes	6 May 97
	C. Mullin	24 Jan 01
	H. Benn	11 Jun 01
	Sally Keeble	29 May 02
	G. Thomas	12 Jun 03
D. Lanc.	**D. CLARK**	3 May 97
(Cabinet	**J. CUNNINGHAM**	27 Jul 98
Office)	**Mo MOWLAM**	11 Oct 99
	(office not in Cabinet 9 Jun 01)	
	Ld MACDONALD	9 Jun 01
	of TRADESTON	
	D. ALEXANDER	12 Jun 03
	A. MILBURN	9 Sep 04
	J. HUTTON	6 May 05
Min. of	D. FOSTER	3 May 97–6 May 97
State	Ld FALCONER	28 Jul 98–11 Jun 01
	I. MCCARTNEY	29 Jul 99–11 Jun 01
	Barbara ROCHE	11 Jun 01–29 May 02
	(also Min. for Women 9 Nov 01)	
	Lady MORGAN	11 Jun 01–9 Nov 01
	(also Min. for Women)	
	D. ALEXANDER	29 May 02–12 Jun 03
	Ruth KELLY	12 Jun 03–16 Dec 04
	D. MILIBAND	16 Dec 04–6 May 05
P.S.	P. Kilfoyle	6 May 97–29 Jul 99
Cabinet O.		
Min.	P. MANDELSON	5 May 97
without	*(office vacant 27 Jul 98)*	
Portfolio	**C. CLARKE**	8 Jun 01
	J. REID	24 Oct 02
	I. MCCARTNEY	13 May 03

Nat. Heritage (renamed Jul 97 Culture, Media and Sport)

	C. SMITH	3 May 97
	Tessa JOWELL	8 Jun 01
Min. of	T. CLARKE	6 May 97–28 Jul 90
State	K.HOWELLS	28 Jul 98–9 Jun 01
	R. CABORN *(Sport)*	9 Jun 01–
	Lady BLACKSTONE	9 Jun 01–17 Jun 03
	(Arts)	
	Estelle MORRIS	18 Jun 03–9 May 05
	(Arts)	
U-S.	M. Fisher	6 May 97–28 Jul 98
(Arts)	A. Howarth	28 Jul 98–9 Jun 01
U-S.	Janet Anderson	28 Jul 98–11 Jun 01
(Tourism)		

U-S.	T. Banks	8 May 97–29 Jun 99
(Sport)	Kate Hoey	29 Jul 99–11 Jun 01
U-S.	Ld McIntosh	12 Jun 03–
	J. Purnell	9 May 05–
	D. Lammy	9 May 05–
Northern	**Mo MOWLAM**	3 May 97
Ireland	**P. MANDELSON**	11 Oct 99
	J. REID	24 Jan 01
	P. MURPHY	24 Oct 02
	P. HAIN *(also Sec. of*	6 May 05
	State Wales)	
Min. of	A. INGRAM	6 May 97–9 Jun 01
State	P. MURPHY	6 May 97–28 Jul 99
	Jane KENNEDY	9 Jun 01–1 Apr 04
	J. SPELLAR	12 Jun 03–9 May 05
	D. HANSON	9 May 05–
	Ld ROOKER	9 May 05–
U-S.	T. Worthington	6 May 97–28 Jul 98
	Ld Dubs	6 May 97–2 Dec 99
	J. McFall	28 Jul 98–2 Dec 99
	G. Howarth	29 Jul 99–9 Jun 01
	D. Browne	11 Jun 01–12 Jun 03
	I. Pearson	23 Oct 02–9 May 05
	Angela Smith	23 Oct 02–
	B. Gardiner	1 Apr 04–9 May 05
	S. Woodward	9 May 05–
Paym.-Gen. (see Treasury)		
Scot. O.	**D. DEWAR**	3 May 97
	J. REID	17 May 99
	Helen LIDDELL	24 Jan 01
	A. DARLING	12 Jun 03
	(also Transport)	
Min. of	H. McLEISH	6 May 97–29 Jul 99
State	B. WILSON	6 May 97–28 Jul 98
	Helen LIDDELL	28 Jul 98–
		17 May 99
	B. WILSON	29 Jul 99–24 Jan 01
	G. FOULKES	24 Jan 01–29 May 02
Advocate-	Lynda CLARK	17 May 99
Gen.		
U-S.	S. Galbraith	6 May 97–29 Jul 99
	M. Chisholm	6 May 97–10 Dec 97
	C. Macdonald	11 Dec 97–29 Jul 99
	Ld Sewel	6 May 97–29 Jul 99
	Ld Macdonald	3 Aug 98–29 Jul 99
	of Tradeston	
	Anne McGuire	29 May 02–
		12 Jun 03
Soc. Sec.	**Harriet HARMAN**	3 May 97
	A. DARLING	27 Jul 98
	(renamed Work and Pensions	
	9 Jun 01)	
	A. SMITH	29 May 02
	A. JOHNSON	15 Sep 04
	D. BLUNKETT	6 May 05

LABOUR GOVERNMENT 1997– (*contd.*)

Min. of	F. FIELD	3 May 97–28 Jul 98		M. O'BRIEN	12 Jun 03–9 May 05	
State	J.DENHAM	28 Jul 98–30 Dec 98		D. ALEXANDER	9 Sep 04–9 May 05	
	S. TIMMS	4 Jan 99–29 Jul 99		(*also in F.O.*)		
	J. ROOKER	29 Jul 99–9 Jun 01		M. WICKS		9 May 05–
	N. BROWN	9 Jun 01–12 Jun 03		I. PEARSON (*also in F.O.*)		9 May 05–
	I. MCCARTNEY	9 Jun 01–13 Mar 03		A. MICHAEL		9 May 05–
	D. BROWNE	12 Jun 03–1Apr 04	U-S.	N. Griffiths	6 May 97–28 Jul 98	
	M. WICKS	12 Jun 03–9 May 05		Barbara Roche	6 May 97–4 Jan 99	
	Jane KENNEDY	1 Apr 04–9 May 05		K. Howells	28 Jul 98–11 Jun 01	
	Margaret HODGE	9 May 05–		Ld Sainsbury		28 Jul 98–
U-S.	K. Bradley	6 May 97–28 Jul 98		M. Wills	4 Jan 99–29 Jul 99	
	J. Denham	6 May 97–28 Jul 98		A. Johnson	29 Jul 99–11 Jun 01	
	Lady Hollis	6 May 97–		N. Griffiths	11 Jun 01–9 May 05	
	Angela Eagle	28 Jul 98–11 Jun 01		Melanie Johnson	11 Jun 01–12 Jun 03	
	S. Timms	28 Jul 98–4 Jan 99		B. Gardiner		9 May 05–
	H. Bayley	4 Jan 99–11 Jun 01		G. Sutcliffe		12 Jun 03–
	M. Wicks	11 Jun 01–12 Jun 03		Meg Munn (*also Deputy*		
	Maria Eagle	11 Jun 01–9 May 05		*Minister for Women*)		9 May 05–
	C. Pond	12 Jun 03–9 May 05	*Transport, Local Govt and the Regions (Dept*			
	Ld Hunt of King's Heath	9 May 05–	*created 8 Jun 01)*			
	J. Plaskitt	9 May 05–		**S. BYERS**		8 Jun 01
	Liz Blackman	9 May 05–	(*Dept. subdivided 29 May 02 See Deputy P.M. and*			
U-S.	Joan Ruddock	11 Jun 97–28 Jul 98	*also Transport)*			
(*Women*)			Min. of S.	J. SPELLAR	9 Jun 01–29 May 02	
Trade	**Margaret BECKETT**	2 May 97		N. RAYNSFORD	9 Jun 01–29 May 02	
	P. MANDELSON	27 Jul 98		Ld FALCONER	9 Jun 01–29 May 02	
	S. BYERS	23 Dec 98	U-S.	D. Jamieson	11 Jun 01–29 May 02	
	(*renamed Trade and Industry 8 Jun 01*)			Sally Keeble	11 Jun 01–29 May 02	
	Patricia HEWITT	8 Jun 01		A. Whitehead	11 Jun 01–29 May 02	
	(*and Min. for Women*)		*Transport (Transport as separate Dept 29 May 02)*			
	A. JOHNSON	6 May 05		**A. DARLING**		29 May 02
Min. for	Ld CLINTON-DAVIS	6 May 97–		(*also Sec of State for Scotland 12 June 03*)		
Trade		29 Jul 99	Min.	J. SPELLAR		29 May 02
	B. WILSON	28 Jul 98–29 Jul 99		K. HOWELLS		12 Jun 03
	R. CABORN	29 Jul 99–9 Jun 01		T.McNULTY		9 Sep 04
Min. for	I. MCCARTNEY	6 May 97–29 Jul 99		S. LADYMAN		9 May 05
Comp.			U-S.	D. Jamieson	29 May 02–9 May 05	
Min. for	Helen LIDDELL	29 Jul 99–24 Jan 01		T. McNulty	12 Jun 02–9 Sep 04	
Energy &				Charlotte Atkins	9 Sep 04–9 May 05	
Competition	P. HAIN	24 Jan 01–9 Jun 01		D. Twigg		9 May 05–
Min. for	J. BATTLE	6 May 97–29 Jul 99		Karen Buck		9 May 05–
Industry			Wales	**R. DAVIES**		3 May 97
Min. for	Patricia HEWITT	29 Jul 99–8 Jun 01		**A. MICHAEL**		27 Oct 98
Small				**P. MURPHY**		29 Jul 99
Business				**P. HAIN**		24 Oct 02
Min. for	Ld SIMON	8 May 97–29 Jul 99		(*also Ld Privy Seal 11 Jun 03; Sec. of*		
Eur.	(*also in Treasury*)		*State Northern Ireland 9 May 05*)			
Min. of	B. WILSON	9 Jun 01–12 Jun 03	U-S.	W. Griffiths	6 May 97–28 Jul 98	
State	A. JOHNSON	9 Jun 01–12 Jun 03		P. Hain	6 May 97–29 Jul 99	
	Lady SYMONS	9 Jun 01–12 Jun 03		J. O. Jones	28 Jul 98–29 Jul 99	
	(*also in F.O.*)			D. Hanson	29 Jul 99–11 Jun 01	
	S. TIMMS	29 May 02–		D. Touhig	11 Jun 01–9 May 05	
	Jacqui SMITH	12 Jun 03–9 May 05		N. Ainger		9 May 05–
	(*also Deputy Minister for Women*)		*Work and Pensions (created 9 Jun 2002; see Soc. Sec.)*			

LABOUR GOVERNMENT 1997– *(contd.)*

Law Officers

Att.-Gen.	J. MORRIS	6 May 97
	Ld WILLIAMS OF MOSTYN	29 Jul 99
	Ld GOLDSMITH	9 Jun 01
Sol.-Gen.	Ld FALCONER	6 May 97
	R. CRANSTON	28 Jul 98
	Harriet HARMAN	9 Jun 01
	M. O'BRIEN	9 May 05
Ld. Adv.	Ld HARDIE	7 May 97–17 May 99
Sol.-Gen. *Scotland*	C. BOYD[1]	7 May 97–17 May 01

Whips

P.S. to *Treasury*	N. BROWN *(office in Cabinet)*	3 May 97
	Ann TAYLOR	27 Jul 98
	Hilary ARMSTRONG	9 Jun 01
Lds of	R. Ainsworth	8 May 97–25 Jan 01
Treasury	G. Allen	8 May 97–28 Jul 98
	J. Dowd	8 May 97–11 Jun 01
	J. McFall	8 May 97–28 Jul 98
	J. O. Jones	8 May 97–28 Jul 98
	C. Betts	28 Jul 98–11 Jun 01
	D. Jamieson	28 Jul 98–11 Jun 01
	Jane Kennedy	28 Jul 98–11 Oct 99
	D. Clelland	2 Feb 01–11 Jun 01
	Anne McGuire	11 Jun 01–29 May 02
	J. Heppell	11 Jun 01–9 May 05
	N. Ainger	11 Jun 01–9 May 05
	T. McNulty	11 Jun 01–29 May 02
	G. Stringer	11 Jun 01–29 May 02
	J. Fitzpatrick	29 May 02–12 Jun 03
	I. Pearson	29 May 02–12 Jun 03
	(also U-S. N. Ireland 23 Oct 02)	
	P. Woolas	29 May 02–12 Jun 03
	J. Murphy	12 Jun 03–9 May 05
	Joan Ryan	12 Jun 03–9 May 05
	D. Twigg	12 Jun 03–16 Dec 04
	Gillan Merron	16 Dec 04–
	V. Coaker	9 May 05–
	T. Watson	9 May 05–
Ass.	C. Betts	8 May 97–28 Jul 98
Whips	D. Clelland	8 May 97–2 Feb 01
	K. Hughes	8 May 97–11 Jun 01
	D. Jamieson	8 May 97–28 Jul 98
	Jane Kennedy	8 May 97–28 Jul 98
	G. Pope	8 May 97–11 Nov 99
	Bridget Prentice	8 May 97–28 Jul 98
	M. Hall	28 Jul 98–11 Jun 01
	D. Hanson	28 Jul 98–29 Jul 99
	K. Hill	28 Jul 98–29 Jul 99

Anne McGuire	29 Jul 99–11 Jun 01
G. Sutcliffe	29 Jul 99–11 Jun 01
T. McNulty	18 Oct 99–11 Jun 01
D. Touhig	17 Nov 99–11 Jun 01
I. Pearson	2 Feb 01–29 May 02
F. Kemp	11 Jun 01–9 May 05
Angela Smith	11 Jun 01–12 Jun 03
(also U-S. N. Ireland 23 Oct 02)	
I. Caplin	11 Jun 01–12 Jun 03
J. Fitzpatrick	11 Jun 01–29 May 02
P. Woolas	11 Jun 01–29 May 02
D. Norris	11 Jun 01–12 Jun 03
J. Murphy	29 May 02–12 Jun 03
Joan Ryan	29 May 02–12 Jun 03
D. Twigg	9 May 02–12 Jun 03
Gillian Merron	27 Oct 02–16 Dec 04
Charlotte Atkins	29 May 02–9 Sep 04
V. Coaker	12 Jun 03–9 May 05
P. Clark	12 Jun 03–9 May 05
Margaret Moran	12 Jun 03–9 May 05
Bridget Prentice	12 Jun 03–9 May 05
J. Purnell	16 Dec 04–9 May 05
F. Roy	9 May 05–
I. Cawsey	9 May 05–
A. Campbell	9 May 05–
D. Watts	9 May 05–
Claire Ward	9 May 05–
P. Dhanda	9 May 05–
T. Cunningham	9 May 05–
K. Brennan	9 May 05–

H.M. Household

Treasurer	G. MUDIE	8 May 97
	K. BRADLEY	28 Jul 98
	K. HILL	11 Jun 01
	R. AINSWORTH	12 Jun 03
Compt.	T. MCAVOY	8 May 97
Vice-	Janet ANDERSON	8 May 97
Chamb.	G. ALLEN	28 Jul 98
	G. SUTCLIFFE	11 Jun 01
	J. FITZPATRICK	12 Jun 03
Cap. Gent.	Ld CARTER[2]	6 May 97
at Arms	Ld GROCOTT[2]	29 May 02
Cap. Yeo.	Ld MCINTOSH	3 May 97
of Guard	Ld DAVIES of OLDHAM	12 Jun 03
Lords in	Ld Haskel	8 May 97–28 Jul 98
Waiting	Lady Farrington	8 May 97–
	Ld Whitty	8 May 97–28 Jul 98
	Lady Gould	8 May 97–18 Dec 98
	Ld Hoyle	8 May 97–9 Apr 99
	Lady Ramsay	18 Dec 98–11 Jun 01

[1] Not a member of the House of Commons.   [2] Attending Cabinet.

LABOUR GOVERNMENT 1997– (*contd.*)

Lady Amos	28 Jul 98–11 Jun 01	Ld Grocott	11 Jun 01–29 May 02
Ld Hunt of King's Heath	28 Jul 98–29 Jul 99	Lady Andrews	29 May 02–9 May 05
Ld Burlison	9 Apr 99–11 Jun 01	Lady Crawley	29 May 02–
Ld Bach	29 Jul 99–20 Nov 00	Ld Evans	12 Jun 03–
Ld Davies of Oldham	20 Nov 00–12 Jun 03	Ld Triesman[1]	19 Dec 03–9 May 05
Ld Bassam	11 Jun 01–	Lady Royall	9 May 05–
Ld Filkin	11 Jun 01–29 May 02	Ld McKenzie	9 May 05–

Ministerial Salaries

	Prime Minister [a]	Secretaries of State [a]	Other Dept. Ministers [a]	Reduced Parl. Salary
1831	£5,000	£5,000	£2,000	–
1937	£10,000	£5,000	£5,000	–
1965	£14,000	£8,500	£8,500	–
1972	£20,000	£13,000	£7,500	–
1978	£22,000	£14,300	£8,250	–
1979	£23,500	£19,650	£12,625	–
1980	£34,650	£23,500	£16,250	–
1981	£36,725	£23,500	£19,775	£6,930
1982	£38,200	£28,950	£20,575	£8,130
1983	£38,200	£28,950	£20,575	£8,460
1984	£38,987	£29,367	£20,867	£11,443
1985	£40,808	£30,188	£20,708	£12,792
1986	£42,745	£31,625	£21,795	£13,375
1987	£44,775	£33,145	£22,875	£13,875
1988	£45,787	£34,157	£23,887	£16,911
1989	£46,109	£34,479	£24,209	£18,148
1990	£46,750	£35,120	£24,850	£20,101
1991	£50,724	£38,105	£26,962	£21,809
1992	£53,007	£39,820	£28,175	£23,227
1994	£54,438	£40,895	£28,936	£23,854
1995	£55,900	£41,994	£29,713	£24,495
1996	£58,557	£43,991	£31,125	£25,660
1997	£100,000	£60,000	£31,125	£43,000
1998	£102,750	£61,650	£31,981	£45,066
1999	£107,179	£64,307	£33,359	£47,008
2000	£110,287	£66,172	£34,326	£48,371
2001	£113,596	£68,157	£35,356	£49,822/£51,822
2002	£116,436	£69,861	£36,240	£55,118
2003	£119,056	£71,433	£37,055	£56,358
2004	£121,437	£72,862	£37,796	£57,485

[a] Not including the salary Ministers receive as Members of Parliament.

[1] Paid as a Parliamentary Secretary.

The figures shown are the full entitlement. In 1979 the Prime Minister chose to forgo any increase and from 1980 to 1991 accepted the same salary as a Cabinet Minister in the Commons. In 1997 the Prime Minister and Cabinet Ministers decided to accept the pre-election salaries of £58,557 (Prime Minister) and £43,991 (Secretaries of State). They also took a reduced salary in each year until 2001, when they agreed to draw their full entitlement.

Opposition Salaries

	Leader of the Opposition [a]	Chief Opposition Whip	
		House of Commons [a]	House of Lords
1937	£2,000	–	–
1957	£3,000	–	–
1965	£4,500	£3,750	£1,500
1972	£9,500	£7,500	£2,500
1978	£10,450	£8,250	£3,248
1979	£16,225	£12,625	£7,124
1980	£20,950	£16,250	£9,950
1981	£20,950	$16,250	£9,950
1982	£24,100	£18,650	£6,925
1983	£26,575	£20,575	£17,840
1984	£26,947	£20,867	£18,770
1985	£27,518	£20,798	£19,710
1986	£28,825	£21,795	£20,645
1987	£30,225	£22,875	£21,570
1988	£31,237	£23,887	£25,618
1989	£31,559	£24,209	£27,377
1990	£32,200	£24,850	£29,971
1991	£34,937	£26,962	£32,519
1992	£36,509	£28,175	£33,982
1994	£37,495	£28,936	£35,099
1995	£38,502	£29,713	£36,239
1996	£40,332	£31,125	£38,313
1997	£55,612	£31,125	£39,462
1998	£56,513	£31,981	£40,547
1999	£56,513	£31,981	£51,181
2000	£60,659	£34,326	£52,645
2001	£62,479	£35,356	£54,224
2002	£64,041	£36,240	£59,630
2003	£65,482	£37,055	£60,972
2004	£66,792	£37,796	£62,191
2005	£68,662	£38,854	£63,933

[a] Not including the Parliamentary salary – see above.

Since 1975 the opposition parties have received financial assistance (known as Short money, after the then Leader of the House) which in 1999 amounted to just under £4,000 per seat. In that year the Neill Committee recommended a substantial increase which more than doubled the amount of assistance – the Conservatives in 1999–2000 received £3,377,973 compared to £1,530,191 paid to Labour in 1996–97.

Ministerial Offices 1979–2005

This list includes almost all specifically named ministerial offices held by Ministers or Ministers of State, apart from appointments in the Royal Household or Ministers of State without a functional title. It does not include offices held by junior ministers. In the 1980s it became increasingly common to give specific titles to Ministers of State in the larger departments, especially in Defence, Environment, Trade, and Transport. Minor variations in these labels were frequent and are not listed here.

Agriculture. Minister of Agriculture, Fisheries and Food, 1979–2001

Armed Forces. Minister for, 1981–

Arts. Minister for Arts, 1979–92; Secretary of State for National Heritage 1992–97; Secretary of State for Culture, Media and Sport 1997–

Attorney-General, 1979–

Aviation. (under Transport) Minister of State for Aviation and Shipping 1990–94

Cabinet Office. Minister for the, 1998–

Civil Service. Minister for the, 1979–

Communities and Local Government. Minister for 2005–

Constitutional Affairs. Secretary of State, 2003–

Construction. (see Environment)

Consumer Affairs. Minister for, 1979– 1983 *(under Trade)*

Corporate Affairs. Minister for, 1990– *(under Trade)*

Culture, Media and Sport. Secretary of State, 1997–

Defence. Secretary of State, 1979–

Defence. Minister for the Armed Forces, 1981–

Defence Support. Minister, 1985–86

Defence Procurement. Minister for, 1981–

Deputy Prime Minister, 1979–88, 1989–90, 1995–

Duchy of Lancaster. Chancellor, 1979–

Education. Secretary of State for Education and Science, 1979–92; Secretary of State for Education 1992–94; Secretary of State for Employment and Education 1994–97; Secretary of State for Education and Skills, 1997–

Employment. Secretary of State, 1979–95

Energy. Secretary of State, 1979–92; Minister for, 1992–94 *(see also under Trade)*

Environment (Transport and the Regions 1997–01). Secretary of State, 1979–2001; (*the titles attached to the two to four Ministers in the Environment Department changed constantly; Construction, Housing, Local Government, Water, Inner Cities, Countryside, Planning, Regions and Regeneration were variously combined, often for short periods and without any change in the ministerial team) (See also Transport)*

Environment, Food, and Rural Affairs. Secretary of State, 2001–

First Secretary of State. 1995–97

Foreign and Commonwealth Affairs. Secretary of State, 1979–

Health. Minister for, 1979–; Secretary of State, 1988–

Health and Social Security. 1979–88. *(See Social Services)*

Heritage. Minister for 1991–92. Secretary of State 1992–97 *(see Culture).*

Home Affairs. Secretary of State, 1979–

Industry. Secretary of State, 1979–83 *(see Trade)*

Information Technology. Minister for Industry and Information Technology, 1981–83; Minister for Information Technology, 1983–87

International Development. Secretary of State, 1997–

Local Government. Minister, 1979– *(under Environment)*

Lord Advocate. 1979–

Lord Chancellor. 1979–

Lord President of the Council. 1979–97

Lord Privy Seal. 1979–

National Heritage. Secretary of State, 1992–97 *(see Culture)*

Northern Ireland. Secretary of State, 1979–

Paymaster-General. 1979–

Portfolio. Minister without Portfolio, 1984–85, 1994–98

President of the Council, 1997–

Prime Minister. 1979–

Privy Council Office. Minister of State, 1983–4, 1985–90

Public Transport. Minister for, 1988– *(under Transport)*

Regions, Minister for, 2002–05

Scotland. Secretary of State, 1979–

Social Security. Secretary of State, 1988–2001; also Minister for Social Security, 1979–2001 (and Disabled People, 1987–2001)

Social Services. Secretary of State, 1979–88

Solicitor-General. 1979–

State, First Secretary of. 1995–97

Trade. President of the Board of Trade, 1992–98; Secretary of State for Trade and Industry, 1983–92, 1998–; Secretary of State for Trade, 1979–83. also Minister for Trade, 1983–; Minister for Trade and Competitiveness in Europe, 1997–2001 *(See Industry)*

Transport. Secretary of State, 1981–97, 2001–; Minister of Transport, 1979–81; Minister of State for Public Transport, 1990–94; Minister of State for Aviation and Shipping, 1990–94; Minister for Railways and Roads (and Public Transport 1996–97), 1994–97

Treasury. Chancellor of the Exchequer, 1979–; Chief Secretary, 1979–; Financial Secretary, 1979–; Economic Secretary, 1981–; Minister of State, 1979–87, 1990–92

Wales. Secretary of State, 1979–99

Women. Minister for, 1997–

Work and Pensions. Secretary of State, 2001–

Holders of Ministerial Offices 1979–2005

Prime Minister
5 Apr 76	J. Callaghan
4 May 79	Margaret Thatcher
28 Nov 90	J. Major
2 May 97	T. Blair

Deputy Prime Minister
4 May 79–10 Jan 88	
	W. Whitelaw
24 Jul 89–1 Nov 90	
	Sir G. Howe
20 Jul 95–2 May 97	
	M. Heseltine
2 May 97–	J. Prescott

Lord President of the Council
8 Apr 76	M. Foot
5 May 79	Ld Soames
14 Sep 81	F. Pym
5 Apr 82	J. Biffen
11 Jun 83	Vt Whitelaw
13 Jun 87	J. Wakeham
10 Jan 88	J. MacGregor
11 Apr 92	A. Newton

(President of the Council)
2 May 97	Ann Taylor
27 Jul 98	Margaret Beckett
8 Jun 01	R. Cook
(18 Mar 03 office vacant)	
4 Apr 03	J. Reid
13 May 03	Baroness Amos

Lord Chancellor
5 Mar 74	Ld Elwyn-Jones
5 May 79	Ld Hailsham
13 Jun 87	Ld Havers
26 Oct 87	Ld Mackay
2 May 97	Ld Irvine
11 Jun 03	Ld Falconer

Lord Privy Seal
10 Sep 76	Ld Peart
5 May 79	Sir I. Gilmour
14 Sep 81	H. Atkins
6 Apr 82	Lady Young
11 Jun 83	J. Biffen
13 Jun 87	J. Wakeham
10 Jan 88	Ld Belstead
28 Nov 90	Ld Waddington
11 Apr 92	J. Wakeham
20 Jul 94	Vt Cranborne
2 May 97	Ld Richard
27 Jul 98	Lady Jay
8 Jun 01	Ld Williams of Mostyn
11 Jun 03	P. Hain
6 May 05	G. Hoon

Chancellor of the Exchequer
25 Mar 74	D. Healey
5 May 79	Sir G. Howe
11 Jun 83	N. Lawson
26 Oct 89	J. Major
28 Nov 90	N. Lamont
27 May 93	K. Clarke
2 May 97	G. Brown

Secretary of State for Foreign and Commonwealth Affairs
21 Feb 77	D. Owen
5 May 79	Ld Carrington
5 Apr 82	F. Pym
11 Jun 83	Sir G. Howe
14 Jun 89	J. Major
26 Oct 89	D. Hurd
5 Jul 95	M. Rifkind
2 May 97	R. Cook
8 Jun 01	J. Straw

Secretary of State for the Home Department
10 Sep 76	M. Rees
5 May 79	W. Whitelaw
11 Jun 83	L. Brittan
2 Sep 85	D. Hurd
26 Oct 89	D. Waddington
28 Nov 90	K. Baker
11 Apr 92	K. Clarke
27 May 93	M. Howard
2 May 97	J. Straw
8 Jun 01	D. Blunkett
15 Dec 04	C. Clarke

Minister of Agriculture, Fisheries and Food
10 Sep 76	J. Silkin
5 May 79	P. Walker
11 Jun 83	M. Jopling
13 Jun 87	J. MacGregor
24 Jul 89	J. S. Gummer
27 May 93	Gillian Shephard
20 Jul 94	W. Waldegrave
5 Jul 95	D. Hogg
3 May 97	J. Cunningham
27 Jul 98	N. Brown
(8 Jun 01 merged into Department of Environment, Food and Rural Affairs)	

Minister of State for the Armed Forces
29 May 81	P. Blaker
13 Jun 83	J. Stanley
13 Jun 87	A. Clark
25 Jul 88	A. Hamilton
27 May 93	J. Hanley
20 Jul 94	N. Soames
6 May 97	J. Reid
28 Jul 98	D. Henderson
27 Jul 99	J. Spellar
12 Jun 01	A. Ingram

Minister for the Arts
14 Apr 76	Ld Donaldson
5 May 79	N. St John-Stevas
5 Jun 81	P. Channon
13 Jun 83	E of Gowrie
2 Sep 85	R. Luce
26 Jul 90	D. Mellor
28 Nov 90	T. Renton
(11 Apr 92 under National Heritage)	

Attorney-General
7 Mar 74	S. Silkin
5 May 79	Sir M. Havers
13 Jun 87	Sir P. Mayhew
15 Apr 92	Sir N. Lyell
3 May 97	J. Morris
27 Jul 99	Ld Williams of Mostyn
11 Jun 01	Ld Goldsmith

Minister for the Public Service
10 Apr 92	W. Waldegrave
20 Jul 94	D. Hunt
5 Jul 95	R. Freeman
(Office wound up May 2 1997)	

(Minister for the Civil Service)
2 May 97	T. Blair

Minister for Consumer Affairs
(under Trade)
8 May 79	Sally Oppenheim
5 Mar 82	G. Vaughan
(office wound up 13 Jun 83)	
20 Jul 94	Earl Ferrers
(Office wound up 6 Jul 95)	

Minister for Corporate Affairs
(under Trade)
24 Jul 89	J. Redwood
(office vacant 15 Apr 92)	

Secretary of State for Defence
10 Sep 76	F. Mulley
5 May 79	F. Pym
5 Jan 81	J. Nott
8 Jan 83	M. Heseltine
9 Jan 86	G. Younger
24 Jul 89	T. King
15 Apr 92	M. Rifkind
5 Jul 95	M. Portillo
2 May 97	G. Robertson
11 Oct 99	G. Hoon
6 May 05	J. Reid

Minister of State for Defence Procurement
29 May 81	Vt Trenchard
6 Jan 83	G. Pattie
11 Sep 84	A. Butler
2 Sep 85	N. Lamont
21 May 86	Ld Trefgarne
13 Jun 87	I. Stewart
24 Jul 89	A. Clark
15 Apr 92	J. Aitken
20 Jul 94	R. Freeman
5 Jul 95	J. Arbuthnot
6 May 97	Ld Gilbert
29 Jul 99	Lady Symons
(office vacant 9 Jun 01)	

Minister for Defence Support
2 Sep 85	Ld Trefgarne
(office wound up 10 Sep 86)	

Secretary of State for Education and Science
10 Sep 76	Shirley Williams
5 May 79	M. Carlisle
14 Sep 81	Sir K. Joseph
21 May 86	K. Baker
24 Jul 89	J. MacGregor
2 Nov 90	K. Clarke

(Secretary of State for Education)

15 Apr 92   J. Patten

(Secretary of State for Education and Employment)

20 Jul 94   Gillian Shephard

(Secretary of State for Education and Skills)

2 May 97   D. Blunkett
8 Jun 01   Estelle Morris
24 Oct 02   C. Clarke
16 Dec 04   Ruth Kelly

Secretary of State for Employment

8 Apr 76   A. Booth
5 May 79   J. Prior
14 Sep 81   N. Tebbit
16 Oct 83   T. King
2 Sep 85   Ld Young of Graffham
13 Jun 87   N. Fowler
3 Jan 90   M. Howard
12 Apr 92   Gillian Shephard
27 May 93   D. Hunt
(office merged with Education 20 Jul 94)

Secretary of State for Energy

10 Jun 75   A. Benn
5 May 79   D. Howell
14 Sep 81   N. Lawson
11 Jun 83   P. Walker
13 Jun 87   C. Parkinson
24 Jul 89   J. Wakeham
(office merged with Trade 15 Apr 92)

Minister for Energy

(under Trade)

15 Apr 92   T. Eggar
(Industry and Energy
20 Jul 94)

Secretary of State for the Environment

8 Apr 76   P. Shore
5 May 79   M. Heseltine
6 Jan 83   T. King
11 Jun 83   P. Jenkin
2 Sep 85   K. Baker
21 May 86   N. Ridley
24 Jul 89   C. Patten
28 Nov 90   M. Heseltine
11 Apr 92   M. Howard
27 May 93   J. S. Gummer

(Environment, Transport and the Regions)

2 May 97   J. Prescott

(Environment, Food and Rural Affairs)

8 Jun 01   Margaret Beckett

Minister for Environment

(under Environment; from 8 Jun 01,
Environment, Food and Rural Affairs)

27 Mar 85   Ld Elton
10 Sep 86   W. Waldegrave

---

13 Jun 87   Ld Belstead
25 Jul 88   M. Howard
24 Jul 89   D. Trippier
14 Apr 92   D. Maclean
27 May 93   T. Yeo
8 Jan 94   R. Atkins
6 Jul 95   Earl Ferrers
3 May 97   M. Meacher
12 Jun 03   E. Morley

Secretary of State for Health and Social Security

5 May 79   P. Jenkin
14 Sep 81   N. Fowler
13 Jun 87   J. Moore

Secretary of State for Health

5 Jul 88   K. Clarke
2 Nov 90   W. Waldegrave
10 Apr 92   Virginia Bottomley
5 Jul 95   S. Dorrell
2 May 97   F. Dobson
11 Oct 99   A. Milburn
11 Jun 03   J. Reid
6 May 05   Patricia Hewitt

Minister for Health

(under Social Services)

7 May 79   G. Vaughan
5 Mar 82   K. Clarke
2 Sep 85   B. Hayhoe
11 Sep 84   A. Newton
10 Sep 86   D. Mellor
(Under Health)
25 Jul 89   Ld Trafford
28 Oct 89   Virginia Bottomley
15 Apr 92   B. Mawhinney
20 Jul 94   G. Malone
6 May 97   Tessa Jowell
11 Oct 99   J. Hutton
9 May 05   Jane Kennedy

Secretary of State for Industry

10 Jun 75   E. Varley
5 May 79   Sir K. Joseph
14 Sep 81   P. Jenkin
(11 Jun 83 office merged
with Trade)

Minister for Industry and Information Technology

13 Jun 83   K. Baker
11 Sep 84   G. Pattie
(office wound up 13 Jun 87)

Minister for Industry

(under Trade and Industry)

13 Jun 83   N. Lamont
2 Sep 85   P. Morrison
13 Jun 87   K. Clarke
24 Jul 88   A. Newton
25 Jul 89   D. Hogg
2 Nov 90   Ld Hesketh
(office vacant 23 May 91)
15 Apr 92   T. Sainsbury

Minister for Industry and Energy

20 Jul 94   T. Eggar
5 Jul 95   G. Knight
(office vacant 2 May 97)

International Development

2 May 97   Clare Short
13 May 03   Lady Amos
7 Oct 03   H. Benn

Chancellor of the Duchy of Lancaster

5 Mar 74   H. Lever
5 May 79   N. St John-Stevas
5 Jan 81   F. Pym
14 Sep 81   Lady Young
6 Apr 82   C. Parkinson[1]
11 Jun 83   Ld Cockfield
11 Sep 84   E of Gowrie
3 Sep 85   N. Tebbit[1]
13 Jun 87   K. Clarke
25 Jul 88   A. Newton
24 Jul 89   K. Baker[1]
28 Nov 90   C. Patten[1]
11 Apr 92   W. Waldegrave
20 Jul 94   D. Hunt
5 Jul 95   R. Freeman
3 May 97   D. Clark
(and Min. for Public Service)
27 Jul 98   J. Cunningham
(and Min. for Cabinet Office)
11 Oct 99   Mo Mowlam
9 Jun 01   D. Alexander
9 Sep 04   A. Milburn
6 May 05   J. Hutton

Secretary of State for National Heritage

11 Apr 92   D. Mellor
24 Sep 92   P. Brooke
20 Jul 94   S. Dorrell
5 Jul 95   Virginia Bottomley
3 May 97   C. Smith
(changed to Min. of Culture, Sport and
the Arts Jul 97)

Secretary of State for Northern Ireland

10 Sep 76   R. Mason
5 May 79   H. Atkins
14 Sep 81   J. Prior
11 Sep 84   D. Hurd
3 Sep 85   T. King
24 Jul 89   P. Brooke
15 Apr 92   Sir P. Mayhew
3 May 97   Mo Mowlam
11 Oct 99   P. Mandelson
24 Jan 01   J. Reid
24 Oct 02   P. Murphy
6 May 05   P. Hain

Minister of (for) Overseas Development

21 Feb 77   Judith Hart
6 May 79   N. Marten
6 Jan 83   T. Raison

---

[1] Also Party Chairman.

10 Sep 86	C. Patten
24 Jul 89–2 May 97	
	Lynda (Lady) Chalker

(the Foreign Secretary was technically the Minister in overall charge while the Minister for Overseas Development took day-to-day charge of the Department. It ceased to be a separate Department from 5 May 79 to 3 May 97 when it was reconstituted; see International Development).

Paymaster-General

8 Apr 76	Shirley Williams
5 May 79	A. Maude
5 Jan 81	F. Pym
14 Sep 81	C. Parkinson
11 Jun 83	*(office vacant)*
11 Sep 84	J. S. Gummer
2 Sep 85	K. Clarke
13 Jun 87	P. Brooke
24 Jul 89	E of Caithness
24 Jul 90	R. Ryder
28 Nov 90	Ld Belstead
15 Apr 92	Sir J. Cope
20 Jul 94	D. Heathcoat-Amory
20 Jul 96	D. Willetts
16 Dec 96	M. Bates
3 May 97	G. Robinson
4 Jan 99	Dawn Primarolo

Minister without Portfolio

11 Sep 84–5 Sep 85	
	Ld Young of Graffham
20 Jul 94–5 Jul 95	
	J. Hanley[1]
5 Jul 95–2 May 97	
	B. Mawhinney[1]
3 May 97–27 Jul 98	
	P. Mandelson
8 Jun 01–24 Oct 02	
	C. Clarke[1]
24 Oct 02–13 May 03	
	J. Reid[1]
13 May 03–	I. McCartney[1]

Minister for Consumer Affairs

(under Trade)

6 May 79	Sally Oppenheim
5 Mar 82	G. Vaughan
(13 Jun 83 office wound up)	

Secretary of State for Scotland

8 Apr 76	B. Millan
5 May 79	G. Younger
11 Jan 86	M. Rifkind
28 Nov 90	I. Lang
5 Jul 95	M. Forsyth
2 May 97	D. Dewar
17 May 99	J. Reid
24 Jan 01	Helen Liddell
(office abolished 11 Jun 03)	

Lord Advocate

8 Mar 74	R. King Murray
7 May 79	J. Mackay *(Ld)*

16 May 84	Ld Cameron of
	Lochbroom
4 Jan 89	Ld Fraser of Carmyllie
15 Apr 92	A. Rodger *(Ld)*
4 May 95	Ld Mackay of
	Drumadoon
7 May 97	Ld Hardie
(office devolved to Scotland 17 May 99)	

Solicitor-General for Scotland

14 Mar 74	J. McCluskey *(Ld)*
7 May 79	N. Fairbairn
28 Jan 82	P. Fraser
4 Jan 89	A. Rodger
15 Apr 92	T. Dawson
4 May 95	D. Mackay
(office ceased to be a political appointment 7 May 97)	

Secretary of State for Social Services

(& Head of the Department of Health and Social Security)

8 Apr 76	D. Ennals
5 May 79	P. Jenkin
14 Sep 81	N. Fowler
13 Jun 87	J. Moore
(office recast 25 Jul 88) (see Health)	

Secretary of State for Social Security

25 Jul 88	J. Moore
23 Jul 89	A. Newton
11 Apr 92	P. Lilley
2 May 97	Harriet Harman
27 Jul 98	A. Darling

(Secretary of State for Work and Pensions)

9 Jun 01	A. Darling
29 May 02	A. Smith
15 Sep 04	A. Johnson
6 May 05	D. Blunkett

Minister for Social Security

(under Social Services)

10 Sep 76	S. Orme
7 May 79	R. Prentice
8 Jan 81	H. Rossi
13 Jun 83	R. Boyson
11 Sep 84	A. Newton
10 Sep 86	J. Major
13 Jun 87	N. Scott
(under Social Security 25 Jul 88)	
20 Jul 94	W. Hague
5 Jul 95	A. Burt
3 May 97	F. Field
(office vacant 28 Jun 98)	
4 Jan 99	S. Timms
29 Jul 99	J. Rooker
9 Jun 01	N. Brown
12 Jun 03	M. Wicks
9 May 05	Margaret Hodge

Solicitor-General

7 Mar 74	P. Archer
5 May 79	Sir I. Percival

13 Jun 83	Sir P. Mayhew
13 Jun 87	Sir N. Lyell
15 Apr 92	Sir D. Spencer
6 May 97	Ld Falconer
28 Jul 98	R. Cranston
9 Jun 01	Harriet Harman
9 May 05	M. O'Brien

Minister with Responsibility for Sport

(U.-S., Educ. & Sci.)

20 Oct 64	D. Howell

(M. of S., Housing & Local Govt.)

13 Oct 69	D. Howell

(U.-S., Housing & Local Govt.)

24 Jun 70	E. Griffiths

(U.-S., Environment)

15 Oct 70	E. Griffiths

(M. of S., Environment)

7 Mar 74	D. Howell

(U.-S., Environment)

7 May 79	H. Monro
15 Sep 81	N. MacFarlane
7 Sep 85	R. Tracy
22 Jun 87	C. Moynihan
26 Jul 90	R. Atkins

(U.-S., Educ. & Sci.)

28 Nov 90	R. Atkins

(U.-S., Nat. Heritage)

14 Apr 92	R. Key
27 May 93	I. Sproat

(U.-S., Environment)

8 May 97	T. Banks

(Min., Culture, Media and Sport)

29 Jul 99	Kate Hoey
9 Jun 01	R. Caborn

First Secretary of State

20 Jul 95	M. Heseltine
2 May 97	*(office vacant)*

Secretary of State for Trade

(see also Industry)

12 Nov 78	J. Smith
5 May 79	J. Nott
14 Sep 81	J. Biffen
5 Apr 82	Ld Cockfield

(Secretary of State for Trade and Industry)

11 Jun 83	C. Parkinson
16 Oct 83	N. Tebbit
2 Sep 85	L. Brittan
24 Jan 86	P. Channon
13 Jun 87	Ld Young of Graffham
24 Jul 89	N. Ridley
14 Jul 90	P. Lilley

(President of the Board of Trade)

11 Apr 92	M. Heseltine
2 May 97	Margaret Beckett

(Secretary of State for Trade)

27 Jul 98	P. Mandelson
23 Dec 98	S. Byers
8 Jun 01	Patricia Hewitt

---

[1] Also Party Chairman.

(Secretary of State for Productivity, Energy and Industry)

6 May 05	A. Johnson

Minister for Trade

7 May 79	C. Parkinson
14 Sep 81	P. Rees
13 Jun 83	P. Channon
24 Jan 86	A. Clark
25 Jul 89	Ld Trefgarne
23 Jul 90	T. Sainsbury
15 Apr 92	R. Needham
6 Jul 95	A. Nelson
6 May 97	Ld Clinton-Davis
28 Jul 98	B. Wilson
29 Jul 99	R. Caborn

(specific title no longer used 9 Jun 01)

Secretary of State for Transport

10 Sep 76	W. Rodgers

(Minister of Transport)

5 May 79	N. Fowler

(Secretary of State for Transport)

5 Jan 81	N. Fowler
14 Sep 81	D. Howell
11 Jun 83	T. King
16 Oct 83	N. Ridley
21 May 86	J. Moore
13 Jun 87	P. Channon
24 Jul 89	C. Parkinson
28 Nov 90	M. Rifkind
15 Apr 92	J. MacGregor
20 Jul 94	B. Mawhinney
5 Jul 95	Sir G. Young

(Minister for Transport)

3 May 97	G. Strang
27 Jul 98	J. Reid
17 May 99	Helen Liddell
29 Jul 99	Ld Macdonald of Tradeston

(Secretary of State for Transport, Local Government and the Regions)

8 Jun 01	S. Byers

(Secretary of State for Transport)

29 May 02	A. Darling

Treasury

(see p. 22 for Chancellor of the Exchequer)

Chief Secretary

7 Mar 74	J. Barnett
5 May 79	J. Biffen
5 Jan 81	L. Brittan
11 Jun 83	P. Rees
2 Sep 85	J. MacGregor
13 Jun 87	J. Major
24 Jul 89	N. Lamont
28 Nov 90	D. Mellor
10 Apr 92	M. Portillo
20 Jul 94	J. Aitken
5 Jul 95	W. Waldegrave
3 May 97	A. Darling
27 Jul 98	S. Byers
23 Dec 98	A. Milburn
11 Oct 99	A. Smith
29 May 02	P. Boateng
6 May 05	D. Browne

Secretary of State for Wales

5 Mar 74	J. Morris
5 May 79	N. Edwards
3 Jun 87	P. Walker
4 May 90	D. Hunt
27 May 93	J. Redwood
5 Jul 95	W. Hague
3 May 97	R. Davies
27 Oct 98	A. Michael
28 Jul 99	P. Murphy
24 Oct 02	P. Hain

Minister for Women[1]

2 May 97	Harriet Harman
27 Jul 98	Lady Jay
8 Jun 01	Patricia Hewitt
6 May 05	Tessa Jowell

Leader of the House of Commons

8 Apr 76	M. Foot
5 May 79	N. St John-Stevas
5 Jan 81	F. Pym
5 Apr 82	J. Biffen
13 Jun 87	J. Wakeham
24 Jul 89	Sir G. Howe
3 Nov 90	J. MacGregor
11 Apr 92	A. Newton

2 May 97	Ann Taylor
27 Jul 98	Margaret Beckett
8 Jun 01	R. Cook

(office vacant 18 Mar 03)

4 Apr 03	J. Reid
11 Jun 03	P. Hain
6 May 05	G. Hoon

Leader of the House of Lords

10 Sep 76	Ld Peart
5 May 79	Ld Soames
14 Sep 81	Lady Young
11 Jun 83	Vt Whitelaw
10 Jan 88	Ld Belstead
28 Nov 90	Ld Waddington
11 Apr 92	Ld Wakeham
20 Jul 94	Vt Cranborne
2 May 97	Ld Richard
27 Jul 98	Lady Jay
8 Jun 01	Ld Williams of Mostyn
7 Oct 03	Lady Amos

Government Chief Whip

(Parliamentary Secretary to the Treasury)

8 Apr 76	M. Cocks
5 May 79	M. Jopling
11 Jun 83	J. Wakeham
13 Jun 87	D. Waddington
28 Oct 89	T. Renton
28 Nov 90	R. Ryder
5 Jul 95	A. Goodlad
3 May 97	N. Brown
27 Jul 98	Ann Taylor
9 Jun 01	Hilary Armstrong

Government Chief Whip in the House of Lords

(Captain of the Gentlemen at Arms)

11 Mar 74	Lady Llewelyn-Davies
6 May 79	Ld Denham
23 May 91	Ld Hesketh
16 Sep 93	Vt Ullswater
20 Jul 94	Ld Strathclyde
6 May 97	Ld Carter
29 May 02	Ld Grocott

Second Church Estates Commissioner

(not a Minister but always an MP from the governing party)

1974	T. Walker
1979	(Sir) W. van Straubenzee
1987	M. Alison
1997	(Sir) S. Bell

[1] Although these were the Ministers responsible at Cabinet level, in practice most of the day-to-day work running the Women and Equality Unit was done at junior minister level. The holders of this office were 11 Jun 97 Joan Ruddock (unpaid), 28 Jul 98 Tessa Jowell, 11 Jun 01 Lady Morgan, 9 Nov 01 Barbara Roche, 12 Jun 03 Jacqui Smith and 9 May 05 Meg Munn (unpaid).

Ministerial Statistics

Size of Cabinets and Governments 1980–2005
(at 1 Jan)

	1980	1990	2000	2005
Cabinet Ministers	22	22	22	21
Min. of State rank	38	33	34	36
Under-Sec. rank	47	48	49	52
MPs in paid posts	86	80	82	91
Peers in paid posts	21	22	24	20
Total paid posts	107	103	106	111
PPSs in Commons	37	47	47	56
Total MPs in Govt	114	111	129	148

Social and Educational Composition of British Cabinets 1976–2005

	No.	Ar.	Class Mid.	Work.	Pub. Sc.	Education Eton	Univ.	O&C
Apr 1976 Lab. Callaghan	22	1	13	7	7	–	15	10
May 1979 Con. Thatcher	22	3	19	–	20	6	18	17
Nov 1990 Con. Major	22	3	17	2	14	2	20	17
May 1997 Lab. Blair	22	–	15	7	8	–	21	3

Women Cabinet Ministers

1970–74 & 1979–90	Margaret Thatcher
1982–83	Lady Young
1992–97	Virginia Bottomley
1992–97	Gillian Shephard
1997–	Margaret Beckett
1997–2001	Ann Taylor
1997–2001	Mo Mowlam
1997–98	Harriet Harman

1997–2003	Clare Short
1998–2001	Lady Jay
2001–	Hilary Armstrong
2001–	Tessa Jowell
2001–03	Helen Liddell
2001–02	Estelle Morris
2003–	Lady Amos
2004–	Ruth Kelly

Durability of Prime Ministers 1979–2005

	Years as PM	Years in Age	Pre-PM Years in HC	Post-PM Years in HC	Years Lived after PM
Margaret Thatcher	11.6	53	20	2	–
J. Major	7.6	47	11	4	–
J. Callaghan	3.1	64	31	8	26
T. Blair	–	43	14	–	–

Long Tenure of Ministerial Office

The following are the only British politicians in this period to have served more than 20 years in ministerial office:

Years	Office	First Office	Last
20	Vt Hailsham	1945	1987
20	K. Clarke	1972	1997

Long Tenure in One Department

18	Vt Long	Ld in Waiting	1979–97
15	W. Roberts	U-S., then Min. Welsh O.	1979–94
12	Ld Hailsham	Ld Chancellor	1970–74, 1979–87
12	Ld Denham (also a Whip 1961–64, 1970–74)	Cap. Gent. at Arms	1979–91
11	Margaret Thatcher	Prime Minister	1979–90
10	Ld Mackay of Clashfern	Ld Chancellor	1987–97

Oldest and Youngest Ministers since 1979

The oldest Cabinet Minister since 1967 was Vt Hailsham (79 in 1989). The youngest Cabinet Minister was W. Hague (35 in 1994). The youngest M.P. to hold any office was D. Lammy (29 in 2002).

Cabinet Members Dying in Office[1]

20 Sep 03	Ld Williams of Mostyn

Cabinet Members Suffering Electoral Defeat while Holding Office

May 1979	Shirley Williams
Apr 1992	C. Patten
May 1997	A. Newton
	M. Forsyth
	R. Freeman
	I. Lang
	M. Portillo
	M. Rifkind
	W. Waldegrave

Ministerial Resignations

Resignations from ministerial office are not easy to classify. A retirement on the ground of ill-health may always conceal a protest or a dismissal. However, there are some cases where ministers have unquestionably left office because they were not willing to continue to accept collective responsibility for some part of Government policy and some cases where the individual actions of ministers have been thought impolitic or unworthy. The following list includes resignations made necessary because of private scandals, but not those stepping down citing personal reasons (such as Estelle Morris, A. Milburn and A. Smith).

[1] J. Smith, the Leader of the Opposition, died on 14 May 1994.

18 May 81   K. Speed (Defence estimates)[1]
21 Jan 82   N. Fairbairn (handling of a Scottish prosecution)
5 Apr 82   Ld Carrington, H. Atkins, R. Luce (Falklands)
8 May 82   N. Budgen (Northern Ireland policy)
11 Oct 83   C. Parkinson (private scandal)
16 Nov 85   I. Gow (Anglo-Irish Accord)
7 Jan 86   M. Heseltine (Westland affair)
22 Jan 86   L. Brittan (Westland affair)
16 Dec 88   Edwina Currie (remarks on salmonella scare)
29 Oct 89   N. Lawson (P.M.'s economic advice)
13 Jul 90   N. Ridley (remarks about Germany)
1 Nov 90   Sir G. Howe (P.M.'s attitude to Europe)
22 Sep 92   D. Mellor (private scandal)
24 Jun 93   M. Mates (links with Asil Nadir)
5 Jan 94   T. Yeo (private scandal)
11 Jan 94   E of Caithness (private scandal)
20 Oct 94   T. Smith (payment for questions)
25 Oct 94   N. Hamilton (payment for questions)
8 Feb 95   A. Stewart (threatening behaviour)
11 Feb 95   C. Wardle (immigration policy)
6 Mar 95   R. Hughes (private scandal)
26 Jun 95   J. Redwood (to contest leadership)
5 Jul 95   J. Aitken (to fight libel action)
2 Jun 96   R. Richards (private scandal)
22 Jul 96   D. Heathcoat-Amory (European policy)
11 Dec 96   D. Willetts (conduct as whip)
4 May 97   D. Foster (ministerial appointment)
10 Dec 97   M. Chisholm (single parent policy)
27 Jul 98   F. Field (ministerial appointment)
27 Oct 98   R. Davies (private scandal)
23 Dec 98   P. Mandelson (private financial arrangements)
23 Dec 98   G. Robinson (private financial arrangements)
24 Jan 01   P. Mandelson (alleged intervention in passport application)
29 Jan 00   P. Kilfoyle (direction of government policy)
17 Mar 03   R. Cook (the decision to go to war over Iraq)
18 Mar 03   Ld Hunt (the decision to go to war over Iraq)
18 Mar 03   J. Denham (the decision to go to war over Iraq)
13 May 03   Clare Short (policy on Iraq)
15 Dec 04   D. Blunkett (private scandal)

---

[1] Technically a dismissal, not a resignation.

Parliamentary Private Secretaries to Prime Ministers

1976–79	R. Stott	1994–97	J. Ward
1979–83	I. Gow	1997–98	⎰ B. Grocott
1983–87	M. Alison	1997–98	⎱ Anne Coffey
1987–88	A. Hamilton	1998–2001	B. Grocott
1988–90	M. Lennox-Boyd	2001–05	D. Hanson
1990–90	P. Morrison	2005–	K. Hill
1990–94	G. Bright		

Biographical Notes

Prime Ministers, Deputy Prime Ministers, Chancellors of the Exchequer, Foreign Secretaries and Leaders of the Opposition.

(Virtually all the most eminent politicians of this period have held one of these four positions. We have also included some who held these posts before 1979 but continued to be prominent in politics after 1979.)

Blair, Anthony Charles Linton
  b. 1953. *Educ.* Fettes; Oxford. Barrister. M.P. (Lab.) for Sedgefield, 1983–; Leader of the Opposition 1994–97; P.M. 1997–.

Brown, (James) Gordon
  b. 1951. *Educ.* Kirkcaldy H.S.; Glasgow Univ. Lecturer, journalist. M.P. (Lab.) for Dunfermline E. 1983–. Chanc. of the Exch. 1997–.

Callaghan, (Leonard) James, Ld Callaghan of Cardiff (Life Peer 1987)
  b. 1912. *Educ.* Elem. and Portsmouth Northern Secondary Schools. M.P. (Lab.) for S. Cardiff 1945–50. M.P. for S.E. Cardiff 1950–83. M.P. for S. Cardiff and Penarth 1983–87. P.S. Min. of Transport, 1947–50. P.S. and F.S. Admiralty, 1950–51. Chanc. of the Exch., 1964–67. Home Sec., 1967–70. For. Sec., 1974–76. P.M., 1976–79. Leader of Opposition 1979–80. d. 2005.

Carrington, 6th Ld (1938), Peter Alexander Rupert Carington
  b. 1919. *Educ.* Eton; Sandhurst. Army 1939–45. Banker. P.S. Min. of Ag. and Fish., 1951–54. P.S. Min. of Defence, 1954–56. High Commissioner to Australia, 1956–59. 1st Ld of Admiralty, 1959–63. Leader of House of Lords, 1963–64. Sec. of State for Defence, 1970–74. Sec. of State for Energy, 1974. Ch. of Con. Party Organisation, 1972–74. For. Sec., 1979–82. Secretary-General of N.A.T.O., 1984–89. European peace negotiator in former Yugoslavia 1991–92.

Clarke, Kenneth
  b. 1940. *Educ.* Nottingham H.S.; Cambridge. Barrister. M.P. (Con.) Rushcliffe 1970–. Asst.Whip, 1972–74. Ld. Com., 1974. P.S. Transport 1979–82. Min. Health 1982–85. Paym. Gen. and Emp. Min., 1985–87. Chanc. of Duchy and Min. Trade 1987–88. Sec. of State Health 1988–90, Sec. of State Educ., 1990–92. Home Sec. 1992–93. Chanc. of Exch., 1993–97.

Cook, Robin (Robert) Finlayson
  b. 1946. *Educ.* Aberdeen G.S.; Edinburgh Univ. M.P. (Lab.) for Edinburgh Cent. 1974–83, for Livingston 1983–2005. Adult educator. For. Sec. 1997–2001. Leader of House of Commons and President of the Council, 2001–03. d. 2005.

Duncan Smith, (George) Iain
  b. 1954. *Educ.* Conway School, Sandhurst. Army officer. M.P. (Con.) for Chingford, 1992–. Leader of the Opposition, 2001–03.

Foot, Michael Mackintosh
  b. 1913. *Educ.* Leighton Park Sch., Reading; Oxford. Journalist. M.P. (Lab.) for Plymouth Devonport, 1945–55. M.P. for Ebbw Vale, 1960–83. M.P. for Blaenau Gwent, 1983–92. Sec. for Employment 1974–76; Lord Pres. of Council and Leader of House of Commons, 1976–79. Leader of Opposition, 1980–83. Dep. Leader of Labour Party, 1976–80. Leader of Labour Party, 1980–83.

Hague, William Jefferson
  b. 1961. *Educ.* Wath-on-Dearne Comp.; Oxford. Management consultant. M.P. (Con.) for Richmond (Yorks) 1989–. U-S. Soc. Sec. 1993–94. Min. of State, Soc. Sec. 1993–95. Sec. of State for Wales, 1995–97. Leader of the Opposition 1997–2001.

Healey, Denis Winston, Lord Healey (Life Peer 1992)
  b. 1917. *Educ.* Bradford G.S.; Oxford. M.P. (Lab.) for Leeds South-East, 1952–55. M.P. for Leeds East, 1955–92. Sec. for Defence, 1964–70. Chanc. of Exch., 1974–79. Dep. Leader of Lab. Party, 1980–83.

Heath, Edward Richard George (Sir)
  b. 1916. *Educ.* Chatham House School, Ramsgate; Oxford. M.P. (Con.) for Bexley, 1950–74. M.P. for Sidcup 1974–83. M.P. for Old Bexley and Sidcup 1983–2001. Con. Whip, 1951–55. Chief Whip, 1955–59. Min. of Labour, 1959–60. Lord Privy Seal, 1960–63. Sec. for Trade & Industry, 1963–64. Leader of the Con. Party, 1965–75. Leader of the Opposition, 1965–70. P.M., 1970–74. Leader of the Opposition, 1974–75. K.G. 1992. d. 2005.

Heseltine, Michael Ray Dibdin
  b. 1933. *Educ.* Shrewsbury; Oxford. Publisher. M.P. (Con.) for Tiverton 1966–74, for Henley 1974–2001. U-S. Transport 1970–72. Min. for Aerospace and Shipping 1972–74. Sec. of State for Environment 1979–83. Sec. of State for Defence 1983–86. Sec. of State for Environment 1990–92. Pres. of B. of Trade 1992–95. First Sec. of State and Deputy P.M. 1995–97.

Howard, Michael
  b. 1941. *Educ.* Llanelli GS, Cambridge. Barrister. M.P. (Con.) for Folkestone and Hythe, 1983–. U-S. Consumer and Corporate Affrs 1985–87, Min. for Local Govt 1987–88, Min. for Water and Planning 1988–90, Sec. of State for Employment 1990–92, Sec. of State for the Environment 1992–93, Home Sec. 1993–97. Leader of the Opposition, 2003–.

Howe, (Richard Edward) Geoffrey (Sir). Ld Howe of Aberavon (Life Peer 1992)
  b. 1926. *Educ.* Winchester; Cambridge. Barrister. M.P. (Con.) for Bebington, 1964–66. M.P. for Reigate, 1970–74. M.P. for Surrey East, 1974–92. Sol.-Gen., 1970–72. Min. for Trade and Consumer Affairs, 1972–74. Chanc. of Exch., 1979–83. For. Sec., 1983–89. Ld Pres. and Deputy P.M. 1989–90. Resigned 1990.

Hurd, Douglas Richard. Lord Hurd of Westwell (1997)
  b. 1930. *Educ.* Eton; Cambridge. Diplomat. Pol. Sec. to E. Heath 1968–73. M.P. (Con.) for Mid-Oxon 1974–83, for Witney 1983–97. Min. of State Foreign Office 1979–83, Home Office 1983–84; Sec. of State for N. Ireland, 1984–85; Home Sec., 1985–89; For. Sec., 1989–95.

Jenkins, Roy Harris. Ld Jenkins of Hillhead (Life Peer 1987)
  b. 1920. *Educ.* Abersychan G.S.; Oxford. Army, 1939–45. M.P. (Lab.) for Central Southwark, 1948–50. M.P. (Lab.) for Stechford, Birmingham, 1950–76. M.P. (S.D.P.) for Glasgow Hillhead, 1982–87. P.P.S. Commonwealth Relations O., 1949–50. Min. of Aviation, 1964–65. Home Sec., 1965–67. Chanc. of Exch., 1967–70. Deputy Leader of Lab. Party, 1970–72. Home Sec., 1974–76. President of European Economic Commission, 1977–81. Leader of SDP, 1982–83. Leader of (Social and) Liberal Democrat Peers 1988–97. d. 2003.

Kinnock, Neil Gordon. Ld Kinnock (Life Peer 2005)
  b. 1942. *Educ.* Lewis Sch., Pengam; U. of Wales (Cardiff). M.P. (Lab.) for Bedwellty, 1970–83. M.P. for Islwyn, 1983–94. P.P.S. to Sec. of State for Employment, 1974–75. Chief Opposition Spokesman on Education, 1979–83. Leader of the Opposition, and Leader of Labour Party, 1983–92. European Commissioner 1994–2004.

Lamont, Norman Stewart Hughson. Ld Lamont (Life Peer 1998)
   b. 1942. *Educ*. Loretto; Cambridge. Merchant banker. M.P. (Con.) for Kingston-on-Thames 1972–97. U-S. Energy 1979–81; Min. of State for Industry, 1981–85; Min. of State (Defence Procurement) 1985–86; Fin. Sec. Treasury 1986–89; Chief Sec. 1989–90; Chanc. of Exch. 1990–93.

Lawson, Nigel. Ld Lawson (Life Peer 1992)
   b. 1932. *Educ*. Westminster; Oxford. Journalist. M.P. (Con.) for Blaby, Feb. 1974–92. Opposition Spokesman on Treasury and Economic Affairs, 1977–79. F.S. to Treasury, 1979–81. Sec. for Energy, 1981–83; Chanc. of Exch., 1983–89. Resigned 1989.

Major, John, Sir
   b. 1943. *Educ*. Rutlish G.S. Banker. M.P. (Con.) for Huntingdon 1979–2001. Whip, 1983–85. U-S. Soc. Sec., 1985–86; Min. of State D.H.S.S., 1986–87; Chief Sec. Treasury, 1987–89; For. Sec., 1989; Ch. of Exch., 1989–90; P.M. and Leader of the Conservative Party, 1990–97. KG 2005.

Owen, David Anthony Llewellyn. Lord Owen (Life Peer 1992)
   b. 1938. *Educ*. Bradfield; Cambridge. Doctor, 1962. M.P. (Lab.) Plymouth Sutton, 1966–74. Plymouth Devonport, 1974–92. U-S. for Navy, 1968–70. U.S. Health and Social Security, 1974. Min. of State Health and Social Security, 1974–76. Min. of State For. O., 1976–77. For. Sec., 1977–79. Leader of SDP, 1983–89.

Prescott, John Leslie
   b. 1938. *Educ*. Grange Sec. Mod., Ellesmere Port. Seaman. M.P. (Lab.) Hull E. 1970–. Dep. Leader of Lab. Party 1994–. Deputy P.M. 1997– and Sec. of State for Environment, Transport and Regions, 1997–2001.

Rifkind, Malcolm Leslie, Sir
   b. 1946. *Educ*. Geo. Watson's; Edinburgh Univ. Advocate. M.P. (Con.) for Edinburgh Pentlands, 1974–97 and for Kensington & Chelsea, 2005–. U-S. Scotland 1979–82; U-S. For. O. 1982–83. Min. of State For. O., 1983–86. Sec of S. Scotland, 1986–90, Sec. of S. Transport, 1990–92. Sec. of State Def, 1992–95. For. Sec. 1995–97. K.C.M.G. 1997.

Smith, John
   b. 1938. *Educ*. Dunoon G.S.; Edinburgh Univ. Barrister. M.P. (Lab.) for N. Lanarkshire, 1970–83. M.P. for Monklands E. 1983–94. U-S. for Energy, 1974–75. Min. of State Energy, 1975–76. Min, Privy Council Off., 1976–78. Sec. of State Trade, 1978–79. Leader of Opposition 1992–94. d. 1994.

Thatcher, Mrs Margaret Hilda (nee Roberts). Lady Thatcher (Life Peeress 1992)
   b. 1925. *Educ*. Grantham Girls' School; Oxford. Research Chemist. Barrister. M.P. (Con.) for Finchley, 1959–92. P.S. to Min. of Pensions and Nat. Insurance, 1961–64. Sec. of State for Education and Science, 1970–74. Leader of the Conservative Party, 1975–90. P.M., 1979–90.

Thorneycroft, (George Edward) Peter. Ld Thorneycroft of Dunston (Life Peer 1967)
   b. 1909. *Educ*. Eton; Woolwich. Barrister, 1935. M.P. (Con.) for Stafford, 1938–45. M.P. (Con.) for Monmouth, 1945–66. P.S. Min. of War Transport, 1945. Pres. of Bd. of Trade, 1951–57. Chanc. of Exch., 1957–58. Resigned, 1958. Min. of Aviation, 1960–62. Min. of Defence, 1962–64. Sec. of State for Defence, 1964. Ch. of Con. Party organisation 1975–81. d. 1994.

Whitelaw, William Stephen Ian. 1st Viscount Whitelaw of Penrith (1983)
   b. 1918. *Educ*. Winchester; Oxford. Landowner. M.P. (Con.) for Penrith and the Border, 1955–83. Whip 1959–62. P.S. Min. of Labour 1962–64. Opposition Chief Whip 1964–70. Ld. Pres. 1970–72. Sec. of State N. Ireland 1972–73. Sec. of State Employment, 1973–74. Dep. Leader of Opposition 1975–79. Deputy P.M. 1979–86. Home Sec. 1979–83. Ld. Pres. and Leader of House of Lords 1983–86. d. 1999.

Index of Ministers

This index records dates of birth and death, as well as university education; where ministers attended an Independent school the fact is indicated. Occupation is a difficult concept. Many politicians have had multiple careers. Here an effort is made to list just one – the last major occupation before entering Parliament or taking up office. The principal sources have been A. Roth and B. Criddle *Parliamentary Profiles*, R. Waller and B. Criddle, the *Almanac of British Politics*, the *Times House of Commons, Dod's Parliamentary Companion*, and *Who's Who*. The choice made in the following pages is necessarily arbitrary. Further information is available in all of the above volumes.

Only one university is cited for the education column. Many ministers attended more than one.

abr	Abroad	Dnd	Dundee	Liv	Liverpool	Shf	Sheffield
Abn	Aberdeen	Edh	Edinburgh	Lon	London	StA	St Andrews
Abw	Aberystwyth	Esx	Essex	Man	Manchester	Slf	Salford
Asr	Aston	Exr	Exeter	Nhm	Nottingham	Sot	Southampton
Bhm	Birmingham	Glw	Glasgow	Nwc	Newcastle	Ssx	Sussex
Bdf	Bradford	H-W	Heriot Watt	OpU	Open University	Stg	Stirling
Blf	Belfast	Hul	Hull	Oxf	Oxford	Swa	Swansea
Bru	Brunel	Kle	Keele	Rdg	Reading	UEA	East Anglia
Cdf	Cardiff	Lds	Leeds	San	Sandhurst	Wwk	Warwick
Cam	Cambridge	Lei	Leicester	Scd	Strathclyde	Yrk	York
Dhm	Durham						

When an individual appears more than once on a page, the frequency is indicated in a superscript^x.

+ denotes a Privy Councillor.

* indicates attendance at an Independent School, as listed in *Whitaker's Almanack*.

Name	Born	Died	Univ.	Occupation	Page
Adonis, Ld (Life Peer 2005) A. Adonis	1959	–	Oxf	political adviser	14
Ainger, N.	1949	–		rigger	16, 17
+Ainsworth, P. M.	1956	–	*Oxf	finance	11
Ainsworth, R. W.	1952	–	–	factory work	13, 14, 17^2
(+)Aitken, J.	1942	–	*Oxf	journalist	8^2
+Alexander, D.	1967	–	Edb	political research	13, 15^2, 16
+Alison, M. J. H.	1926	2004	*Oxf	political research	3, 4^2
Allen, G. W.	1953	–	Lds	union official	17^2
+Amos, Lady (Life Peer 1997) Valerie Amos	1954	–	Wwk	local govt	12, 13, 15, 18
+Ancram, E of (1965). M. A. J. F. Kerr (*known as M. Ancram*) 13th Marquess of Lothian (2004)	1945	–	*Oxf	advocate	5, 10^2
Anderson, Janet	1949	–	Abr	political adviser	15, 17
Andrews, Lady (Life Peer 2000) Elizabeth K.Andrews	1943	–	Cdf	political adviser	12, 18

Annaly, 6th Ld (1990). L. R. White	1954	–	*San	army officer	12
+Arbuthnot, J. N.	1952	–	*Cam	barrister	8, 10, 11
+Armstrong, Hilary	1952	–	Bhm	lecturer	14, 17
Arran, 9th E of, (1983). A. D. G. Gore	1938	–	*Oxf	director	3, 7, 9², 10, 12
Ashton of Upholland, Lady (Life Peer 2000), Catherine Ashton	1956	–	Lon	administrator	12, 14
Astor, 4th Vt (1966). W. W. Astor	1952	–	*–	director	7, 10², 12
Atkins, Charlotte	1950	–	Lon	social worker	16, 18
+Atkins, Sir H. E. (KCMG 1983). Ld Colnbrook (Life Peer 1987)	1922	1996	*–	naval officer	1, 4
Atkins, Sir R. J. (Kt 1997)	1948	–	*–	insurance	4, 6², 9², 10
Avon, 2nd E of (1977) Vt Eden (1961). N. Eden	1930	1985	*–	army officer	3, 4, 7
Bach, Ld (Life Peer 1998). W. G. Bach	1946	–	*Oxf	barrister	12, 13, 14, 18
+Baker of Dorking, Ld (Life Peer 1997). K.W.Baker	1934	–	*Oxf	advertising	3³, 4², 5, 8
Baker, Sir N. B. (Kt 1997)	1938	1997	*Oxf	solicitor	7, 8, 11
Baldry, A. B.	1950	–	*Ssx	barrister	3, 8², 9
Banks, A. L. Ld Stratford (Life Peer 2005)	1945	–	*Yrk	union official	15
Bassam of Brighton, Ld (Life Peer 1997). (J.) S. Bassam	1953	–	Ssx	local govt	13, 18
Bates, M–	1944	–	–	investment adviser	9, 10, 11²
*Battle J. D.	1951	–	Lds	political adviser	13, 16
Bayley, H.	1952	–	*Brl	broadcaster	16
Beaverbrook, 3rd Ld (1985). M. W. H. Aitken	1951	–	*Cam	director	7
+Beckett, Margaret	1943	–	Man	political research	12, 13, 16
Bellwin, Ld (Life Peer 1979). I. Bellow	1923	2001	Lds	local govt	3, 4
+Belstead, 2nd Ld (1958). J. J. Ganzoni	1932	–	*Oxf	politician	1², 2², 3, 10²
+Benn, H.	1953	–	Ssx	political adviser	13, 15³
Bennett, N. J.	1949	–	Lon	schoolmaster	11
Beresford, Sir P. (Kt 1990)	1946	–	abr	dentist	9
Berry, Sir A. G. (Kt 1983)	1925	1984	*Oxf	journalist	7³
Betts, C. J. C.	1950	–	*Cam	local govt	17²
+Biffen, Ld (Life Peer 1997). J. Biffen	1930	–	Cam	business	1³, 5
Blackman, Liz	1949	–	–	teacher	16
+Blackstone, Lady (Life Peer 1987). Tessa Blackstone	1942	–	Lon	lecturer	14, 15
+Blair, A. C. L.	1953	–	*Oxf	barrister	12
+Blaker, Ld (Life Peer 1994). Sir P. A. R. Blaker (KCMG 1983)	1922	–	*Oxf	diplomat	1, 2
+Blatch, Lady (Life Peer 1987). Emily Blatch	1937	2005	–	local govt	4, 7, 8, 9³
Blears, Hazel	1956	–	–	solicitor	13, 14
+Blunkett, D.	1947	–	Shf	local govt	13, 14, 15
+Boateng, P. Y.	1951	–	Brl	barrister	13³, 14
Bonsor Sir N. (4th Bt)	1942	–	*Oxf	barrister	8
Boscawen, R. T.	1923	–	*Cam	underwriter	6, 7³
Boswell, T. E.	1944	–	*Oxf	farmer	7, 8, 9, 11²
Bottomley, P. J.	1944	–	*Cam	director	3, 5, 6
+Bottomley of Nettlestone, Lady (Life Peer 2005). Virginia Bottomley	1948	–	*Esx	social worker	4², 9², 10
Bowis, J.	1945	–	*Oxf	party official	9, 11
+Boyd, C.	1953	–	*Edh	advocate	17

+Davis, D. M.	1945	–	Lon	director	8, 9, 11
+Davis, S. C., Ld Clinton-Davis (Life Peer 1990)	1928	–	Lon	solicitor	16
Dawson, T.	1948	–	*Edb	advocate	11
+Denham, 2nd Ld (1948). B. S. M. Bowyer	1927	–	*Cam	writer	7, 11
*Denham, J. Y.	1953	–	Sot	lobbyist	13, 14, 16²
Denton of Wakefield, Lady, (Life Peer 1991). Jean Denton	1935	2001	Lon	solicitor	9, 10², 12
+Dewar, D. G.	1937	2000	*Glw	solicitor	15
Dhanda, P.	1971	–	Nhm	engineer	17
+Dobson, F.	1940	–	Lon	administrator	14
Donoughue, Ld (Life Peer 1984). B. Donoughue	1937	–	Oxf	lecturer	13
+Dorrell, S. J.	1952	–	*Oxf	director	4, 6, 7, 8, 9², 10
+Douglas-Hamilton, Ld J., Ld Selkirk (Life Peer 1997) (Disclaimed E of Selkirk, 1995)	1942	–	*Oxf	advocate	5, 6, 10²
Dowd, J. P.	1951	–	–	systems analyst	17
Drayson, Ld (Life Peer 2004). P. R. Drayson	1960	–	–	businessman	14
Dubs, Ld (Life Peer 1994). A. Dubs	1932	–	Lon	local govt	15
Dundee, 12th E of (1983). A. H. Scrymgeour, Vt Dudhope (1953)	1949	–	*StA	landowner	7
Dunn, R. J.	1946	2003	Slf	director	3
Durant, Sir (R.) T. (Kt 1991)	1928	–	* –	party official	6, 7²
Eagle, Angela	1961	–	Oxf	union official	13, 14, 16
Eagle, Maria	1961	–	Oxf	solicitor	14, 16
+Edwards, (R.) N., Ld Crickhowell (Life Peer 1987)	1934	–	*Cam	director	6
+Eggar, T. J. C.	1951	–	*Cam	director	2, 3², 9, 10
Elton, 2nd Ld (1973). R. Elton	1930	–	*Oxf	teacher	2², 3, 4, 5
Evans, J.	1950	–	Lon	solicitor	8, 10², 11
Evans of Temple Guiting, Ld (Life Peer 2000). M. Evans	1941	–	LSE		18
Eyre, Sir R. E. (Kt 1983)	1924	–	*Cam	solicitor	5, 6
Fairbairn, Sir N. (Kt 1988)	1933	1995	*Edb	advocate	6
Fairgrieve, Sir (T.) R. (Kt 1981)	1924	1999	*–	director	5
Falconer of Thoroton, Ld (Life Peer 1997). C. L. Falconer	1951	–	*Cam	barrister	12, 13, 15, 16, 17
Fallon, M.	1952	–	*StA	director	3, 6, 7, 9
Farrington of Ribbleton, Lady (Life Peer 1997). Josephine Farrington	1940	–	–	local govt	17
Fatchett, D.	1945	1999	*Bhm	lecturer	13
Fenner, Dame P. E.	1922	–	–	local govt	2
+Ferrers, 13th E (1954). R. W. S. Ferrers	1929	–	* Cam	director	2², 8, 9, 10
+Field, F.	1942	–	Hul	lobbyist	16
Filkin, Ld (Life Peer 1999). D. G. N. Filkin	1944	–	*Cam	local govt	12, 13, 14, 18
Finsberg, Ld (Life Peer 1992). Sir G. Finsberg (Kt 1984)	1926	1996	*Lon	director	4²
Fisher, M.	1944	–	*Cam	lecturer	15
Fitzpatrick, J.	1952	–	–	fireman	12, 17³
Fletcher, Sir A. M. (Kt 1986)	1929	1989	–	accountant	5²
Flint, Caroline	1961	–	UEA	researcher	13, 15

+Hamilton of Epsom, Ld (Life Peer 2005). Sir A. Hamilton (Kt 1994)	1941	–	*Oxf	director	2, 3, 6, 7, 8
Hamilton, (M.) N.	1949	–	Cam	barrister	7, 10, 11
+Hanley, Sir J. J. (Kt 1997)	1945	–	*–	director	8^2, 10^2
Hanson, D. G.	1959	–.	Hul	lobbyist	15, 16, 17
Hardie, Ld (Life Peer 1997). A. R. Hardie	1946	–	Edb	solicitor	17
+Harman, Harriet	1950	–.	*Yrk	lobbyist	12, 15, 17
Haskel, Ld (Life Peer 1993). S. Haskel	1934		Slf	director	17
+Havers, Ld (Life Peer 1987). Sir (R.) M. O. Havers (Kt 1973)	1923	1992	*Cam	barrister	1, 6
Hayhoe, Ld (Life Peer 1992). Sir B. J. Hayhoe (Kt 1987)	1927	–	–	engineer	1^2, 2, 4
+Hayman, Lady (Life Peer 1996). Helen Hayman	1949	–	*Cam	lobbyist	13, 14^2
Heald, O.	1954	–	*Cam	barrister	10
Healey, J.	1960	–	*Cam	union official	13^2, 14
+Heathcoat-Amory, D. P.	1949	–	*Oxf	accountant	4, 6, 7, 8^2, 9, 10, 11
Henderson, D. J.	1949	–	Glw	union official	13, 14
Henley, 8th Ld (1977). O. M. R. Eden	1953	–	*Dhm	barrister	5, 7, 9^3, 10
Heppell, J.	1948	–	–	fitter	17
+Heseltine, Ld (Life Peer 2001). M. R. D. Heseltine	1933	–	*Oxf	publisher	2, 3, 8, 9, 10
+Hesketh, 3rd Ld (1955). T. A. Fermor-Hesketh	1950	–	*–	director	4, 5, 7, 10, 11
+Hewitt, Patricia	1948	–	Cam	researcher	13, 14, 16^2
+Hill, K.	1943	–	Oxf	union official	12, 14, 17^2
Hodge, Margaret	1944	–	*Lon	business	14^2, 16
Hoey, Kate	1946	–	–	lecturer	13, 15
+Hogg, D. M. (3rd Vt Hailsham 2001)	1945	–	*Oxf	barrister	2^2, 5, 7, 8^2
+Hogg, Q. M., 2nd Vt Hailsham (1950–63), Ld Hailsham of St Marylebone (Life Peer 1970)	1907	2001	*Oxf	barrister	1
+Hollis of Heigham, Lady (Life Peer 1990). Patricia Hollis	1941	–	Cam	lecturer	16
+Hoon, G. W.	1953	–	Cam	barrister	12^3, 13, 14
Hooper, Lady (Life Peer 1985). Gloria Hooper	1935	–	Sot	solicitor	3^2, 4, 7, 9
Hope, P.	1955	–	Exe	consultant	12, 14
Horam, J. R.	1939	–	*Cam	journalist	9^2
+Howard, M.	1941	–	Cam	barrister	3^3, 4, 6, 8, 9^2
+Howarth of Newport, Ld (Life Peer 2005). A. T. Howarth	1944	–	*Cam	party official	3, 6, 7, 9, 14, 15
Howarth, G. E.	1949	–	–	engineer	13, 15
Howe, 7th E (1984). F. R. P. Curzon	1951	–	*Oxf	director	8, 9, 12
+Howe of Aberavon, Ld (Life Peer 1992). Sir (R. E.) G. Howe (Kt 1970)	1926	–	*Cam	barrister	1^3
+Howell of Guildford, Ld (Life Peer 1997). D. A. R. Howell	1936	–	*Cam	journalist	3, 6
Howells, K. S.	1946	–	Wwk	union official	13, 14^2, 15, 16^2
Hoyle, Ld (Life Peer 1997). (E.) D. H. Hoyle	1940	–	–	sales engineer	17
*Hughes, Beverley	1950	–	Man	lecturer	13^2, 14^2
Hughes, K.	1952	–	–	miner	17
Hughes, R. G.	1951	–	–	film producer	9, 11

Leigh, E. J. E.	1950	–	*Dhm	barrister	6, 10
Le Marchant, Sir S. (Kt 1984)	1931	1986	*–	stockbroker	7
Lennox-Boyd, M. A.	1943	–	*Oxf	barrister	2, 6, 7, 8
Leslie, C.	1972	–	Lds	political adviser	12²
Lester, Sir J. T. (Kt 1996)	1932	–	*–	business	3
Lewis, I.	1967	–	–	lobbyist	13, 14
+Liddell, Helen	1950	–	Scd	party official	13, 14, 15², 16
Lightbown, Sir D. L. (Kt 1995)	1932	1995	–	director	6, 7², 11
+Lilley, P. B.	1943	–	*Cam	director	1², 5, 10²
Lindsay, 16th E of (1989). J. R. Lindesay-Bethune	1955	–	*Edb	director	10, 12
Lloyd, A. J.	1950	–	Nhm	lecturer	13
Lloyd, Sir P. R. C. (Kt 1995)	1937	–	*Oxf	business	2, 5, 6, 7, 8²
Lock. D. A.	1960	–	Cam	barrister	12
Long, 4th Vt (1967). R. G. Long	1929	–	*–	landowner	7, 12
Lucas of Chilworth, 2nd Ld (1967). M. W. G. Lucas	1926	2001	–	engineer	6, 7
Lucas of Crudwell, 11th Ld (1991). R. Palmer	1951		*Oxf	director	12
+Luce, Ld (Life Peer 2000). Sir R. N. Luce (Kt 1991)	1936	–	*Cam	director	1³, 2
Lyell, 3rd Ld (1943). C. Lyell	1939	–	*Oxf	accountant	5, 7
+Lyell, Ld (Life Peer 2005). Sir N. Lyell (Kt 1987)	1938	–	*Oxf	barrister	4, 6, 11²
+McAvoy, T. M.	1943	–	–	storeman	17
+McCartney, I.	1951	–	–	political organiser	15², 16²
Macdonald, C.	1956	–	Edb	academic	15
+Macdonald of Tradeston, Ld (Life Peer 1998). A. J. Macdonald	1935	–	–	journalist	14, 15²
+McFall, J.	1944	–	Scd	teacher	15, 17
Macfarlane, (D.) N.	1936	–	–	director	3, 4
+MacGregor, Ld (Life Peer 2001). J. R. R. MacGregor	1937	–	*StA	city banker	1², 2², 3, 4, 6, 8, 10
McGuire, Anne	1949	–	–	social worker	12, 15, 17²
+McIntosh of Haringey, Ld (Life Peer 1983). A. R. McIntosh	1933	–	*Oxf	market research	15, 17
+Mackay of Ardbrecknish, Ld (Life Peer 1991). J. J. Mackay	1938	2001	Glw	teacher	5, 10, 11
+Mackay of Clashfern, Ld (Life Peer 1979). J. P. H. Mackay	1927	–	*Edb	advocate	1, 6, 8
Mackay of Drumadoon, Ld (Life Peer 1995). D. S. Mackay	1946	–	*Edb	advocate	11⁴
+Mackay, A. J.	1949	–	*–	estate agent	18
+Maclean, D. J.	1953	–	Abn	businessman	2, 6, 7, 8², 9
+McLeish, H. G.	1948	–	H-W	local govt	15
McLoughlin, P. A.	1957	–	–	miner	6, 9, 10, 11³
McNulty, T.	1958	–	–	lecturer	12, 13, 16², 17²
MacShane, D. J.	1948	–	*Oxf	union official	13²
MacTaggart, Fiona	1953	–	Lon	teacher	13
+Major, Sir J. (K.G.2005)	1943	–	–	banker	1³, 4², 6, 7, 8
Malone, P. B.	1950	–	Glw	journalist	7, 9
+Mandelson, P. B.	1953	–	Oxf	party official	15², 16

+Smith, Jacqui	1962	–	Oxf	teacher	15
Smith, T. J.	1947	–	*Oxf	accountant	14^3, 16
+Soames, Ld (Life Peer 1978).	1920	1987	*San	diplomat	10
Sir (A.) C. J. Soames (GCMG 1972)					
Soames, A. N. W.	1948	–	*–	director	1, 8, 9
Speed, Sir (H.) K. (Kt 1992)	1934	–	–	party research	2
+Spellar, J. F.	1947	–	*Oxf	union official	14^2, 15, 16^2
Spencer, Sir D.	1936	–	Oxf	barrister	11
Spicer, Sir (W.) M. H. (Kt 1996)	1943	–	*Cam	party official	3^2, 6
Sproat, I. M.	1938	–	*Oxf	journalist	5, 10^2
Squire, R. C.	1944	–	–	accountant	9^2
+Stanley, Sir J. P. (Kt 1988)	1942	–	*Oxf	director	2, 3, 5
Stewart, (J.) A.	1942	–	StA	lobbyist	5, 10
+ Stewart, (B. H.) I. H., Ld Stewartby	1935	–	*Cam	banker	1, 2, 3, 5
(Life Peer 1992)					
*Strang, G. S.	1943	–	*Edh	agric. research	14
Stratford, Ld (Life Peer 2005). T. Banks	1943		Yrk	union official	15
Strathclyde, 2nd Ld (1985).	1960	–	*E.A	insurance	3, 4, 5, 7,
T. G. D. Galbraith					9, 10^3, 12
Strathcona & Mount Royak,	1923	–	*Cam	consultant	2
4th Ld. (1959). D. E. P. Howard					
Strathmore, 16th E of (1987).	1957	–	Abn	landowner	7, 12^2
M. F. Bowes-Lyon					
+Straw, J. W.	1946	–	*Lds	political adviser	13^2
Streeter, G.	1955	–	Lon	solicitor	8, 11
Stringer	1950	–	Shf	chemist	17
Stuart, Gisela	1955	–	Lon	law lecturer	14
Sutcliffe, G. M.	1953	–	Bfd	union official	16, 17^2
Swinton, 2nd E of (1972).	1937	–	*–	landowner	7
J. Cunliffe-Lister, Ld Masham (1955)					
+ Symons of Vernham Dean,	1951	–	*Cam	union official	13^2, 14, 16
Lady (Life Peer 1996). Elizabeth					
Symons					
+Taylor of Bolton, Lady (Life Peer	1947	–	*Bfd	teacher	12, 17
2005). Ann Taylor					
Taylor, I.	1945	–	Kel	director	10
Taylor, J. M.	1941	–	*–	solicitor	6, 7, 8, 10, 11
+Tebbit, Ld (Life Peer 1992).	1931	–	–	pilot	3, 4^2, 5^2
N. B. Tebbit					
+Thatcher, Lady (Life Peer 1992).	1925	–	Oxf	barrister	1
Margaret H. Thatcher					
Thomas, G.	1967	–	Abw	teacher	15
Thomas, Sir J. S. (Kt 1985)	1925	1991	*Lon	farmer	6, 7
Thompson, Sir D. (Kt 1992)	1931	–	–	director	2, 6, 7
Timms, S.	1955	–	Cam	computers	13^2, 14, 16^3
Tipping, P.	1949	–	Nhm	social worker	12
Touhig, D.	1947	–	–	journalist	12, 14, 16, 17
Tracey, R. P.	1948	–	–	public relations	4
Trafford, Ld (Life Peer 1987).	1932	1989	*Lon	doctor	4
Sir J. A. Trafford (Kt 1985)					
+Trefgarne, 2nd Ld (1960).	1941	–	*abr	director	2^3, 4, 5^2, 7
D. G. Trefgarne					
Trenchard, 2nd Vt (1956). T. Trenchard	1923	1987	*–	city banker	2^2, 4
Triesman Ld (Life Peer 2003).	1941	–	Esx	union official	13, 18
D. Triesman					

II
Parties

Conservative Party

Party Leaders

11 Feb 75	Margaret Thatcher	13 Sep 01	I. Duncan Smith
28 Nov 90	J. Major	6 Nov 03	M. Howard
19 Jun 97	W. Hague		

Conservative Party Leadership Elections

In 1965 the Conservative Party introduced a procedure for the leader to be elected by a ballot of M.P.s. If there was no clear winner on the first ballot (defined by having over 50% of the votes, and being 15% clear of the second placed candidate), the rules stated that the election should go to a second ballot; if there was still no winner with over 50%, it should go to a run-off between the best-placed candidates. This procedure was used in 1965 and 1975 and four times since then. But after the election of W. Hague in 1997 the arrangements were modified to provide for party members voting between the two candidates who came top in the M.P.s poll.

1989	*1st ballot[1]*				
5 Dec 89	Margaret Thatcher	314			
	Sir A. Meyer	33			
1990	*1st ballot*			*2nd ballot*	
20 Nov 90	Margaret Thatcher	204	27 Nov 90	J. Major	185[2]
	M. Heseltine	152		M. Heseltine	131
				D. Hurd	56
1995	*1st ballot[3]*				
4 Jul 95	J. Major	218			
	J. Redwood	89			

[1] There were 27 abstentions.
[2] Although the rules required a larger majority, both M. Heseltine and D. Hurd withdrew in favour of J. Major when the results of the second ballot were known.
[3] There were 22 abstentions.

1997	*1st ballot*			*2nd ballot*			*3rd ballot*	
10 Jun 97	K. Clarke	49	17 Jun 97	K. Clarke	64	19 Jun 97	W. Hague	92
	W. Hague	41		W. Hague	62		K. Clarke	70
	J. Redwood	27		J. Redwood	38			
	P. Lilley	24						
	M. Howard	23						

	1st Ballot			*2nd Ballot*	
12 Jul 01	M. Portillo	50	13 Jul 01	K. Clarke	59
	I. Duncan Smith	42		I. Duncan Smith	54
	K. Clarke	39		M. Portillo	53
	M. Ancram	18			
	M. Howard	17			

	Party Member vote	
13 Sep 01	I. Duncan Smith	60.7%
	K. Clarke	39.3%
6 Nov 03	M. Howard	*unopposed*

Deputy Leaders

12 Feb 75–4 Aug 91	W. Whitelaw *(Vt)*
1 Jun 98–15 Jun 99	P. Lilley

Leaders in the House of Lords

1973	Ld Carrington	1990	Ld Waddington
1979	Ld Soames	1992	Ld Wakeham
1981	Lady Young	1994	Vt Cranborne
1983	Vt Whitelaw	1998	Ld Strathclyde
1988	Ld Belstead		

Principal Party Officials

Chairmen of the Party Organisation

Jun 74–Feb 75	W. Whitelaw	Jul 94–Jul 95	J. Hanley
Feb 75–Sep 81	Ld Thorneycroft	Jul 95–Jun 97	B. Mawhinney
Sep 81–Sep 83	C. Parkinson	Jun 97–Oct 98	Ld Parkinson
Oct 83–Sep 85	J. S. Gummer	Oct 98–Sep 01	M. Ancram
Sep 85–Jun 87	N. Tebbit	Sep 01–Jul 02	D. Davis
Jun 87–Jul 89	P. Brooke	Sep 02–Nov 03	Theresa May
Jul 89–Nov 90	K. Baker	Nov 03–May 05	{ L. Fox
Nov 90–Apr 92	C. Patten	Nov 03-May 05	{ Ld Saatchi
Apr 92–Jul 94	Sir N. Fowler	May 05–	F. Maude

Deputy Chairman

Mar 75–May 79	A. Maude	Jul 94–Jul 95	J. Maples
Nov 77–May 79	Lady Young	Jul 95–Jun 98	M. Trend
May 79–Jun 83	A. McAlpine *(Ld)*	Mar 98–Mar 00	R. Hodgson
Jun 83–Sep 84	M. Spicer	Jun 98–Oct 98	M. Ancram
Sep 85–Oct 86	J. Archer	Jun 99–Jun 02	D. Prior
Sep 85–Jul 89	P. Morrison	Aug 02–Mar 03	J. Taylor
Jul 89–May 90	Ld Young of Graffham	Aug 02–Nov 03	Gillian Shephard
May 90–Nov 90	D. Trippier	Mar 03–May 05	R. Monbiot
Nov 90–Apr 92	Sir J. Cope	Nov 03–May 05	C. Hendry
Apr 92–Jul 95	Dame A. Rumbold	Nov 03–	D. Cameron
May 92–Jul 94	G. Malone	Sep 04–Mar 05	H. Flight
Jul 94–Jul 95	M. Dobbs	May 05–	A. Mackay

Treasurers

Aug 75–Nov 90	A. McAlpine *(Ld)*	Mar 93–Jun 97	C. Hambro *(Ld)*
May 79–Jun 83	Ld Boardman	Mar 93–Jun 97	Ld Harris of Peckham
Apr 82–Apr 90	Sir O. Wade	Jun 97–Jun 98	Sir G. Kirkham
Dec 84–Jan 88	Sir C. Johnston *(Ld)*	Jun 98–Jul 01	M. Ashcroft *(Ld)*
Jan 88–Mar 93	Ld Laing	Jul 01–Jun 03	S. Kalms *(Ld)*
Apr 90–Jul 92	Vt Beaverbrook	Jun 03–Nov 03	G. Magan
Apr 91–Apr 92	Sir J. Cope	Nov 03–	Ld Hesketh
Jul 92–Feb 93	T. Smith		

Chairman of Conservative Party Foundation

Dec 03–   Ld Hesketh

Chairman of Executive Committee of the Party

Jul 76	Sir C. Johnston
Jul 81	Sir R. Sanderson *(Ld)*
Jul 86	Sir P. Lane *(Ld)*
Jul 91	Sir B. Feldman *(Ld)*
Mar 96	R. Hodgson

(*post abolished Mar 98*)

Director of Organisation

Feb 76–Jun 88   (Sir) A. Garner

Director of Organisation and Campaigning

Jun 88–May 92   (Sir) J. Lacy

Director of Campaigning

Jun 92–Jul 98   (Sir) T. Garrett

Director of (Field) Operations

Jul 98–Nov 03	S. Gilbert
Nov 03–	G. Barwell

Director of Strategy

1999–2001	A. Cooper
2002–03	D. Cummings

Director of Policy

1999–2001	D. Finkelstein
2001–03	G. Clark

Director-General

Nov 92–Jun 95	P. Judge

Chief Executive

Jul 98	A. Norman
May 99	D. Prior
Jan 02	M. Macgregor
Feb 03	B. Legg
May 03	*(vacant)*

Director of Publicity & Communications

1978	G. Reece	1990	S. Woodward
1980	Sir H. Boyne	1991	T. Collins
1982	A. Shrimsley	1994	H. Colver
1985	H. Thomas	1995	T. Collins *(acting)*
1986	M. Dobbs	1996	C. Lewington
1989	B. Bruce	1997	*(post vacant)*

Director of Political Operations and Communications

1997–99	A. Cooper

Director of Media

1998	G. Mackay
1999	Amanda Platell
2001	N. Wood
2003	*(post vacant)*

Press Secretary

2003	G. Black

Director of Strategic Communications

2003	(Jan–Nov) P. Baverstock

Conservative Research Department

Director

1974–79	C. Patten	1989–95	A. Lansley
1979–82	A. Howarth	1995–99	D. Finkelstein
1982–84	P. Cropper	1999–2003	R. Nye
1984–85	*(post vacant)*	2003–	G. Clark
1985–89	R. Harris		

SOURCES:- Annual Conference Reports of the National Union of Conservative and Unionist Associations, and information from the Conservative Research Department.

Chief Whips in the House of Commons

1973	H. Atkins	1990	R. Ryder
1979	M. Jopling	1994	A. Goodlad
1983	J. Wakeham	1997	J. Arbuthnot
1987	D. Waddington	2001	D. Maclean
1989	T. Renton		

Chief Whips in the House of Lords

1977	Ld Denham	1994	Ld Strathclyde
1991	Ld Hesketh	1998	Ld Henley
1993	Vt Ullswater	2001	Ld Cope

SOURCES:- *Dod's Parliamentary Companion*, 1900–. For a full list of whips see F. M. G. Wilson, 'Some Career Patterns in British Politics; Whips in the House of Commons, 1906–66', *Parliamentary Affairs*, 24 (Winter 1970–71) pp. 33–42.

Chairmen of 1922 Committee[1]

Nov 72–Nov 84	E. du Cann
Nov 84–Apr 92	C. Onslow
Apr 92–May 97	Sir M. Fox
May 97–Jun 01	Sir A. Hamilton
Jun 01–	Sir M. Spicer

[1] Or the Conservative (Private) Members' Committee. This is an organisation of the entire membership of the Conservative Party in the Commons. It acts as a sounding board of Conservative opinion in the House, but has no official role in formulating policy for the party.

SOURCES:- *The Times Index*, 1923–, information from the 1922 Committee, R. T. Mackenzie, *British Political Parties* (1955) pp. 57–61, P. Goodhart, *The 1922* (1973) and Conservative Research Department.

Conservative Shadow Cabinets

1997–2001

W. Hague (1997–2001)

P. Ainsworth (1998–2001)
M. Ancram (1997–2001)
Angela Browning
(1999–2001)
Vt Cranborne (1997–98)
D. Curry (1997–98)
S. Dorrell (1997–98)
I. Duncan-Smith
(1997–2001)
Sir N. Fowler (1997–99)
L. Fox (1998–2001)
Sir A. Goodlad (1997–98)
D. Heathcoat-Amory
(1999–2001)
Ld Henley (1999–2001)
M. Howard (1997–99)
B. Jenkin (1999–2001)
A. Lansley (1999–2001)
P. Lilley (1997–99)
A. Mackay (1997–2001)
J. Maples (1997–2001)
F. Maude (1997–2001)
Sir B. Mawhinney
(1997–98)
Theresa May (1999–2001)
Ld Parkinson (1997–98)
J. Redwood (1997–2001)
Gillian Shephard (1997–99)

Ld Strathclyde
(1998–2001)
G. Streeter (1999–2001)
Ann Widdecombe
(1997–2001)
D. Willetts (1998–2001)
T. Yeo (1999–2001)
Sir G. Young (1997–2001)
(J. Arbuthnot *Chief Whip*)
(Secretary)
D. Finkelstein (1997–98)
D. Finkelstein (1998–2001)
(joint)
R. Nye (1998–2001) *(joint)*

2001–

I. Duncan Smith
(2001–03)
M. Howard (2003–)
P. Ainsworth (2001–02)
M. Ancram (2001–)
J. Bercow (2001–02)
D. Cameron (2004–)
T. Collins (2001–03,
2004–05)
Ld Cope (2001–03)
D. Curry (2003–05)
Q. Davies (2001–03)
D. Davis (2001–05)
A. Duncan (2005–)

N. Evans (2001–03)
O. Heald (2002–)
H. Flight (2002–05)
L. Fox (2001–)
D. Green (2001–03)
C. Grayling (2005–)
P. Hammond (2005–)
J. Hayes (2002–03)
M. Howard (2001–03)
B. Jenkin (2001–03)
Julie Kirkbride (2004–04)
A. Lansley (2004–)
Jacqui Lait (2001–03)
O. Letwin (2001–)
D. Lidington (2002–03)
D. Maclean (2001–)
Theresa May (2001–)
A. Mitchell (2005–)
E. Pickles (2001–03)
J. Redwood (2004–)
Sir M. Rifkind (2005–)
Ld Saatchi (2003–05)
N. Soames (2004–05)
Caroline Spelman
(2001–03, 2004–)
Ld Strathclyde (2001–)
D. Willetts (2001–)
Ann Winterton (2001–02)
J. Whittingdale (2001–03)
T. Yeo (2001–05)

SOURCE:- press reports.

Party Membership

In 1982 an internal study suggested that the membership was just under 1.2 million and a similar figure was found in 1984. Estimates in the press in 1993 suggested that previous suggested membership totals had been greatly exaggerated, and that the figure had in any case fallen sharply, so that in 1997 there were probably only a quarter of a million members.

SOURCES:- Nuffield Election Studies; *Committee on Financial Aid to Political Parties* (Cmnd 6601/1976 p. 31); M. Pinto-Duschinsky, *British Political Finance 1830–1980* (1980); P. Whiteley and P. Seyd, *True Blues* (1994).

Party Finance

The routine expenditure annually reported since 1979 has been:

1978–79	£4,800,000	1988–89	£10,200,000	1998–99	£13,300,000
1979–80	£5,200,000	1989–90	£10,800,000	1999–2000	£13,300,000
1980–81	£5,500,000	1990–91	£14,900,000	2000–01	£23,800,000
1981–82	£4,200,000	1991–92	£23,400,000	2001–02	£23,294,000
1982–83	£4,700,000	1992–93	£11,500,000	2002 (last	£9,928,000
1983–84	£8,600,000	1993–94	£14,100,000	9 months)	
1984–85	£5,600,000	1994–95	£15,300,000	2003	£13,619,000
1985–86	£5,500,000	1995–96	£21,400,000	(calendar)	
1986–87	£7,500,000	1996–97	£42,500,000		
1987–88	£15,600,000	1997–98	£13,200,000		

SOURCES:- Conservative Party Headquarters; Electoral Commission; M. Linton, *Money and Votes* (Institute for Public Policy Research 1994).

Party Structure

Until 1998 the Conservative Central Office (answerable to the Leader of the Party) and the National Union of Conservative Associations had a separate but symbiotic relationship. Formally the Leader alone promulgated party policy and appointed the chief party officials. In 1998 the party organisation and the National Union merged under a 15-person Board of Management, a minority of whom were appointed by the Leader.

National Union of Conservative and Unionist Associations

Annual Conferences, 1979–97; National Convention 1998–

Date	Place	President	Chairman
9–12 Oct 79	Blackpool	F. Pym	D. D-Handley
11–15 Oct 80	Brighton	Sir T. Constantine	Dame A. Springman
13–16 Oct 81	Blackpool	E. du Cann	F. Hardman
12–15 Oct 82	Brighton	Sir J. Taylor	D. Walters
11–14 Oct 83	Blackpool	Sir G. Howe	P. Lane
9–12 Oct 84	Brighton	Sir A. Graesser	Dame P. Hunter
8–11 Oct 85	Blackpool	Sir H. Atkins	Sir B. Feldman
7–10 Oct 86	Bournemouth		P. Lawrence
6–9 Oct 87	Blackpool	G. Younger	Dame J. Seccombe
11–14 Oct 88	Brighton	Dame S. Roberts	Sir I. McLeod
10–13 Oct 89	Blackpool	Vt Whitelaw	Sir S. Odell
9–12 Oct 90	Bournemouth	Sir D. D-Handley	Dame M. Fry
7–10 Oct 91	Blackpool	J. Wakeham	Sir J. Barnard
6–9 Oct 92	Brighton	Sir D. Walters	J. Mason
5–8 Oct 93	Blackpool	Dame W. Mitchell	Sir B. Feldman

11–14 Oct 94	Bournemouth	B. Stuttaford	Sir B. Feldman
10–13 Oct 95	Blackpool	D. Kelly	Sir B. Feldman
8–11 Oct 96	Bournemouth	Dame H. Byford	R. Hodgson
7–10 Oct 97	Blackpool	J. Taylor	R. Hodgson
6–9 Oct 98	Bournemouth	G. Park	R. Hodgson
4–7 Oct 99	Blackpool	B. Hanson	R. Hodgson
2–5 Oct 00	Bournemouth	R. Monbiot	J. Taylor
8–11 Oct 01	Blackpool	Jean Searle	J. Taylor
7–10 Oct 02	Bournemouth	Caroline Abel-Smith	J. Taylor
6–9 Oct 03	Blackpool	D. Porter	R. Monbiot
4–7 Oct 04	Bournemouth	R. Stephenson	R. Monbiot

Labour Party

Party Leaders and Deputy Leaders

Leader of the Parliamentary Party

1976	J. Callaghan

Leader of the Labour Party

10 Nov 80	M. Foot
1 Oct 83	N. Kinnock
18 Jul 92	J. Smith
12 May 94	Margaret Beckett *(acting)*
21 Jul 94	T. Blair

Deputy Leader

1976	M. Foot
1980	D. Healey
1983	R. Hattersley
1992	Margaret Beckett
1994	J. Prescott

Leadership Elections

From 1922 to 1981 the Parliamentary Labour Party, when in opposition, elected its Leader and Deputy Leader at the beginning of each session. Most elections were uncontested, but there were these exceptions (The figures in brackets show the result of the first ballot. The date is for the final ballot).

Leader

1980	*1st ballot*			*2nd ballot*	
4 Nov 80	D. Healey	112	10 Nov 80	M. Foot	139
	M. Foot	83		D. Healey	129
	J. Silkin	38			
	P. Shore	32			

Deputy Leader

1980		
13 Nov 80	D. Healey	unopposed

At a special conference at Wembley, 24 January 1981, the Labour Party endorsed a procedure by which the party's Leader and Deputy Leader should be re-elected each year by the Party Conference with 40% of the vote allocated to the trade unions, 30% to the Parliamentary Party and 30% to the constituency parties.

The system was first used on 1 October 1981 when D. Healey defeated T. Benn for the Deputy Leadership.

Deputy Leader

1 Oct 1981	*1st ballot*					2nd ballot			
	TU	CLP	MP	Total		TU	CLP	MP	Total
D. Healey	24.696	5.367	15.306	45.369	D. Healey	24.994	5.673	19.759	50.426
T. Benn	6.410	23.483	6.734	36.627	T. Benn	15.006	24.327	10.241	49.574
J. Silkin	8.894	1.150	7.959	18.004					

The first time the procedure was used for electing both Leader and Deputy Leader was on 2 October 1983.

Leader

1 Oct 1983	*1st ballot*			
	TU	CLP	MP	Total
N. Kinnock	29.042	27.452	14.778	71.272
R. Hattersley	10.878	0.577	7.833	19.288
E. Heffer	0.046	1.971	4.286	6.303
P. Shore	0.033	0.000	3.103	3.137

Deputy Leader

1 Oct 83	*1st ballot*			
	TU	CLP	MP	Total
R. Hattersley	35.237	15.313	16.716	67.266
M. Meacher	4.730	14.350	8.806	27.886
D. Davies	0.000	0.241	3.284	3.525
Gwyneth Dunwoody	0.033	0.096	1.194	1.323

There was another leadership election on 2 October 1988, when T. Benn challenged N. Kinnock for the Leadership and E. Heffer and J. Prescott challenged R. Hattersley for the Deputy Leadership.

Leader

2 Oct 88	*1st ballot*			
	TU	CLP	MP	Total
N. Kinnock	39.660	24.128	24.842	88.630
T. Benn	0.340	5.872	5.158	11.370

Deputy Leader

2 Oct 88 *1st ballot*

	TU	CLP	MP	Total
R. Hattersley	31.339	18.109	17.376	66.823
J. Prescott	8.654	7.845	7.195	23.694
E. Heffer	0.007	4.046	5.430	9.483

After the 1992 general election N. Kinnock and R. Hattersley stood down as Leader and Deputy Leader. An election was held on 18 July 1992, at a special conference in London.

Leader

18 Jul 92 *1st ballot*

	TU	CLP	MP	Total
J. Smith	38.518	29.311	23.187	91.016
B. Gould	1.482	0.689	6.813	8.984

Deputy Leader

18 Jul 92 *1st ballot*

	TU	CLP	MP	Total
Margaret Beckett	25.394	19.038	12.871	57.303
J. Prescott	11.627	7.096	9.406	28.129
B. Gould	2.979	3.866	7.723	14.568

At the 1993 Party Conference the party approved a change in the rules under which trade unions and constituency parties were obliged to ballot members individually in leadership elections and divide their votes accordingly (one member one vote). In addition the proportions in the electoral college were adjusted to three equal thirds for each of the constituent elements. This new procedure was used for the first time in July 1994 following the death of J. Smith. The results were declared on 21 July 1994.

Leader

21 Jul 94 *1st ballot*

	TU	CLP	MP	Total
T. Blair	52.3	58.2	60.5	57.0
J. Prescott	28.4	24.4	19.6	24.1
Margaret Beckett	19.3	17.4	19.9	18.9

Deputy Leader

21 Jul 94 *1st ballot*

	TU	CLP	MP	Total
J. Prescott	55.6	59.4	53.7	56.5
Margaret Beckett	43.4	40.6	46.3	43.5

SOURCES:- 1988 Party Annual Conference Reports, Labour Year Books; *Keesing's Contemporary Archive, Keesing's U.K. Record.*

Leaders in the House of Lords

1976	Ld Peart	1998	Lady Jay
1982	Ld Cledwyn	2001	Ld Williams
1992	Ld Richard	2003	Lady Amos

Chief Whips in the House of Commons

1976	M. Cocks	1997	N. Brown
1985	D. Foster	1998	Ann Taylor
1995	D. Dewar	2001	Hilary Armstrong

Chief Whips in the House of Lords

1973	Lady Llewelyn-Davies
1982	Ld Ponsonby
1990	Ld Graham of Edmonton
1997	Ld Carter
2002	Ld Grocott

SOURCES:- *Dod's Parliamentary Companion*, 1900–; Labour Party Annual Conference Reports.

Labour Party – National Executive Committee

The Chairman of the National Executive Committee is listed as Chairman of Annual Conference at end of his or her year in office; (see p. 60). In 2001 the party leader created the position of party chairman, as effectively a Cabinet appointment in his own gift.

Chairman

2001	C. Clarke
2002	J. Reid
2003	I. McCartney

General Secretary

1972	R. Hayward
1982	J. Mortimer
1985	L. Whitty
1995	T. Sawyer (Ld)
1998	Margaret McDonagh

2001	D. Triesman (Ld)
2003	M. Carter

Deputy General Secretary

1997	Margaret McDonagh
1998	*(office vacant)*
2003	C. Lennie

Treasurer

1976	N. Atkinson
1981	E. Varley

1984	A. Booth
1984	S. McCluskie
1992	T. Burlison
1996	Margaret Prosser
2000	J. Elsby
2004	J. Dromey

National Agent

1972	R. (Ld) Underhill
1979	D. Hughes
1985	Joyce Gould

(Director, Organisation and Development)

1990	Joyce Gould
1993	P. Coleman
1996	D. Gardner

Assistant Gen. Sec. (Organisation)

1998	D. Gardner
2001	Carol Linforth

Director of Campaigns and Elections

1994	Joy Johnson
1995	Sally Morgan
1996	*(post vacant)*

Research Secretary

1974	G. Bish
1993	R. Wales
1996	M. Taylor

(Director of Policy and Campaigns)

1997	M. Taylor

(Assistant Gen Sec. Policy)

1997	M. Taylor
1998	*(post vacant)*
1999	N. Pecorelli
2001	L. Bruce

Director of Publicity (Communications)

1964	P. Clark
1979	M. Madden
1982	N. Grant
1983	*(post vacant)*
1985	P. Mandelson
1990	J. Underwood
1990	D. Hill[1]
1993	Joy Johnson

(Chief Party Spokesperson)

1994	D. Hill
1998	M. Craven *(acting)*
1998	*(post vacant)*
1999	P. Murphy

(Director of Communications)

2000	L. Price

(Assistant Gen. Sec. Communications)

2001	E. Morgan

(Chief Press and Broadcasting Officer)

2003–05 M. Doyle

[1] In 1993 D. Hill took the title 'Chief Spokesperson'.

SOURCES:- Labour Representation Committee Annual Conference Reports, 1900–05, and Labour Party Annual Conference Reports, 1906–.

Parliamentary Labour Party – Parliamentary Committee

Parliamentary Labour Party – Executive Committee

The figures denote the order of successful candidates in the ballot.

1979–88[a]

	Jun 1979	Nov 1990	Nov 1981[a]	Nov 1982	Nov 1983	Oct 1984	Oct 1985	Oct 1986	Jun 1987	Nov 1988
P. Archer	–	–	14	9	8	7	10	9	–	–
A. W. Benn	–	(13)[b]	–	–	–	–	–	–	–	–
A. Booth	7	8	8	6	–	–	–	–	–	–
G. Brown	–	–	–	–	–	–	–	–	11	1
D. Clark	–	–	–	–	–	–	–	11	14	4
R. Cook	–	–	–	–	10	15	5	–	8	5
J. Cunningham	–	–	–	–	5		9	8	11	14
D. Davies	–	–	–	–	–	12	13	3	6	–
F. Dobson	–	–	–	–	–	–	–	–	10	7
Gwyneth Dunwoody	–	–	15	13	12	10	–	–	–	–
B. Gould	–	–	–	–	–	–	–	14	1	7
R. Hattersley	4	1	3	4	–	–	–	–	–	–
D. Healey	1	–	–	–	1	2	3	4	–	–
E. Heffer	–	–	13	15	11	–	–	–	–	–
R. Hughes	–	–	–	–	–	–	15	–	7	–
B. John	–	–	10	12	–	–	–	–	–	–
B. Jones	–	–	–	–	9	8	11	6	–	12
G. Kaufman	–	3	2	1	2	1	1	1	4	3
N. Kinnock	–	12	7	2	–	–	–	–	–	–
R. Mason	11	10	–	–	–	–	–	–	–	–
M. Meacher	–	–	–	–	13	11	12	15	3	10
B. Millan	–	–	12	14	–	–	–	–	–	–
S. Orme	6	6	11	10	15	4	2	5	–	–
D. Owen	10	–	–	–	–	–	–	–	–	–
J. Prescott	–	–	–	–	6	8	4	12	2	13
G. Radice	–	–	–	–	14	13	8	10	–	–
M. Rees	9	4	6	11	–	–	–	–	–	–
Jo Richardson	–	–	–	–	–	–	–	–	11	15
W. Rodgers	8	9	–	–	–	–	–	–	–	–
P. Shore	3	5	1	3	3	6	–	–	–	–
J. Silkin	2	7	4	7	7	–	–	–	–	–
J. Smith	12	11	9	8	4	5	7	2	5	2
J. Straw	–	–	–	–	–	–	–	–	15	11
E. Varley	5	2	5	5	–	–	–	–	–	–

[a] The PLP Committee was enlarged from 12 to 15 elected members in 1981.

[b] A. Benn took over the place vacated by W. Rodgers when he joined the SDP.

1989–97

In 1989 the rules for the election of the Parliamentary Committee were changed in favour of women M.P.s; the total size was increased to 18, at least three of whom had to be women. In 1993 the rules were further amended so that M.P.s had to vote for at least four women candidates.

	Nov 1989	Nov 1990	Nov 1991	Jul 1992	Oct 1993	Nov 1994	Nov 1995	Jul 1996
Margaret Beckett	17	3	6	–	–	2	1	1
A. Blair	4	8	8	2	6	–	–	–
D. Blunkett	–	–	–	15	17	15	11	17
G. Brown	1	2	1	1	4	3	3	14
D. Clark	1	7	10	18	7	13	9	9
T. Clarke	–	–	–	17	13	–	19	18
Ann Clwyd	14	11	4	10	–	–	–	–
R. Cook	3	4	2	3	1	1	2	5
J. Cunningham	8	13	12	12	18	10	–	12
R. Davies	–	–	(19)[a]	11	12	4	11	11
D. Dewar	15	8	10	14	11	4	5	6
F. Dobson	10	16	6	4	2	6	8	7
B. Gould	9	17	5	6	–	–	–	–
Harriet Harman	–	–	–	6	–	5	18	19
B. Jones	16	13	17	–	–	–	–	–
G. Kaufman	5	5	12	–	–	–	–	–
Joan Lestor	6	–	–	–	15	16	14	–
M. Meacher	12	10	15	13	10	11	15	10
Mo Mowlam	–	–	–	6	5	8	6	8
J. Prescott	11	18	15	5	2	–	–	–
G. Robertson	–	–	–	–	16	7	17	16
Jo Richardson	7	15	18	–	–	–	–	–
Clare Short	–	–	–	–	–	–	16	3
C. Smith	–	–	–	6	9	9	7	15
J. Smith	2	1	3	–	–	–	–	–
G. Strang	–	–	–	–	–	17	12	4
J. Straw	18	6	14	16	8	14	13	13
Ann Taylor	–	12	9	11	14	18	10	2

[a] R. Davies was elected to the Shadow Cabinet as a result of a by-election in November 1992 following the resignation of B. Gould.

Chair, Parliamentary Labour Party

Jun 1979	F. Willey	May 1997	C. Soley
Nov 1983	J. Dormand	Jun 2001	Jean Corston
Jul 1987	S. Orme	May 2005	Ann Clywd
Jul 1992	D. Hoyle		

Secretary, Parliamentary Labour Party

1979	B. Davies
1992	A. Haworth
2004–05	S. Gordon

Labour Party – Annual Conferences, 1979–

Date	Place	Chairman
1–5 Oct 79	Brighton	F. Allaun
29 Sep–3 Oct 80	Blackpool	Lady Jeger
27 Sep–2 Oct 81	Brighton	A. Kitson
27 Sep–1 Oct 82	Blackpool	Dame J. Hart
3–8 Oct 83	Brighton	S. McCluskey
1–5 Oct 84	Blackpool	E. Heffer
29 Sep–4 Oct 85	Bournemouth	A. Hadden
28 Sep–3 Oct 86	Blackpool	N. Hough
27 Sep–2 Oct 87	Brighton	S. Tierney
2–7 Oct 88	Blackpool	N. Kinnock
1–6 Oct 89	Brighton	D. Skinner
30 Sep–5 Oct 90	Blackpool	Jo Richardson
29 Sep–4 Oct 91	Brighton	J. Evans
27 Sep–2 Oct 92	Blackpool	T. Clarke
26 Sep–1 Oct 93	Brighton	D. Blunkett
3 Oct–7 Oct 94	Blackpool	D. Hoyle
29 Apr 95[1]	London	G. Colling
2 Oct–6 Oct 95	Brighton	G. Colling
30 Sep–4 Oct 96	Blackpool	Diana Jeuda
29 Sep–3 Oct 97	Brighton	R. Cook
28 Sep–2 Oct 98	Blackpool	R. Rosser
27 Sep–1 Oct 99	Brighton	Brenda Etchells
24–28 Sep 00	Brighton	V. Hince
30 Sep–4 Oct 01	Brighton	Maggie Jones
29 Sep–3 Oct 02	Blackpool	Margaret Wall
29 Sep–2 Oct 03	Bournemouth	Diana Holland
26–30 Sep 04	Brighton	Mary Turner
25–29 Sep 05	Brighton	I. McCartney

[1] Special Conference on the Party Constitution.

SOURCES:- Labour Party Annual Conference Reports.

Party Membership

Year	Constit. & Central Parties	Total Indiv. Members (000s)[a]	No.	T.U.s Members (000s)	No.	Soc. & Co-op Socs. Members (000s)	Total Membership (000s)
1979	623	666	59	6,511	9	58	7,236
1980	623	348	54	6,407	0	56	6,811
1981	623	277	54	6,273	0	58	6,608
1982	623	274	50	6,185	0	57	6,516
1983	633	295	47	6,101	0	59	6,456
1984	633	323	46	5,844	9	60	6,227
1985	633	313	44	5,827	9	60	6,200
1986	633	297	44	5,778	9	58	6,133
1987	633	289	44	5,564	9	55	5,908

Year	Constit. & Central Parties	Total Indiv. Members (000s)[a]	T.U.s No.	Members (000s)	Soc. & Co-op Socs. No.	Members (000s)	Total Membership (000s)
1988	633	266	44	5,481	9	56	5,804
1989	633	294	44	5,335	9	53	5,682
1990	633	311	44	4,922	9	54	5,287
1991	634	261	34	4,811	13	54	5,126
1992	634	280	38	4,634	14	51	4,965
1993	634	266	b	b	b	b	b
1994	634	305					
1995	641	365					
1996	641	400					
1997	641	405					
1998	641	388					
1999	641	361					
2000	641	311					
2001	641	272					
2002	641	248					
2003	641	215					
2004	628	201					

[a] The membership figure is for 31 December each year.
[b] From 1993 the reports to conference from the NEC stopped including data on affiliates.

SOURCES:- Labour Party Annual Conference Reports. But see P. Seyd, *Labour's Grassroots* (1992).

The Labour Party – Organisation and Constitutions

The Labour Representation Committee was formed on 27 February 1900 to promote a distinct Labour group in Parliament, representing the affiliated trade unions and socialist societies. The sovereign body of the party was the annual conference, and between conferences the ruling body was the National Executive Committee. The Leader (since 1929) and the Deputy Leader (since 1953), both elected by the Parliamentary Labour Party, are ex officio members of the N.E.C. Other members were elected by the trade unions and constituency parties at conference. In 1981 the procedure for the election of Leader and Deputy Leader was changed (see p. 54).

In 1990 the Party Conference agreed in principle to a changed pattern of policy-making with the establishment of a Policy Forum and the production of a rolling programme of party policy. The National Policy Forum met first in May 1993. In 1997, some drastic changes were made following an N.E.C. document *Partnership in Power*. The National Conference remained supreme in policy-making, considering reports from a 175-member (later 183-member) National Policy Forum, elected for a two-year term. The National Executive was restructured. The women's section was abolished but half the representatives from the T.U. section, the Constituency Labour Parties, the new Local Government section and the Parliamentary Labour Party were to be women. M.P.s were barred from most sections.

SOURCES:- H. Pelling, *The Origins of the Labour Party, 1880–1900* (1954); F. Bealey and H. Pelling, *Labour and Politics, 1900–1906* (1958); P. Poirier, *The Advent of the Labour Party* (1958); G. D. H. Cole, *A History of the Labour Party from 1914* (1948); R. T. McKenzie, *British Political Parties* (1955); L. Minkin, *The Labour Party Conference* (1978). Since 1918 complete lists of Labour Party publications have been given in the Labour Party Annual Conference Reports. See also I. Bulmer-Thomas, *The Growth of the British Party System* (1965).

Sponsored M.P.s

The following table summarises information on the number of Labour M.P.s with Trade Union or Co-operative financial sponsorship. Such sponsorship was discontinued in 1995.

	Oct 1974	1979	1983	1987	1992
NUM	18	16	14	13	14
TGW	22	22	25	33	38
NUR	6	12	10	8	12
TSSA	3	3	2	2	2
GMW	13	14	11	11	17
ASW	3	1	1	–	–
USDAW	5	5	2	8	3
I & S	1	2	1	1	–
AEU	16	21	17	12	13
ASSET	12	10	8	10	13
ETU	3	3	4	3	3
APEX	6	6	5	3	–
NUPE	6	6	7	4	12
Others	13	11	8	22	16
T.U. sponsored	129	132	115	130	143
Co-op. sponsored	16	17	8	10	14
Unsponsored	172	120	86	139	114
Total MPs	319	269	209	229	271

Party Finance

Labour Party Central Annual Expenditure

1980	£2,720,000	1995	£15,525,000
1985	£4,542,000	2000	£27,424,000
1990	£6,563,000	2003	£24,281,000

In 1990 Trade Union affiliation fees provided 67% of the Labour Party's routine annual income; in 2003 the figure had fallen to 25%.

SOURCES:- The Labour Party has always published Accounts in its Annual Conference Reports. M. Pinto-Duschinsky, *British Political Finance 1830–1980* (1981); Labour Party Annual Reports; M. Linton, *Money and Votes* (Institute for Public Policy Research, 1994); Labour History Archive and Study Centre, University of Manchester.

Liberal Party

The Alliance and the Merger

From 1981 to 1987 the Liberal party was linked in the Alliance with the newly formed Social Democratic Party (see pp. 72–3). On 14 June 1987 the Liberal leader D. Steel proposed merging the two parties. On 17 September 1987 the Liberal Conference in Harrogate voted to start negotiations. On 23 January 1988 a special Liberal Assembly convened in Blackpool voted to proceed with merger. This took place on 3 March 1988 following an affirmative ballot by the membership of both parties (see below for Social and Liberal Democrats).

Leaders and Deputy Leaders of the Party

Leaders		Deputy Leaders	
7 Jul 76	D. Steel	1985–88	A. Beith

Leaders in the House of Lords

1967	Ld Byers
1984	Lady Seear

Principal Office-holders

Liberal Party Organisation, 1979–88		Chairman of Party 1979–88	
Head		1976	G. Tordoff
1977	H. Jones *(Sec.-General)*	1980	R. Pincham
1983	J. Spiller *(Sec.-General)*	1983	Joyce Rose
1985	A. Ellis *(Sec.-General)*	1984	P. Tyler
		1986	T. Clement-Jones

Treasurer

1977–83	Ld Lloyd of Kilgerran
1977–83	M. Palmer
1983–86	A. Jacobs
1986–88	C. Fox
1986–88	T. Razzall

Chief Whips in the House of Commons

1977	A. Beith
1985	D. Alton
1987	J. Wallace

Chief Whips in the House of Lords

1977	Ld Wigoder
1984	Ld Tordoff

SOURCE:- *Dod's Parliamentary Companion*, 1900–.

Annual Conferences, 1979–88

Date	Place	President
28–29 Sep 79	Margate	M. Steed
8–13 Sep 80	Blackpool	Joyce Rose
14–19 Sep 81	Llandudno	R. Holme
20–25 Sep 82	Bournemouth	V. Bingham
19–24 Sep 83	Harrogate	J. Griffiths
17–22 Sep 84	Bournemouth	Ld Tordoff
16–21 Sep 85	Dundee	A. Watson
21–26 Sep 86	Eastbourne	D. Penhaligon
13–18 Sep 87	Harrogate	D. Wilson
22–23 Jan 88	Blackpool *(Special Assembly)*	A. Slade

(Social and) Liberal Democrats

On 2 March 1988 the result of a ballot was published in which Liberal Party members voted by 46,376 to 6,365 to merge with the Social Democratic Party (which voted by 18,722 to 9,929 to do the same). The new party was officially launched the following day (3 March 1988). Its full title was the Social and Liberal Democrats (SLD), with the short title 'the Democrats'. On 16 October 1989, following a membership ballot, the party announced that it was henceforth to be known as the Liberal Democrats (although for formal, legal purposes, it retained its full title).

Leaders and Deputy Leaders of the Party

Leader
28 Jul 88   P. Ashdown
(Postal ballot: P. Ashdown 41,401 (71%), A. Beith 16,202 29%).
9 Aug 99   C. Kennedy
(Postal ballot, single transferable vote 1st round: C. Kennedy 22,724,
S. Hughes 16,223, M. Bruce 4,643, Jackie Ballard 3,928, D. Rendel 3,428;
4th round: C. Kennedy 28,425 (57%), S. Hughes 21,833 (43%)
Turnout: 61.6%.)

Deputy Leader of Parliamentary Party
1988	A. Beith
2002	(Sir) M. Campbell

Principal Office-holders
President
1988	I. Wrigglesworth	1998	Lady Maddock
1990	C. Kennedy	1999	Ld Dholakia
1994	R. McLennan	2004	S. Hughes

Leader in the House of Lords
1988	Ld Jenkins of Hillhead
1997	Ld Rodgers
2001	Lady Williams
2004	Ld McNally

Treasurer
1988	T. Razzall *(Ld)*

General Secretary
1988	A. Ellis
1989	G. Elson

(Chief Executive)
1998	Elizabeth Pamplin
1999	H. Rickard
2003	Ld Rennard

Director of (Media) Communications
1989	Olly Grender
1995	*(Office vacant)*
1997	Jane Bonham-Carter
1998	D. Walter
2004	S. Walkington
2005	*(Office vacant)*

Party Conferences
25–29 Sep 88	Blackpool	21–25 Sep 97	Eastbourne
3–5 Mar 89	Bournemouth	14–15 Mar 98	Southport
9–15 Sep 89	Brighton	20–24 Sep 98	Brighton
10–11 Mar 90	Cardiff	5–7 Mar 99	Edinburgh
15–20 Sep 90	Blackpool	19–23 Sep 99	Harrogate
15–17 Mar 91	Nottingham	17–19 Mar 00	Plymouth
9–12 Sep 91	Bournemouth	17–21 Sep 00	Bournemouth
7–8 Mar 92	Glasgow	16–18 Mar 01	Torquay
13–17 Sep 92	Harrogate	23–27 Sep 01	Bournemouth
29–31 May 93	Nottingham	8–10 Mar 02	Manchester
19–23 Sep 93	Torbay	22–26 Sep 02	Brighton
12–13 Mar 94	Cardiff	14–16 Mar 03	Torquay
18–22 Sep 94	Brighton	21–25 Sep 03	Brighton
11–12 Mar 95	Scarborough	19–21 Mar 04	Southport
17–21 Sep 95	Glasgow	19–23 Sep 04	Bournemouth
15–17 Mar 96	Nottingham	4–6 Mar 05	Harrogate
22–26 Sep 96	Brighton	18–22 Sep 05	Blackpool
8–9 Mar 97	Cardiff		

Party Finance

	Total net central income	Membership
1988–89	£1.2m	
1989–90	£1.4m	
1990–91	£1.6m	
1991–92	£1.9m	
1992–93	£3.0m	
1993	£1.8m	
1994	£2.4m	
1995	£2.3m	
1996	£2.7m	
1997	£3.8m	
1998	n/a	
1999	n/a	
2000	n/a	
2001	£5.2m	73,276
2002	£3.4m	71,636
2003	£4.0m	73,505

Minor Parties

Co-operative Party

The Co-operative Party is Labour's sister party. It is the only other party to which Labour Party members are allowed to belong. Its programme focuses on co-operative and mutual forms of enterprise. In 2005 there were 30 Labour and Co-operative M.P.s, 8 M.S.P.s, 5 Welsh Assembly Members and over 700 councillors, and a membership of 8,000.

	M.P.s	Candidates
1979	17	25
1983	8	17
1987	10	20
1992	14	26
1997	26	26
2001	30	30
2005	29	32

SOURCES:- Reports of the Annual Co-operative Congress 1900–.

Green Party

The Green Party was founded in 1985 as the successor to the Ecology Party (founded in 1975). It describes itself as the only party committed to ecological sustainability and social justice. It has never had one 'Leader' but has nominated two or more 'main speakers' from its executive. The party made its mark in the 1989 European Elections when it secured 15% of the national vote and pushed the Liberal Democrats into fourth place in every constituency but one. The party suffered from internal disagreements and, despite some success in local elections, it made little impact in Westminster elections (although in 2001, Ten Green candidates saved their deposits). It did however make considerable progress in elections where proportional representation was used, with members elected to the European Parliament, Scottish Parliament, and Greater London Assembly from 1999 onwards.

Ecology/Green Vote

	Candidates	% of UK vote	% per candidate
1979	53	0.1	1.5
1983	108	0.1	1.0
1987	133	0.2	1.4
1992	254	0.5	1.3
1997	95	0.2	1.4
2001	145	0.6	2.7
2005	229	1.0	2.8

Irish Parties

The SDLP, founded in 1970, became the main party representing the Republican or Nationalist aspirations of the Roman Catholic minority. From the early 1980s it faced an increasingly stiff challenge from Provisional Sinn Fein, the political arm of the Provisional IRA, which adopted a strategy known as 'the Armalite and the ballot box'. The SDLP nevertheless remained the larger of the two main nationalist parties in terms of votes until the 2005 General Election, although Sinn Fein overtook it in the Northern Ireland Assembly election of November 2003.

Sinn Fein M.P.s

1983–92	G. Adams	2001–	Michelle Gildernew
1997–	G. Adams	2001–	P. Doherty
1997–	M. McGuinness		

Independent Socialist M.P.

| 2005– | C. Murphy |
| 1979–83 | G. Fitt |

SDLP M.P.s

1983–2005	J. Hume
1986–2005	S. Mallon
1987–	E. McGrady
1992–97	J. Hendron
2005–	M. Durkan
2005–	A. McDonnell

Independent Republican M.P.s

Oct 1974–81	F. Maguire (Independent Unity)
1981–81	R. Sands (Anti H-Block)
1981–83	O. Carron (Anti H-Block)

In October 1974 H. West who had acted as Unionist Leader was the only one of the 11 Ulster Unionists to be defeated. J. Molyneaux succeeded him as parliamentary leader. In 1979 3 Paisleyites, 1 Independent Unionist (J. Kilfedder), 1 UUUP and 5 official Unionists were successful. In 1983 3 Paisleyites, 11 Official Unionists and J. Kilfedder were successful. In 1986 all 15 Unionists resigned their seats to force by-elections in protest at the Anglo-Irish Agreement; one, the Official Unionist M. Robinson in Newry and Armagh, lost his seat to the SDLP. At the 1987 election 9 Official Unionists, 3 Democratic Unionists and J. Kilfedder were elected; all these seats were retained in 1992, despite a strong challenge in North Down from the Conservative Party, which had been organising in the area since 1987 and received official blessing at the 1991 Conservative Party Conference.

After the death in 1995 of Sir J. Kilfedder, R. McCartney was elected in North Down as an Independent Unionist. He retained his seat in 1997 along with two DUP M.P.s (I. Paisley and P. Robinson) and 10 Official Unionists.

At the 2001 election R. McCartney lost his seat to the UUP, while the DUP and Sinn Fein made progress at the UUP's expense; the total Unionist representation was 6 UUP, and 5 DUP.

In Northern Ireland Assembly elections in 1999 (for full results see p. 229) the SDLP outpolled Sinn Fein among nationalist voters (24 seats to 18), and the UUP were comfortably ahead of the DUP (28–20) on the unionist side. The UUP leader D. Trimble became First Minister of Northern Ireland. The situation was reversed in the 2003 when the DUP edged ahead of the UUP (30–27) and Sinn Fein overtook the SDLP (24–18).

At the 2005 election the UUP lost four seats to the DUP and one to the SDLP, leaving it with only one; D. Trimble, who had himself lost his seat, resigned as UUP leader. The DUP had nine seats. Sinn Fein emerged with five M.P.s and the SDLP with three.

Alliance Party of Northern Ireland

The non-Sectarian Alliance Party, founded in 1970, was joined by S. Mills, a Unionist M.P., in 1972. He did not stand in February 1974. The Alliance Party leaders have been O. Napier (1973–84), followed by J. Cushnahan (1984–87), J. Alderdice (1987–98), S. Neeson (1998–2001) and D. Ford (2001–).

Election	Candidates	Lost Deposits	% of N.I. vote
Feb 74	3	2	n.a.
Oct 74	5	1	6.4
1979	12	7	11.9
1983	11	7	8.0
1987	16	4	9.9
1992	16	5	8.7
1997	17	6	8.0
2001	10	5	3.6
2005	12	5	3.9

Militant

Militant, known internally as the Revolutionary Socialist League, secretly infiltrated the Labour Party for almost forty years, using the Trotskyist tactic of 'entryism'. The RSL was established in 1955, a democratic centralist Marxist-Leninist Party with its own central committee and annual conference. The Militant newspaper was founded in 1964. Leading figures were its General Secretary P. Taaffe, and T. Grant. At its peak in the mid 1980s, Militant had more than 8,000 members, and achieved prominence in leading Liverpool City Council's resistance to Government spending controls. Two Militant members, D. Nellist and T. Fields, were elected as Labour M.P.s in 1983, and a third P. Wall in 1987. Both Taaffe and Grant were expelled from the Labour Party in 1983, the first of around 200 expulsions over the next decade culminating in the two surviving M.P.s in 1991 (both lost their seats to official Labour candidates at the 1992 election). In 1992 Grant and several of his followers were expelled from Militant itself for opposing its decision to abandon 'entryism' and work mainly outside the Labour Party under the name Militant Labour. In Scotland it has since had several local councillors elected, and went on to form the core of the Scottish Socialist Party, with representation in the Scottish Parliament.

SOURCE:- M. Crick, *The March of Militant* (1986).

The National Front and British National Party

The National Front was formed by a merger of the League of Empire Loyalists and the British National Party in 1966. The Greater Britain Movement joined in 1967. The leader of the League of Empire Loyalists, A. K. Chesterton, President of the British National Party, became Executive Director. In 1970 A. K. Chesterton was succeeded by J. O'Brien, who was succeeded in 1972 by J. Tyndall (previously leader of the Greater Britain Movement). In 1974 J. Read ousted J. Tyndall but the courts ruled the ouster illegal. J. Read formed the National Party and J. Tyndall resumed as leader with M. Webster as National Activities Organiser. In 1982 a breakaway faction under J. Tyndall, the New National Front, merged with other groups to form the British National Party.

National Front Candidates

	No.	Av. % vote	Highest % vote
1979	303	1.3	7.6
1983	60	1.1	2.4
1987	–	–	–
1992	14	0.8	1.2
1997	6	1.0	1.6
2001	5	1.5	2.2
2005	16	1.1	2.0

British National Party Candidates

	No.	Av. % vote	Highest % vote
1983	54	0.5	1.2
1987	2	0.6	0.8
1992	13	1.2	3.6
1997	57	1.3	7.5
2001	33	3.9	16.4
2005	130	3.5	16.9

SOURCE: M. Walker, *The National Front* (1977); C. Husbands, *Racial Exclusionism in the Cities: Support for the National Front* (1983).

Natural Law Party

The British branch of the world wide Natural Law Party was formed in 1992. It is dedicated to finding solutions to problems through Natural Law, following the teachings of Maharashi Mahesh Yogi and through yogic flying.

The party has fought elections extensively but with no success.

Chair: 1992 G. Clements

	Candidates	% of UK vote	% per candidate
1992	309	0.4	0.2
1997	193	0.3	0.1

Plaid Cymru (Welsh Nationalist Party)

The party was founded in 1925 and has fought elections consistently since then, but without any success at the Parliamentary level until a by-election victory in Carmarthen in 1966. The seat was lost in 1970 but in the February 1974 election, two seats, Caernarvon and Merioneth were won. Carmarthen was recaptured in October 1974, lost in 1979, and recaptured in 2001. In 1987 Plaid Cymru gained Ynys Mon (Anglesey) – which they lost in 2001 – and in 1992 Ceredigion and Pembroke North.

The party's great breakthrough came in the 1999 Welsh Assembly elections, in which they secured 17 seats and 30.6% of the vote, becoming the main opposition to Labour in Wales. In the 2003 Assembly elections the Plaid Cymru vote fell back to 19.7%.

Welsh Nationalist Candidates

	Candidates	Seats won	% of Welsh vote
1979	36	2	8.1
1983	38	2	7.8
1987	38	3	7.3
1992	38	4	8.8
1997	40	4	9.9
2001	40	4	14.3
2005	40	3	12.6

Plaid Cymru	M.P.s
Oct 74–79	G. Evans
Feb 74–01	D. Wigley
Feb 74–92	D. Thomas
1987–2001	W. Jones
1992–	E. Llwyd
1992–2001	C. Dafis
2001–05	S. Thomas
2001–	H. Williams
2001–	A. Price

Referendum Party

The Referendum Party was founded by Sir J. Goldsmith in October 1995 with the sole object of forcing a Referendum on British membership of the European Union. Sir J. Goldsmith devoted £20 million to the enterprise. The party attracted considerable attention during the 1997 election. In June 1997 Sir J. Goldsmith died and the party announced that it would devote its efforts to propaganda rather than to parliamentary candidacies.

	Candidates	Lost Deposits	% of UK vote	% per candidate
1997	547	505	2.6	3.1

Scottish National Party

The party was formed in 1928 as the National Party of Scotland. In 1934 it merged with a body called the Scottish Party (founded 1932) and the name was then changed to the Scottish National Party. Its first success was in the Motherwell by-election of April 1945; but the victor, R. McIntyre, was defeated in the General Election three months later. In 1967 a seat was won in the Hamilton by-election but lost in 1970. In 1970, however, a Scottish Nationalist won Western Isles. In November 1973 the Govan, Glasgow, seat was won in a by-election but lost four months later. In the General Elections of 1974 the Scottish Nationalists made great advances in votes and seats, but fell back sharply in 1979. The SNP did well in the 1999 Scottish Parliament election, achieving 27.3% of the top-up vote, just 6.3% behind Labour; but they fell back in 2003 to 20.9% of the top-up vote.

	Candidates	Seats	% of Scottish vote
1979	71	2	17.3
1983	72	2	11.8
1987	71	3	14.0
1992	72	3	21.5
1997	72	6	22.1
2001	72	5	20.1
2005	59	6	17.7

Scottish National Party M.P.s

1970–87	D. Stewart
Feb 74–87	G. Wilson
Oct 74–79, 1987–2001	Margaret Bain (Margaret Ewing)
Oct 74–79, 1987–2001	A. Welsh
1987–	A. Salmond
1988–92	J. Sillars
1990–92	D. Douglas
1995–2001	Roseanna Cunningham
1997–2001	J. Swinney
1997–2001	A. Morgan
2001–05	Annabelle Ewing
2001–	P. Wishart
2001–	A. Robertson
2001–	M. Weir
2005–	S. Hosie
2005–	A. MacNeil

Social Democratic Party

The Social Democratic Party was launched by four former Labour Cabinet Ministers following the Labour Party Special Conference on 24 January 1981. In its first year it recruited a total of 25 sitting Labour M.P.s and one Conservative M.P. and two of its founders (Shirley Williams and R. Jenkins) won parliamentary by-elections. It formed an Alliance with the Liberal Party and shared out constituencies with them in the 1983 general election, when the two parties jointly won 26% of the votes and 23 seats (six SDP). The SDP won two further seats in by-elections in 1984 and early 1987 but in the General Election of 1987 only six SDP M.P.s survived. The party was seriously split over the Liberal Party's proposal in June 1987 that the two parties should merge. On 6 August 1987 the membership voted narrowly to proceed with merger negotiations, whereupon D. Owen resigned as leader. R. Maclennan (one of only two SDP M.P.s to support merger) was elected leader unopposed on 29 August 1988. A draft constitution for a new merged party was published on 11 December 1987, and an amended version on 18 January 1988; both were rejected by D. Owen and his supporters. The Council for Social Democracy voted to put the merger proposals to the party membership on 31 January 1988 and a vote in favour of merger was announced on 2 March 1988. The Social Democratic Party was formally subsumed into the Social and Liberal Democrats on 3 March 1988.

Three of the five SDP M.P.s (D. Owen, J. Cartwright and Rosie Barnes) refused to be involved in the merged party and relaunched a continuing SDP on 8 March 1988. The party had limited success in by elections and after disappointing results in local elections in May 1989 the party wound down its operations, conceding it could no longer operate as a national party. It formally suspended operations in June 1990. Although attempts were later made to revive it, from June 1990 on the three M.P.s sat as independent Social Democrats. D. Owen did not contest his seat in the 1992 General Election. J. Cartwright and Rosie Barnes fought the 1992 election as Independent Social Democrats but lost.

Leader
1982   R. Jenkins
1983   D. Owen

SOURCE:- I. Crewe and A. King, *SDP* (1996).

United Kingdom Independence Party (UKIP)

The United Kingdom Independence Party was founded in August 1993 to campaign against British membership of the European Union. It secured 3.3% of the vote in the 24 constituencies it fought in the 1994 Euro-elections. In 1997 it was overshadowed by the much better funded Referendum Party, which was wound up shortly after the 1997 election. In the 1999 Euro-elections it secured 7.0% of the GB vote with two M.E.P.s elected, and in the 2004 Euro-elections it went up to 16.2% with 12 M.E.P.s elected.

	Candidates	% of UK vote	% per candidate
1997	194	0.3	1.2
2001	428	1.5	2.2
2005	549	2.3	2.7

Independent M.P.s

Only four times since 1979 have M.P.s without affiliation to any national party been elected in GB constituencies (not including the Speaker). In 1997 M. Bell won in Tatton on an anti-sleaze ticket after Labour and Lib Dem candidates had withdrawn. He did not contest the seat in 2001. In 2001 R. Taylor won in Wyre Forest on a 'Save Kidderminster Hospital' platform; he was re-elected in 2005. Also in 2005 P. Law won in Blaenau Gwent, having run against the official Labour candidate in protest at the imposition of an all-women shortlist. In addition, G. Galloway won the seat of Bethnal Green and Bow in 2005 – although he was not strictly an independent, because his party 'Respect' put up 26 candidates across the country.

Independent
1997   M. Bell
2001   R. Taylor
2005   R. Taylor
2005   P. Law

Minor Parties – Representation in the House of Commons

Year	Total	Ir. N.	SNP	PC	UU/DUP	Other
1979	16	2	2	2	10	–
1983	21	2	2	2	15	–
1987	23	3	3	3	14	–
1992	24	4	3	4	13	–
1997	29	5	6	4	13	1
2001	28	7	5	4	11	1
2005	30	8	6	3	10	3

Other Minor Parties Contesting Parliamentary Elections

(England, Scotland and Wales)

Every effort has been made to give accurate figures for minor party candidacies, but in many cases it is virtually impossible to ascertain whether a candidate is genuinely affiliated to the party whose label they bear.

Name	Date of founding	Principal founder or key policy	(MPs elected)	Candidates First	Last	No.	Lost Deposits
Anti-Federalist League	1991	A. Sked		1992	1997	19	19
Cornish Nationalist Pty	1975	J. Whetter		1979	1983	2	2
English Democrats	2002	Support for English Parliament		2004	2005	25	25
Islamic Party	1989			1990	1992	5	5
Liberal Party	1988	M. Meadowcroft		1988	2005	280	279
Mebyon Kernow	1951	Cornish Independence		1970	2005	19	19
Natural Law Party	1992	Transcendental meditation		1992	1999	519	519
Pro-Life	1996	Anti-abortion		1997	1997	53	53
Red Front	1987	Alliance of left groups		1987	1987	14	14
Referendum Party	1995	Sir J. Goldsmith		1997	1997	547	505
Respect	2004	Successor to Socialist Alliance	(1)	2005	2005	29	24
Revolutionary Communist Party	1981			1983	1992	15	15
Socialist Alliance	1999	Alliance of small left-wing groups		2001	2005	199	199
Scottish Militant Labour	1992	Militant tendency		1992	1992	1	0
Scottish Socialist Party	1997			1997	2005	151	137
Social Democratic Party	1988	D. Owen; opponents of Lib/SDP merger		1988	1991	9	5
Socialist Labour Party	1996	A. Scargill		1997	2005	321	319
Veritas	2005	R. Kilroy-Silk; anti-Europe		2005	2005	66	65
Wessex Regional Party	1979	A. Thynne		1979	1983	16	16
Workers' Revolutionary Party	1959			1974	2005	133	133

SOURCES:- BBC Political Research Unit.

Political Pressure Groups

The following is a selection of pressure groups with a more generalised remit:

Fabian Society 1884–   Affiliated to the Labour Party.
Tory Reform Group   Centrist, one-nation Conservative.
Bow Group 1951–   Mainstream Conservative.
Institute of Economic Affairs 1955–   Free market, economic liberal.
Centre for Policy Studies 1974–   Free market, closely associated with Margaret Thatcher.
Adam Smith Institute 1977–   Free market; non-party but closer to Conservatives.
PSI (Policy Studies Institute) 1978–   Non-party.
Charter 88 1988–   Civil liberties and democratic reform.
Institute for Public Policy Research 1989–   Left-leaning, close links to Labour modernisers.
Social Market Foundation 1989–   Initially SDP, later Conservative leaning, now non-party.
Demos 1993–   Initially left-leaning, but avoids party political agenda.
Politeia 1995–   Conservative, specialising in education and social policy.
Conservative Mainstream 1996–   Founded by Michael Heseltine; centrist Conservative.
Policy Exchange 2002–   Founded by supporters of Michael Portillo; 'modernising' Conservative.
Reform 2002–   Conservative, free market-inclined.

Registration of Political Parties

Under the *Registration of Political Parties Act, 1998*, all parties wishing to put forward candidates for election were required to record their title and responsible officials with the Registrar of Companies. Inititially 70 parties registered. The Registrar's function was taken over by the Electoral Commission under the Political Parties, Elections and Referendums Act, 2000.

III
Parliament

House of Commons

Speakers and Their Deputies

Speaker of the House of Commons

3 Feb 76	G. Thomas (Vt Tonypandy)	Lab.
15 Jun 83	B. Weatherill (Ld Weatherill)	Con.
17 Apr 92	Betty Boothroyd (Lady Boothroyd)	Lab.
23 Oct 00	M. Martin	Lab.

Chairman of Ways and Means

1976	O. Murton	Con.
1983	(Sir) H. Walker	Lab.
1992	M. Morris	Con.
1997	Sir A. Haselhurst	Con.

Deputy Chairman of Ways and Means

1976	Sir M. Galpern	Lab.	1992	G. Lofthouse	Lab.
1979	G. Irvine	Con.	1997	M. Martin	Lab.
1982	E. Armstrong	Lab.	2001	Sylvia Heal	Lab.
1987	Sir P. Dean	Con.			

Second Deputy Chairman of Ways and Means

1976	G. Irvine	Con.	1987	Betty Boothroyd	Lab.
1979	R. Crawshaw	Lab.	1993	Dame J. Fookes	Con.
1981	E. Armstrong	Lab.	1997	(Sir) M. Lord	Con.
1982	(Sir) P. Dean	Con.			

Officers of the House of Commons

Clerk

1976	(Sir) R. Barlas		1994	(Sir) D. Limon
1979	(Sir) C. Gordon		1997	(Sir) W. McKay
1983	(Sir) K. Bradshaw		2003	R. Sands
1987	(Sir) C. Boulton			

Librarian		Serjeant-at-Arms	
1976	D. Menhennet	1976	(Sir) P. Thorne
1991	D. Englefield	1982	(Sir) V. Le Fanu
1993	Jennifer Tanfield	1989	Sir A. Urwick
2000	Priscilla Baines	1995	(Sir) P. Jennings
2004	J. Pullinger	2000	(Sir) M. Cummins

Parliamentary Sessions

In 1930 both Houses agreed that they should adjourn between July and October, and that the session should last from September or October to the September or October of the following year. During the adjournments the Speaker or the Lord Chancellor has the power to give notice of an earlier meeting of his House if it is in the national interest.

Commons Hours of Sitting

For most of the period since the Second World War, Parliament sat from 2.30 until around 10pm Mon–Thurs, and 11am until 3pm on Friday. The Friday start time was brought forward to 9.30am in 1980. From December 1994 to November 1999 the House also met from 10am on Wednesday mornings to deal with private members' business. In 1998 the House voted to sit from 11.30am until 7.30pm on Thursdays. In October 2002 the House voted to extend the 11.30–7.30 sitting hours to Tuesday and Wednesday from January 2003. In January 2005 M.P.s voted to revert to sitting from 2.30 to 10 pm on Tuesdays, while keeping the earlier hours on Wednesdays and Thursdays.

If the House sits beyond the time scheduled for the next day's sitting the next day's business is lost. This has happened on these occasions since 1979:

4 Aug 80	Consolidated Fund Bill
1 Apr 80	British Telecommunications Bill
22 May 84	Local Government Bill
5 Mar 85	Water (Fluoridation) Bill
10 Dec 86	Teachers' Pay Bill
10 Nov 87	Felixstowe Dock and Railway Bill
14 Jun 88	Housing Bill
10 Mar 05	Prevention of Terrorism Bill

Westminster Hall

In 1999 the old Grand Committee Room off Westminster was set up as an additional debating forum where issues of policy and administration can be ventilated by M.P.s. Westminster Hall sits for four hours on Tuesdays and Wednesdays and for three hours on Thursdays.

Emergency Recalls of the House of Commons

Under Standing Order No 12, which dates from 1948, the Speaker on request from ministers may give notice that the House of Commons will sit earlier than the date agreed on adjournment if the public interest requires it. This Standing Order has been used on these occasions:

3 Apr, 14 Apr 82	Falkland Islands
6–7 Sep 90	Kuwait
24–25 Sep 92	Exchange rate policy, UN operations
2–3 Sep 98	Passage of Anti-Terrorism legislation
14 Sep 01	Sep 11 terrorist attacks in the U.S.
4 and 8 Oct 01	Coalition against international terrorism
3 Apr 02	Death of Queen Mother
24 Sep 02	Iraq crisis

Broadcasting of Parliament

In February 1975 the House of Commons approved (354–152) a four-week experiment in the live radio broadcasting of its proceedings and this took place from 9 June to 4 July 1975. On 16 March 1976 the House approved (299–124) the idea of permanent sound broadcasting. A select committee of six M.P.s (Chairmen: 1978: R. Mellish; 1979: Sir A. Royle; 1983: Sir P. Goodhart) was set up on 6 February 1978 to supervise the arrangements to be made with the broadcasting authorities. Regular sound broadcasting began on 3 April 1978. Private members have since introduced Ten Minute Rule bills to test opinion on televising proceedings, as follows:

4 Jul 1978:	defeated (181–161)
30 Jan 1980:	first reading carried (202–201) on deputy speaker's casting vote
15 Dec 1981:	defeated (176–158)
13 Apr 1983 (select committees only):	first reading carried (153–138)
2 Nov 1983:	first reading carried (164–159)

On 8 December 1983, the Lords voted (74–24) for the public televising of some of its proceedings for an experimental period, and the select committee recommended a six-month experiment which began on 23 January 1985. On 22 July 1985 the House of Lords extended the experiment and on 12 May 1986 agreed to make television a permanent feature.

There were regular attempts by supporters of the televising of the House of Commons to air the issue, using Ten Minute Rule bills. On 20 November 1985 a motion moved by Dame J. Fookes to allow the televising of proceedings was narrowly defeated (275–263). On 9 February 1988 the House voted, 318–264, to allow a limited experiment in televising proceedings under strict conditions, laid down by a newly appointed select committee on televising the proceedings of the House. Televising began on 21 November 1989. The Select Committee reviewed the first six months of the experiment, and when the House approved their report (19 July 1990) it effectively ended the debate on whether televising was desirable; it was formally made permanent on 1 May 1991. Under the permanent arrangements put in place in 1991, integrated coverage of both Houses of Parliament was undertaken by the Parliamentary Broadcasting Unit Limited (PARBUL), financed by the broadcasting companies. Although the strict conditions laid down by the House of Commons when it first approved the televising experiment were subsequently relaxed slightly, television directors were not allowed to show reaction shots during question time or ministerial statements, or to show any scenes of disturbances.

Main Occupations of Members of Parliament
1979–2005 (percentages)

	Conservative							Labour						
	79	*83*	*87*	*92*	*97*	*01*	*05*	*79*	*83*	*87*	*92*	*97*	*01*	*05*
Professional	45	45	42	39	37	39	38	43	42	40	42	45	43	40
Business	34	36	37	38	39	36	38	7	9	10	8	9	8	7
Miscellaneous	20	19	20	22	23	25	23	14	16	21	28	33	36	43
Manual Work	1	1	1	1	1	1	1	36	33	29	22	13	12	10
	100	100	100	100	100	100	100	100	100	100	100	100	100	100

SOURCE:- Nuffield Studies.

Education of Conservative and Labour M.P.s
1979–2005 (percentages)

	Conservative		Labour	
	Public school	*University educated*	*Public school*	*University educated*
1979	77	73	17	57
1983	70	71	14	53
1987	68	70	14	56
1992	62	73	14	61
1997	61	81	16	66
2001	64	83	17	67
2005	60	81	17	64

SOURCE:- Nuffield Studies.

House of Commons Business

Sessions		Allocation of Time			Bills		Questions Daily Av. Starred		
Date of Meeting	Date Prorogued	Sitting Days	Length of Day	Private MPs' Days	Total Introduced	Royal Assent	Yes	No	Total
31 Oct 78	7 Apr 79	86	8h 17m	15	115	50	54	153	17,851

Dissolution 7 Apr 79. Duration 4 years 5 months 16 days

9 May 79	13 Nov 80	244	8h 55m	25	217	102	51	164	52,635
20 Nov 80	30 Oct 81	163	9h 7m	22	145	78	50	139	30,863
4 Nov 81	28 Oct 82	174	8h 8m	22	143	59	52	135	32,430
3 Nov 82	13 May 83	115	8h 34m	17	134	56	53	149	23,220

Dissolution 13 May 1983. Duration 4 years 4 days

15 Jun 83	31 Oct 84	213	8h 59m	24	181	76	63	188	53,995
6 Nov 84	30 Oct 85	172	9h 06m	25	153	75	86	183	46,314
5 Nov 85	7 Nov 86	172	8h 56m	25	162	69	101	185	49,140
12 Nov 86	18 May 87	109	8h 32m	17	124	51	12	196	34,537

Dissolution 18 May 87. Duration 3 years 11 months 4 days

17 Jun 87	15 Nov 88	159	11h 31m	26	168	62	110	219	72,666
22 Nov 88	16 Nov 89	136	11h 38m	25	179	46	136	225	63,472
21 Nov 89	1 Nov 90	127	11h 32m	25	162	45	148	248	66,045
7 Nov 90	22 Oct 91	125	10h 50m	24	171	69	173	205	37,644
31 Nov 91	16 Mar 92	63	11h 02m	12	97	47	97	193	18,433

Dissolution 16 Mar 1992. Duration 4 years 5 months 30 days

27 Apr 92	17 Nov 93	240	8h 16m	25	220	68	30	236	63,684
18 Nov 93	3 Nov 94	154	8h 10m	25	142	41	30	267	45,610
16 Nov 94	8 Nov 95	159	8h 16m	20	102	54	31	283	49,897
15 Nov 95	17 Oct 96	146	8h 45m	13d	147	60	31	246	40,307
23 Oct 96	21 Mar 97	86	8h 21m	7d	121	59	30	214	21,061

Dissolution 8 Apr 97. Duration 4 years 11 months 11 days

7 May 97	19 Nov 98	241	8h 47m	13	202	62	34	219	60,765
4 Nov 98	11 Nov 99	149	9h 15m	13	135	35	34	216	37,157
17 Nov 99	30 Nov 00	170	8h 29m	13	144	45	34	216	42,528
6 Dec 00	11 May 01	83	8h 19m	9	89	21	33	201	19,197

Dissolution 12 May 01. Duration 4 years 4 days

13 Jun 01	7 Nov 02	201	7h 40m	13	162	47	32	362	79,433
10 Nov 02	21 Nov 03	162	7h 57m	13	138	46	25	342	59,554
26 Nov 03	18 Nov 04	157	7h 44m	13	131	38	23	349	58,562
23 Nov 04	7 Apr 05	65	8h 7m	4	88	21	22	343	25,243

Dissolution 11 Apr 05 Duration 3 years 9 months 28 days

Fathers of the House of Commons

		Length of service			
	M.P. until	as M.P.		as Father	
		y.	m.	y.	m.
G. Strauss[a]	Apr 1979	46	11	5	0
J. Parker	May 1983	46	7	4	1
J. Callaghan	May 1987	41	10	4	0
Sir B. Braine	Mar 1992	42	1	3	10
Sir E. Heath	May 2001	51	3	9	0
T. Dalyell	Apr 2005	42	10	3	11
Sir P. Tapsell[a]	(sat 1959–64 and then from 1966)				

[a] By tradition the title of Father of the House goes to the member with the longest continuous service. G. Strauss sat in 1929–31 and then from 1934–79.

Long-service M.P.s

The following M.P.s served 38 years or more:

Years			Years		
51	Sir E. Heath	50–01	40	Sir E. Taylor	64–79, 80–05
50	T. Benn	50–79,80–01	40	D. Healey	52–92
47	J. Parker	35–83	39	Sir H. Fraser	45–84
47	G. Strauss	29–31,34–79	39	J. Amery	50–66,69–92
45	J. Parker	35–87	39	Sir R. Body	55–59,66–01
43	T. Dalyell	62–05	39	K. Macnamara	66–05
42	M. Foot	45–55,60–92	38	Sir J. Langford-Holt	45–83
42	J. Callaghan	45–87	38	A. Lewis	45–83
42	Sir J. Morris	59–01	38	G. Thomas	45–83
42	Sir B. Braine	50–92	38	J. Silverman	45–83
42	J. Callaghan	45–87	38	F. Willey	45–83
41	Sir G. Johnson-Smith	59–64, 65–01	38	Sir H. Wilson	45–83
41	Sir P. Emery	59–66,67–01	38	Sir D. Walker-Smith	45–83
41	A. Williams	64–05			

In 2005 Sir P. Tapsell (1959–64, 1966–) was the only M.P to have sat for over 38 years.

Oldest and Youngest M.P.s

Sir E. Heath (84 in 2001), D. Weitzman (81 in 1979) and P. Khabra (81 in 2005) have been the oldest M.P.s to serve since 1979.

C. Kennedy (23 in 1983), M. Taylor (24 in 1987), Claire Ward (25 in 1997), C. Leslie (25 in 1997) and Jo Swinson (25 in 2005) have been the youngest M.P.s elected since 1979.

Family Connections of M.P.s

Many M.P.s have had extended family connections with other present or past M.P.s. Often, when through the female line, these are difficult to check. However, the following include the most outstanding examples of parliamentary families.

Aitken	J. Aitken (1974–97) s. of Sir W. Aitken (1950–64) nephew of Sir W. Aitken (1910–16) who was father of M. Aitken (1945–50).
Benn	(Vt Stansgate) H. Benn (1999–) s. of A. Wedgwood Benn (1950–60, 1963–83, 1984–01); s. of W. Benn (1906–31, 1937–41); s. of Sir J. Benn (1892–95, 1904–10).
Butler	Sir A. Butler (1970–92); s. of R. A. Butler (1929–65), nephew of Sir G. Butler (1923–29).
Cecil	(M of Salisbury) Vt Cranborne (1979–87); s. of Vt Cranborne (1950–54); s. of Vt Cranborne (1929–41); s. of Vt Cranborne (1885–92, 1893–1903); s. of Vt Cranborne (1853–68); s. of Vt Cranborne (1813–23); s. of Vt Cranborne (1774–80).
Channon	(Sir) P. Channon (1959–97); s. of Sir H. Channon (1935–58) and g.s. of Countess of Iveagh (1927–35) and Vt Elveden (1908–10, 1912–27). This is the only example of a seat, Southend, being held successively by four members of one family.
Churchill	(D of Marlborough) W. Churchill (1970–97); s. of R. Churchill (1940–45); s. of Sir W. Churchill (1900–22, 1924–64); s. of Ld R. Churchill (1874–94); s. of M of Blandford (1844–45, 1847–57); s. of M of Blandford (1818–20, 1826–30, 1832–35, 1838–40); s. of M of Blandford (1790–96, 1802–04).
Clifton Brown	G. Clifton Brown (1992–); g.s. of G. Clifton Brown (1945–50); nephew of H. Clifton Brown (1922–23, 1924–45); and D. Clifton Brown (1918–23, 1924–51); s. of J. Clifton Brown (1876–80); g.s. of Sir W. Brown (1846–59).
Cryer	J. Cryer (1997–2005), s. of Anne Cryer (1997–) and R. Cryer (1974–83, 1987–94)
Foot	M. Foot (1945–55, 1960–92); b. of (Sir) D. Foot (1931–45, 1957–70) and s. of I. Foot (1922–24, 1929–35).
Hogg	(Vt Hailsham) D. Hogg (1979–); s. of Q. Hogg (1938–50, 1963–70); s. of Sir D. Hogg (1922–28); nephew of Sir J. Hogg (1865–68, 1871–87), and grandson of Sir J. Hogg (1835–57).
Hurd	N. Hurd (2005–); s. of D. Hurd (1974–2001); s. of Sir A. Hurd (1945–64); s. of (Sir) P. Hurd (1918–23, 1924–45).
Keen	Ann Keen (1997–) sister of Sylvia Heal (1990–92, 1997–) and wife of A. Keen (1992–).
Morris	Estelle Morris (1992–2005), d. of C. Morris (1963–83) and niece of A. Morris (1964–97).
Morrison	C. Morrison (1963–92); b. of P. Morrison (1974–92); s. of J. Morrison (1942–64); s. of H. Morrison (1918–23, 1924–31); b. of J. Morrison (1900–06, 1910–12).
Nicholson	Emma Nicholson (1987–97); d. of Sir G. Nicholson (1931–35, 1937–66); nephew of J. Nicholson (1921–24) and O. Nicholson

	(1924–31); sons of W. Nicholson (1897–1935); s. of W. Nicholson (1866–74, 1880–85).
Ridley	N. Ridley (1959–92); grandson of M. Ridley (1900–05); s. of Sir M. Ridley (1868–00); s. of Sir M. Ridley (1859–68) and b. of G. Ridley (1856–60) and E. Ridley (1878–80); s. of Sir M. Ridley (1812–36); s. of Sir M. Ridley (1768–1812) s. of M. Ridley (1747–74).
Silkin	J. Silkin (1963–83) and S. Silkin (1964–83); sons of L. Silkin (1936–50).
Sinclair	J. (Ld) Thurso) (2001–); g.s. of Sir A. Sinclair (1922–45); g.s. of Sir J. Sinclair (1870–85), s. of Sir G. Sinclair (1811–41), s. of Sir J. Sinclair (1780–1811).
Younger	G. Younger (1964–1992), nephew of K. Younger (1945–59); g.s. of Sir G. Younger (1896–1923).

Spouse's Succession

In the following case a wife took over at a by-election the seat being left vacant by her husband's death, elevation to the peerage, disqualification, or resignation.

1982	Helen McElhone (Glasgow, Queen's Park)
1986	Llin Golding (Newcastle-under-Lyme)
1990	Irene Adams (Paisley North)

The only cases of husband and wife sitting together in the House of Commons have been:

N. and Anne Winterton	1983–
P. and Virginia Bottomley	1984–05
G. and Bridget Prentice	1992–2000
R. and Julie Morgan	1997–2001
A. and Anne Keen	1997–
A. Mackay and Julie Kirkbride	1997–
P. and Iris Robinson	2001–
E. Balls and Yvette Cooper	2005–

Shirley Summerskill (1964–83) sat with her ex-husband J. Ryman (1974–87).

Bridget Prentice (1992–) continued to sit with her ex-husband G. Prentice (1992–) following divorce in 2000.

A. Lyon (1966–83) and Clare Short (1983–), though married, did not sit in the same House.

Some M.P.s have married after one had left the House: N. Fisher (1950–83) and Patricia Ford (1953–55); J. Sillars (1970–79, 1988–92) and Margo Macdonald (1973–74); A. Beith (1973–) and Lady Maddock (1993–97).

Filial Succession

In two cases a daughter was nominated to fill a vacancy left by a parent.

1983	Sarah Palmer *Lab.* (Bristol N.W.) (defeated)
1987	Hilary Armstrong *Lab.* (Durham N.W.)

Dual Mandates

From 1973 to 1979 all the UK members of the European Assembly were nominated from the House of Commons or the House of Lords. In the first direct elections, seven M.P.s were elected as M.E.P.s as well as three Peers. Since 1979 the following M.P.s have served simultaneously at Westminster and Strasbourg.

1979–04	I. Paisley (Dem.U.)	1983–84	R. Boyes (Lab)
1979–05	J. Hume (SDLP)	1983–84	Anne Clwyd (Lab)
1979–89	J. Taylor (UU)	1983–84	R. Caborn (Lab)
1979–84	Sir B. Rhys-Williams (Con)	1983–84	W. Griffiths (Lab)
1979–87	T. Normanton (Con)	1983–84	A. Rogers (Lab)
1979–84	Elaine Kellett-Bowman (Con)	1987–89	Joyce Quin (Lab)
1979–84	J. Spicer (Con)	1992–94	G. Hoon (Lab)
1983–84	R. Jackson (Con)	1992–94	L. Smith (Lab)
1983–84	D. Harris (Con)	1992–94	G. Stevenson (Lab)
1979–84	D. Curry (Con)	1997–99	Anne McIntosh (Con)
1983–84	J. Taylor (Con)	2005–	Theresa Villiers (Con)
1983–84	E. Forth (Con)	2005–	C. Huhne (LibDem)

In the period 1999–2001 a number of M.P.s continued at Westminster although elected to the Scottish Parliament or Welsh Assembly. Many N. Ireland M.P.s also sat at Stormont.

Critical Votes in the House of Commons since 1979

Votes in the House of Commons have only rarely disturbed or threatened to disturb a government or to prevent its implementing its programme. The following occasions do not constitute an exhaustive list but they include most that caused a serious stir.

28 Mar 1979	311–310	Government defeated on Conservative vote of No Confidence
23 Apr 1980	477–49	Government faces rebellion on closed shop
15 Dec 1982	290–272	Government defeated on amendment to immigration rules (51 Cons voting with Opposition or abstaining)
19 Jul 1983	226–218	Government advice on delaying M.P.s pay increase rejected
11 Apr 1984	300–208	Government win against challenge on TU ballot rules but 90 M.P.s cross vote
14 Apr 1986	296–282	Government defeated on Second Reading of Shops Bill (Sunday trading)
4 Nov 1992	319–316	Government win paving motion on Maastricht Treaty
22 Jul 1993	324–316	Defeat of Government motion on Social Policy Protocol of Maastricht Treaty. (On the next day the decision was reversed 339–301 on a confidence motion)
5 Dec 1994	319–311	Government defeated on extension of V.A.T. on fuel and power for charities (7 Conservatives voted against)
6 Nov 1995	299–297	Government defeated on E.U. fisheries 'take note' motion (3 Conservatives Noes and 7 abstentions)

26 Feb 1996	320–319	Government wins by one vote over Scott Report on Arms for Iraq (three Conservatives vote against)
10 Jun 1996	302–123	One of three Government defeats on 'free' votes on M.P.s' pay
10 Dec 1997	457–197	Government wins vote on lone parents' benefit (47 Labour M.P.s vote against)
20 May 1999	310–270	Government wins vote on disability cuts (67 Labour M.P.s vote against)
3 Nov 1999	320–262	One of three Government victories on Welfare Reform Bill (55 Labour M.P.s vote against)
16 Jul 2001	221–308	On a free vote 125 Labour MPs defied their frontbench line to vote against the government's choice of membership of the Transport Committee; 118 then also did so in respect of the Foreigh Affairs committee (232–301)
21 Nov 2001	325–89	32 Labour MPs rebel in the largest of 22 revolts against the Anti-Terrorism Bill
6 Feb 2002	87–405	46 Labour MPs rebel over faith schools during Education Bill
24 Sep 2002	6–64	56 Labour MPs rebel over possible military action in Iraq
18 Mar 2003	217–396	Following six votes from Nov 02 to Feb 03 in which from 30 to 121 Labour MPs voted against the Government over Iraq, 139 supported a critical motion in the largest back-bench rebellion since the Corn Laws
7 May 2003	117–297	65 Labour MPs vote against foundation hospitals
27 Jan 2004	316–311	72 Labour MPs voted against Student Top-Up Fees
2 Nov 2004	75–424	49 Labour MPs rebel over physical chastisement of children
28 Feb 2005	253–267	62 Labour MPs rebel in largest of 27 revolts against the Prevention of Terrorism Bill

SOURCE:- P. Cowley and M. Stuart; <www.revolts.co.uk>.

Government Defeats on the Floor of the House of Commons 1979–

1979–83	1	1992–97	9
1983–87	2	1997–01	–
1987–92	1	2001–05	–

Confidence Motions since 1979

Many motions before the House of Commons are implicitly treated as questions of confidence.

	For Government	*Against Government*	*Issue*
28 Mar 79	310	311	General confidence
28 Feb 80	327	268	Economic management
27 Jul 81	334	262	Economic management
28 Oct 81	312	250	Economic management
31 Jan 85	395	222	Economic management
22 Nov 90	367	247	General confidence
27 Mar 91	358	238	Poll tax
24 Sep 92	322	296	Economic management

	For Government	Against Government	Issue
23 Jul 93	339	299	Maastricht Treaty
1 Dec 93	282	95	(HL) General confidence
28 Nov 94	329	44	European Communities Bill

Guillotine and Programme Motions since 1979

From 1945 to 1993 the average number of guillotine motions was little more than three per year. But with arrival of 'programme motions' in 1999 and the general timetabling of all legislation in the years that followed the numbers greatly increased.

Session	Guillotine motions	Session	Guillotine motions
1978–79	–	1992–93	5
1979–80	7	1993–94	6
1980–81	4	1994–95	–
1981–82	5	1995–96	1
1982–83	3	1996–97	4
1983–84	3	1997–98	6
1984–85	2	1998–99	13
1985–86	3	1999–2000	21
1986–87	2	2000–01	52
1987–88	9	2001–02	57
1988–89	13	2002–03	74
1989–90	6	2003–04	66
1990–91	3	2004–05	31
1991–92	8		

M.P.s' Suspension

Members acting in sustained defiance of the Chair or breaking the rules of the House can be named and suspended from the service of the House of Commons, with loss of pay – normally for five sitting days. The following list includes all that have occurred since 1979. Two of the suspensions – R. Brown in 1981 and T. Dalyell in 1988 – were extended because they were the second suspension for the same member within one session. The suspensions listed here should be distinguished from the occasions when members have withdrawn for the remainder of the day's sitting after showing disorderly conduct (it usually seems to be refusal to withdraw an unparliamentary remark).

Date	Member	Period	Reason
12 Feb 81	I. Paisley	5 days	Order in the House
8 Apr 81	R. Brown	5 days	Order in the House
15 Jul 81	R. Brown	20 days	Order in the House
16 Nov 81	J. McQuade, P. Robinson, I. Paisley	5 days	Order in the House
26 May 82	A. Faulds	5 days	Order in the House
2 May 84	T. Dalyell	5 days	Order in the House

17 Jul 84	D. Skinner	5 days	Order in the House
31 Jul 84	M. Flannery	5 days	Order in the House
11 Nov 85	B. Sedgemore	5 days	Order in the House
20 Jan 86	D. Wigley	5 days	Order in the House
12 Nov 87	T. Dalyell	5 days	Order in the House
24 Nov 87	D. Wigley	5 days	Order in the House
11 Jan 88	J. Hughes	5 days	Order in the House
25 Jan 88	K. Livingstone	5 days	Order in the House
18 Feb 88	H. Cohen	5 days	Order in the House
15 Mar 88	A. Salmond	5 days	Order in the House
13 Apr 88	D. Nellist	5 days	Order in the House
20 Apr 88	R. Brown	20 days	Damage to the mace and conduct towards the Chair
25 July 88	T. Dalyell	20 days	Order in the House
14 Mar 89	J. Sillars	5 days	Order in the House
24 Jul 89	T. Dalyell	5 days	Order in the House
7 Mar 90	J. Browne	20 days	Members' Interests Committee report (HC135–90)
23 Jul 90	D. Douglas	5 days	Order in the House
20 Apr 95	D. Tredinnick	20 days	Privileges Committee report (HC 351 1994–95)
20 Apr 95	G. Riddick	10 days	Privileges Committee report (HC 351 1994–95)
30 Oct 97	R. Wareing	1 week	Standards & Privileges Committee report (HC 182 1997–98)
12 Jul 99	E. Ross	10 days	Standards & Privileges Committee report (HC 607 1988–99)
21 Oct 99	D. Touhig	3 days	Standards & Privilages Committee report (HC 747 1998–99)
21 Oct 99	Kali Mountford	5 days	Standards & Privileges Committee report (HC 747 1998–99)
1 Mar 00	Teresa Gorman	1 month	Standards & Privileges Committee report (HC 260 1999–2000)
31 Oct 01	G. Robinson	3 weeks	Standards & Privileges Committee report (HC 297 2001–02)
13 Feb 02	K. Vaz	1 month	Standards & Privileges Committee report (HC 605 2001–02)
27 Feb 03	M. Trend	2 weeks	Standards & Privileges Committee report (HC 435 2002–03)
17 Jul 03	C. Betts	7 days	Standards & Privileges Committee report (HC 947 2002–03)
8 Feb 05	J. Sayeed	2 weeks	Standards & Privileges Committee report (HC 233 & 473 2004–05)

Select Committees

Select Committees have been appointed for many purposes and have a long history in both Houses. In the Commons Select Committees have been used in connection with public expenditure, parliamentary procedure, legislation, and for ad hoc inquiries, sometimes of a quasi-judicial character.

The Public Accounts Committee has existed continuously since 1862.

An Estimates Committee, later subsumed in the Expenditure Committee, was set up in one form or another in most sessions from 1912 to 1979.

In 1979 a new structure of Select Committees was established to cover the work of each major Government Department.

Chairmen's Liaison Committee

The Chairmen of Select Committees meet from time to time to discuss subjects of common interest such as the allocation of funds available for overseas visits. Since 2004 the Prime Minister has faced them regularly for questioning.

Committee of Selection, 1840–

Chairman (since 1979)

1976	F. Willey
1979	(Sir) P. Holland
1984	(Sir) M. Fox
1992	Sir F. Montgomery
1997	J. McWilliam

Committee of Public Accounts, 1862–

Chairman

1974	E. du Cann
1979	J. Barnett
1983	R. Sheldon
1997	D. Davis
2001	E. Leigh

The Committee is made up of no more than 15 members, including the Chairman, and meets on about 30 days each session. The Chairman is usually a member of the Opposition with Treasury experience.

Comptroller and Auditor-General

1976	Sir D. Henley
1981	(Sir) G. Downey
1989	(Sir) J. Bourn

Public Accounts Commission 1984–

The Public Accounts Commission was set up by National Audit Act 1983. It is composed of nine members of the House of Commons of whom two – the Chairman of the Public Accounts Committee and the Leader of the House – are ex-officio. The remaining seven, none of whom may be Ministers of the Crown, are appointed by the House. The Act gave the Commission three main functions: to appoint an accounting officer for the National Audit Office; to appoint an auditor for the National Audit Office; and to examine the National

Audit Office Estimates and lay them before the House, with such modifications as it thinks fit. In this last capacity, the Commission can examine all the expenses of the Office, including such things as accommodation, salaries of staff, superannuation provision.

Chairman

1984	(Sir) E. du Cann
1987	Sir P. Hordern
1996	Sir T. Higgins
1997	R. Sheldon
2001	E. Leigh

Committee on European Secondary Legislation, 1974–76; European Legislation etc., 1976–98; European Scrutiny Committee 1998–

Chairman

1979	J. Silverman
1983	N. Spearing
1992	J. Hood

The Committee's membership since 1974 has been 16. There are currently three sub-committees.

Procedure (Sessional) Committee, 1976–

Chairman

1979	T. Higgins
1983	Sir P. Emery
1997	Sir N. Winterton

The Committee has 15 members and a quorum of four.

House of Commons Services Committee, 1965–92

Chairman

1979	N. St John-Stevas
1981	F. Pym
1982	J. Biffen
1987	J. Wakeham
1989	Sir G. Howe
1990	J. MacGregor
1992	A. Newton

The Committee consisted of 19 members. The Leader of the House was always Chairman of the Committee. The Committee usually appointed four main Sub-Committees: the Accommodation and Administration Sub-Committee, the Catering Sub-Committee, the Library Sub-Committee and the Computer Sub-Committee. The Catering Sub-Committee replaced the 'Select Committee on Kitchen and Refreshment Rooms' appointed every session since the late nineteenth century.

House of Commons Commission 1978–

Under the House of Commons (Administration) Act of 1978, a House of Commons Commission was appointed to control the internal finances of the House. Independent of Government, it comprises the Speaker, the Leader of the House, one M.P. nominated by the Leader of the Opposition, and three other non-ministerial M.P.s (including one, in practice, nominated by the minority parties).

Domestic Committees

Accommodation Committee

Chairman

1992   R. Powell
1997   Sir S. Chapman
2001   D. Conway
2005   (*subsumed into Administration Committee*)

Administration Committee

Chairman

1992   J. Hood
1997   Dame M. Roe
2005   F. Doran

Broadcasting

Chairman

1983   (Sir) P. Goodhart
1992   A. Newton
2000   E. Clarke
2001   D. Lepper
2005   (*subsumed into Administration Committee*)

Catering

Chairman

1991   C. Shepherd
1997   D. Turner
2005   (*subsumed into Administration Committee*)

Other Committees
Finance and Services Committee

Chairman

1993   P. Channon
1997   L. Moonie
2000   (Sir) S. Bell

Information Committee

Chairman

199	G. Waller
1998	R. Allan
2001	M. Jack
2004	R Key
2005	(*subsumed into Administration Committee*)

Modernisation

Chairman

1997	Ann Taylor
1998	Margaret Beckett
2001	R. Cook
2003	J. Reid
2003	P. Hain
2005	G. Hoon

Regulatory Reform

Chairman

1997	R. Pike
2005	A. Miller

Environmental Audit

Chairman

1997	J. Horam
2003	P. Ainsworth

Committee on Members' Interests, 1975–95

This Committee was established to scrutinise a new Register of Members' outside interests.

In 1995 its functions were taken over by the Committee on Standards.

Chairman

1975	F. Willey
1983	(Sir) G. Johnson-Smith

Committee of Privileges, c.1630–1995

The Committee of Privileges only met when prima facie breaches of privileges were referred to it by the House. Unlike other committees it included senior members from both the Front Benches. It was ordered to be appointed by long-standing tradition on the first day of every session. The Chairman was usually the Leader of the House.

Chairman

1979	N. St John-Stevas	1989	Sir G. Howe
1981	F. Pym	1990	J. MacGregor
1982	J. Biffen	1992	A. Newton
1987	J. Wakeham		

The following include all Reports of the Select Committee of Privileges and a few from Ad Hoc Committees.

1980–81	D. Campbell-Savours: Conversation about British Steel policy towards Workington
1980–81	R. Parry: Important letter from solicitors to M.P.
1982–83	T. Davis: Behaviour of witnesses before Select Committee on Abortion (Amendment) Bill
1982–83	R. Brown: Comments by K. Livingstone and other GLC members
1982–83	Sir A. Kershaw: Leak of Foreign Affairs Committee report on Falklands
1983–84	T. Jessel: Threat by GLC Chairman to penalise constituencies of London members voting in a particular way
1984–85	Sir E. Gardner: Publication by the Times of Home Affairs Committee draft Report on police special powers
1985–86	Environment Committee: Leak of draft Report of Environment Committee on radio-active waste
1986–87	Mr. Speaker: Showing of Zircon film within the Palace of Westminster
1988–89	Clare Short: Alleged misconduct of a Parliamentary Agent
1989–90	Education Committee: Premature disclosure of proceedings of Education Committee
1989–90	Public Accounts Committee: Premature disclosure of proceedings of Public Accounts Committee
1990–91	K. Barron: Guidelines issued by Yorkshire N.U.M.
1994–95	T. Benn: Publication of Committee proceedings
1994–95	D. Tredinnick and G. Riddick: Payment for putting Questions

Committee on Standards and Privileges, 1995–

Following a Report from the Committee on Standards in Public Life under Ld Nolan, the House voted to replace the Committee on Privileges and the Select Committee on Members' Interests with a Committee on Standards and Privileges and appointed a Parliamentary Commissioner for Standards to report to it.

Chairman

1995	A. Newton
1998	R. Sheldon
2001	Sir G. Young

Parliamentary Commission for Standards

1994	Sir G. Downey
1999	Elizabeth Filkin
2002	Sir P. Mawer

The following matters have been reported on:

1995–96	The Code of Conduct and the Guide to the Rules relating to the Conduct of Members
1995–96	J. Aitken: Failure to register a directorship
1995–96	R. Thomason: Failure to declare an interest
1995–96	Mo Mowlam: Failure to register a payment
1995–96	W. Cash: Alleged breach of advocacy rules
1995–96	C. Goodson-Wickes: Failure to declare an interest

1995–96	P. Nicholls: Alleged breach of advocacy rules
1996–97	D. Atkinson: Failure to register an interest
1996–97	A. Mitchell: Alleged improper pressure on Select Committee members
1996–97	M. Howard: Alleged conflict of interest
1996–97	D. Willetts: Alleged improper pressure on Select Committee members
1999–00	B. George: Failure to account for expenses
1999–00	B. Wells: Failure to declare an interest
1999–00	W. Hague: Failure to record use of Ld Archer's gym
2002–03	G. Galloway: Alleged acceptance of payments from Iraqi government
2002–03	I. Duncan Smith: Employment of his wife on parliamentary expenses

Statutory Instruments 1947–
(since 1972 a Joint Committee of both Houses)
Chairman

1974	G. Page	1987	R. Cryer
1979	R. Cryer	1994	A. Bennett
1983	A. Bennett	1997	D. Tredinnick

The Committee has had between 7 and 11 members, meeting fortnightly on about 16 days each session. The Chairman has always been an opposition member.

Terms of Reference: The vast majority of Statutory Instruments are considered by a Joint Committee of Members of both Houses. However, the Statutory Instruments Committee still exists to consider instruments on which proceedings are subject to proceedings in the House of Commons only. The Joint Committee has power to consider every instrument which is laid before each House of Parliament and upon which proceedings may be or might have been taken in either House of Parliament in pursuance of an Act of Parliament. It also has power to draw the attention of the House of Commons to other Statutory Instruments on any of the following grounds:

(i) that they involve public money; (ii) that they are immune from challenge in the courts; (iii) that they have effect retrospectively; (iv) that there seems to have been an unjustifiable delay in publication of the SI or in laying it before Parliament; (v) that there seems to have been an unjustifiable delay in sending notification to the Speaker; (vi) that it appears to make unusual or unexpected use of the powers conferred by the Statute under which it is made; (vii) if elucidation is considered necessary; (viii) that the drafting appears to be defective.

Statutory Instruments	
1970	2,044
1980	2,051
1990	2,667
1991	2,953
1992	3,359
1993	3,276
1994	3,334

Statutory Instruments (cont.)		
1995	3,345	
1996	3,291	
1997	3,114	
1998	3,319	
1999[a]	3,488	(SP SIs 204)
2000	3,424	(SP SIs 454)
2001	4,147	(SP SIs 494)
2002	3,271	(SP SIs 575)
2003	3,354	(SP SIs 622)
2004	3,452	(SP SIs 565)

[a] Creation of Scottish Parliament.

Committee on Parliamentary Commission for Administration, 1967–97

Chairman

1974   (Sir) A. Buck
1992   J. Pawsey
1997   (*see* Select Committee on Public Administration below)

The Committee had 10 members and a quorum of 4.

Parliamentary Commissioner for Administration (Ombudsman)

The Parliamentary Commissioner for Administration is appointed by Letters Patent under the provisions of the Parliamentary Commissioner Act, 1967, which came into force on 7 April 1967. His or her function is to investigate complaints referred by Members of the House of Commons from members of the public who claim to have sustained injustice in consequence of maladministration in connection with actions taken by or on behalf of Government Departments.

Parliamentary Commissioner

3 Jan 79	(Sir) C. Clothier	1 Jan 97	(Sir) M. Buckley
1 Jan 85	(Sir) A. Barrowclough	1 Jan 02	Ann Abraham
1 Jan 90	(Sir) W. Reid		

Ombudsman Cases

Year	No. of cases disposed of during the year	Member informed case outside jurisdiction	Member informed case is discontinued	Investigation completed and result reported to Member
1979	801	541	22	238
1980	927	686	16	225
1981	929	694	7	228
1982	784	574	8	202

1983	809	605	6	198
1984	850	658	9	183
1985	788	606	5	177
1986	719	549	2	168
1987	656	509	2	145
1988	657	529	8	120
1989	639	502	11	126
1990	724	535	12	177
1991	769	580	6	183
1992	857	661	6	190
1993	926	715	3	208
1994	1,105	870	9	226
1995	1,474	1,226	3	245
1996	1,679	1,413	6	260
1997	1,679	1,303	4	376
1998	1,134	762	–	372

After 1998, data was collected and presented in a different way.

New cases received:

1998–99	2,002	2001–02	2,582
1999–2000	2,108	2002–03	2,567
2000–01	2,228	2003–04	2,319

SOURCE:- Annual Reports of the Parliamentary Commissioner for Administration.

Select Committees since 1979

Fourteen Select Committees were appointed in 1979 'to examine the expenditure, administration and policy of the principal government departments ... and associated public bodies'. In January 1980 a Liaison Select Committee, comprising the chairman of the Committees (and some additional members) was appointed. Their membership varied between 9 and 11 until 1983 when all Committees except Scottish Affairs (13) were allotted 11 members. Only the Foreign Affairs, Home Affairs, and Treasury Committees were empowered to appoint a sub-committee.

Agriculture 1979–2001 (9) (11)
(See Environment, Food, and Rural Affairs)

1979	Sir W. Elliott
1983	J. Spence
1986	Sir R. Body
1987	(Sir) J. Wiggin
1997	P. Luff
2000	D. Curry

Defence (10) (11)

1979	Sir J. Langford-Holt
1981	C. Onslow
1982	Sir T. Kitson

1983	Sir H. Atkins
1987	M. Mates
1992	Sir N. Bonsor
1996	M. Colvin
1997	B. George
2005	J. Arbuthnot

Education, Science and Arts (9) (11)
(Education, 1992–96) (Education and Employment 1996–) (Education and Skills 2001–)

1979	C. Price
1983	Sir W. Van Straubenzee

1987	T. Raison
1989	(Sir) M. Thornton
1997–98	Margaret Hodge (joint)
1997–2001	D. Foster (joint)
1998–99	M. Wicks (joint)
1999–01	B. Sheerman (joint)
2001	B. Sheerman

Education and Employment Sub-Committee 1996–97 (8)

1996	E. Ross

Education Sub-Committee 1997–2001 (8)

1997	Margaret Hodge
1998	M. Wicks
1999	B. Sheerman

Employment Sub-Committee 1997–2001 (8)

1997	E. Ross
1997	D. Foster

Employment 1979–94 (9) (11)

1979	J. Golding
1982	J. Craigen
1983	R. Leighton
1992	G. Janner

Energy 1981–92 (10) (11)

1979	(Sir) I. Lloyd
1989	M. Clark

Environment 1980–97 (10) (11)

1979	B. Douglas-Mann
1981	R. Freeson
1983	Sir H. Rossi
1992	R. Jones
1995	A. Bennett

Environment Transport and Regional Affairs 1997–2001 (17)

1997–2001	A. Bennett (joint)
1997–2001	Gwyneth Dunwoody (joint)

Environment Sub-Committee 1997–2001 (11)

1997	A. Bennett

Transport Sub-Committee 1997–2001

1997	Gwyneth Dunwoody

Environment, Food and Rural Affairs 2001–

2001	D. Curry
2003	M. Jack

Foreign Affairs (11)

1979	Sir A. Kershaw
1987	D. Howell
1997	D. Anderson
2005	M. Gapes

Foreign Affairs Overseas Development Sub-Committee (5)

1979	K. McNamara
1982	F. Hooley
1983	*(not reconstituted)*

Health

1991	N. Winterton
1992	Marion Roe
1997	D. Hinchcliffe
2005	K. Barron

Home Affairs (11)

1979	Sir G. Page
1981	Sir J. Eden
1983	Sir E. Gardner
1987	Sir J. Wheeler
1992	Sir I. Lawrence
1997	C. Mullin
1999	R. Corbett
2001	C. Mullin
2003	J. Denham

Home Affairs Sub-Committee on Race Relations and Immigration 1980–97 (5)

1979	J. Wheeler
1992	J. Greenway

International Development 1997– (11)

1997	B. Wells
2001	T. Baldry
2005	M. Bruce

National Heritage 1992–97 (Culture, Media and Sport 1997–) (11)

1992	G. Kaufman
2005	J. Whittingdale

Northern Ireland 1994– (13)

1994	Sir J. Kilfedder
1995	C. Soley
1997	P. Brooke
2001	M. Mates
2005	Sir P. Cormack

Office of the Deputy P.M.

2002	A. Bennett
2005	Phyllis Starkey

Public Service 1995–97 (11)

1995   G. Radice

Public Administration 1997– (11)

1997   R. Morgan

1999   T. Wright

Science and Technology 1992– (11)

1992   Sir G. Shaw

1997   M. Clark

2001   I. Gibson

Scottish Affairs (13)

1979   D. Dewar

1981   R. Hughes

1982   D. Lambie

(In abeyance 1987–92)

1992   W. McKelvey

1997   D. Marshall

2001   Irene Adams

Social Services (9) (11) (Social Security and Health 1988–91) Social Security 1991–2002

1979   Renee Short

1987   F. Field

1997   A. Kirkwood

(See Work and Pensions)

Trade and Industry (11) (Industry and Trade 1979–83)

1979   Sir D. Kaberry

1983   K. Warren

1992   R. Caborn

1997   M. O'Neill

2005   P. Luft

Transport 1979–97 (10) (11)

1979   T. Bradley

1983   H. Cowans

1985   G. Bagier

1987   D. Marshall

1992   R. Adley

1993   P. Channon

(see Environment 1997–2001)

Transport, Environment and the Regions 2001–

2001   Gwyneth Dunwoody

Urban Affairs Sub-Committee 2001

2001   A. Bennett

Treasury and Civil Service 1979–95 (11)

1979   E. du Cann

1983   T. Higgins

1992   J. Watts

1994   Sir T. Arnold

Treasury and Civil Service Sub-Committee 1979–95 (5)

1979   R. Sheldon

1981   J. Bray

1982   M. Meacher

1983   A. Mitchell

1987   G. Radice

Treasury 1996–

1996   M. Carrington

1997   G. Radice

2001   J. McFall

Treasury Sub-Committee 1998–

1998   Sir P. Lloyd

1998   Sir M. Spicer

2001   M. Fallon

Welsh Affairs (11)

1979   L. Abse

1981   D. Anderson

1983   G. Wardell

1997   M. Jones

2005   H. Francis

Work and Pensions 2002–

2002   (Sir) A. Kirkwood

2005   T. Rooney

Joint Committees (with Lords)

Intelligence and Security

1994   T. King

2001   Ann Taylor

2005   B. Ainsworth

Human Rights

2001   Jean Corston

2005   A. Dismore

Payment of M.P.s

1983: M.P.s' pay linked to Civil Service rates. Secretarial allowance raised to £12,000 and other allowances increased.

1992: Following a Top Salaries Review Board inquiry into office costs, the House voted for a substantial increase in the allowance for office, Research and

Secretarial Costs. M.P.s with constituencies in Inner London are entitled to a payment of £1,222 a year; M.P.s with constituencies outside London are entitled to claim up to £10,958 a year for staying overnight away from home.

	M.P.s' basic pay	Office costs[1]	Staffing costs (maximum)
1979	£9,450	£4,600	
1980	£11,750	£8,000	
1981	£13,950	£8,480	
1982	£14,510	£8,820	
1983	£15,308	£11,364	
1984	£16,106	£12,437	
1985	£16,904	£13,211	
1986	£17,702	£20,140	
1987	£18,500	£21,302	
1988	£22,548	£22,588	
1989	£24,107	£24,903	
1990	£26,701	£27,166	
1991	£28,970	£28,986	
1992	£30,854	£39,960	
1993	£30,854	£40,380	
1994	£31,687	£41,308	
1995	£33,189	£42,754	
1996	£43,000	£48,464	
1997	£43,860	£47,568	
1998	£45,086	£49,232	
1999	£47,008	£50,264	
2000	£48,371	£51,572	
2001	£51,822	£52,760	£70,000
2002	£55,118	£53,466	£72,310
2003	£56,358	–	£74,985
2004	£57,485	–	£77,534
2005	£59,095	–	£77,534

See p. 18 for Ministers' pay, and reduced parliamentary salaries payable to Ministers and other paid office-holders.

House of Lords

Lord Chairmen of Committees

(Deputy Speaker of the House of Lords. The Lord Chancellor (see p. 22) acts as Speaker.)

1976	Ld Aberdare	2000	Ld MacKay of Ardbrecknish
1992	Ld Ampthill	2001	Ld Tordoff
1994	Ld Boston of Faversham	2002	Ld Brabazon of Tara

[1] Office costs allowance renamed staffing costs allowance and reformed in 2001.

Principal Deputy Chairman of Committees

(Salaried Chairman of Select Committee on European Communities –
European Union Committee from 1999)

1977	Ld Greenwood of Rossendale	1992	Ld Boston of Faversham
1989	Lady White	1994	Ld Tordoff
1982	Lady Llewelyn-Davies of Hastoe	2001	Ld Brabazon of Tara
1986	Lady Serota	2002	Ld Grenfell

Officers of the House of Lords

Clerk of the Parliaments

1974	(Sir) P. Henderson (Lord	1991	(Sir) M. Wheeler-Booth
	Henderson of Brompton)	1997	(Sir) M. Davies
1983	(Sir) J. Sainty	2003	P. Hayter

Librarian

1977   R. Morgan
1991   D. Jones

Gentleman Usher of the Black Rod

1978	Sir D. House	1995	Sir E. Jones
1985	Sir J. Gingell	2001	Sir M. Willcocks
1992	Sir R. Thomas		

SOURCES:- *Dod's Parliamentary Companion*; *Whitaker's Almanack*; House of Lords Biographies; Hansard.

Composition of the House of Lords

To 1999 *(including minors)*

Year	Duke	Marq	Earl	Vt	Baron	Life Peer	Law Ld	Bishops	Total
1980	28	29	157	105	477	330	19	26	1,171
1990	27	27	156	102	471	358	19	26	1,186
1999	28	27	174	103	420	485	26	26	1,296

1999–

	Hereditary Statutory	Elected	Life Peer	Law Ld	Bishop	Total
2000	2	90	522	27	26	667
2005	2	89	561	28	26	706

By the *House of Lords Act 1999* hereditary peers ceased to be members of the House of Lords as of Right (except for the Earl Marshal and the Lord Great

Chamberlain). But the hereditary peers were allowed to elect 88 of their own number, proportionately by party, to sit in the Lords.

See p. 158 for not on the House of Lords Appointments Commission.

Creation of Peerages

		Law Lords	Hereditary	Life Peers	Life peerages for hereditaries[a]	Total
Thatcher	1979–90	11	4	201	–	216
Major	1990–97	11	–	160	–	171
Blair	1997–2005[b]	9	1	280	17	307

[a] When hereditary peers lost the automatic right to sit in the Lords in 1999, a number were given life peerages.
[b] Up to and including dissolution 2005 honours.

Party Strengths in the House of Lords

	Con	Lab	Lib Dem	Cross Bench	Other
1975	292	149	30	281	387
1985	376	122	76	245	360
1990	425	110	74	234	353
1995	472	114	55	280	279
1999	483	194	73	354	107
2000	232	197	63	164	39
2005	203	202	69	183	49

SOURCE:- *Dod's Parliamentary Companion.*

House of Lords Sittings and Business

See p. 101 for House of Lords Sittings and Business.

House of Lords Sittings and Business

| | Sessions and Settings | | Membership and Attendance | | | | Work of the House | | | | | |
Session[a]	Sittings	Average sitting	Total membership	Without writ of summons[c]	On leave of absence	Average attendance	Public bills first in Lords	Govt. bills first in Lords[b]	Divisions	Starred questions	Written questions	Unstarred (debatable) questions
1979–80	206	6hrs 9m.	1,171	85	172	290	50	11	303	765	1277	68
1980–81	143	6hrs 43m.	1,179	87	160	296	48	12	184	537	857	31
1981–82	147	6hrs 20m.	1,174	91	150	284	42	10	146	531	1098	50
S1982–83	94	6hrs 35m.	1,181	97	143	294	40	11	89	357	619	36
L1983–84	178	7hrs 13m.	1,183	99	153	321	48	14	237	691	1350	60
1984–85	151	6hrs 47m.	1,174	95	142	320	40	12	145	573	1142	45
1985–86	165	7hrs 21m.	1,171	89	135	317	34	16	250	631	1182	44
S1986–87	84	6hrs 38m.	1,185	89	133	325	26	14	80	317	622	24
L1987–88	192	7hrs 6m.	1,185	84	169	333	21	9	279	742	1405	51
1988–89	153	7hrs 2m.	1,183	93	149	316	24	11	12	572	1202	35
1989–90	147	7hrs 18m.	1,186	86	139	318	23	8	186	551	1204	31
1990–91	137	6hrs 28m.	1,196	78	136	324	26	10	104	531	1304	42
S1991–92	74	7hrs 1m.	1,196	80	133	337	28	5	83	276	664	22
L1992–93	194	6hrs 52m.	1,208	85	82	379	39	12	165	739	2567	90
1993–94	142	6hrs 51m.	1,204	84	77	378	24	6	136	540	1974	56
1994–95	142	6hrs 22m.	1,190	85	68	376	43	11	106	515	2172	42
1995–96	136	6hrs 53m.	1,207	80	66	372	38	13	110	498	2471	26
1996–97	79	6hrs 40m.	1,204	74	63	381	36	7	67	262	1349	27
1997–98	228	7hrs 2m.	1,297	68	63	417	44	18	179	832	5729	129
1998–99	154	7hrs 36m.	1,290	63	52	446	29	9	99	539	4322	83
1999–00	177	7hrs 29m.	693	n/a[c]	3	352	34	14	192	630	4511	
S2000–01	76	6hrs 41m.	679	n/a	4	347	18	9	40	270	1993	
L2001–02	200	6hrs 58m.	694	n/a	11	370	29	12	171	713	5798	
2002–03	174	7hrs 15m.	682	n/a	11	362	26	10	226	687	5084	
2003–04	157	6hrs 58m	707	n/a	14	368	24	12	176	634	4524	758
2004–05	63	7hrs 17m.	706	n/a	14	388	16	9	67	229	1877	406

[a] S beside the date of a session indicates a shortened session drawn to an early conclusion by a General Election. L shows a prolonged session usually following an election.

[b] Excludes Consolidation Bills, on average an extra seven per session.

[c] Since the departure of the hereditaries the number without writs is of little interest. It used to represent those who had succeeded to title but not sought to take up a seat in the House. Now it covers a tiny category: bishops who have yet to get round to getting a writ; bankrupts; and any new Earl Marshal or Lord Great Chamberlain in the period before receiving a writ.

SOURCE:- House of Lords Information Office.

Critical Votes in the House of Lords

The following represent outstanding occasions when the House of Lords has set itself against the House of Commons. In cases of repeated defiance on the same issue the final vote alone is normally recorded.

13 Mar 80	216-112	Clause of the Education (No. 2) Bill to give local authorities power to charge for home-to-school transport rejected.
9 Apr 84	235-153	Amendment to 2nd Reading of Rates Bill (stating that it would 'result in damaging constitutional changes in the relationship between central and local government', etc.) rejected.
11 Jun 84	238-217	Amendment to 2nd Reading of Local Government (Interim Provisions Bill) (stating that the Bill was a 'dangerous precedent', etc.) rejected.
28 Jun 84	191-143	Amendment carried to insert a clause postponing the coming into force of the Local Government (Interim Provisions) Bill until the passing of the main Act to abolish the GLC and Metropolitan County Councils.
7 May 85	152-135	Amendment to Local Government Bill preserving some environmental powers of GLC. This was the first of four amendments to the Bill carried against the Government.
23 May 88	317-184	Amendment on poll tax.
4 Jun 90	207-74	Amendment to War Crimes Bill (technically on a free vote)
18 Apr 91	177-79	Amendment to the Criminal Justice Bill on life sentence for murder.
20 Oct 92	125-100	Motion for enquiry into pit closures.
26 Jun 95	142-126	Amendment to give right of appeal against mandatory life sentence.
5 Feb 96	223-105	Motion to ensure the public broadcasting of 'listed' sporting events.
21 Jan 97	158-135	One of four government defeats on the Firearms Bill.
21 Jul 97	149-132	Amendment to limit revenue-raising powers of the Scottish Parliament.
27 Jan 98	207-97	Motion to revoke the ban on selling beef on the bone.
7 Jul 98	319-108	Amendment to curtail the charging of tuition fees in Scottish Universities.
20 Oct 98	165-140	First of six Government defeats on the European Communities Bill.
15 Dec 98	167-73	European Parliamentary Elections Bill rejected at Second Reading.
27 Jul 99	353-203	Motion to refer House of Lords Act to Committee of Privileges.
26 Oct 99	221-61	Passage of the House of Lords Act.
7 Feb 00	210-165	Amendment to retain 'Section 28' of 1988 Local Government Act.
9 Mar 00	144-82	Amendment to Local Government Bill not to compel councils to adopt a systems of mayors and cabinets.
14 Mar 00	166-161	Amendment to Learning and Skills Bill to block further grammar school ballots.
26 Oct 00	112-90	Amendment to Transport Bill to delay public–private partnership of air traffic control.

10 Dec 01	240-141	Rejection of a new offence of incitement to religious hatred.
2 Jun 03	109-105	Amendment to Sexual Offences Bill to give anonymity to rape defendants.
15 Jul 03	210-136	Amendment to Criminal Justice Bill to reject restrictions on trial by jury; subsequently rejected again five more times.
6 Nov 03	150-100	Rejection of Foundation hospitals.
30 Mar 04	136-130	Final insistence that three rather than four regions have all-postal voting in European elections; last of six government defeats on this issue.
10 Mar 05	200-129	Last of eighteen Government defeats in three days on the Prevention of Terrorism.

Landmarks in the Reform of the House of Lords since 1997

1999 (Jan)   Publication of the White Paper: *Modernising Parliament: Reforming the House of Lords* (Cmd.4183). Appointments Commission and Royal Commission established.

1999 (11 Nov)   House of Lords Act removes the right of all but 92 hereditary peers to sit in the House of Lords.

2000 (20 Jan)   Royal Commission on the Reform of the House of Lords (Wakeham Commission) publishes its report, *A House for the Future* (Cm 4534).

2000 (May)   Members of House of Lords Appointments Commission appointed.

2001 (Feb)   House of Lords established a Constitution Committee.

2001 (Apr)   House of Lords Appointments Commission nominates 15 non-party peers.

2001 (Nov)   Publication of the White Paper, *The House of Lords, Completing the Reform* (Cm 5291).

2002 (9–10 Jan) Debates in House of Commons and House of Lords on White Paper.

2002 (13 May)   Joint Committee on House of Lords Reform announced. (First Report published 11 Dec.)

2003 (4 Feb)   House of Commons and House of Lords debate proposals (was this when the House of Commons failed to choose any option?)

2003 (12 Jun)   Abolition of post of Lord Chancellor announced

2004 (8 Mar)   House of Lords votes to refer Constitutional Reform Bill [HL] to a Select Committee which reported inconclusively (24 Jun 04).

Peerages disclaimed:

Between 1963 and 1978 16 peerages were disclaimed. Since 1979 the only disclaimers have been 1995 E of Selkirk (since 1997 sits as Life Peer, Ld Selkirk of Douglas)

1995 Vt Camrose (M. Berry, who sat as a Life Peer, Ld Hartwell, since 1968) (d. 2001). His son resumed the title

2002 Ld Silkin (C. Silkin disclaimed the title he inherited from his uncle, A. Silkin, who had previously disclaimed, and died in Nov 2001)

After the House of Lords Act, 1999, hereditary peers were no longer barred from standing for election to the House of Commons, so the issue of disclaiming peerages largely disappeared.

In 1998, 10 living peers had disclaimed, but three of these sat in the House of Lords by virtue of other titles.

Royalty

Royalty and Politics

H.M. Queen Elizabeth II. Born 21 Apr 1926, married to Philip, D of Edinburgh on 20 Nov 1947, succeeded to the throne 6 Feb 1952, crowned at Westminster Abbey 2 Jun 1953. Children: (i) H.R.H. Prince Charles, Prince of Wales (26 Jun 1958), D of Cornwall, born 14 Nov 1948, married (1) Lady Diana Spencer 29 Jul 1981. Separated 9 Dec 1992. Divorced 15 Jul 1996. Children: Prince William, born 21 Jun 1982; Prince Henry (Harry), born 15 Sep 1984. Married (2) Mrs Camilla Parker-Bowles 9 Apr 2005. (ii) H.R.H. Princess Anne, the Princess Royal (13 Jun 1987), born 15 Aug 1950, married (1) Mark Phillips 14 Nov 1973. Divorced 23 Apr 1992. Children: Peter Phillips, born 15 Nov 1977; Zara Phillips, born 15 May 1981. Married (2) Timothy Lawrence 12 Dec 1992. (iii) H.R.H. Prince Andrew, Duke of York (23 Jul 1986), born 19 Feb 1960, married Sarah Ferguson 23 Jul 1986. Separated 19 Mar 1992. Divorced 1996. Children: Princess Beatrice of York, born 8 Aug 1988; Princess Eugenie of York, born 23 Mar 1990. (iv) H.R.H. Prince Edward, Earl of Wessex (19 June 1999) born 10 Mar 1964. Married Sophie Rhys-Jones 19 Jun 1999. Child: Princess Louise, born 8 Nov 2003.

Throughout Queen Elizabeth II's reign, great efforts have been made to avoid involving the Crown in politics. But there have been a few occasions when, unavoidably or deliberately, politics and the monarchy have come into contact. No list of such occasions can be very satisfactory. It may omit times when in private audience the Sovereign expressed strong views to the Prime Minister. It may include times when, despite all the formality of consultation, the Sovereign had no real opportunity of affecting the outcome.

Jul 1986	Elizabeth II's reference to her role as head of the Commonwealth, interpreted as a reproach to the Prime Minister Margaret Thatcher over the issue of sanctions on South Africa.
Dec 1992	Prime Minister J. Major announces to Parliament that the Prince and Princess of Wales are to separate.
Aug 1997	Prime Minister T. Blair comments on the death of the Princess of Wales: 'Truly she was the people's princess.'
Apr–Jun 2002	Newspaper allegations that Downing Street is seeking a greater role for the Prime Minister in the Queen Mother's funeral lead to a complaint to the Press Complaints Commission, later dropped.
Nov 2004	A memo from Prince Charles emerges in the course of an Employment Tribunal: 'What is wrong with everyone nowadays? Why do they all seem to think they are qualified to do things far beyond their actual capabilities?' In response Education Secretary C. Clarke accused Prince

Charles of being 'out of touch' in a broadcast interview: 'We can't all be born to be king, but we can aspire to do the best we possibly can.'

Private Secretaries to the Sovereign

1977–86	Sir P. Moore	1990–99	Sir R. Fellowes
1986–90	Sir W. Heseltine	1999–	Sir R. Janvrin

Lord Chamberlains

1971	Ld Maclean	1998	Ld Camoys
1984	E of Airlie	2000	Ld Luce

Civil List of the Crown

The annuities payable to the Sovereign and Members of the Royal Family are known as the Civil List which is granted by Parliament upon the recommendation of a Select Committee. Specific sums are allocated to named members of the Royal Family. In 1981 the Queen undertook to bear the cost of the Civil List vote to three of her cousins (the Duke of Kent, the Duke of Gloucester and Princess Alexandra), by refunding to the Exchequer an equivalent sum. On 11 February 1993 the Prime Minister announced that from 6 April 1993 the Queen would refund the Civil List payments to all other members of her family except the Queen Mother, the Duke of Edinburgh and herself. At the same time he announced that the Queen's personal income from investments and other sources would henceforth be taxed, along with such revenues from the Privy Purse and the Duchy of Cornwall as were to be used for personal purposes. The Prince of Wales receives no money from the state, and voluntarily pays tax on his income from the Duchy of Cornwall (£7,827,000 in 2002).

Year	Total voted	Total retained by Queen
1979	£2,609,200	
1980	£3,527,550	
1981	£4,249,200	£3,964,200
1982	£4,612,883	£4,308,183
1983	£4,833,900	£4,515,600
1984	£5,017,000	£4,686,000
1985	£5,180,000	£4,838,000
1986	£5,387,300	£5,031,700
1987	£5,661,200	£5,289,500
1988	£5,922,300	£5,535,700
1989	£6,195,300	£5,795,200
1990	£6,762,000	£6,327,000

In 1990 the total Civil List was set at £7.9 million for the next ten years. When the settlement was reviewed in 2000, it was decided to freeze it at that figure.

Total Head of State Expenditure

Head of State expenditure is the official expenditure relating to the Queen's duties as Head of State and Head of the Commonwealth. Head of State expenditure is met from public funds in exchange for the surrender by the Queen of the revenue from the Crown Estate. In the financial year to 31 March 2004 the revenue surplus from the Crown Estate paid to the Treasury amounted to £176.9 million.

Head of State expenditure for 2003–04 was £36.8 million. This was 1.7% higher than in the previous year (a decrease of 1% in real terms). The slight increase is mainly attributable to increased expenditure on State Visits, major overseas tours and ceremonial costs. This is offset by the exclusion of one-off Golden Jubilee expenditure in 2002–03. Head of State expenditure has reduced significantly over the past decade, from £87.3 million (expressed in current pounds) in 1991–92.

A summary of Head of State expenditure met from public funds in the year to 31 March 2004 reads as follows:

	2004 £m	2003 £m
The Queen's Civil List (figures are for calendar years 2003 and 2002)	9.9	9.8
Parliamentary Annuities	0.4	0.4
Grants-in-aid	21.6	21.4
Expenditure met directly by Government Departments and the Crown Estate	4.9	4.6
	36.8	36.2

SOURCES:- *Imperial Calendar; Whitaker's Almanack; Dictionary of National Biography; Who Was Who; Who's Who; Keesing's UK Record;* <www.royal.gov.uk/output/Page308.asp>.

IV
Elections

General Election Statistics

It is impossible to present election statistics in any finally authoritative way. Until 1998 British statutes made no acknowledgement of the existence of political parties, and in most general elections the precise allegiance of at least a few of the candidates has been in doubt. This, far more than arithmetic error, explains the minor discrepancies between the figures provided in various works of reference. Election figures suffer much more from being inherently confusing than from being inaccurately reported. The complications that arise from variations in the number of candidates put up by each party is the most serious hazards in psephological interpretation. However, since 1979 the three main parties have nominated almost full slates – except in Northern Ireland.

In the figures which follow an attempt is made to allow for these factors by a column which shows the average vote won by each opposed candidate. All Northern Ireland candidates are classed as 'Other', and the votes for the few Conservative candidates are left in that category.

General Election Results, 1979–2001

	Total votes	M.P.s elected	Candidates	% Share of total vote	Vote per opposed candidate
1974 Thurs. 10 Oct					
Conservative	10,464,817	277	623	35.8	36.7
Labour	11,457,079	319	623	39.2	40.2
Liberal	5,346,754	13	619	18.3	18.9
Communist	17,426	–	29	0.1	1.5
Plaid Cymru	166,321	3	36	0.6	10.8
Scot. Nat. P.	839,617	11	71	2.9	30.4
National Front	113,843	–	90	0.4	2.9

Others (G.B.)	81,227	–	118	0.3	1.5
Others (N.I.)	702,094	12	43	2.4	27.9
Elec. 40,072,971	29,189,178	635	2,252	100.0	–
Turnout 72.8%					

1979 Thurs. 3 May

Conservative	13,697,690	339	622	43.9	44.9
Labour	11,532,148	269	623	36.9	37.8
Liberal	4,313,811	11	577	13.8	14.9
Communist	15,938	–	38	0.1	0.9
Plaid Cymru	132,544	2	36	0.4	8.1
Scot. Nat. P.	504,259	2	71	1.6	17.3
National Front	190,747	–	303	0.6	1.6
Ecology	38,116	–	53	0.1	2.0
Workers Rev. P.	13,535	–	60	0.1	0.5
Others (G.B.)	85,338	–	129	0.3	1.3
Others (N.I.)[a]	695,889	12	64	2.2	18.8
Elec. 41,093,264	31,220,010	635	2,576	100.0	–
Turnout 76.0%					

1983 Thurs. 9 Jun

Conservative	13,012,315	397	633	42.4	43.5
Labour	8,456,934	209	633	27.6	28.3
Liberal	4,210,115	17	322	13.7	27.7
Social Democrat	3,570,834	6	311	11.6	24.3
(Alliance)	(7,780,949)	(23)	(633)	(25.4)	(26.0)
Communist	11,606	–	35	0.04	0.8
Plaid Cymru	125,309	2	36	0.4	7.8
Scot. Nat. P.	331,975	2	72	1.1	11.8
National Front	27,065	–	60	0.1	1.0
Others(G.B.)	193,383	–	282	0.6	1.4
Others (N.I.)[a]	764,925	17	95	3.1	17.9
Elec. 42,197,344	30,671,136	650	2,579	100.0	–
Turnout 72.7%					

1987 Thurs. 11 Jun

Conservative	13,763,066	376	633	42.3	43.4
Labour	10,029,778	229	633	30.8	31.2
Liberal	4,173,450	17	327	25.5	12.8
Social Democrat	3,168,183	5	306	9.7	20.6
(Alliance)	(7,341,633)	(22)	(633)	(22.5)	(23.2)
Plaid Cymru	123,599	3	38	0.3	7.3
Scot. Nat. P.	416,473	3	71	1.3	14.0
Others (G.B.)	151,519	–	241	0.5	1.2
Others (N.I.)[a]	730,152	17	77	2.2	22.1
Elec. 43,181,321	32,529,568	650	2,325	100.0	–
Turnout 75.3%					

1992 Thurs. 8 Apr

Conservative	14,482,283	336	634	41.9	42.3
Labour	11,559,735	271	634	34.4	35.2
Liberal Democrat	5,999,384	20	632	17.8	18.3
Plaid Cymru	154,439	4	38	0.5	8.8
Scot. Nat. P.	629,552	3	72	1.9	21.5
Others (G.B.)	436,207	–	838	1.0	1.3
Others (N.I.)[a]	740,485	17	100	2.2	17.2
Elec. 43,249,721	33,612,693	651	2325	100.0	–
Turnout 77.7%					

1997 Thurs. 1 May

Conservative	9,600,940	165	640	30.7	31.0
Labour	13,517,911	419	639	43.2	44.5
Liberal Democrat	5,243,440	46	639	16.8	17.3
Plaid Cymru	161,030	4	40	0.5	12.4
Scot. Nat. P.	622,260	6	72	2.0	22.1
Referendum	811,827	–	547	2.6	3.1
Others (G.B.)	549,874	1	1139	1.7	1.0
Others (N.I.)[a]	790,778	18	117	2.5	15.3
Elec. 43,784,559	31,287,702	659	3724	100.0	–
Turnout 71.5%					

2001 Thurs. 7 June

Conservative	8,357,615	166	640	31.7	32.7
Labour	10,724,953	413	640	40.7	41.9
Liberal Democrat	4,814,321	52	639	18.3	18.9
Plaid Cymru	195,583	4	40	0.7	14.3
Scot. Nat. P.	464,314	5	72	1.8	20.1
UKIP	390,159	–	428	1.5	2.3
Others (G.B.)	610,064	1	660	2.3	1.4
Others (N.I.)[a]	810,374	18	100	3.1	18.0
Elec. 43,212,229	25,557,009	659	3219	100.0	–
Turnout 59.1%					

2005 Thurs. 5 May

Conservative	8,772,473	198	627	32.4	33.3
Labour	9,547,944	356	628	35.2	36.2
Liberal Democrat	5,981,874	62	627	22.0	26.6
Plaid Cymru	174,838	3	40	0.6	12.6
Scot. Nat. P.	412,267	6	59	1.5	17.7
UKIP	612,707	497	2.2	2.8	3.6
Others (G.B.)	906,665	3	977	3.3	5.2
Others (N.I.)*	714,884	18	100	2.6	17.9
Elec. 44,261,545	27,123,652	646	3560	100.0	
Turnout 61.3%					

[a] No candidates in Northern Ireland are included in the major party totals.

General Election Results by Regions

	Feb 1974	Oct 1974	1979	1983	1987	1992	1997	2001	2005
London									
(GLC'66)									
Con.	42	41	50	56	58	48	11	13	21
Lab.	50	51	42	26	23	35	57	55	44
Lib.	–	–	–	2	3	1	6	6	8
Other	–	–	–	–	–	–	–	–	1
Rest of S.									
England									
Con.	136	128	146	168	170	161	109	107	120
Lab.	21	29	13	3	3	10	59	58	45
Lib.	5	5	3	5	3	6	22	25	25
Other	–	–	–	–	–	[	–	–	–
Midlands									
Con.	43	40	57	70	67	57	28	28	34
Lab.	54	58	41	30	33	43	74	71	64
Lib.	–	–	–	–	–	–	1	3	4
Other	1	–	–	–	–	–	–	1	1
North of									
England									
Con.	47	44	53	68	63	53	13	15	19
Lab.	112	117	107	89	96	107	139	137	133
Lib.	4	3	4	6	4	3	5	6	10
Other	1	–	–	–	–	–	1	–	–
Wales									
Con.	8	8	11	14	8	6	–	–	3
Lab.	24	23	22	20	24	27	34	34	29
Lib.	2	2	1	2	3	1	2	2	4
Other	3	2	22	2	3	4	4	4	4
Scotland									
Con.	21	16	22	21	10	11	–	1	1
Lab.	40	41	44	41	50	49	56	56	41
Lib.	3	3	3	8	9	9	10	10	11
Other	7	11	2	2	3	3	6	5	6
Northern									
Ireland									
Con.	–		–	–	–	–	–	–	–
Lab.	–	–	–	–	–	–	–	–	–
Lib.	–	–	–	–	–	–	–	–	–
Other	12	12	12	17	17	17	18	18	18

	Feb 1974	*Oct 1974*	*1979*	*1983*	*1987*	*1992*	*1997*	*2001*	*2005*
Total									
Con.	297	277	339	397	376	336	165	166	198
Lab.	301	319	269	209	229	271	419	413	356
Lib.	14	13	11	23	22	18	46	52	62
Other	23	26	16	21	23	26	29	28	30
Total	635	635	635	650	650	651	659	659	646

The vertical lines indicate redistributions of seats.

Northern England includes Cheshire, Lancashire Yorkshire, and all counties to their north.

Midlands includes Hereford, Worcs., Warwickshire, Northants., Lincs., Notts., Leics., Staffs., Salop, Derbyshire.

Southern England includes the rest of England, except for the Greater London Council area.

In 1992 there was an extra English Seat added (in Milton Keynes) without any general redistribution. In 2005, 13 seats were taken from Scotland in a purely Scottish redistribution.

Referendum on E.E.C. Membership
(Thursday 5 June 1975)
'Do you think that the United Kingdom should stay in the European Community (the Common Market)?'

	Total electorate[a]	*Total votes*[b]	*% turnout*[a]	*%*[b] *'yes'*	*Highest 'yes'*	*Lowest 'yes'*
England	33,339,959	21,722,222	64.6	68.7	76.3	62.9
Wales	2,015,766	1,345,545	66.7	64.8	74.3	56.9
Scotland	3,698,462	2,286,676	61.7	58.4	72.3	29.5
N. Ireland[b]	1,032,490	498,751	47.4	52.1	52.1	–
U.K.[a]	40,086,677	29,453,194	64.5	64.5	76.3	29.5

[a] The electorate figures are for the civilian electorate only. The 370,000 service votes are included only in the total votes and the 'Yes' percentages.

[b] The votes were counted on a county basis except in Northern Ireland which was treated as a single unit. In 66 of the 68 counties there was a 'Yes' majority (Shetland voted 56.3% 'No' and Western Isles 70.5% 'No').

(For the 1979 and 1997 referendums in Scotland and Wales see pp.223–7).

See also the Devolution chapter for details of Scottish, Welsh and Northern Ireland Referendums.

Party Changes between Elections

The party composition of the House of Commons changes continuously partly owing to Members changing their allegiance and partly owing to by-election results. The following table shows the net change due to both causes during the life of each Parliament. (Seats vacant at dissolution are included under the last incumbent's party.)

		Con.	Lib.	Lab.	Others
1974–79	Election	277	13	319	26
	Dissolution	284	14	309	28
1979–83	Election	339	11	269	16
	Dissolution	336	(42)[a]	240	17
1983–87	Election	397	(23)[a]	209	21
	Dissolution	393	(27)[a]	208	22
1987–92	Election	376	23	229	23
	Dissolution	369	23	231	28
1992–97	Election	336	20	271	24
	Dissolution	324	26	275	26
1997–01	Election	165	46	419	29
	Dissolution	162	47	418	32
2001–05	Election	166	52	413	28
	Dissolution	163	54	412	30
2005–	Election	198	62	356	30

[a] SDP/Liberal Alliance.

M.P.s' Changes of Allegiance

The difficulties in compiling an exact and comprehensive list of all floor-crossings, Whip withdrawals, Whip resignations, and Whip restorations are enormous. The list which follows is probably fairly complete as far as floor-crossings go, but it certainly omits a number of Members who relinquished the Whip for a time. It also omits cases of M.P.s who stood without official party support in their constituencies but who remained in good standing with the Whips. Throughout this list the test, in so far as it can be applied, is whether the M.P. was officially in receipt of the weekly documentary Whip.

Parliament of 1979–83

Nov 79	G. Fitt	Belfast W.	SDLP	Ind. Soc.
Feb 81	T. Ellis	Wrexham	Lab.	SDP
Feb 81	R. Crawshaw	Liv. Toxteth	Lab.	SDP
Mar 81	T. Bradley	Leicester E.	Lab.	SDP
Mar 81	J. Cartwright[1]	Woolwich E.	Lab.	SDP
Mar 81	J. Horam	Gateshead W.	Lab.	SDP
Mar 81	R. Maclennan[1]	Caithness & Sutherland	Lab.	SDP
Mar 81	J. Roper	Farnworth	Lab.	SDP
Mar 81	D. Owen[1]	Devonport	Lab.	SDP
Mar 81	W. Rodgers	Stockton	Lab.	SDP
Mar 81	N. Sandelson	Hayes & H.	Lab.	SDP

Mar 81	M. Thomas	Newcastle E.	Lab.	SDP	
Mar 81	I. Wrigglesworth[1]	Thornaby	Lab.	SDP	
Mar 81	E. Lyons	Bradford W.	Lab.	SDP	
Mar 81	C. B-Fowler	Norfolk N.W.	Con.	SDP	
Jul 81	J. Wellbeloved	Erith & C.	Lab.	SDP	
Sep 81	M. O'Halloran	Islington N.	Lab.	SDP	Became I. Lab. Mar 83
Oct 81	D. Mabon	Greenock	Lab.	SDP	
Oct 81	R. Mitchell	Soton, Itchen	Lab.	SDP	
Oct 81	D. Ginsburg	Dewsbury	Lab.	SDP	
Oct 81	J. Dunn	Liv. Kirkdale	Lab.	SDP	
Oct 81	T. McNally	Stockport S	Lab.	SDP	
Oct 81	E. Ogden	Liv. W. Derby	Lab.	SDP	
Nov 81	J. Grant	Islington C.	Lab.	SDP	
Nov 81	G. Cunningham	Islington S.	Lab.	I. Lab	Became SDP Jun 82
Dec 81	R. Brown	Hackney S.	Lab.	SDP	
Dec 81	J. Thomas	Abertillery	Lab.	SDP	
Dec 81	E. Hudson-Davies	Caerphilly	Lab.	SDP	
Dec 81	B. Douglas-Mann	Mitcham	Lab.	Ind. SDP	Lost by elec. Jun 82
Jan 82	B. Magee	Leyton	Lab.	Ind. Lab	Became SDP Mar 82
Aug 82	R. Mellish	Bermondsey	Lab.	Ind. Lab	Resigned seat Jan 83

Parliament of 1983–87
[None]

Parliament of 1987–92

Mar 88	R. Maclennan	Caithness & S	SDP	(Lib)Dem	
Mar 88	C. Kennedy	Ross, Crom. & S	SDP	(Lib)Dem	
May 88	R. Brown	Leith	Lab.	–	Whip withdrawn for 3 months
Mar 90	R. Douglas	Dunf'line W.	Lab.	I. Lab.	Joined SNP Oct 90
Dec 91	D. Nellist	Cov'try S.E	Lab.	–	Expelled from Party
Dec 91	T. Fields	Broad Green	Lab.	–	Expelled from Party
Mar 92	J. Browne	Winchester	Con.	–	Whip withdrawn

Parliament of 1992–97

Jul 93	R. Allason	Torbay	Con.	–	Whip withdrawn; restored Jul 94
Nov 94	Teresa Gorman	Billericay	Con.	–	
Nov 94	N. Budgen	Wolv'ton SW	Con.	–	
Nov 94	M. Cartiss	Gt. Yarmouth	Con.	–	Whip withdrawn;
Nov 94	C. Gill	Ludlow	Con.	–	restored Apr 95
Nov 94	R. Shepherd	Aldridge-B.	Con.	–	
Nov 94	A. Marlow	North'ton N.	Con.	–	
Nov 94	J. Wilkinson	Ruislip-Nd	Con.	–	
Nov 94	Sir R. Body	Holland-w-B.	Con.	–	Resigned whip; whip restored Apr 96
Oct 95	A. Howarth[2]	Stratford/Avon	Con.	Lab.	
Dec 95	Emma Nicholson	Devon W. & T.	Con.	Lib. D.	
Feb 96	P. Thurnham	Bolton N.E.	Con.	Ind.	Joined Lib.D. Oct 96
Nov 96	Sir J. Gorst	Hendon N.	Con.	–	Said 'Free from Whip'
Mar 97	Sir G. Gardiner	Reigate	Con.	Ref.	

Parliament of 1997–2001

Nov 97	P. Temple-Morris	Leominster	Con.	Ind.	Took Lab. Whip Jun 98
Jun 97	R. Wareing	Liv. W. Derby	Lab.	–	Suspended till Nov 97
Jun 97	M. Sarwar	Glasgow, Govan	Lab.	–	Whip withdrawn; restored Mar 99
Apr 97	D. Canavan	Falkirk W.	Lab.	–	Whip withdrawn
Aug 98	T. Graham	Renfrewshire W.	Lab.	–	Whip withdrawn
Dec 99	S. Woodward[2]	Witney	Con.	Lab.	
Apr 00	K. Livingstone	Brent E.	Lab.	–	Expelled from party

Parliament of 2001–05

Dec 01	P. Marsden	Shrewsbury	Lab.	Lib. D	Rejoined Lab Apr 05
Mar 04	G. Galloway[2]	Glasgow, Kelvin	Lab.	Ind.	Founded RESPECT
Jan 04	J. Donaldson[1]	Antrim S.	UUP	DUP	
Dec 04	A. Hunter	Basingstoke	Con.	DUP	
Feb 05	R. Jackson	Wantage	Con.	Lab.	
Mar 05	J. Sayeed	Mid-Beds	Con.	–	Whip withdrawn
Mar 05	H. Flight	Arundel & S. D.	Con.	–	Whip withdrawn

[1] Elected for the same seat at the next general Election.
[2] Elected for a different seat at the next General Election.
[3] Defeated for a different seat at the next general election.

M.P.s Elected under New Label

In addition to the floor crossings recorded above there are the following instances of ex-M.P.s, after an interval out of Parliament, returning to the House under a designation basically different from the ones under which they had previously sat.

J. Horam	Lab.70–81,	SDP 81–83	Con. 92–
R. Jenkins	Lab. 48–77	SDP 82–87	
E. Powell	Con. 50–74	U.U. 74–87	
J. Sillars	Lab. 70–76	Sc. Lab. 76–79	S.N.P 88–92
Shirley Williams	Lab. 64–79	SDP 81–83	

M.P.s Denied Party Renomination

When a sitting M.P. does not stand again, it is often unclear whether the retirement is entirely voluntary. Irreparable conflicts with the local party may lie behind formal statements about reasons of health or age or business. At least in the following cases, there is little doubt that the local party failed to renominate a sitting and willing M.P. who was still in receipt of the party whip at Westminster. It is plain that in the overwhelming majority of cases the disagreement could be ascribed to personal rather than ideological considerations. In several of the 1983 and 1997 cases, the M.P.s were seeking renomination in a substantially redrawn constituency, often against another sitting M.P.

Conservative

1979	B. Drayson (Skipton)
1979	R. Cooke (Bristol W.)
1983	T. Benyon (Wantage)
1983	M. Brotherton (Louth)
1983	J. Bruce-Gardyne (Knutsford)
1983	R. Mawby (Totnes)
1983	G. Morgan (Clwyd N.W.)
1983	W. Rees-Davies (Thanet North)
1983	K. Stainton (Sudbury)
1987	C. Murphy (Welwyn & Hatfield)
1992	Sir A. Meyer (Clwyd N.W.)
1992	J. Browne (Winchester)[1]
1997	H. Booth (Finchley)
1997	W. Churchill (Davyhulme)
1997	Dame J. Fookes (Plymouth, Drake)
1997	M. Stephen (Shoreham)
1997	Sir C. Townsend (Bexleyheath)
1997	Sir J. Wheeler (Westminster N.)
1997	D. Ashby (Leics. N.W.)
1997	Sir N. Scott (Kensington & C.)
1997	Sir G. Gardiner[1] (Reigate)
2001	C. Wardle (Bexhill)
2005	N. Hawkins (Surrey Heath)
2005	J. Sayeed (Mid-Beds)
2005	H. Flight (Arundel & South Downs)

Labour

1979	Sir A. Irvine (Liverpool, Edge Hill)[2]
1983	F. Tomney (Hammersmith N.)
1983	J. Barnett (Heywood & Royton)
1983	S. Cohen (Leeds S.E.)
1983	S. C. Davies (Hackney C.)
1983	M. English (Nottingham W.)
1983	B. Ford (Bradford N.)[1]
1983	R. Fletcher (Ilkeston)
1983	F. Hooley (Sheffield, Heeley)
1983	A. Lewis (Newham N.W.)
1983	Helen McElhone (Glasgow, Queens Park)
1983	A. McMahon (Glasgow, Govan)
1983	C. Morris (Manchester, Openshaw)
1983	F. Mulley (Sheffield, Park)
1983	E. Ogden (Liverpool, W. Derby)
1983	R. Race (Tottenham)
1983	J. Sever (Birmingham, Ladywood)
1983	A. Stallard (St Pancras N.)
1983	J. Tilley (Lambeth & Vauxhall)
1987	R. Freeson (Brent E.)
1987	M. Maguire (Makerfield)
1987	N. Atkinson (Tottenham)
1987	M. Cocks (Bristol S.)
1987	A. Woodall (Hemsworth)
1987	E. Roberts (Hackney N.)
1987	J. Forrester (Stoke N.)
1992	D. Nellist (Coventry S.E.)[1]
1992	R. Brown (Edinburgh, Leith)[1]
1992	T. Fields (Liverpool, Broad Green)[1]
1992	J. Hughes (Coventry N.E.)[1]
1992	S. Bidwell (Southall)
1997	R. Hughes (Aberdeen C.)
1997	M. Madden (Bradford W.)
1997	B. Davies (Oldham C. & Royton)
1997	Muriel Gordon (Bow & Poplar)
1997	N. Spearing (Newham S.)
1997	M. Watson (Glasgow, C.)
1997	J. Dunnachie (Glasgow, Pollok)
1997	D. Young (Bolton S.E.)
2005	Jane Griffiths (Reading E.)

[1] Stood as an Independent and lost.
[2] Died before the next election.

By-elections

	Total By-el.	Changes	Con. +	Con. −	Lib. +	Lib. −	Lab. +	Lab. −	Oth. +	Oth. −	No. per year	% with change
1974–79	30	7	6	–	1	–	–	7	–	–	6	23
1979–83	20	7	1	4	4	–	1	1	1	2	5	35
1983–87	31[a]	6	–	4	4	–	1	1	1	1	8	19[a]
1987–92	23	8	–	7	3	–	4	1	1	–	4	35
1992–97	17	8	–	8	4	–	3	–	1	–	3	47
1997–01	17	2	–	1	1	–	1	–	–	1	4	12
2001–05	6	2	–	–	2	–	–	2	–	–	1	33

[a] 15 of the 31 by-elections were in N. Ireland. In mainland G.B. there were 16 by-elections – an annual incidence of 4 with a turnover rate of 31%.

Seats Changing Hands at By-elections

Date	Constituency	Gen. el.	By-el.
General Election 10 Oct 74			
26 Jun 75	Woolwich W.	Lab.	Con.
4 Nov 76	[a]Walsall N.	Lab.	Con.
14 Nov 76	[a]Workington	Lab.	Con.
31 Mar 77	[a]Birmingham Stechford	Lab.	Con.
28 Apr 77	[a]Ashfield	Lab.	Con.
2 Mar 78	Ilford N.	Lab.	Con.
29 Mar 79	Liverpool, Edge Hill	Lab.	Lib.
General Election 3 May 79			
9 Apr 81	Fermanagh & S. Tyrone	Ind.	Anti-H Block
22 Oct 81	[a]Croydon N.W.	Con.	Lib.
26 Nov 81	[a]Crosby	Con.	SDP
25 Mar 82	Glasgow, Hillhead	Con.	SDP
3 Jun 82	Mitcham & Morden (see p. 118)	Lab.	Con.
8 Oct 82	[a]Birmingham Northfield	Con.	Lab.
24 Feb 83	Bermondsey	Lab.	Lib.
General Election 9 June 83			
14 Jun 84	[a]Portsm'th S.	Con.	SDP
4 Jul 85	Brecon & Radnor	Con.	Lib.
26 Jan 86	Newry & Armagh	U.U.	SDLP
4 Apr 86	[a]Fulham	Con.	Lab.

Date	Constituency	Gen. el.	By-el.
8 May 86	ᵃRyedale	Con.	Lib.
26 Feb 87	Greenwich	Lab.	SDP
General Election 11 Jun 87			
10 Nov 88	ᵃGlasgow, Govan	Lab.	SNP
4 Apr 89	ᵃVale of Glamorgan	Con.	Lab.
22 Mar 90	ᵃMid Staffs	Con.	Lab.
16 Mar 91	ᵃMonmouth	Con.	Lab.
8 Oct 90	ᵃEastbourne	Con.	Lib. D.
7 Mar 91	ᵃRibble V.	Con.	Lib. D.
7 Nov 91	ᵃLangbaurgh	Con.	Lab.
7 Nov 91	ᵃKincardine & Deeside	Con.	Lib. D.
General Election 9 Apr 92			
6 May 93	Newbury	Con.	Lib. D.
29 Jul 93	ᵃChristchurch	Con.	Lib. D.
9 Jun 94	Eastleigh	Con.	Lib. D.
15 Dec 94	Dudley W.	Con.	Lab.
25 May 95	Perth	Con.	SNP
15 Jun 95	N. Down	UPUP	UKU
27 Jul 95	Littleborough & Saddleworth	Con.	Lib. D.
11 Apr 96	Staffs S.E.	Con.	Lab.
28 Feb 97	Wirral S.	Con.	Lab.
General Election 1 May 1997			
4 May 00	Romsey	Con.	Lib. D.
21 Sep 00	ᵃS. Antrim	UU	DUP
23 Nov 00	W. Bromwich W.	Spkr	Lab.
General Election 7 June 2001			
18 Sep 03	Brent E.	Lab	Lib. D.
15 Jul 04	Leicester S.	Lab	Lib. D.
General election 5 May 2005			

ᵃ Seat regained at subsequent General Election.

Notable Retentions of Seats in By-elections

In addition, there have over the years been a number of by-elections where the seat did not change hands, but which were seen as having great significance at the time. These are outstanding examples:

28 Apr 77	Grimsby	Lab held seat unexpectedly when it was losing safer seats elsewhere.
16 Jul 82	Warrington	Lab held seat despite enormous swing to newly founded SDP (R. Jenkins).

| 8 Mar 83 | Darlington | Lab held seat in three-cornered race when defeat could have ended M. Foot's leadership. |

M.P.s Resigning to Fight By-elections

The following M.P.s on changing their party, or for other reasons, voluntarily resigned their seats to test public opinion in a by-election:

Date of by-election	M.P.	Constituency	Former label	New label	Whether successful
3 Jun 82	B. Douglas-Mann	Mitcham	Lab. Ind.	SDP	No
23 Jan 86	15 M.P.s	N. Ireland	Un.	Un.	14 Yes

Electoral Administration

The one major examination of the electoral system was the 1997–98 Commission on Alternative Voting Systems under Lord Jenkins (Cm. 4090/98).

Many aspects of the election process have come under scrutiny from the Electoral Commission since its inception (under the Chairmanship of S. Younger) in February 2001 and its numerous reports are available on the web <www.electoralcommission.org.uk>.

Parliamentary Franchise

Year	Population over 18	Registered electorate	Percentage of population[a]
1979	41,352,000	41,572,705	100.8
1980	41,634,900	41,840,527	100.8
1981	41,885,600	42,122,009	100.9
1982	42,089,500	42,462,316	101.1
1983	42,382,200	42,703,516	101.0
1984	42,709,100	42,983,727	100.8
1985	43,023,900	43,130,535	100.5
1986	43,282,500	43,392,617	100.5
1987	43,528,600	43,666,375	100.4
1988	43,721,200	43,705,071	99.9
1989	43,962,000	43,613,960	99.3
1990	44,154,000	43,663,423	98.8
1991	44,319,000	43,556,783	98.4
1992	44,413,900	43,724,886	98.4
1993	44,491,000	43,718,537	98.3
1994	44,554,600	43,786,734	98.4
1995	44,624,900	43,896,208	98.4
1996	44,694,700	43,984,745	98.6
1997	44,820,300	44,203,604	98.7
1998	45,002,700	44,296,793	98.5

Year	Population over 18	Registered electorate	Percentage of population[a]
1999	45,227,100	44,388,885	98.2
2000	45,479,700	44,423,440	97.8
2001[b]	45,757,000	44,545,654 (Feb)	97.5
		44,695,764 (Dec)	
2002	46,011,400	44,363,353	96.7
2003	46,300,300	44,136,652	95.5
2004	46,600,000	44,162,080	95.0

[a] The UK resident population over 18 includes many people not eligible to vote in UK parliamentary elections – principally those who are not citizens of the UK or the Irish Republic. British citizens living abroad have the right to vote in parliamentary elections, and people with two addresses can register in both places.
[b] In 2001 the reference date for electoral statistics was changed from 1 February to 1 December. Both figures are included here.

Redistribution

The House of Commons elected in 1974 had 635 constituencies. In 1977 the Boundary Commissioners began work on a fresh general revision of boundaries and in February 1978 a Speaker's Conference recommended that the representation of Northern Ireland should be increased from 12 to 17 seats. An Act authorising the Boundary Commissioners to proceed on this basis was passed in March 1979. In 1983 the general revision resulted in a House of Commons of 650. The laws on Redistribution were consolidated in the *Parliamentary Constituencies Act, 1986.* In 1992 the number of seats rose to 651 because of an extra seat created to cope with the over-large constituencies around Milton Keynes. In 1991 the Boundary Commissions initiated a further redrawing of boundaries to be completed in 1995; but in 1992 the *Redistribution Act 1992* required them to report by the end of 1994; it also reduced the maximum interval between reviews from 15 to 12 years. The redistribution of seats, completed in 1996, increased the size of the House to 659. A new Redistribution begun in 2000 was due for completion in 2006 but an interim redistribution in Scotland reduced the House from 659 to 646 in 2005 according to the Provisions of the *Scotland Act 1999.*

Election Expenses

Candidates' Election Expenses

Year	Total Expenditure	Candidates	Average per Candidate	Con.	Lab.	Lib. D.
Oct 74	2,168,514	2,252	963	1,275	1,163	725
1979	3,557,441	2,576	1,381	2,190	1,897	1,023
1983	6,145,264	2,579	2,383	3,320	2,927	2,520
1987	8,305,721	2,325	3,572	4,400	3,900	3,400
1992	10,443,407	2,948	3,542	5,840	5,090	3,169

Year	Total Expenditure	Candidates	Average per Candidate	Con	Lab.	Lib. D.
1997	12,929,207	3,724	3,471	6,211	6,011	3,144
2001	11,885,794	3,319	3,581	6,484	5,860	3,029

These figures are based on the official returns from the candidates. What constitutes an election expense is a matter of judgment, particularly since there have been no petitions to test the law on expenses since 1929.

Central Party Expenses

Party headquarters have provided separate estimates of the amount spent centrally in general elections. (See also pp. 52 and 62.) The first official statements of central campaign expenditure was provided by the Electoral Commission in 2001.

Con.	£12,751,813
Lab.	£10,945,119
Lib. D.	£1,361,377
UKIP	£743,903
SNP	£226,203
PC	£71,949

The whole question of party and election finance came under review by the Neill Committee on Standards in Public Life which reported in October 1998 (Cd.4057/1998). Responsibilitry for monitoring party income and expenditure was given to the Electoral Commission in 2001.

Lost Deposits

The *Representation of the People Act*, 1918, provided that any parliamentary candidate would have to deposit, on nomination, £150 in cash with the Returning Officer. This money would be forfeit to the state unless the candidate received one-eighth of the valid votes cast. In 1985 the deposit was raised from £150 to £500 but the condition of forfeiture was lowered from one-eighth to one-twentieth (5%).

	Con.	Lab.	Lib. (Dem.)	Other	Total	% of all cands
1979	3	22	303	673	1,001	38.1
1983	5	10	119	605	739	28.7
1987	–	–	10	307	308	12.4
1992	3[a]	–	1	888	903	30.6
1997	7[a]	1	11	1,576	1,393	42.8
2001	3[a]	–	10	1,164	1,177	35.5
2005	2[a]	–	1	1,539	1,542	43.3

[a] All in N. Ireland.

Women Candidates and MPs 1974–2005

	Con.		Lab.		Lib.+		Other		Total	
	Cands	MPs	Cands	MPs	Cands	MPs	Cands	MPs	Cands	MPs
Oct 74	30	7	50	18	49	–	32	2	161	27
1979	31	8	52	11	51	–	76	–	210	19
1983	40	13	78	10	115	–	87	–	280	23
1987	46	17	92	21	106	2	85	1	329	41
1992	59	20	138	37	144	2	227	1	568	60
1997	66	13	156	102	139	2	311	2	672	120
2001	92	14	149	95	139	5	256	4	636	118
2005	123	17	166	98	145	10	128	3	562	128

Election Petitions and Challenges

In 1992 Sinn Fein unsuccessfully petitioned against the result in West Belfast.

In 1997 the Conservative in Winchester (G. Malone) who had lost by two votes petitioned against the result. A by-election was agreed before the petition was fully heard. M. Oaten's Lib. Dem. majority of two was turned into 21,556.

In 1998 M. Sarwar for Glasgow Govan lost the whip while court cases were pursued over his selection and election. He was exonerated.

On 19 March 1999 Fiona Jones, M.P. for Newark, automatically lost her seat on being convicted of presenting fraudulent expense accounts for the 1997 election. On 15 April 1999 the conviction was reversed on appeal and on 29 April 1999 she was reinstated as an M.P. She lost the seat at the 2001 election.

Sources on Electoral Matters

Official returns, listing candidates' votes and expenses, have been published as Parliamentary Papers about one year after every General Election, 1979–80 (374), 1983–84 (130), 1987–88 (426), 1992–93 (408), 1998–99 (260).

More usable returns, identifying candidates by party and supplying supplementary data, are to be found in *Dod's Parliamentary Companion*, Vacher's *Parliamentary Companion*, and *Whitaker's Almanack*, all issued annually (or more often) and in *The Times House of Commons*, published after every election.

All by-election results up to 1997 are listed in C. Cook and J. Ramsden, *By-elections in British Politics* (2nd edn 1997), and up to 1990 in P. Norris, *British By-elections* (1990).

From 1945, the results of each election have been analysed in statistical appendices to the Nuffield College series of studies; see *The British General Election of 1979* (1980), *The British General Election of 1983* (1984), *The British*

General Election of 1987 (1988), *The British General Election of 1992* (1992), *The British General Election of 1997* (1997), *The British General Election of 2001* (2001), and *The British General Election of 2005* (2005). For 2001 see also R. Waller and B. Criddle, *The Almanack of British Politics* (7th edn 2002); I. Crewe and A. Fox, *British Parliamentary Constituencies: A Statistical Compendium* (1984).

Further data is to be found in: R. Leonard and R. Mortimore, *Elections in Britain*, (5th edn 2005); C. Rallings and M. Thrasher, *British Electoral Facts 1832–1999* (2000); the Report of the Independent Commission on the Voting System (Cm 4090/98).

Census data arranged on a constituency basis is available in Census 1971: *General and Parliamentary Constituency Tables* (1974); in Census 1981: *General and Parliamentary Constituency Tables* (1983); in Census 1991: *General and Parliamentary Constituency Tables* (1994); and in Census 2001: *General and Parliamentary Constituency Tables* (2003).

See also I. McLean and D. Butler, *Fixing the Boundaries* (1995) and D. Rossiter et al., *The Boundary Commissions: Redrawing the UK's Map of Parliamentary Constituencies* (1999).

Public Opinion Polls

Many polling companies have been affiliated to the Market Research Society. Since 2004 almost all have been affiliated to the British Polling Council (www.britishpollingcouncil.org).

Gallup Poll

The British Institute of Public Opinion was established in 1937. Its name was changed in 1952 to Social Surveys (Gallup Poll) Ltd. It then became known as the Gallup Organisation. From 1961 to 2001 its findings were published regularly in the *Daily Telegraph* and the *Sunday Telegraph*. It has been relatively inactive in published political polling since 2001.

National Opinion Polls (NOP)

National Opinion Polls were established in 1957 as an affiliate of Associated Newspapers Ltd and political findings were published in the *Daily Mail* intermittently until 1961 and then regularly until 1979. In 1979 Associated Newspapers sold NOP to MAI; MAI merged NOP with another research company under the name MAI Research. NOP are now owned by United Business Media. Political polls continue to be published under the NOP name, published intermittently by the *Daily Mail* and the *Mail on Sunday* and later by the BBC. In 1998 they polled for the *Sunday Times*, and subsequently the *Independent*. Findings from the regular political surveys and from other ad hoc political opinion polls were published in the bi-monthly NOP *Social Political and Economic Review* until 1992. Since the 1990s Philip (Lord) Gould has operated as the Labour Party's private pollster through NOP. NOP is now based at Ludgate House, 245 Blackfriars Road, London SE1 9UL <www.nop.co.uk>.

Marplan Ltd/ICM Research

Marplan (present address 5–13 Great Suffolk Street, London SE1) was founded in 1959 as a subsidiary of Interpublic and later of Research International. It published opinion polls for various newspapers from 1962 onwards. After 1980 its polls were reported regularly in the *Guardian*. In 1989 its principal political researchers (led by N. Sparrow) left to form ICM Research, and their polls continued to be carried by the *Guardian*. At times after 1996 ICM acted as the Conservatives' private pollster. ICM Research is now based at Knighton House, 56 Mortimer St, London W1N 7DG <www.icmresearch.co.uk>.

Opinion Research Centre (ORC)

The Opinion Research Centre was founded in 1965. It subsequently conducted private polls for the Conservative Party ever since. It published a regular monthly poll in the *Evening Standard* and other newspapers from 1967 to 1976. It merged with Louis Harris in 1983 to form the Harris Research Centre.

Louis Harris Research Ltd/Harris Research Centre

In 1969 the *Daily Express* abandoned the poll which since the 1940s it had run from within its own office and joined with the Opinion Research Centre and the American expert Louis Harris in setting up an independent new polling organisation, Louis Harris Research Ltd. In 1972 the *Daily Express* sold its shares. Louis Harris Research Ltd and the Opinion Research Centre shared a single Managing Director, and the two companies merged in 1983 to form the Harris Research Centre. In 1994 it was bought by the French research company SOFRES, now merged with Taylor Nelson AGB. In addition to carrying out private polling for the Conservative Party until the 1990s, it also published polls in the *Observer* and for London Weekend and Thames Television's current affairs programmes. In 1997 it polled for the *Independent*. The Harris Research Centre has not been active in political polling in Britain since 2000.

Market & Opinion Research
International (MORI)

MORI, under the chairmanship of (Sir) R. Worcester, conducted extensive political surveys from 1969, including private studies for the Labour Party (from 1969 to 1998). From 1978 it published regular polls in the *(Evening) Standard* and the *Sunday Times*, as well as occasional polls for *The Times*, *Daily Express* and *Daily Star*, the *Scotsman*, *The Economist* and the BBC. In the 1980s and 1990s it published regular polls for *The Times*. MORI is now based at 79-81 Borough Rd, London SE1 1FY <www.mori.com>. 0207 347 3000.

YouGov

YouGov, founded in 2001 under the chairmanship of P. Kellner, has conducted extensive political surveys including a regular poll for the *Daily Telegraph*. It has been an innovator in the use of internet panels. It is based at 1 West Smithfield, London EC1A 9JW <www.yougov.com>. 0207 618 3010.

Populus

Populus, founded in 2001 under the chairmanship of A. Cooper, has published polls for *The Times* since 2002. It uses ICM's fieldforce, but frames its own questionnaires and research methodology. It is based at 10 Northbugh St, London EC1V OAT <www.populuslimited.com>.

Polling Archives

Most opinion polling companies preserve an archive of their findings on their websites. A more comprehensive archive of academic and commercial survey research findings is maintained at the University of Essex.

Polls on Voting Intentions

In the 1990s there were three regularly published monthly series of poll finding on voting intention; Gallup in The *Daily Telegraph*, ICM in the *Guardian* and MORI in *The Times*. Soon after the 2001 election YouGov took over at the *Daily Telegraph* and Populus at *The Times*. However MORI continued with its series which offers a continuous record from 1978 onwards. Our previous volume *Twentieth Century British Political Facts 1900–2000* reproduces the Gallup series from 1946 to 1999. But here we turn to the MORI time series. To preserve a continuous time-series, we report their basic figures. But it should be pointed out that since November 2004 their headline figure has been changed; falling turnout figures have led MORI (alone among polling companies) only to report the intentions of those 'absolutely certain to vote'.

How would you vote if there were a General Election tomorrow?

	Con. %	Lab. %	Lib. %	SDP %	Alliance %	Other %	Lab. lead ±	Combined Alliance
1979								
Aug	44	45	9	–	–	2	+1	
Sep	42	43	12	–	–	2	+1	
Oct	41	46	11	–	–	2	+5	
Nov	40	45	13	–	–	3	+5	
1980								
Jan	40	43	14	–	–	3	+3	
Feb	38	46	14	–	–	2	+8	
Mar	38	46	13	–	–	3	+8	
Apr	39	44	14	–	–	3	+5	
Jun	41	43	13	–	–	3	+2	
Jul	37	47	13	–	–	2	+10	
Aug	37	48	13	–	–	2	+11	
Sep	37	46	15	–	–	2	+9	
Oct	34	50	15	–	–	2	+16	
Nov	36	50	13	–	–	1	+14	
1981								
Jan	35	45	17	–	–	4	+10	
Feb	33	41	17	8	–	2	+8	
Mar	28	38	17	15	–	2	+10	
Apr	30	38	17	12	–	3	+8	
Jun	31	39	16	12	–	3	+6	
Jul	30	36	13	18	–	2	+6	
Aug	30	39	13	16	–	2	+9	
Sep	27	38	16	17	–	2	+11	
Oct	27	31	14	26	–	2	+4	
Nov	27	27	8	16	19	2	0	44
Dec	27	29	11	19	13	1	+2	43
1982								
Jan	29	30	12	15	13	1	+1	40
Feb	30	33	12	11	11	3	+3	34
Mar	34	34	11	11	8	2	0	30
Apr	35	30	10	11	12	2	−5	33
May	44	30	10	7	7	1	−14	25
Jun	48	28	10	8	6	1	−20	23
Jul	45	31	10	4	8	1	−14	22
Aug	44	30	9	6	8	2	−14	24
Sep	42	30	13	4	10	1	−12	27
Oct	43	32	10	6	8	2	−11	23
Nov	43	35	9	6	6	2	−8	21
Dec 9–12	42	35	10	6	6	2	−7	21
1983								
Jan 20–26	44	36	8	5	6	a	−8	19
Feb 17–23	46	32	10	5	6	a	−14	21

	Con. %	Lab. %	Lib. %	SDP %	Alliance %	Other %	Lab. lead ±	Combined Alliance
Mar 17–23	43	28	9	8	10	1	−15	28
Apr 17–23	46	33	10	4	7	1	−13	20
May 5–11	46	32	9	4	9	a	−14	22
Jun 16–20	43	27	11	6	12	1	−16	29
Jul 21–25	44	30	11	6	8	1	−14	25
Aug 18–22	46	30	9	5	8	2	−16	22
Sep 22–26	45	27	13	5	8	1	−18	26
Oct 20–24	42	37	8	4	7	2	−5	19
Nov 17–21	39	37	10	5	7	2	−2	22
Dec 05–09	42	37	10	3	7	1	−5	19
1984								
Jan 05–09	42	37	10	3	7	1	−5	19
Feb 16–20	41	38	10	4	6	2	−3	19
Mar 14–20	41	40	8	3	6	1	−1	17
Apr– May 25–01	40	39	10	3	7	a	−1	20
May 24–29	40	38	8	4	9	1	−2	21
Jun 21–25	39	39	7	3	11	1	0	21
Jul 19–23	37	40	7	4	9	2	+3	20
Aug 16–20	39	39	9	4	8	1	0	21
Sep 17–21	42	36	9	3	7	2	−6	20
Oct 18–22	44	35	7	4	9	2	−9	20
Nov 15–19	43	35	8	4	7	3	−8	19
Dec 06–10	40	36	8	5	9	2	−4	22
1985								
Jan 02–07	42	34	9	4	8	3	−8	21
Feb 19–24	39	35	10	4	10	2	−4	24
Mar 19–24	36	40	9	4	10	1	+4	23
Apr 25–28	38	37				1	−1	24
May 21–26	33	35	11	6	13	2	+2	30
Jun 18–23	35	36	10	5	12	2	+1	27
Jul 16–21	33	34	12	8	12	2	+1	31
Aug 13–18	31	35	10	9	12	3	+4	31
Sep 17–22	30	33	10	7	18	2	+3	35
Oct 15–20	37	36	9	5	11	2	−1	25
Nov 19–24	36	36	9	6	11	2	0	25
Dec 03–08	35	35	9	7	13	2	0	28
1986								
Jan 04–08	33	38	10	6	12	2	0	28
Feb 22–26	34	35	8	7	15	1	+1	30
Mar 22–26	34	36	7	5	15	2	+2	28
Apr 19–22	34	39	7	6	12	2	+5	25
May 17–21	32	40	8	3	15	2	+8	26
Jun 20–24	34	40	8	5	11	2	+6	23
Jul 18–22	36	37	10	4	11	2	+1	25
Aug 15–19	37	37	9	4	11	2	0	24
Sep 19–23	35	37	7	6	13	2	+2	26
Oct 17–22	39	41	6	4	7	2	+2	17

	Con. %	Lab. %	Lib. %	SDP %	Alliance %	Other %	Lab. lead ±	Combined Alliance
Nov 20–26	41	39	7	4	8	2	−2	18
Dec 18–30	39	38	10	6	6	2	−1	21
1987								
Jan 23–28	39	38	7	5	9	2	−1	21
Feb 06–10	39	36	5	5	13	2	−3	23
Mar 20–25	41	35	6	3	11	3	−6	21
Mar 06–10	41	32	6	6	13	2	−9	21
Mar 26–2 Apr	41	29	8	4	17	1	−12	29
Apr 24–30	44	31	8	4	12	2	−13	23
Jun 25–Jul 01	49	31	7	3	8	3	−18	17
Jul 21–28	49	33	6	2	8	3	−16	17
Aug 21–26	48	36	7	3	4	2	−12	14
Sep 24–30	49	36	6	2	4	3	−13	12
Oct 21–26	47	37	7	2	5	2	−10	14
Nov 19–25	50	38	7	2	3	1	−12	11
Dec 29–30	48	36	6	3	6	1	−12	15
1988								
Jan 22–26	50	36	7	2	3	2	−14	12
Feb 26–Mar 01	46	38	7	2	5	3	−8	14

	Con.	Lab.	Lib. D	SDP		Other	Lab. lead	
Mar 24–28	46	37	8	6		3	−9	
Apr 22–26	44	42	6	5		3	−2	
May 27–01 Jun	44	40	7	6		3	−4	
Jun 22–28	48	38	7	5		2	−10	
Jul 21–25	46	41	8	4		1	−5	
Aug 18–22	50	36	8	4		2	−14	
Sep 21–26	44	39	8	6		3	−5	
Oct 26–31	44	39	8	6		3	−5	
Nov 25–30	45	37	8	6		4	−8	
Dec 28–29	46	36	6	7		5	−10	
1989								
Jan 26–30	47	36	8	5		4	−11	
Feb 23–28	42	39	9	7		3	−3	
Mar 15–19	44	40	6	6		4	−4	
Apr 20–24	41	41	9	6		3	0	
May 18–22	41	43	7	4		5	+2	

	Con.	Lab.	Lib. D	SDP	Green	Other	Lab. lead	
June 22–27	37	47	4	3	7	2	+10	
July 20–26	36	45	4	4	8	3	+9	
Aug 17–21	40	45	4	3	6	2	+5	
Sep 21–26	38	43	6	3	7	3	+5	
Oct 19–23	38	48	5	3	5	1	+10	

	Con. %	Lab. %	Lib. D. %	SDP %	Green %	Other %	Lab. lead ±
Nov 23–27	42	46	5	3	3	1	+4
Dec 27–28	39	46	6	3	4	2	+7
1990							
Jan 18–22	36	48	5	3	5	3	+12
Feb 15–19	34	51	5	4	4	2	+17
Mar 15–20	30	54	6	4	4	2	+24
Apr 19–24	31	54	6	3	4	2	+23
May 17–21	35	48	8	4	4	1	+13
Jun 13–18	38	49	8	n/a	3	2	+11
Jul 19–23	38	46	10	n/a	4	2	+8
Aug 16–20	35	50	10	n/a	4	1	+15
Sep 20–24	38	45	12	n/a	3	2	+7
Oct 18–22	33	49	14	n/a	2	2	+16
Nov 15–19	38	46	12	n/a	2	2	+8
Dec 27–28	41	45	9	n/a	2	3	+4
1991							
Jan 18–21	46	41	9	n/a	2	2	−5
Feb 22–25	44	41	11	n/a	1	3	−3
Mar 21–25	40	40	16	n/a	2	2	0
Apr 18–22	42	40	15	n/a	1	2	−2
May 24–28	37	43	16	n/a	2	a	+6
Jun 21–24	39	41	15	n/a	1	4	+2
Jul 19–22	38	43	15	n/a	2	2	+5
Aug 23–27	42	40	14	n/a	2	2	−2
Sep 20–24	39	39	17	n/a	1	4	0
Oct 18–21	39	45	12	n/a	2	2	+6
Nov 22–25	40	42	15	n/a	1	2	+2
Dec 27	38	44	14	n/a	2	2	+6
1992							
Jan 17–21	42	39	16	n/a	1	2	−3
Feb 21–25	39	40	18	n/a	1	2	+1
Mar 20–24	38	41	17	n/a	1	3	+3
Apr 25–28	43	38	16	n/a	a	2	−5
May 21–26	43	38	16	n/a	1	2	−5
Jun 19–23	42	39	16	n/a	1	2	−3
Jul 23–28	39	43	15	n/a	1	2	+4
Aug 27-Sep 1	41	44	13	n/a	1	1	+3
Sep 25–29	37	43	16	n/a	1	3	+6
Oct 23–27	35	45	15	n/a	1	4	+10
Nov 27–Dec 1	34	47	15		1	1	+13
Dec 11–15	34	47	16		1	2	+13
1993							
Jan 21–25	37	45	14		1	3	+8
Feb 18–22	34	46	16		1	3	+12
Mar 25–29	32	47	17		1	3	+15

	Con. %	Lab. %	Lib. D. %	Green %	Other %	Lab. lead ±
Apr 22–26	32	46	20	a	2	+14
May 20–24	28	44	24	1	3	+16
Jun 24–28	28	46	23	1	2	+18
Jul 22–26	27	44	25	1	3	+17
Aug 19–23	28	42	25	1	3	+14
Sep 16–20	29	43	25	1	2	+14
Oct 21–25	29	45	23	1	2	+16
Nov 18–22	29	47	22	1	2	+18
Dec 9–13	29	47	20	1	3	+18
1994						
Jan 20–24	28	48	20	1	3	+20
Feb 24–28	28	47	21	1	3	+19
Mar 24–28	27	49	20	1	3	+22
Apr 21–25	26	47	23	1	3	+21
May 19–23	27	46	23	1	3	+19
Jun 16–20	24	52	20	1	3	+28
Jul 14–18	23	51	21	1	4	+28
Aug 18–22	23	56	18	1	2	+33
Sep 22–26	25	54	17	1	3	+29
Oct 20–24	25	57	14	1	3	+32
Nov 17–21	24	55	17	1	3	+31
Dec 15–19	22	61	13	1	3	+39
1995						
Jan 20–23	27	56	14	1	2	+29
Feb 17–20	24	58	14	1	3	+34
Mar 17–20	25	57	13	1	4	+32
Apr 21–24	26	56	15	1	2	+30
May 19–22	22	58	16	1	3	+36
Jun 23–26	29	56	13	1	2	+27
Jul 21–24	26	59	12	1	2	+33
Aug 25–28	25	56	15	1	3	+31
Sep 22–25	28	51	16	1	4	+23
Oct 20–23	27	56	13	1	3	+29
Nov 17–20	26	56	14	1	3	+30
Dec 1–4	28	55	13	1	3	+27
1996						
Jan 19–22	29	55	13	1	1	+26
Feb 23–26	26	57	14	1	2	+31
Mar 22–25	28	57	13	a	2	+29
Apr 19–22	28	54	14	1	3	+26
May 23–26	27	54	15	1	3	+27
Jun 21–24	31	52	12	1	4	+21
Jul 23–28	29	53	12	1	5	+24
Aug 20–25	30	51	13	1	4	+21
Sep 20–23	29	52	14	1	3	+23

	Con. %	Lab. %	Lib. D. %	Green %	UKIP %	Other %	Lab. lead ±
Oct 25–28	28	56	12		1	2	+28
Nov 8–11	33	50	12		1	3	+17
Dec 6–9	30	51	13		1	3	+21
1997							
Jan 24–28	30	55	11	1	1	2	+25
Feb 21–24	31	52	11	1	1	1	+21
Mar 21–24	29	50	14	1	3	1	+21
Apr 1*	28	55	11	1	2	4	+27
Apr 8*	34	49	12	a	1	4	+15
Apr 15*	32	49	13	1	2	3	+17
Apr 22*	27	48	17	1	3	4	+21
Apr 29*	27	51	15	1	2	4	+24
Jun 20–23	24	58	15	1	a	2	+34
Jul 25–28	23	57	15	1	a	4	+34
Aug 21–25	28	54	15	a	1	2	+26
Sep 26–29	25	59	13	a	a	3	+34
Oct 24–27	24	60	12	a	a	3	+36
Nov 21–24	24	56	16	1	a	3	+32
Dec 12–15	26	55	15	1	a	4	+29
1998							
Jan 23–26	28	54	14	1	a	3	+26
Feb 20–23	28	52	15	1	a	4	+24
Mar 20–23	28	53	14	1	a	4	+25
Apr 24–27	27	55	14	1	a	3	+28
May 21–24	26	55	14	1	0	4	+29
Jun 25–30	27	56	13	1	a	4	+29
Jul 17–21	28	53	14	1	1	4	+25
Aug 21–24	28	52	14	1	0	5	+24
Sep 18–21	24	56	15	1	a	3	+32
Oct 23–26	26	53	16	1	a	4	+27
Nov 20–23	29	53	13	1	a	3	+24
Dec 11–14	27	54	12	1	a	5	+27
1999							
Jan 22–25	24	56	14	1	a	5	+32
Feb 19–22	30	51	14	a	1	1	+21
Mar 19–22	27	54	13	1	a	4	+27
Apr 23–26	25	56	13	1	1	4	+31
May 21–24	28	52	14	1	1	4	+24
June 18–21	28	51	13	2	1	5	+23
July 23–26	28	51	14	2	1	4	+23
Aug 20–23	27	49	17	2	a	5	+22
Sep 24–27	25	52	17	1	a	5	+27
Oct 22–25	28	56	11	2	1	2	+28
Nov 19–22	25	55	14	1	a	4	+30
Dec 10–14	28	54	13	1	a	4	+26

	Con. %	Lab. %	Lib. D. %	Green %	UKIP %	Other %	Lab. lead ±
2000							
Jan 21–24	30	50	15	1	a	4	+20
Feb 17–22	29	50	15	1	1	4	+21
Mar 23–28	29	50	14	1	1	5	+21
Apr 13–18	27	51	15	2	1	1	+24
May 18–23	32	48	15	1	a	4	+16
Jun 22–27	33	47	13	2	1	3	+14
Jul 20–24	33	49	12	1	a	5	+16
Aug 17–21	29	51	15	1	1	3	+22
Sep 21–26	35	37	21	1	a	6	+2
Oct 19–23	32	45	17	1	1	4	+13
Nov 23–28	33	48	13	1	a	4	+15
Dec 7–12	34	46	14	1	1	4	+12
2001							
Jan 18–22	31	50	14	1	a	4	+19
Feb 15–20	30	50	14	1	1	4	+20
Mar 22–27	31	50	14	1	a	4	+19
Apr 19–24	30	50	13	2	1	4	+20
May 8	30	54	13	1	1	1	+24
May 15	28	54	12	1	a	5	+26
May 22	30	55	11	1	1	2	+25
May 29	30	48	16	1	2	1	+18
Jun 5	30	45	18		7		+15
Jun 21–26	25	49	19	1	1	5	+24
Jul 19–23	25	52	17	1	1	4	+27
Aug 23–28	25	53	16	2	a	4	+28
Sept 20–25	27	53	15	1	a	4	+26
Oct 18–22	25	57	13	1	1	3	+32
Nov 22–27	25	56	15	1	a	4	+31
2002							
Jan 24–28	27	51	16	1	a	4	+24
Feb 21–26	28	51	16	1	a	4	+23
Mar 21–26	28	47	19	1	a	4	+19
Apr 18–22	27	50	16	1	1	5	+23
May 23–28	30	46	17	2	1	4	+16
Jun 20–24	29	48	17	1	a	5	+18
Jul 18–24	27	48	18	1	a	1	+21
Sep 19–24	27	49	17	2	0	2	+22
Oct 17–21	26	49	21	1	a	1	+23
Nov 14–19	27	47	18	2	1	5	+20
Dec 12–17	29	43	23	1	1	3	+14
2003							
Jan 23–27	27	44	20	2	1	6	+17
Feb 20–25	25	44	22	2	1	6	+19
Mar 20–24	27	46	20	2	1	4	+19

	Con. %	Lab. %	Lib. D. %	Green %	UKIP %	Other %	Lab. lead ±
Apr 24–28	26	47	20	1	a	6	+21
May 22–28	28	43	22	2	1	4	+15
June 19–24	27	43	22	2	1	5	+16
July 17–22	32	40	21	2	1	4	+8
Aug 28–Sep 2	30	40	21	2	1	6	+10
Sep 11–16	29	43	21	2	1	4	+14
Oct 23–28	31	42	20	1	1	5	+11
Nov 20–25	31	41	21	1	1	5	+10
Dec 11–17	28	43	22	1	1	5	+15
2004							
Jan 15–20	31	41	20	2	1	5	+10
Feb 12–16	32	39	20	2	1	6	+7
Mar 11–16	32	40	22	2	1	3	+8
Apr 15–19	31	40	21	2	1	5	+9
May 27–Jun 1	30	37	20	3	3	7	+7
Jun 24–29	28	37	20	4	6	5	+9
Jul 22–27	28	36	23	3	5	5	+8
Aug 12–16	30	38	21	2	4	5	+8
Sep 10–14	29	37	24	2	3	5	+8
Oct 21–27	27	40	22	3	3	1	+13
Nov 4–8	29	39	22	3	3	4	+10
Dec 2–6	27	40	24	3	3	3	+13
2005							
Jan 20–24	27	42	22	2	2	5	+15
Feb 17–21	37	39	18	2	1	3	+2
Mar 17–22	33	39	21	2	1	4	+6
Apr 1–3	33	38	23	2	2	2	+5
Apr 7–9	35	39	21	2	1	2	+4
Apr 7–9	33	40	19	2	2	4	+7
Apr 15–18	32	40	21	2	1	4	+8
Apr 18–19	32	39	22	2	1	4	+7
Apr 21–25	34	36	23	2	2	3	+2
Apr 28–29	33	36	22	2	2	5	+3
Apr 29–May 1	29	39	22	2	3	5	+10
May 3–4	33	38	23	1	2	3	+5

a Less than 0.5%.
* Election campaign polls.

Opinion Poll Accuracy in General Elections

The following is a list of all major poll predictions of general election results.

	Actual Result (G.B.)	Gallup	NOP	Harris	ORC
1974, Oct					
Con.	36.7	−0.7	−5.7	−2.1	−2.3
Lab.	40.2	+1.3	+5.3	+2.8	+1.6

	Actual Result (G.B.)	Gallup	NOP	Harris	ORC	
Lib.	18.8	+0.2	+0.7	+0.5	+0.6	
Other	4.3	−0.8	−0.3	−1.2	+0.1	
1979				*MORI*	*Marplan*	
Con.	44.9	−1.9	+1.1	−0.5	+0.1	
Lab.	37.8	+3.2	+1.2	+1.0	+0.8	
Lib.	14.1	−0.6	−1.6	−0.6	−0.6	
Other	3.2	−0.7	−0.7	−0.1	−0.3	
1983						*Harris*
Con.	43.5	+2.0	+3.5	+0.3	+2.5	+3.5
Lab.	28.3	−1.8	−3.3	−0.3	−2.3	−3.3
Alln	26.0	0.0	0.0	0.0	0.0	0.0
Other	2.2	−0.2	−0.2	−0.2	+2.0	+2.0
1987						
Con.	43.3	−2.3	−1.3	+0.7	−1.3	−1.3
Lab.	31.5	+2.5	+3.5	+0.5	+3.5	+3.5
Alln	23.1	+0.4	−2.1	−1.1	−2.1	−2.1
Other	2.1	−0.6	−0.1	−0.1	−0.1	−0.1
1992	*ICM*					
Con.	42.8	−4.3	−3.8	−4.0	−4.0	
Lab.	35.2	+2.8	+6.8	+3.8	+2.8	
Lib. D.	18.3	+1.7	−1.3	−1.7	−1.7	
Other	3.7	−0.2	−1.7	−1.7	+0.3	
1997						
Con.	31.4	+1.6	−3.4	1.4	1.6	0.4
Lab.	44.4	+2.6	+5.6	+2.6	−1.4	+3.6
Lib. D.	17.2	−3.2	−3.2	+1.8	+0.8	−2.2
Other	7.0	−1.0	+1.0	−2.0	−1.0	−1.0
2001						*Rasmussen*
Con.	32.7	−2.7	−2.7	−2.7	−0.7	−0.3
Lab.	42.0	+5.0	+5.0	+3.0	+3.0	+2.0
Lib. D.	18.8	−0.8	−0.8	−0.8	+0.3	−2.8
Other	8.5	−3.5	−1.5	−1.5	−2.5	−1.5
2005	*Result*	*ICM*	*NOP*	*MORI*	*Populus*	*YouGov*
Con.	33.2	−1.2	−0.2	−0.2	−1.2	−1.2
Lab.	36.2	+1.8	−0.2	+1.8	+1.8	+0.8
Lib. D.	22.6	−0.6	+0.4	−0.4	−1.6	+0.6
Other	8.0	0	0	−2.0	+1.0	−1.0

SOURCES:- Each of the Nuffield *British General Election* series includes analyses of the polls. But R. Worcester *British Public Opinion* (1991) provides the fullest record of political polling since 1945; see also Market Research Society's report on the 1992 performance of the polls (1994).

V
Civil Service

Heads of Departments and Public Offices

Except where stated otherwise, all these had the title of Permanent Secretary or Permanent Under-Secretary. The Permanent Secretary is the official head and usually the accounting officer of the Department and is responsible to the Minister for all the Department's activities. In some Departments, e.g. Defence since 1964, there are also Second Permanent Secretaries who are official heads and usually accounting officers for large blocks of work. Except where stated otherwise, all the following had the title of Permanent Secretary or Permanent Under-Secretary. The name is that by which they were known while in office; if a title was acquired while in office it is placed in brackets.

Agriculture, Fisheries & Food

1978	(Sir) B. Hayes
1983	(Sir) M. Franklin
1987	(Sir) D. Andrews
1993	(Sir) R. Packer
2000	B. Bender

(*2001 see Environment, Food and the Regions*)

Cabinet

(*Secretary to the Cabinet*)

1973	Sir J. Hunt
1979	Sir R. Armstrong
1988	Sir R. Butler
1998	Sir R. Wilson
2003	Sir A. Turnbull
2005	Sir G. O'Donnell

(*Permanent Secretary to the Cabinet Office*)

1998	R. Mountfield
1999	B. Bender
2000	Mavis McDonald
2002	Sir D. Omand

(Chief *Scientific Adviser*)

1974	(*post vacant*)
1986	(Sir) J. Fairclough
1990	Sir W. Stewart
1995	Sir R. May
2000	Sir D. King

(*Head of Government Statistical Service*)

1978	(Sir) A. Boreham
1986	(Sir) J. Hibbert
1992	W. McLennan
1995	T. Holt
2000	L. Cook

(*See Office for National Statistics*)

Central Policy Review Staff

(*Director-General*)

1974	Sir K. Berrill
1980	R. Ibbs
1982	J. Sparrow
1983	(*post vacant*)

(see pp. 190–1 for *Economic Advisers*)

Civil Service Commission
(*First Commissioner*)
1974	F. Allen
1981	A. Fraser
1983	D. Trevelyan
1989	J. Holroyd
1994	Anne Bowtell
1995	Sir M. Bett
2000	Lady Prashar

Head of the Home Civil Service
1978	Sir I. Bancroft
1981	{ Sir R. Armstrong
1981	{ Sir D. Wass
1983	Sir R. Armstrong
1988	Sir R. Butler
1998	Sir R. Wilson
2003	Sir A. Turnbull
2005	Sir G. O'Donnell

Civil Service Department
1978	Sir I. Bancroft
1981	(*post vacant*)

Commissioner for Public Appointments
1999	Dame R. Fritchie

Constitutional Affairs
2003	Sir H. Phillips
2004	A. Allan

Culture, Media & Sport
(*see National Heritage*)
1997	(Sir) H. Phillips
1998	R. Young
2001	N. Kroll (*acting*)
2001	Sue Street

Board of Customs and Excise
1978	(Sir) D. Lovelock
1983	(Sir) A. Fraser
1987	(Sir) B. Unwin
1993	(Dame) V. Strachan
2003	M. Eland

(*merged with Inland Revenue as HM Revenue and Customs, 2005*)

Defence
1976	Sir F. Cooper
1983	(Sir) C. Whitmore
1988	Sir M. Quinlan
1993	Sir C. France
1995	R. Mottram
1998	(Sir) K. Tebbit

Defence (Procurement)
(*Chief Executive*)
1975	(Sir) C. Cornford
1980	(Sir) D. Cardwell
1983	D. Perry
1985	(Sir) P. Levene
1991	M. McIntosh
1996	Sir R. Walmsley
2003	Sir P. Spencer

Office of the Deputy Prime Minister
2002	(Dame) Mavis McDonald

Education (and Science 1964–92)
1976	(Sir) J. Hamilton
1983	(Sir) D. Hancock
1989	(Sir) J. Caines
1992	Sir D. Holland
1994	Sir T. Lankester

(Education and Employment)
1996	(Sir) M. Bichard
2001	D. Normington

Employment
1975	(Sir) K. Barnes
1983	(Sir) M. Quinlan
1988	(Sir) G. Holland
1993–95	(Sir) N. Monck

(*see Education*)

Energy (–1995)
1974	Sir J. Rampton
1980	Sir D. Maitland
1983	Sir K. Couzens
1985	(Sir) P. Gregson
1989	G. Chipperfield
1991–92	J. Guinness

(*1995 under Trade*)

Environment (Transport and the Regions)
1978	Sir J. Garlick
1981	(Sir) G. Moseley
1985	(Sir) T. Heiser
1992	(Sir) R. Wilson
1994	A. Turnbull
1998	Sir R. Mottram

Environment Food and Rural Affairs
2001   Sir B. Bender
(*see also Transport and Office of the Deputy Prime Minister*)

Foreign and Commonwealth Office
(*Also Head of Diplomatic Service*)
1975   Sir M. Palliser
1982   Sir A. Acland
1986   Sir P. Wright
1991   Sir D. Gillmore
1994   Sir J. Coles
1997   Sir J. Kerr
2002   Sir M. Jay

Forestry Commission
(*Chairman*)
1976   J. Mackie
1979   Sir D. Montgomery
1989   (Sir) R. Johnstone
1994   Sir P. Hutchison
2001   Ld Clark of Windermere

Government Accountancy Service
1984   (Sir) A. Wilson
1989   Sir A. Hardcastle
1993   (Sir) A. Likierman
2004   Mary Keegan

Health & Social Security
1975   Sir P. Nairne
1981   Sir K. Stowe
1987   Sir C. France
(Health)
1988   Sir C. France
1992   (Sir) G. Hart
1997   C. Kelly
2000   (Sir) N. Crisp

Home Office
1977   (Sir) R. Armstrong
1979   Sir B. Cubbon
1988   Sir C. Whitmore
1994   (Sir) R. Wilson
1998   (Sir) D. Omand
2001   J. Gieve

Industry (–1983)
1976–83 Sir P. Carey
(*see Trade and Industry*)

Central Office of Information
(*Director-General*)
1978   J. Groves
1982   D. Grant
1985   N. Taylor
1989   G. Devereux
(*Chief Executive*)
1996   A. Douglas
1998   Carol Fisher
2003   A. Bishop

Board of Inland Revenue
(*Chairman*)
1976   Sir W. Pile
1980   Sir L. Airey
1986   Sir A. Battishill
1997   (Sir) N. Montagu
(*merged with Customs and Excise to create Revenue and Excise 2005*)

International Development
1997   (Sir) J. Vereker
2002   S. Chakrabati

Secretary to the Ld Chancellor & Clerk of the Crown in Chancery
1977   (Sir) W. Bourne
1982   (Sir) D. Oulton
1989   (Sir) T. Legg
1999   Sir H. Phillips
(*Ld Chancellor's Department subsumed into Department of Constitutional Affairs 2003*)
2004   A. Allan

National Health Service Management Board
(*Chairman*)
1985   V. Paige
2000   N. Crisp

National Heritage
1992   H. Phillips
(*see Culture*)

National Statistics
(*Chief executive*)
1996	T. Holt
1999	L. Cook

Northern Ireland
1976	(Sir) B. Cubbon
1979	Sir P. Woodfield
1984	(Sir) R. Andrew
1988	Sir J. Blelloch
1990	(Sir) J. Chilcot
1997	(Sir) J. Pilling

Overseas Development
1976	(Sir) P. Preston
1982	Sir W. Ryrie
1984	Sir C. Tickell
1987	J. Caines
1989	(Sir) T. Lankester
1994	J. Vereker

(*see 1997 International Development*)

Prices and Consumer Protection
1974–79	(Sir) K. Clucas

Privy Council
(*Clerk of the Council*)
1974	(Sir) N. Leigh
1984	(Sir) G. de Deney
1992	N. Nicholls
1998	A. Galloway

Property Services
1979	Sir R. Cox
1981	A. Montague
1984	Sir G. Manzie
1990	P. Brown
1991	(Sir) G. Chipperfield
1993	P. Fletcher

(*sold to private sector, 1994*)

Office of Public Service (and Science 1992–95)
1992	R. Mottram
1995	(Sir) R. Mountfield

(*merged with Cabinet Office 1998*)

General Register Office
(*Registrar-General for England and Wales*)
1978	A. Thatcher
1986	Gillian Banks
1990	P. Wormald
1996	T. Holt
1999	L. Cook

HM Revenue and Excise
2005	D. Varney

Scottish Office
1978	(Sir) W. Fraser
1988	(Sir) R. Hillhouse
1998	M. Russell

(*Scottish Executive took over 1 Jul 99*)

Social Security
1968–88	(*see Health & Social Security*)
1988	(Sir) M. Partridge
1996	Dame A. Bowtell
1999	Dame R. Lomax

(*see Work and Pensions*)

Board of Trade
1977	(Sir) L. Pliatzky
1979	Sir K. Clucas

(Trade and Industry)
1979	Sir P. Carey
1983	{ Sir B. Hayes
1983	{ Sir A. Rawlinson
1985	Sir B. Hayes
1989	Sir P. Gregson
1996	(Sir) M. Scholar
2001	(Sir) R. Young
2005	Catherine Bell

Transport
1976	(Sir) P. Baldwin
1982	(Sir) P. Lazarus
1986	(Sir) A. Bailey
1991	(Sir) P. Brown

(*Dept merged with Environment 1997; separated off again 2002*)
2003	D. Rowlands

Treasury

1974	(Sir) D. Wass
1983	(Sir) P. Middleton
1991	Sir T. Burns
1998	Sir A. Turnbull
2002	G. O'Donnell

University Grants Committee (Chairman)

1978	(Sir) E. Parks
1983	Sir P. Swinnerton-Dyer

(Higher Education Funding Council)

1992	Sir R. Dearing
1993	B. Gough

1997	Sir M. Checkland
2001	D. Young

Welsh Office

1971	(Sir) H. Evans
1980	(Sir) T. Hughes
1985	(Sir) R. Lloyd-Jones
1993	M. Scholar
1996	Rachel Lomax
1999	J. Shortridge

(*office modified July 1999*)

Work and Pensions

2002	Sir R. Mottram

Salary of Permanent Secretary in the Civil Service

1980	£33,500
1990	£89,500
1998	£95,720–£164,110
2004	£121,100–£256,550

Prime Minister's Principal Private Secretary

1975	K. Stowe
1979	C. Whitmore
1982	R. Butler
1985	N. Wicks
1988	A. Turnbull
1992	A. Allan
1997	(Sir) J. Holmes
1999	J. Heywood
2003	I. Rogers

Chief of Staff

1979–85	D. Wolfson
1997	J. Powell

Appointments Secretary

1972	C. Peterson
1982	(Sir) J. Catford
1993	J. Holroyd
1999	W. Chapman

Prime Minister's Staff

In addition to an official Civil Service Principal Private Secretary, all Prime Ministers have made their own arrangements for advice and help. These cannot be consistently categorised. The following have played significant roles.

Head of Policy Unit

1974	B. Donoughue
1979	J. Hoskyns
1983	F. Mount
1983	J. Redwood
1985	B. Griffiths
1990	Sarah Hogg
1995	N. Blackwell
1997	D. Miliband (*acting 97–98*)
2001	A. Adonis
2003	M. Taylor

(*See also Heads of Central Policy Review Staff p. 134*)

Specialist Advisers

1982–83	Sir A. Parsons (Foreign Policy)
1984–92	Sir P. Cradock (Foreign Policy)
1983–89	Sir A. Walters (Economics)
1983–89	Sir D. (Ld) Rayner (Efficiency)
1983–88	Sir R. Ibbs (Efficiency)
1988–92	Sir A. Fraser (Efficiency)
1992–97	Sir P. Levene (Efficiency and Competition)
1992–93	Sir R. Braithwaite (Foreign Policy)
1991–3	Sir S. Wall (Foreign Policy)
2000–4	Sir S. Wall (European Policy)
2001–3	Sir D. Manning (Foreign Policy)
2003–	Sir N. Sheinwald (Foreign Policy)

Political Secretary/Adviser

1976–79	T. McNally

1979–81	R. Ryder
1981–83	D. Howe
1983–87	S. Sherbourne
1987–90	J. Whittingdale
1990–92	Judith Chaplin
1992–94	J. Hill
1994–97	H. James
1997–01	Sally (Bness) Morgan
2001–05	P. McFadden
2005–	J. McTernan

Director of Government Relations

2001–05	Bness Morgan
2005–	J. McTernan

Press Officers

Press Secretary

1976	T. McCaffrey

Chief Press Secretary

1979	B. Ingham
1990	G. O'Donnell
1994	C. Meyer
1996	J. Haslam

Prime Minister's Official Spokesman

1997	A. Campbell
2001–03 {	G. Smith
2001–03 {	T. Kelly
2003	T. Kelly

Director of Communications Strategy

2001	A. Campbell
2003	D. Hill

Special or Political Advisers to Ministers

Many Ministers have brought in unofficial advisers and secretaries but political advisers only became established in an official way after 1974 (although in 1970–74 six or seven Conservative ministers had full-time assistants paid from party funds). During H. Wilson's 1974 ministry it was agreed that any Cabinet minister could appoint political advisers with a tenure that lasted only as long as he or she continued in office. From 1979 to 1990 Margaret Thatcher limited Cabinet ministers to one political adviser – except for the Treasury, the Home Office, the Foreign Office and the Department of the Environment. In May 1997 the incoming Labour Government agreed that each Cabinet Minister could have two Special Advisers and there was a significant increase in the number employed in the Prime Minister's Office. Two Special

Advisers (A. Campbell and J. Powell) were dispensed from the restriction on Special Advisers having any authority over civil servants.

Number of Special Advisers

Nov 1974	28
Jan 1980	14
Oct 1990	20
Feb 1997	38 (8 working in 10 Downing St)
Jul 1999	74 (25 working in 10 Downing St)
Apr 2003	80 (27 working in 10 Downing St)
Jun 2005	72 (24 working in 10 Downing St)

SOURCE: Ninth report of the Committee on Standards in Public Life (Cm. 5775); 10 Downing St.

Size of Civil Service

The transfer of functions between departments makes comparisons of one year with another potentially misleading. These figures are liable to slight error as they are estimates and not reports of the actual staff employed. In each case they are estimates for the year ending 31 March of the following year (e.g. under the column headed '1 Apr 1990' the estimates are for 1990–91). The figures in this table should be used with great caution because of the considerable differences in the sources. In particular, the growth of Next Steps agencies (see below) has led to apparent sharp drops in the number of civil servants in some areas which are quite misleading. Where possible – in other words, where the Civil Service websites record the information in that way – we have given the total figure for each department, including the agencies which come under it. In 2004 73% of civil servants worked in agencies established on Next Steps lines.

Number of Civil Servants

	1980 1 Apr	1990 1 Apr	2000 1 Apr	2004 1 Apr
Total non-industrial	547,486	495,000	445,980	–
Total industrial	157,417	67,000	29,440	–
Total Civil S. Staff	704,903	562,388	475,420	523,580
Defence	118,450	141,373	100,330	91,430
Foreign & C.O.	11,291	9,491	5,470	5,970
International Dev.	–	–	1,210	1,780
Northern Ireland	194	223	190	170
Scottish Off.	9,990	10,274	40	80
Scottish Executive	–	–	10,850	12,140
Welsh O.[a]	2,324	2,284	30	–[a]

	1980 1 Apr	1990 1 Apr	2000 1 Apr	2004 1 Apr
Welsh Assembly	–	–	2,570	4,290
Treasury	1,044	3,135	830	1,030
Home Office	30,289	42,721	12,540	24,010
Prison Service	–	–	40,560	45,280
Agriculture[b]	13,273	9,881	9,590	9,690[b]
Education	2,594	2,560	4,970	5,130
Energy	1,252	1,024	–	–
Environment[c]	28,177	6,074	17,070[c]	
Health[d]	95,923	5,422	5,160	4,180
(& Soc. Sec.)				
Social Security/Work &				
Pensions	–	80,890	83,530	125,170
Employment[e]	48,718	48,138	31,090[e]	
Security & Intelligence	–	–	4,520	4,490
Trade & Ind.	–	11,793	8,840	9,640
Trade	7,163	–	–	–
Industry	8,499	–	–	–
Transport	12,792	15,513	–	15,760
Customs & Ex.	27,232	26,864	21,910	22,590
Inland Revenue	78,282	66,063	62,460	80,110
H.M.S.O.	3,070	3,201	–	–
Civil Serv. Dpt	3,210			
Cabinet Office	580	1,484	1,980	2,090
C.S.O./O.N.S.[f]	–	999	2,870	3,450
C.P.S.[g]	–	4,710	5,450	7,540
Ld Chancellor/DCA[a]	–	10,454	10,640	11,950
Culture, Media & Sport[h]	–	–	620	730

[a] In 2003 the Lord Chancellor's Department became the Department for Constitutional Affairs. It included the vestiges of the old Welsh Office.

[b] 2004 figure is for Environment, Food and Rural Affairs.

[c] Department of Environment, Transport and the Regions; includes many civil servants previously classified as Transport.

[d] The Department of Health and Social Security split into its two constituent parts in 1988.

[e] 2000 figures are for the Employment service within the Department for Education and Employment. For 2004 the successor departments are included in the Department for Work and Pensions total.

[f] The Central Statistical Office was established on 31 Jul 89. It later became the Office for National Statistics.

[g] The Crown Prosecution Service was established on 20 Jul 87.

[h] The Department of National Heritage was established on 3 Jul 92. It became the Department of Culture Media and Sport in Jul 97.

SOURCE: <http://www.civilservice.gov.uk/management_information/statistical_information/ statistics/ publications/pdf/staff/staff_apr00.pdf>

<http://www.civilservice.gov.uk/management_information/statistical_information/statis- tics/ publications/xls/staff/staff_apr04_4nov04.xls>

Civil Service Agencies

Next Steps

In 1987 the Prime Minister commissioned a report into Civil Service reform, published in 1988 under the title *Improving Management in Government: The Next Steps* (The Ibbs Report). It proposed that many of the functions currently performed by the Civil Service could be undertaken more efficiently by semi-autonomous agencies managing themselves outside the main Civil Service structure. The programme began the same year, and was given legislative effect by the *Government Trading Act, 1990*. By 1 January 1998 383,290 civil servants were operating on *Next Steps* lines.

	Launched	*Wound up/sold*
Attorney-General		
Public (Crown) Prosecution Service[a]	1 Oct 88	
Government Property Lawyers	1 Apr 93	30 Sep 99
Serious Fraud Office[a]	1 Apr 88	
Treasury Solicitor's Department	1 Apr 96	
Cabinet Office		
Central Office of Information	5 Apr 90	
Government Car and Despatch	1 Apr 97	
Chancellor of the Exchequer		
Buying Agency	31 Oct 91	31 Mar 01
Central Computer & Telecom.	1 Apr 96	31 Mar 01
Central Statistical Office	19 Nov 91	31 Mar 96
National Savings	1 Jul 96	
Office of Government Commerce	1 Apr 00	31 Mar 01
Office for National Statistics	1 Apr 96	
OGC Buying Solutions	1 Apr 01	
Paymaster	1 Apr 93	1 Apr 97
Property Advisers to Civil Estate	1 Apr 96	31 Mar 01
Royal Mint	2 Apr 90	
UK Debt Management Office	1 Apr 98	
Valuation Office	30 Sep 91	
Department of Constitutional Affairs		
Court Service	3 Apr 95	
HM Land Registry	2 Jul 90	
National Archives	1 Apr 03	
Public Guardianship Office	1 Apr 01	
Public Record Office	1 Apr 92	31 Mar 03
Public Trust Office	1 Jul 94	31 Mar 01
Culture, Media and Sport		
Historic Royal Palaces	1 Oct 89	30 Mar 98
Royal Parks	1 Apr 93	

	Launched	Wound up/sold
Defence		
Armed Forces Personnel Admin.	1 Apr 97	
Army Base Repair Organisation	1 Apr 93	
Army Base Storage and Distribution	4 Apr 95	31 Mar 99
Army Personnel Centre	2 Dec 96	
Army Technical Support	19 Oct 95	1 Apr 00
Army Training & Recruiting	1 Jul 97	
British Forces Post Office	1 Jul 99	
Chemical & Biological Defence	1 Apr 91	1 Apr 95
Defence Accounts	1 Apr 91	1 Feb 96
Defence Analytical Services	1 Jul 92	
Defence Animal Centre	1 Jun 93	31 Mar 99
Defence Aviation Repair	1 Apr 99	
Defence Bills	1 Jan 96	
Defence Clothing and Textiles	22 Nov 94	1 Oct 00
Defence Codification	20 Jun 96	31 Mar 99
Defence Communication Services	1 Apr 98	
Defence Dental	1 Mar 96	
Defence Estates	18 Mar 97	
Defence Geographic and Imagery Intelligence	1 Apr 00	
Defence Housing Executive	1 Apr 99	
Defence Intelligence & Security	1 Oct 96	
Defence Medical Training	1 Apr 97	31 Mar 03
Defence Medical Education and Training	1 Apr 03	
Defence Evaluation and Research	1 Apr 95	1 Jul 01
Defence Operational Analysis	1 Jul 92	1 Apr 95
Defence Postal & Courier Service	1 Jul 92	30 Jun 99
Defence Procurement	1 Apr 99	
Defence Research	2 Apr 91	1 Apr 95
Defence Secondary Care	30 Apr 96	31 Mar 03
Defence Science and Technology Laboratory	1 Apr 01	
Defence Storage and Distribution	1 Apr 99	
Defence Transport & Movements Agency	1 Apr 99	
Defence Transport & Movements Exec.	4 Apr 95	31 Mar 99
Defence Vetting	1 Apr 97	
Disposal Services	1 Oct 94	
Duke of York's Royal Military Sch.	1 Apr 92	
Hydrographic Office	6 Apr 90	
Joint Air Reconnaissance Intell.	19 Apr 96	31 Mar 00
Logistic Information Systems	21 Nov 94	31 Mar 01
Medical Supplies	1 Mar 96	
Meteorological Office	2 Apr 90	
Military Survey	2 Apr 91	31 Mar 00
MOD Police	1 Apr 96	
Naval Aircraft Repair Org.	1 Apr 92	31 Mar 99
Naval Bases and Supply	11 Dec 96	31 Mar 01
Naval Manning	1 Jul 96	
Naval Recruiting and Training	1 Apr 95	

	Launched	*Wound up/sold*
Pay and Personnel	1 Feb 96	
Queen Victoria School	1 Apr 92	
RAF Logistic Support	9 Dec 96	31 Mar 00
RAF Maintenance Group	1 Apr 91	31 Mar 99
RAF Personnel Management	2 Feb 97	
RAF Signals Engineering	22 Nov 94	31 Mar 00
RAF Training Group	1 Apr 94	
Service Children's Education	24 Apr 91	
Ships Support	11 Nov 96	31 Mar 01
Specialist Procurement Services	1 Jun 97	31 Mar 99
Veterans Agency	8 Jun 01	
Warship Support	2 Apr 01	
Education		
Teachers' Pensions	1 Apr 92	30 Sep 96
Environment, Food and Rural Affairs ADAS	1 Apr 92	2 Apr 97
Central Science Laboratory	1 Apr 92	
Centre for Environment, Fisheries and Aquaculture Science	1 Apr 97	
Farming and Rural Conservation	1 Apr 97	31 Mar 01
Forest Enterprise – England	1 Apr 03	
Intervention Board	2 Apr 90	16 Nov 01
Meat Hygiene Service	1 Apr 95	
Pesticides Safety Directorate	1 Apr 93	
Rural Payments Agency	16 Oct 01	
Veterinary Laboratories	2 Apr 90	
Veterinary Medicines Directorate	2 Apr 90	
Office of Deputy Prime Minister		
Fire Service College[b]	1 Apr 92	
Ordnance Survey	1 May 90	
Planning Inspectorate	1 Apr 92	
Rent Office	1 Oct 99	
QEII Conference Centre	6 Jul 89	
Foreign Office		
Wilton Park	1 Sep 91	
Forestry Commission[c]		
Forest Research	1 Apr 97	
Health		
Medical Devices	29 Sep 94	31 Mar 03
Medicines Control	11 Jul 91	31 Mar 03
Medicines and Healthcare Products Regulatory	1 Apr 03	
NHS Estates	1 Apr 91	
NHS Pensions	20 Nov 92	
NHS Purchasing and Supply	1 Apr 00	

	Launched	*Wound up/sold*
Home Office		
Criminal Records Bureau	1 Apr 03	
Forensic Science Service	1 Apr 91	
HM Prison Service (see p. 165)	1 Apr 93	
UK Passport Service	2 Apr 91	
International Development		
Natural Resources Institute	2 Apr 90	1 May 96
Northern Ireland		
Business Development Service	1 Oct 96	
Compensation	1 Apr 92	
Construction Service	1 Apr 96	31 Mar 02
Driver and Vehicle Licensing	2 Aug 93	
Driver and Vehicle Testing	1 Apr 92	
Child Support	5 Apr 93	
Environment & Heritage Service	1 Apr 96	
Forensic Science	1 Sep 95	
Forest Service of NI	1 Apr 98	
Government Purchasing	1 Apr 96	31 Mar 02
Health Estates	2 Oct 95	
Industrial Research & Technology	3 Apr 95	2 Apr 02
Land Registers	1 Apr 96	
Ordnance Survey	1 Apr 92	
Planning Service	1 Apr 96	
Prison Service	1 Apr 95	
Public Record Office	3 Apr 95	
Rate Collection	1 Apr 91	
Rivers	1 Oct 96	
Roads Service	1 Apr 96	
Social Security	1 Jul 91	
Statistics and Research	1 Apr 96	
Training and Employment	2 Apr 90	30 Apr 02
Valuation and Lands	1 Apr 93	
Water	1 Apr 96	
Scotland		
Communities Scotland	1 Nov 01	
Fisheries Research Services	1 Apr 97	
Forest Enterprise	1 Apr 96	31 Mar 03
Forest Enterprise – Scotland	1 Apr 03	
Historic Scotland	2 Apr 91	
National Archives of Scotland	1 Apr 03	
Registers of Scotland	6 Apr 90	
Scottish Agricultural Science	1 Apr 92	
Scottish Court Service	3 Apr 95	
Scottish Fisheries Protection	12 Apr 91	
Scottish Prison Service	1 Apr 93	

	Launched	*Wound up/sold*
Scottish Public Pensions	1 Apr 93	
Student Awards	5 Apr 94	
Trade and Industry		
Accounts Services	1 Oct 91	1 Apr 95
Companies House	3 Oct 88	
Employment Tribunals	1 Apr 97	
Insolvency Service	21 Mar 90	
Govt. Chemistry Lab.	30 Oct 89	31 Mar 96
National Physical Lab.	3 Jul 90	1 Oct 95
Nat. Weights & Measures Lab.	18 Apr 89	
Patent Office	1 Mar 90	
Radiocommunications	2 Apr 90	31 Dec 03
Small Business Service	1 Apr 01	
Warren Spring Laboratory	20 Apr 89	31 Mar 94
Transport		
Building Research	2 Apr 90	19 Mar 97
Coastguard	1 Apr 94	31 Mar 98
Driver and Vehicle Licencing	2 Apr 90	
Driving Standards	2 Apr 90	
Highways	1 Apr 94	
Marine Safety	1 Apr 94	31 Mar 98
Maritime and Coastguard Agency	1 Apr 98	
Security Facilities Executive	15 Oct 91	30 Jun 98
Transport Research Laboratory	2 Apr 92	31 Mar 96
Vehicle Certification	2 Apr 90	
Vehicle Inspectorate	1 Aug 88	31 Mar 03
Vehicle and Operator Services	1 Apr 03	
Welsh Assembly		
Cadw: Welsh Historic Monuments	2 Apr 91	
Health Commission Wales	1 Apr 03	
Work and Pensions		
Appeals Service	3 Apr 00	
Benefits	2 Apr 91	31 Mar 02
Child Support	5 Apr 93	
Contributions	2 Apr 91	31 Mar 99
Employment Service	2 Apr 90	31 Mar 02
Information Technology Services	2 Apr 90	31 Mar 00
Jobcentre Plus	1 Apr 02	
Pensions Service	1 Apr 02	
Resettlement	24 May 89	31 Mar 96
War Pensions[d]	1 Apr 94	8 Jun 01
Others		
Chessington Computer Centre	1 Apr 93	31 Jul 96
Civil Service College	6 Jun 89	1 Apr 00

	Launched	Wound up/sold
HM Customs and Excise[a]	1 Apr 91	
HMSO	14 Dec 88	30 Sep 96
Inland Revenue[a]	1 Apr 92	
Occupational Health Service	2 Apr 90	18 Sep 96
Recruitment & Assessment Services	2 Apr 91	30 Sep 96
Security Facilities Executive	15 Oct 93	1 Jul 98

[a] Not strictly a Next Steps agency, but operating on Next Steps lines.
[b] An agency under the Home Office until April 2000.
[c] Responsible to DEFRA in England, the Scottish Parliament and the Welsh Assembly.
[d] Became the Veterans Agency and transferred to the Ministry of Defence.

SOURCES:- Executive Agencies 2004 (Cabinet Office), *Improving Management in Government: The Next Steps. A Report to the Prime Minister* (Ibbs Report), HMSO 1988; National Audit Office: *Report by the Comptroller and Auditor General – The Next Steps Initiative*, HMSO 1989.

VI
Justice and Law Enforcement

Major Criminal Justice Legislation 1979–

Criminal Attempts Act, 1981. This replaced the common law offence of attempt with a statutory offence and modified the statutory definition of criminal conspiracy. It also implemented the recommendation by the Home Affairs Committee of the House of Commons that the offence of 'sus' be repealed; it is partially replaced by a new offence of vehicle interference.

Criminal Justice Act, 1982. This created a completely new framework of custodial offences for offenders under 21, superseding imprisonment, Borstal training and detention in detention centres. It also amended the law on suspended sentences and introduced a new scale of standard maximum fines for summary offences.

Police and Criminal Evidence Act, 1984. This derives largely from various recommendations made by the Royal Commission on Criminal Procedure, the Criminal Law Revision Committee, and Lord Scarman's Report on the Brixton disorders. It reforms the law relating to police powers to stop and search, police powers of entry, search and seizure, powers of arrest and detention, the treatment, interrogation and identification of suspects, the admissibility of evidence obtained during police questioning, and public complaints against the police.

Prosecution of Offences Act, 1985. This established an independent Crown Prosecution Service under the Director of Public Prosecutions.

Public Order Act, 1986. This abolished the Common Law offences of riot, unlawful assembly and affray and established new statutory offences relating to public order.

Criminal Justice Act, 1987. Established the Serious Fraud Office.

Criminal Justice Act, 1988. This empowered the Attorney General to refer unduly light sentences to the Court of Appeal.

Criminal Justice Act, 1991. This set up a new structure for dealing with juvenile offenders, introduced a system of 'unit' fines related to ability to pay, and altered the rules on sentencing persistent offenders, making it harder for courts to take previous offences into account.

Criminal Justice Act, 1993. This repealed the provisions of the 1991 Act relating to unit fines and sentencing persistent offenders.

Criminal Justice Act, 1994. This lowered the age of consent below which homosexual acts are illegal from 21 to 18, and introduced a number of changes to the composition of police authorities.

Crime and Disorder Act, 1998. This introduced Antisocial Behaviour Orders (ASBOs) and a new category of racially aggravated offences.

Youth Justice and Criminal Evidence Act, 1999. This established a Young Offenders Panel to deal with first-time offenders, and provided for greater use of television links.

Criminal Justice and Court Services Act, 2000. This established a National Probation Service, and introduced disqualification orders to prevent people convicted of some offences from working with children.

Terrorism Act, 2000. This replaced the *Prevention of Terrorism Act, 1974*, with a new framework for detaining those suspected of terrorist offences.

Criminal Justice and Police Act, 2001. This gave police new powers to give 'penalty notices' to any person of 18 and over who committed one of ten specific offences; restricted alcohol consumption in public places, with a new summary offence; introduced travel restrictions for drug trafficking offenders; created new offences of intimidation, harming or threatening witnesses during the course of proceedings; cracked down on activities connected with prostitution; and amended the *Bail Act* so that Justices now had to give reasons why they grant bail, rather than withholding it.

Anti-Terrorism, Crime and Security Act, 2001. This gave the Government a number of new powers to deal with the threat of international terrorism, in particular the right to detain foreign nationals without trial.

Criminal Justice Act, 2003. This extended the maximum possible period of detention without charge under the *Terrorism Act, 2000* from 7 to 14 days, tightened the law on defendants who reoffend on bail or fail to turn up at court, introduced measures against jury nobbling, laid out clearer rules on sentencing, setting out the purposes and principles of sentencing in statute for the first time, introduced longer sentences for murder, sexual and violent offences, persistent offenders, firearms offences and dangerous drivers who kill, and provided for new alternatives to custody.

Prevention of Terrorism Act, 2005. This revised the *Anti-Terrorism, Crime and Security Act, 2001*, in the light of a House of Lords ruling. It introduced a system of control orders for suspects, widely (but not strictly accurately) described as house arrest.

SOURCES:– K. Smith and D. J. Keenan, *English Law* (10th edn, 1992); J. Smith and B. Hogan, *Criminal Law* (7th edn, 1992); C. McCrudden, *Individual Rights in the U.K.* (1993).

Major Legislation Relating to the Administration of Civil Justice, 1979–

The Legal Aid Act, 1979. This extended the 'green form' legal advice and assistance scheme to cover representation in inferior courts and tribunals.

The Contempt of Court Act, 1981. This implemented with modifications the Phillimore Report on Contempt of Court (Cmnd. 5794, 1974) and harmonised the law of England and Wales with the European Court's judgment in the *Sunday Times* (Thalidomide) case, 1973.

The Supreme Court Act 1981. This consolidated and significantly updated the legislation relating to the Supreme Court, superseding the Act of 1925 (see above).

Courts and Legal Services Act, 1990. This laid down a framework to give some solicitors rights of audience in the higher courts, removed the bar on solicitors becoming High Court judges, and allowed lawyers to take on cases on a 'no win, no fee' basis. It also removed the upper limit on the jurisdiction of the County Court in most cases.

Human Rights Act, 1998. This enshrined the provisions of the European Convention on Human Rights in British law, allowing British citizens to pursue civil human rights claims in British courts.

Access to Justice Act, 1999. This greatly extended 'no win, no fee' and solicitors' rights of audience in the higher courts.

Courts Act, 2003. This brought the magistrates' courts under the same management structure as the Courts' Service.

Constitutional Reform Act, 2005. This redefined the functions of the Lord Chancellor and established a Supreme Court to replace the judicial functions of the House of Lords.

SOURCES:– R. M. Jackson, *The Machinery of Justice in England* (8th edn, ed. J. R. Spencer, 1989); D. Pannick, *Judges* (1987); J. Griffith, *The Politics of the Judiciary* (4th edn, 1991); M. Berlins and C. Dyer, *The Law Machine* (3rd edn, 1989).

Cases of Political Significance

The number of lawsuits that have had major domestic political implications is not great. Most of the celebrated ones have involved trade unions and are listed on pp. 177–8. Successful election petitions are listed on p. 121. But these cases also seem to have left a significant mark on the political scene.

Mead v. Haringey [1979]. All E.R. 1016 A.C. The Court of Appeal held that it was arguable that a local authority might be in breach of its statutory duty to provide for children's education when it failed to do so by reason of the industrial action of School caretakers.

Duport Steels Ltd. v. Sirs [1980] 1 All E.R. 529. In the course of a pay dispute with the British Steel Corporation, the trade unions involved took secondary industrial action against private steel firms in the hope of causing a total shut-down of the industry. The Court of Appeal granted injunctions to the private steel companies, but the House of Lords reversed the decision, holding that the secondary action was 'in furtherance of a trade dispute' within the meaning of the *Trade Union and Labour Relations Act, 1974*. The Thatcher Government sub-sequently reversed the decision by legislation (see p. 176).

Williams v. *Home Office [1981] 1 All E.R. 151*. Following the principles laid down in *Conway* v. *Rimmer* (above), the judge ordered the disclosure of internal Home Office documents relating to experimental control units, in an action brought against the department by a prisoner.

Harman v. *Home Office [1982] 2 All E.R. 151*. A solicitor was given confidential policy documents by way of discovery in the course of a civil action brought against the Home Office, and undertook not to disclose them outside the course of the proceedings. The documents were read out in open court and the solici-tor then showed them to a journalist. The House of Lords affirmed, by a 3–2 majority, the lower courts' finding that this amounted to contempt of court.

Norwich City Council v. *Secretary of State for the Environment [1982] 1 All E.R. 737*. The Court of Appeal upheld the exercise of default powers by a minister against a local authority in circumstances where the minister adjudged the authority to have been dilatory in fulfilling statutory obligations to sell council houses to tenants.

O'Reilly v. *Mackman [1982] 3 All E.R. 1182 (H.L.)* There is a fundamental dis-tinction between private law and public law proceedings which cannot be evaded by seeking a private law remedy against a public authority in circumstances where a public law remedy is appropriate.

Bromley London Borough Council v. *GLC [1983] A.C. 768 (H.L.)*. The GLC 'Fares Fair' case. The Council acted ultra vires the *Transport (London) Act, 1969*, and in breach of its fiduciary duty towards ratepayers by its decision to cut fares by 25%.

Pickwell v. *Camden Borough Council [1983] 1 All E.R. 602*. A local authority, responding to a strike by its employees, agreed a pay settlement that turned out to be more generous than the settlement agreed nationally. The Queen's Bench Divisional Court denied the district auditor's claim that the action of the coun-cil was ultra vires.

Air Canada v. *Secretary of State for Trade [1983] 1 All E.R. 910*. Action brought by foreign airlines disputing increases in fees at Heathrow Airport. The House of Lords declined to order disclosure of ministerial documents on the grounds that the plaintiffs had failed to show that the documents were likely to assist their case.

The Council of Civil Service Unions v. *Minister for the Civil Service [1984] Industrial Cases Reports 1985, 15*. The House of Lords decided that the 'reasonable expectations' of the Civil Service unions to be consulted before the Government banned union membership at GCHQ were overridden by considerations of national security. However, their Lordships held, contrary to the Government's contentions, that ministerial actions based on the royal prerogative could, in principle, be reviewed by the courts.

Attorney General v. *Guardian Newspapers Ltd [1987] 3 All E.R. 316; Attorney General* v. *Guardian Newspapers (no. 2) [1988] 3 All E.R. 545.* The House of Lords first upheld by a 3–2 majority the Attorney General's efforts to prevent publication of extracts from the book 'Spycatcher' on the grounds that a member of the Security Service owed a lifelong duty of confidentiality to the Crown. In the second case they removed the ban on the grounds that the material was now in the public domain.

Barber v. *Guardian Royal Exchange Insurance Group [1990] 2 All E.R. 660; E.C.J. C-262/88.* The European Court of Justice ruled since occupational pensions constitute a form of pay, any unjustified discrimination in benefits paid under the scheme are illegal (with implications for different pension ages). The ruling was modified in the case of *Neath* v. *Hugh Sleeper Ltd E.C.J. C-152/1991*, which ruled that actuarial factors such as women's longer life expectancy could be taken into account.

Brind v. *Secretary of State for the Home Department [1991] 1 All E.R. 720.* The House of Lords upheld the decision of the Home Secretary banning the direct broadcasting of words spoken in support of terrorist organisations (in effect banning interviews with Sinn Fein).

Factortame Ltd v. *Secretary of State for Transport [1991] E.C.J. C-213/89.* The European Court of Justice ruled in a case concerning a Spanish fishing firm that where a British Act of Parliament conflicts with European legislation the Act of Parliament is not enforceable in the courts.

Regina v. *Bartle and the Commissioner of Police for the Metropolis and others EX Parte Pinochet [1999].* The House of Lords ruled that the former ruler of Chile General Pinochet was not immune from prosecution or extradition, although he did have immunity for crimes committed before 1988.

A (FC) and others v. *Secretary of State for the Home Department [2004] UKHL 56.* This related to a number of non-British citizens detained at Belmarsh prison indefinitely without trial under the *Anti-terrorism, Crime and Security Act, 2001.* The House of Lords concluded that orders made on this act could not be compliant with the European Convention on Human Rights.

Principal Judges

Lord Chancellor
(See p. 22)

Vice Chancellor

1976	Sir R. Megarry	1994	Sir R. Scott
1985	Sir N. Browne-Wilkinson	2000	Sir R. Morritt
1991	Sir D. Nicholls		

Master of the Rolls

1962	Ld Denning
1982	Sir J. Donaldson (*Ld*)
1992	Sir T. Bingham
1996	Ld Woolf
2000	Ld Phillips of Worth Matravers

President of the Family Division

1971	Sir G. Baker
1979	Sir J. Arnold
1988	Sir S. Brown
1999	Dame E. Butler-Sloss

Lord Chief Justice

1971	Ld Widgery
1980	Ld Lane
1992	Ld Taylor of Gosforth
1996	Ld Bingham
2000	Ld Woolf

Lord Chief Justice of Northern Ireland

1971	Sir R. Lowry (*Ld*)
1988	Sir B. Hutton
1997	Sir R. Carswell
2004	Sir B. Kerr

Lord President of the Court of Session

1974	G. Emslie (*Ld*)
1989	Ld Hope
1996	Ld Rodger
2001	Ld Cullen

Lord Justice Clerk

1972	Ld Wheatley
1985	Ld Ross
1997	Ld Cullen
2001	Ld Gill

Lords of Appeal in Ordinary

1964–82	Ld Wilberforce	1992–96	Ld Woolf
1968–85	Ld Diplock	1993–99	Ld Lloyd
1969–80	Vt Dilhorne	1994–98	Ld Nolan
1972–80	Ld Salmon	1994–	Ld Nicholls of Birkenhead
1974–81	Ld Edmund-Davies	1995–	Ld Steyn
1975–85	Ld Fraser of Tullybelton	1995–	Ld Hoffman
1975–82	Ld Russell of Killowen	1996–	Ld Hope of Craighead
1977–96	Ld Keith of Kinkel	1996–2001	Ld Clyde
1977–86	Ld Scarman	1997–2004	Ld Hutton
1979–80	Ld Lane	1997–	Ld Saville of Newdigate
1980–86	Ld Roskill	1998–2004	Ld Hobhouse of Woodborough
1980–92	Ld Bridge of Harwich		
1981–91	Ld Brandon of Oakbrook	1998–2004	Ld Millett
1982–86	Ld Brightman	1999–2000	Ld Phillips of Worth Matravers
1982–94	Ld Templeman		
1985–93	Ld Griffiths	2000–	Ld Bingham
1985–87	Ld Mackay of Clashfern	2000–	Ld Scott of Foscote
1986–93	Ld Ackner	2001–	Ld Rodger of Earlsferry
1986–98	Ld Goff of Chieveley	2002–	Ld Walker of Gestingthorpe
1986–92	Ld Oliver of Aylmerton		
1988–96	Ld Jauncey of Tullichettle	2004–	Lady Hale of Richmond
1988–94	Ld Lowry	2004–	Ld Carswell
1991–2000	Ld Browne-Wilkinson	2004–	Ld Brown of Eaton-under-Heywood
1992–97	Ld Mustill		
1992–2002	Ld Slynn of Hadley		

Any peers of Parliament as are holding or have held, high judicial office are also entitled to take part in cases before the House of Lords.

Lords Justices of Appeal

1969–83	Sir J. Megaw	1988–92	Sir P. Taylor
1970–83	Sir D. Buckley	1988–99	Dame E. Butler-Sloss
1971–85	Sir J. Stephenson	1988–2000	Sir M. Stuart-Smith
1971–80	Sir A. Orr	1988–97	Sir C. Staughton
1971–80	Sir E. Roskill	1988–95	Sir M. Mann
1972–86	Sir F. Lawton	1989–95	Sir D. Farquharson
1974–83	Sir R. Ormrod	1989–97	Sir A. McCowan
1974–83	Sir P. Browne	1989–2000	Sir R. Beldam
1974–79	Sir G. Lane	1990–97	Sir A. Leggatt
1975–80	Sir W. Goff	1991–94	Sir M. Nolan
1975–80	Sir N. Bridge	1991–94	Sir R. Scott
1975–82	Sir S. Shaw	1992–95	Sir J. Steyn
1976–84	Sir G. Waller	1992–	Sir P. Kennedy
1976–85	Sir R. Cumming-Bruce	1992–95	Sir L. Hoffman
1977–85	Sir E. Eveleigh	1992–99	Sir D. Hirst
1978–81	Sir H. Brandon	1992–2004	Sir S. Brown
1978–82	Sir S. Templeman	1992–2000	Sir A. Evans
1979–82	Sir J. Donaldson	1992–	Sir C. Rose
1979–82	Sir J. Brightman	1993–97	Sir J. Waite
1980–86	Sir D. Ackner	1993–2000	Sir J. Roch
1980–84	Sir R. Dunn	1993–	Sir P. Gibson
1980–86	Sir P. Oliver	1993–98	Sir J. Hobhouse
1980–93	Sir T. Watkins	1993–2002	Sir D. Henry
1980–89	Sir P. O'Connor	1994–98	Sir M. Saville
1980–85	Sir H. Griffiths	1994–2000	Sir S. Thomas
1981–92	Sir M. Fox	1994–2000	Sir A. Morritt
1981–89	Sir M. Kerr	1995–2001	Sir P. Otton
1982–89	Sir J. May	1995–	Sir R. Auld
1982–91	Sir C. Slade	1995–	Sir M. Pill
1982–93	Sir F. Purchas	1995–2004	Sir W. Aldous
1982–86	Sir R. Goff	1995–	Sir A. Ward
1982–99	Sir B. Dillon	1995–99	Sir M. Hutchison
1983–88	Sir S. Brown	1995–2004	Sir K. Schiemann
1983–92	Sir R. Parker	1995–99	Sir N. Phillips
1983–85	Sir N. Browne-Wilkinson	1995–	Sir M. Thorpe
1984–89	Sir D. Croom-Johnson	1996–	Sir M. Potter
1984–93	Sir A. Lloyd	1996–	Sir H. Brooke
1985–92	Sir M. Mustill	1996–	Sir I. Judge
1985–96	Sir B. Neill	1996–	Sir M. Waller
1985–95	Sir I. Glidewell	1996–	Sir J. Mummery
1985–2001	Sir M. Nourse	1997–2004	Sir C. Mantell
1985–95	Sir A. Balcombe	1997–	Sir J. Chadwick
1985–94	Sir R. Gibson	1997–2002	Sir R. Walker
1986–91	Sir D. Nicholls	1997–	Sir R. Buxton
1986–92	Sir T. Bingham	1997–	Sir A. May
1986–92	Sir J. Stocker	1997–	Sir S. Tuckey
1986–92	Sir H. Woolf	1998–	Sir A. Clarke
1987–96	Sir P. Russell	1999–	Sir J. Laws

Lords Justices of Appeal (*contd.*)

1999–	Sir S. Sedley	2002–	Sir R. Carnwath
1999–	Sir J. Mance	2002–	Sir S. Baker
1999–2004	Dame B. Hale	2002–	Dame J. Smith
2000–	Sir D. Latham	2003–	Sir R. Thomas
2000–04	Sir J. Kay	2003–	Sir R. Jacob
2000–	Sir B. Rix	2004–	Sir N. Wall
2000–	Sir J. Parker	2004–	Sir D. Neuberger
2000–	Dame M. Arden	2004–	Sir M. Kay
2000–	Sir D. Keene	2004–	Sir A. Hooper
2001–	Sir J. Dyson	2004–	Sir W. Gage
2001–	Sir A. Longmore		

The Lord High Chancellor (President), the Lord Chief Justice, the Master of the Rolls, and the President of the Family Division serve *ex officio* on the Court of Appeal.

SOURCES:– *The Law List*; *Who Was Who*; *Who's Who*; *Whitaker's Almanack*; <www.dca.gov.uk/judicial/senjudfr.htm#senjud>.

Other Legal and Law Enforcement Officials

Law Commission
Chairman

1978	Sir M. Kerr
1981	Sir R. Gibson
1985	Sir R. Beldam
1990	Sir P. Gibson
1993	Sir H. Brooke
1996	Dame Mary Arden
1999	Sir R. Carnwath
2002	Sir R. Toulson

Police Complaints Board
Chairman

1977	Ld Plowden
1981	Sir C. Philips

(Police Complaints Authority)

1985	Sir C. Clothier
1989	F. Petre
1992	Sir L. Peach
1996	P. Moorehouse
2000	Sir A. Graham

(Independent Police Complaints Commission)

2004	N. Hardwick

Director of Public Prosecutions

1978	(Sir) T. Hetherington
1987	A. Green
1992	(Dame) Barbara Mills
1998	D. Calvert-Smith
2003	K. Macdonald

Serious Fraud Office
Director

1988	Sir J. Wood
1990	Barbara Mills
1992	G. Staple
1997	Rosalind Wright
2003	R. Wardle

Monopolies and Mergers Commission
Chairman

1975	(Sir) J. Le Quesne
1988	Sir S. Lipworth
1993	(Sir) G. Odgers

(Competition Commission)

1998	D. Morris
2004	P. Geroski

Commissioner of Metropolitan Police

1977	(Sir) D. McNee
1982	Sir K. Newman
1987	(Sir) P. Imbert
1993	(Sir) P. Condon
2000	Sir J. Stevens
2005	Sir I. Blair

Criminal Injuries Compensation Board
 Chairman

| 1975 | M. Ogden |
| 1989 | Ld Carlisle of Bucklow |

(Criminal Injuries Compensation Authority)
 Chief Executive

| 1996 | P. Spurgeon |
| 1999 | H. Webber |

Criminal Cases Review Commission

| 1997 | Sir F. Crawford |
| 2003 | G. Zellick |

Procurator General and Treasury Solicitor

1975	(Sir) B. Hall
1980	Sir M. Kerry
1984	(Sir) J. Bailey
1988	J. Nursaw
1992	G. Hooke
1997	A. Hammond
2000	Juliet Wheldon

Clerk of the Crown in Chancery[1]

1885	(Sir) K. Mackenzie
1915	(Sir) C. Schuster
1944	(Sir) A. Napier
1954	(Sir) G. Coldstream
1968	(Sir) D. Dobson
1977	(Sir) W. Bourne
1982	(Sir) D. Oulton
1989	(Sir) T. Legg
1998	Sir H. Phillips
2004	A. Allan

[1] Full title, Permanent Secretary to the Chancellor and Clerk of the Crown in Chancery. *See also* p. 136.

Royal Commissions, Committees of Inquiry and Tribunals

Investigatory Process

The public investigation of problems can take a number of forms – Royal Commissions, Tribunals, ad hoc departmental Committees and special parliamentary conferences or committees. This chapter does not deal with purely parliamentary bodies such as the Speaker's Conferences (on Electoral Reform (see p. 118) and on Devolution (see p. 223)) or like the Select Committees set up from time to time by the House of Commons and/or the House of Lords. But there is an attempt at an exhaustive listing of all domestic Royal Commissions. There is also an arbitrary selection from the many ad hoc and statutory Committees of Inquiry appointed since 1979. It is, however, important to remember that the decision whether to refer a problem to a Royal Commission or a Committee is not necessarily determined by the importance of the subject. Royal Commissions are listed fully here because the number is not excessive. Departmental Committees, which have been much more numerous, often deal with relatively narrow and limited matters; the selection here covered only a few which seem plainly to be as important as the average Royal Commission. No reference is made to the committees and sub-committees appointed by

Royal Commissions and by standing governmental advisory bodies, though these include some reports of importance.

Advisory Committees appointed by the Government are of two basic types (apart from those which are just internal committees of Civil Servants): (a) standing committees, set up to give advice on such matters, usually within some general class of subjects, as may from time to time be referred to them or otherwise come to their attention; and (b) ad hoc committees, which are appointed to carry out some specific mandate and which come to an end when that mandate is discharged. These committees may be appointed directly by the Minister in his own name or indirectly in the name of the Crown. Finally, standing and ad hoc committees may both be appointed in two different ways: namely, by virtue of conventional or (in the case of the Crown) prerogative powers, or by virtue of authority conferred by Parliament by means of a statute.

Royal Commissions

Royal Commissions are ad hoc advisory committees formally appointed by the Crown by virtue of its prerogative powers. All such committees appointed since the mid 1970s are listed in the table below, along with the name of their chairman, their size, the dates of their appointment and adjournment, and the Command number of their final report. There is no 'official' title for a Royal Commission, so that usage may vary slightly from the names given below. Where there were two successive chairmen for a single committee, both are listed. The size of a Royal Commission is given as of the date of its appointment; subsequent changes in membership are not shown. The date of appointment is the date on which the Royal Warrant appointing the committee was signed, and the date of adjournment is the date of signature of the last report issued (or, failing that, the date of its presentation to the House of Commons). Command numbers in the late twentieth century form part of successive series, each of which is marked by a different abbreviation of the word 'Command' as follows:

1956–86: Cmnd. 1 to Cmnd. 9271
1986–: Cm. 1–

Gambling	Vt Rothschild	10 Feb 76	Jul 78	7200
National Health Service	Sir A. Merrison	16 May 76	Jul 79	7613
Legal Services	Sir H. Benson	15 Jul 76	Oct 79	7648
Criminal Procedures	Sir C. Philips	16 Dec 77	Jan 81	8092
Criminal Justice	Ld Runciman	11 Jun 91	Jul 93	2263
Care of the elderly	Sir S. Sutherland	12 Dec 97	Mar 99	4192
Reform of the House of Lords	Ld Wakeham	11 Feb 99	Jan 00	4534

Permanent and Operating Commissions

Certain Royal Commissions have an enduring existence:

The Royal Commission on Historical Manuscripts set up in 1869 sits under the ex officio Chairmanship of the Master of the Rolls. It was reconstituted with extended powers in 1959. Its task is to advise and assist in the preservation of historical manuscripts and to publish them.

The Royal Commission on Ancient and Historical Monuments was set up for England in 1908 with similar bodies for Scotland (reconstituted 1948) and Wales and Monmouthshire. Their task is to maintain an inventory of Ancient Monuments.

The Royal Fine Arts Commission was set up in 1924 (reconstituted in 1933 and 1946) and the Royal Fine Art Commission for Scotland in 1927 (reconstituted 1948): their task is to inquire into questions of public amenity and artistic importance.

The Royal Commission for the Exhibition of 1851, surviving from the winding up of the affairs of the Great Exhibitions, still distributes the income from surplus funds to promote scientific and artistic education.

The Royal Commission on Environmental Pollution was established in 1970. It produces regular reports on pollution issues – 25 by early 2005.

In 1994 The Committee on Standards in Public Life was set up (Chair: Ld Nolan 1994–97; Ld Neill 1997–2001; Sir N. Wicks 2001–04; Sir A. Graham 2004–). It has produced ten major reports: Cm. 2850/95; Cm. 3270/96; Cm. 3702/97; Cm. 4057/98; Cm. 4413/99; Cm. 4817/00; HL68/01; Cm. 5663/02; Cm. 5775/03; and Cm. 6407/05.

Following the Government's White Paper *Modernising Parliament: Reforming the House of Lords* (Cm. 4183, January 1999) the House of Lords Appointments Commission was established in 2000 to identify candidates to be non-party peers ('People's Peers') and to vet the nominations of political nominees to verify that there was nothing improper about the appointment (Chair: Ld Stevenson 2000–).

Departmental Committees

Departmental Committees are ad hoc advisory committees appointed by Ministers by virtue of their conventional powers. As such they are the direct counterpart of Royal Commissions. In the table below are listed some of the more important Departmental Committees appointed since 1979. As with Royal Commissions, there is no 'official' title for a Departmental Committee, so usage may vary slightly; where there were two successive chairmen, both are listed; and the dates of appointment and report as well as the Command number are derived in the same manner as for Royal Commissions.

A Select List of Departmental Committees

In the absence of any single official title for a Committee we have tried to select the most commonly used short title. The Command number given is that of the final report. The last four are not strictly speaking Departmental Committees.

	Chairman	Date appointed	Date of report no.	Cd.
Age of Consent	Sir G. Waller	Dec 75	Apr 81	8216
Genetic Manipulation	Sir G. Wolstenholme	Dec 76	Sep 82	8665
Insolvency Law	Sir K. Cork	Jan 77	Jun 82	8558
Functioning of Financial Institutions	Sir H. Wilson	Jan 77	Jun 80	7937
Financing of Small Firms	Sir H. Wilson	Jan 77	Mar 78	7503
Obscenity and Film Censorship	B. Williams	Jul 77	Nov 79	7772
Ownership of Agricultural Land	Ld Northfield	Sep 77	Jul 79	7599
Police Pay	Ld Edmund-Davies	Oct 77	Jul 78	7283
Police Interrogation in Northern Ireland	H. Bennett	Jun 78	Mar 79	7497
Public Records	Sir D. Wilson	Aug 78	Mar 81	804
UK Prison Service	Sir J. D. May	Nov 78	Oct 79	7673
Education of Ethnic Minority Children	A. Rampton Ld Swann	Mar 79	Feb 85	9403
Local Government in Scotland	Sir A. Stodart	Dec 79	Jan 81	8115
Postgraduate Education	Sir P. Swinnerton-Dyer	Dec 79	Apr 82	8537
University Scientific Research	Sir A. Merrison	Mar 80	Jun 82	8567
Police Complaints	Ld Plowden	Jul 80	Mar 81	8193
Brixton Disorders	Ld Scarman	Apr 81	Nov 81	8427
Civil Service Pay	Sir J. Megaw	Jun 81	Jul 82	8590
Review of 1976 Terrorism Act	Earl Jellicoe	Mar 82	Feb 83	8803
Cable Television	Ld Hunt of Tanworth	Apr 82	Oct 82	8679
Fertilisation of Human Embryos	Dame M. Warnock	Jul 82	Jul 84	9314
Falkland Islands Review	Ld Franks	Jul 82	Jan 83	8787
Protection of Military Information	Sir H. Beach	Feb 83	Dec 83	9112
Education of Children from Minority Groups	Ld Swann	Mar 87	Mar 85	9453
Crowd Safety at Football Grounds	Sir O. Popplewell	May 85	Jan 86	9710
Academic Valuation of Degree Courses	Sir N. Lindop	Apr 84	Apr 85	9501
Conduct of Local Authority Business	D. Widdecombe	Feb 85	Jun 86	9797
Financing the B.B.C.	A. Peacock	Mar 85	Jul 86	9824
Public Health in England	Sir D. Acheson	Jan 86	Jan 88	289
Child Abuse in Cleveland	Dame E. Butler-Sloss	Jul 87	Jul 88	412
King's Cross Underground Fire	D. Fennell	Nov 87	Nov 88	499
Parole System in England & Wales	Ld Carlisle of Bucklow	Sep 87	Feb 89	532
Banking Services	R. Jack	Jan 87	Feb 88	622
War Crimes	Sir T. Hetherington	Feb 88	Jul 89	744
Clapham Junction Railway Accident	A. Hidden	Dec 88	Nov 90	820
N. Ireland Emergency Provisions Acts	Vt Colville		Jul 90	1115
The Piper Alpha Disaster	Ld Cullen	Jul 88	Nov 90	1330
River Safety	J. Hayes	Dec 91	Jul 92	1991
Press Self-Regulation	Sir D. Calcutt	Jul 92	Jan 93	2135
Police Responsibilities and Rewards	Sir P. Sheehy	Jul 92	Jun 93	2263
Pollution from Merchant Shipping	Ld Donaldson	Jan 93	May 94	2560
Escapes from Whitemoor Prison	Sir J. Woodcock	Sep 94	Dec 94	2741
Sinking of MV *Derbyshire*	Ld Donaldson	Mar 95	Dec 95	3128
Criminal Appeals and Miscarriages of Justice in Scotland	Sir S. Sutherland	Nov 94	Jun 96	3245
Dunblane School Massacre	Ld Cullen	Mar 96	Oct 96	3386
Review of Hillsborough Inquiry	Sir M. Stewart-Smith	Jun 97	Feb 98	3878
Crown Prosecution Service	Sir I. Glidewell	Jul 97	Jun 98	3960
Money in Politics	Ld Neill	Nov 97	Oct 98	4057

	Chairman	Date appointed	Date of report no.	Cd.
Electoral Systems	Ld Jenkins	Dec 97	Nov 98	4090
Murder of Stephen Lawrence	Sir W. Macpherson	Jul 97	Feb 99	4262
Hunting with Dogs	Lord Burns	Dec 99	Jun 00	4763
Hinduja passport	Sir A. Hammond	Jan 01	Mar 01	HC287
Funding of health care	D. Wanless	Mar 01	Apr 02	
Death of David Kelly	Ld Hutton	Jul 03	Jan 04	HC247
Intelligence on WMD	Ld Butler	Jan 04	Jul 04	HC 898
Home Office issue of Passport (D. Blunkett)	Sir A. Budd	Dec 04	Dec 04	HC 175

(Political) Honours Scrutiny Committee 1924–2005

The Political Honours Scrutiny Committee was established in 1924, following scandals over the 'sale of honours'. It was to 'consider before they are submitted to the King, the names and particulars of persons recommended for appointment to any dignity or honours on account of political services ... and to report ... whether such persons ... are fit and proper persons to be recommended'. Its activities were virtually never reported but they continued after H. Wilson announced the ending of 'political honours' in 1966 and again in 1974. In 1976, following agitation over Sir H. Wilson's resignation honours list, there was a complete change of membership. In 1998 its name was changed to the Honours Scrutiny Committee. From 2000 the House of Lords Appointments Commission took over the scrutiny of appointments to the House of Lords. In 2005 the Committee was wound up, and its functions largely transferred to the Appointments Commission. It always had three members:

1976–92	Ld Shackleton *(Ch 1976–92)*	1987–99	Ld Pym *(Ch 1992–99)*
		1992–99	Ld Cledwyn
1976–87	Ld Carr	1992–2005	Ld Thomson *(Ch 1999–)*
1976–87	Ld Banks	1998–2005	Bness Dean
1987–92	Ld Grimond	2000–05	Ld Hurd

SOURCE:- *Whitaker's Almanack.*

Intelligence Services

MI5 (the Security Service) and MI6 (the Secret Intelligence Service) can trace their origins back to 1909, and the establishment of the Secret Service Bureau with domestic and foreign intelligence arms. In 1916 the internal arm, known as MO 5, was reorganised within the the Military Intelligence Directorate, and became known as MI5. The Secret Intelligence Service was given the acronym MI 1 (c) in 1916, but by the 1920s had become known as MI6. In 1989 MI5 was put on a statutory footing by the *Security Service Act*. In 1994 MI6 was put on a similar statutory footing by the *Intelligence Services Act*, which also established a joint committee of both houses to bring the intelligence services under parliamentary scrutiny for the first time.

Security Service (MI5)		**Secret Intelligence Service (MI6)**	
Director General		*Director General*	
1972	(Sir) M. Hanley	1978	(Sir) A. Franks
1979	Sir H. Smith	1981	(Sir) C. Figurres
1981	(Sir) J. Jones	1985	(Sir) C. Curwen
1985	Sir A. Duff	1989	(Sir) C. McColl
1988	Sir P. Walker	1993	(Sir) D. Spedding
1992	Mrs S. Rimington	1999	(Sir) R. Dearlove
1996	(Sir) S. Lander	2004	J. Scarlett
2002	Eliza Manningham-Buller		

SOURCES:– <www.mi5.gov.uk>; *Whitaker's Almanack.*

Security Commission

The Security Commission was set up by Sir A. Douglas-Home in January 1964. In a statement to the House of Commons (HC Deb vol 687, col 1271) he set out terms of reference; 'If so requested by the Prime Minister, to investigate and report upon the circumstances in which a breach of security is known to have occurred in the public service, and upon any related failure of departmental security arrangements or neglect of duty; and in the light of any such investigation, to advise whether any change in security arrangements is necessary or desireable.' There were minor amendments to these terms of reference in 1965 and 1969 to take account of difficulties investigating matters which were before the courts. Its role was redefined under the *Security Service Act*, 1989.

	Chairman
1971	Ld Diplock
1982	Ld Bridge of Harwich
1985	Ld Griffiths
1992	Sir A. Lloyd (Ld)
1999	Dame E. Butler-Sloss

Number of Judges
(England and Wales)

Year	*Lords of Appeal Lord Justices & ex officio judges*	*High Court Judges*	*County Court/Circuit Judges*
1980	31	75	333
1990	40	83	420
2000	51	101	553
2004	52	107	609

SOURCES:– *Criminal Statistics, Civil Judicial Statistics.*

Volume of Civil Proceedings
Appellate Courts: Appeals entered in selected years since 1978, by nature of court

	1978	1988	1990	1999	2000	2001	2002	2003
Nature of court								
Judicial Committee								
of the Privy Council	52	61	52	69	90	102	103	73
House of Lords:								
From courts in								
England & Wales	77	75	54	77	63	80	243	228
Elsewhere	6	15	7	5	16	4	10	9
Court of Appeal:								
Civil Division	1,401	1,645	1,580	1,339	1,420	1,358	1,251	1,276
Criminal Division[a]–			6,307	8,274	7,740	7,440	9,720	7,451
High Court:								
Chancery Division–	74	111	161	149	147	107	145	120
Queen's Bench								
Division[b]	510	1,800	2,738	5,566	4,734	5,293	5,947	6,899
Family Division–	247	240	235	21	12	13	62[c]	60[c]
Total	8,466	11,182	11,134	15,500	14,222	14,397	15,479	16,116

[a] Includes applications.
[b] Includes judicial review, appeals by way of case stated and statutory appeals.
[c] Includes appeals under s94 *Children Act* 1989.

The Growth of Judicial Review

Applications for leave to apply for judicial review			
1979	410	1992	2,439
1980	491	1993	2,886
1981	533	1994	3,208
1982	685	1995	3,604
1983	850	1996	3,901
1984	915	1997	3,848
1985	1,169	1998	4,539
1986	816	1999	4,959
1987	1,529	2000	4,247
1988	1,229	2001	4,732
1989	1,580	2002	5,377
1990	2,129	2003	5,949
1991	2,028		

SOURCE:– *Judicial Statistics*.

Recorded Crime, 1980–2004

England and Wales

	Violent crime (000s)	Property crime (000s)	Car[a] crime (000s)	Total crime (000s)
1980	133	2,547	619	2,688
1981	140	2,815	712	2,964
1982	151	3,102	800	3,262
1983	154	3,079	750	3,247
1984	159	3,325	800	3,499
1985	171	3,424	846	3,612
1986	178	3,653	988	3,847
1987	199	3,674	1,048	3,892
1988	216	3,477	987	3,716
1989	240	3,603	1,022	3,871
1990	250	4,263	1,267	4,544
1991	265	4,976	1,495	5,276
1992	284	5,268	1,549	5,592
1993	294	5,191	1,523	5,526
1994	310	4,895	1,384	5,253
1995	311	4,739	1,322	5,100
1996	345	4,636	1,293	5,037
1997	347	4,191	1,118	4,598
1997/98[b,c]	353	4,131	1,096	4,545
1998/99[c]	332	4,087	1,072	4,482
1998/99[d]	606	4,304	1,078	5,109
1999/00	703	4,411	1,044	5,301
2000/01	733	4,261	968	5,171
2001/02	813	4,525	983	5,525
2002/03[e,f]	992	4,694	976	5,899
2003/04	1,109	4,610	889	5,935

[a] Vehicle-related crime includes aggravated vehicle taking, theft from a vehicle and theft or unauthorised taking of a motor vehicle.

[b] Change from calendar year to financial year.

[c] The number of crimes recorded in that financial year using the coverage and rules in use until 31 March 1998.

[d] The number of crimes recorded in that financial year using the expanded offence coverage and revised counting rules which came into effect on 1 April 1998.

[e] Numbers of recorded crimes will be affected by changes in reporting and recording. The national impact of recording changes in 2002/03 was estimated to be 10% for total recorded crime. This impact will vary for different types of offences.

[f] Some forces have revised their 2002/03 data and totals may not therefore agree with those previously published.

SOURCES:– *Criminal Statistics*, <www.homeoffice.gov.uk/rds/pdfs04/hosb1004.pdf>.

British Crime Survey, 1981–2004

England and Wales

Numbers (thousands) and percentage changes

	1981	*1991*	*1995*[a]	*1997*	*1999*	*2001/02*	*2002/03*	*2003/04*
PROPERTY CRIME								
Vandalism[b]	2,713	2,759	3,366	2,866	2,861	2,600	2,530	2,465
Burglary[c]	749	1,380	1,770	1,621	1,290	967	972	943
All vehicle thefts	1,751	3,845	4,350	3,511	3,009	2,491	2,361	2,121
Bicycle theft	216	569	673	541	400	367	358	370
Other household theft	1,518	1,857	2,267	2,024	1,880	1,443	1,358	1,283
Theft from the person	434	438	680	621	636	603	689	622
Other thefts of personal property	1,586	1,739	2,069	1,935	1,554	1,405	1,342	1,321
VIOLENCE								
Common assault (includes some with minor injuries)[d]	1,403	1,751	2,924	2,455	2,322	1,722	1,699	1,654
Wounding	508	624	914	804	650	648	708	655
Robbery	164	182	339	334	406	356	302	283
All BCS violence[e]	2,160	2,635	4,256	3,675	3,436	2,799	2,798	2,708
ALL HOUSEHOLD CRIME	6,947	10,410	12,426	10,562	9,441	7,868	7,578	7,181
ALL PERSONAL CRIME	4,094	4,733	6,926	6,148	5,569	4,733	4,741	4,535
Old comparable crime[f]	6,535	9,796	12,093	10,297	9,253	8,031	7,920	7,459
Comparable crime[f]	n/a	n/a	n/a	n/a	11,575	9,753	9,619	9,113
ALL BCS CRIME	11,041	15,142	19,353	16,711	15,009	12,601	12,319	11,716

[a] Note that estimates for 1995 to 2002/03 vary from those previously published due to revisions to the weighting of the data and revisions to population and numbers of household estimates. Figures for 1991 to 2003/04 are based on estimates of population and the number of households in England and Wales, that have been revised in light of the 2001 Census.

[b] For vandalism, burglary, vehicle thefts, bicycle thefts and other household thefts the 2003/04 numbers are derived by multiplying offence rates (incidence rates) by 22,320,681 households in England and Wales. For common assault, wounding, robbery, snatch thefts, stealth thefts, all BCS violence and other thefts of personal property the 2003/04 numbers are derived by multiplying incidence rates by 42,333,000 adults in England and Wales.

[c] Burglary with entry plus attempted burglary add up to total burglary. Burglary with loss plus attempts and no loss also add up to total burglary.

[d] The BCS common assault definition includes minor injuries. From 2002/03 the recorded crime definition does not include minor injuries.

[e] All BCS violence includes common assault, wounding, robbery and snatch theft.

[f] Old comparable crime includes vandalism, burglary, all vehicle thefts, bicycle theft, snatch and stealth thefts from the person, wounding and robbery. Comparable crime also includes common assault which became a notifiable offence from 1 April 1998.

Prison Population in England and Wales

	Average total in custody[a]	*Of which under sentence (30 Jun)*	*Violence against the person*	Sentenced prisoners convicted of			
				Rape and other sexual offences	*Burglary*	*Robbery*	*Drug offences*
1979	42,220	35,728	6,459	1,692	10,285	2,363	768
1980	42,264	36,637	6,869	1,654	10,498	2,362	813
1981	43,311	36,669	6,738	1,510	11,096	2,495	854
1982	43,754	36,000	6,572	1,394	10,937	2,554	995
1983	43,772	35,438	6,725	1,412	10,571	2,542	1,181
1984	43,349	35,496	6,639	1,486	9,938	2,694	1,631
1985	46,278	37,344	7,144	1,663	10,096	3,027	2,343
1986	46,889	36,450	7,554	1,897	8,848	3,429	2,825
1987	48,963	39,303	8,239	2,329	8,954	3,847	3,456
1988	49,949	38,548	8,833	2,692	7,914	3,988	3,207
1989	48,610	38,013	8,667	3,005	7,106	4,233	3,313
1990	45,636	35,220	7,678	3,029	5,936	4,103	3,147
1991	45,897	35,114	7,134	3,109	5,121	4,036	2,856
1992	45,817	35,564	7,077	3,156	5,400	4,230	3,158
1993	44,565	33,046	7,489	3,180	4,729	4,933	3,208
1994	48,794	35,763	7,992	3,279	5,135	5,185	3,512
1995	51,047	39,379	8,781	3,668	5,953	5,372	4,256
1996	55,281	43,055	9,585	3,951	6,422	5,715	5,755
1997	61,114	48,805	10,424	4,077	8,077	6,438	7,174
1998	65,298	52,269	10,944	4,795	8,656	6,626	7,893
1999	64,771	51,393	10,858	2,946	8,780	6,331	8,169
2000	64,602	53,180	11,217	5,090	8,982	6,353	8,473
2001	66,301	54,212	11,744	5,107	8,570	6,784	9,148
2002	70,861	57,306	12,202	5,305	9,151	7,506	10,055

[a] Including those in police cells and unsentenced prisoners.

HM Chief Inspector of Prisons
1987	S. Tumim
1995	Sir D. Ramsbotham
2001	Anne Owers

Director General of the Prison Service
1993	D. Lewis
1995	R. Tilt
1999	M. Narey
2003	P. Wheatley

Parole Board, 1967–

Chairman

1967	Ld Hunt
1974	Sir L. Petch
1979	Ld Harris of Greenwich
1982	Ld Windlesham
1988	Vt Colville of Culross
1992	Ld Belstead
1997	Baroness Prashar
2001	(Sir) D. Hatch
2004	Sir D. Nichol

Police Force

	England & Wales		Scotland		Northern Ireland	
	No. of forces	No. of Police	No. of forces	No. of Police	No. of forces	No. of Police
1980	43	115,900	8	13,200	1	6,900
1990	43	125,646	8	13,981	1	8,243
2000	43	124,576	8	14,870	1	8,500
2003	43	136,797[a]	8	15,324[b]	1	7,469[c]

[a] Figures at 30 September 2003.
[b] Figure for 30 September 2002.
[c] Figure for 31 March 2003.

SOURCES:– *The War against Crime in England and Wales 1959–64*, Cmnd. 2296/1964; C. Reith, *A Short History of the British Police* (1948); J. M. Hart, *The British Police* (1951); B. Whitaker, *The Police* (1965); M. Banton, *The Police and the Community* (1964); Sir F. Newsam, *The Home Office* (2nd edn 1955); *Royal Commission on Police Powers and Procedure* Cmd. 3297/1929; *Royal Commission on the Police*, Cmnd. 1728/1962; G. Marshall, *Police and Government* (1965); R. Reiner, *The Politics of the Police* (2nd edn 1992); Annual Reports of HM Inspectors of Constabulary for England and Wales; Further information from Scottish Office and Northern Ireland Office.

VII
Population, Health and Employment

UK Population and Migration 1979–

	Total UK population (000s[a])	Net migration (000s)	Asylum applications (000s)
1979	56,240	6	–
1980	56,330	–55	–
1981	56,357	–79	–
1982	56,291	–56	–
1983	56,316	17	–
1984	56,409	37	–
1985	56,554	58	4.4
1986	56,684	37	4.3
1987	56,804	2	4.3
1988	56,916	–21	4.0
1989	57,076	44	11.6
1990	57,237	36	26.2
1991	57,439	73	44.8
1992	57,585	–11	24.6
1993	57,714	–2	22.4
1994	57,862	109	32.8
1995	58,025	75	44.0
1996	58,164	54	29.6
1997	58,314	47	32.5
1998	58,475	139	46.0
1999	58,684	163	71.2
2000	58,886	163	80.3
2001	59,113	172	71.0
2002	59,322	153	84.1
2003	59,554	151	49.4

[a] Mid-year estimates.

SOURCE:- *Annual Abstract of Statistics.*

Geographical Distribution

Government Office regions

	1981	1991	2001
North-East	2,636	2,603	2,515
North-West	6,940	6,885	6,730
Yorkshire & Humberside	4,918	4,983	4,965
East Midlands	3,853	4,035	4,172
West Midlands	5,187	5,265	5,267
London	6,806	6,890	7,172
South-West	4,381	4,718	4,928
East	4,854	5,150	5,388
South-East	7,245	7,679	8,001
Wales	2,813	2,891	2,903
Scotland	5,180	5,107	5,062
Northern Ireland	1,543	1,607	1,685
Major Cities:			
Belfast	315	294	277[a]
Birmingham	1,021	1,007	977
Bristol	401	397	381
Cardiff	281	294	305
Edinburgh	446	440	453[a]
Glasgow	774	689	609[a]
Hull	274	267	244
Leeds	718	717	715
Leicester	283	285	280
Liverpool	517	481	439
Manchester	463	439	393
Newcastle	284	278	260
Nottingham	278	281	267
Plymouth	253	254	241
Sheffield	548	529	513
Stoke-on-Trent	252	253	241

[a] Mid-year estimates.

SOURCE:- *Annual Abstract of Statistics*; <www.statistics.gov.uk>.
1981 and 1991 figures are mid-year estimates. 2001 figures for England and Wales are from the Census.

Births, Deaths and Marriages in the UK

	Births	*% outside marriage*	*Marriages*	*Divorces*	*Deaths per 000*	*Infant mortality*	*Life expectancy*	
							Male	*Female*
1981	731	12.5%	398	156	658	11.2	70.8	76.8
1986	755	20.4%	394	168	661	9.5	71.9	77.7
1991	792	29.8%	350	174	646	7.4	73.2	78.7
1996	733	35.5%	318	172	636	6.1	74.2	79.4
2001	669	40.1%	286	157	602	5.5	75.3	80.1

SOURCE:- *Population Trends*.

Causes of Death
England and Wales

	1980	*1985*	*1990*	*1995*	*2000*
Total Deaths	581	591	565	570	536
Of which:					
Lung cancer	35	36	34	32	29
Breast cancer	12	14	14	13	11
Other cancer	83	92	97	96	95
Heart disease	290	287	259	243	207
Respiratory illness	83	65	61	91	92
Violent causes	20	19	18	16	17

SOURCE:- *Annual Abstract of Statistics*.

Racial Composition of the UK Population

The last three censuses have each adopted a different approach to ascertaining the composition of the ethnic minority population. The 1981 Census could only establish the number of people living in households whose head was born outside the UK. On this measure there were 295,179 people of Caribbean origin, 628,589 from the subcontinent, and 342,382 from other Commonwealth countries (the largest contingents being Australians, Cypriots, New Zealanders and Maltese). Since this approach did not identify any second generation households, it could not be taken as an accurate assessment of the non-white population. The 1991 Census asked people to categorise themselves in terms of colour. It yielded:

Black (Caribbean)	*Black (other)*	*Indian*	*Pakistani*	*Bangladeshi*	*Other non-white*
499,964	290,763	840,255	476,555	162,835	644,678[a]

[a] Of which the largest components are 'other Asian' and Chinese.

The 2001 Census adopted a similar approach, but took more account of people having mixed racial origins, so its findings are not strictly comparable. It concluded that the population components were:

'000s

White	Mixed	Indian	Pakistani	Other Asian	Caribbean	Other black	Chinese	Other
54,154	677	1,053	747	531	566	583	247	231
92.1%	1.2%	1.8%	1.3%	0.9%	1.0%	1.0%	0.4%	0.4%

Acceptances for Settlement in the United Kingdom
Country of Origin

Year	Europe	USA	Other Americas	Africa	Indian subcontinent	Middle East	Other Asia	Oceania	All
1979	9,550	3,540	3,950	5,490	24,130	2,070	5,860	5,870	69,670
1980	8,180	3,420	3,210	4,550	22,220	2,310	6,130	5,960	69,750
1981	6,580	3,510	2,820	4,060	21,370	2,560	6,120	4,500	59,060
1982	7,100	3,350	2,470	4,120	20,180	2,580	5,020	4,220	53,870
1983	6,520	3,940	2,590	4,670	16,690	3,280	5,070	4,660	53,460
1984	6,370	3,750	2,690	4,380	14,840	2,870	4,870	6,040	50,950
1985	6,270	4,170	2,960	4,710	17,510	3,580	5,000	6,660	55,360
1986	5,240	3,790	2,590	4,130	14,550	3,030	5,030	5,380	47,790
1987	5,060	3,710	2,640	5,150	11,620	2,690	5,600	5,710	45,980
1988	5,620	3,750	2,730	5,840	12,180	2,810	6,020	6,190	49,280
1989	4,820	3,030	2,410	6,390	12,360	3,590	5,860	6,830	49,060
1990	5,130	3,750	3,050	8,310	13,170	3,030	7,430	5,350	53,200
1991	5,530	3,910	3,310	9,580	14,290	2,900	7,720	2,440	53,900
1992	4,630	3,850	3,410	8,980	15,070	2,570	7,620	2,340	52,570
1993	5,010	4,060	3,600	10,790	14,090	2,590	8,680	2,650	55,640
1994	4,620	3,990	3,900	11,880	14,070	2,620	9,210	2,850	55,010
1995	4,250	3,960	4,220	12,000	14,450	2,880	8,790	3,450	55,480
1996	7,500	4,030	4,440	12,970	13,590	4,790	9,500	3,520	61,730
1997	7,740	3,900	3,890	13,200	13,080	4,160	8,370	3,100	58,720
1998	7,570	3,940	6,840	16,090	16,420	4,180	9,520	3,690	69,790
1999	15,990	3,760	4,760	27,020	21,440	5,590	13,060	4,120	97,120
2000	15,155	4,585	6,965	44,845	22,840	7,230	17,850	4,905	125,945
2001	13,990	4,385	7,590	31,925	23,020	4,830	16,305	5,455	108,410
2002	11,740	4,355	7,325	39,165	24,665	5,345	16,575	6,250	115,965
2003	15,390	5,695	11,040	45,835	30,190	4,985	20,015	7,185	141,490

SOURCE:- *Annual Abstract of Statistics* (table 5.10).

Education Spending – England and Wales

Year ending Mar 31	Schools (current expenditure) (£m)[a]	Schools (capital) (£m)[a]	Further education (£m)[b]	Higher Education (£m)[c]	Total (£m)
1980	5,670	391	1,301	981	10,511
1981	7,031	481	1,591	1,265	12,941
1982	7,793	395	1,812	1,332	14,041
1983	8,297	392	1,987	1,388	15,037
1984	8,702	399	2,157	1,497	15,946
1985	9,023	390	2,260	1,562	16,516
1986	9,504	412	2,375	1,605	17,288
1987	10,518	397	2,625	1,654	18,802
1988	11,610	416	2,895	1,824	20,401
1989	12,584	474	3,277	1,958	22,137
1990	13,729	749	3,729	2,104	24,102
1991	14,726	854	4,128	2,265	26,728
1992	16,279	904	4,454	2,437	29,550
1993	17,963	934	4,136	3,361	31,576
1994	18,747	930	3,072[b]	4,908[c]	33,544
1995	19,420	1,119	3,200	5,192	35,367
1996	19,689	1,030	3,392	5,472	36,810
1997	20,469	1,049	3,694	5,729	37,953
1998	21,382	1,191	3,718	5,693	39,078
1999	23,069	1,357	5,064	4,726	38,981
2000	24,441	1,472	5,216	5,166	40,895
2001	27,066	1,762	5,194	5,843	44,350
2002	30,227	2,044	6,810	5,628	49,733
2003	31,546	2,185	6,085	6,239	53,815

[a] Includes nursery, primary, secondary and special schools.
[b] Includes all further education, adult education, teacher training, polytechnics and other higher education until 1993.
[c] Includes all higher education from 1994 onwards.

SOURCE:- *Annual Abstract of Statistics*, table 10.19

Maintained Secondary Schools by Religious Character

England Only

Year	C. of E.	Catholic	Jewish	Other	Total schools
1982	159	456	4	168	3,963
1987	233	434	5	163	4,221
1992	219	330	4	182	3,847
1997	199	359	4	174	3,569
2002	192	357	5	32	3,547
2004	199	352	5	34	3,409

SOURCE:- *Statistics of Education 2004*, table 23b, and preceding years' equivalent tables back to table A10 for 1982.

Pupils in Full-time Education (000s)
England

	Primary			State secondary			Independent		
	Schools	Pupils	Teachers	Schools	Pupils	Teachers	Schools	Pupils	Teachers
1979	21,309	4,371	192,462	4,694	3,872	231,404	2,361	512	39,710
1980	21,242	4,210	188,603	4,680	3,866	232,457	2,348	517	41,159
1981	21,018	4,021	181,310	4,654	3,840	230,928	2,339	516	41,597
1982	20,650	3,839	174,240	4,622	3,798	228,397	2,338	510	42,261
1983	20,384	3,661	168,514	4,553	3,741	227,084	2,344	503	42,902
1984	20,020	3,571	165,637	4,444	3,646	224,648	2,331	501	43,757
1985	19,734	3,542	164,429	4,382	3,526	218,605	2,311	501	44,520
1986	19,549	3,548	165,318	4,286	3,389	212,641	2,285	504	45,233
1987	19,432	3,577	168,385	4,221	3,240	207,180	2,276	515	46,102
1988	19,319	3,618	169,700	4,153	3,070	199,584	2,273	523	47,151
1989	19,232	3,667	172,414	4,035	2,945	192,841	2,269	532	48,741
1990	19,162	3,734	175,599	3,976	2,863	187,646	2,283	540	50,204
1991	19,047	3,782	176,295	3,897	2,853	183,508	2,287	546	51,692
1992	18,926	3,811	177,873	3,847	2,906	183,555	2,269	546	52,558
1993	18,828	3,879	179,420	3,773	2,965	184,036	2,261	539	52,995
1994	18,683	4,242	180,558	3,629	2,934	178,780	2,266	534	52,746
1995	18,551	4,312	181,910	3,614	2,993	181,445	2,259	533	53,055
1996	18,480	4,389	182,626	3,594	3,010	180,868	2,264	534	53,399
1997	18,392	4,429	182,442	3,569	3,042	181,692	2,271	541	53,676
1998	18,312	4,461	181,394	3,567	3,073	181,853	2,242	546	54,789
1999	18,234	4,460	182,646	3,560	3,122	183,578	2,229	547	56,163
2000	18,158	4,435	183,762	3,550	3,182	185,429	2,202	550	57,196
2001	18,069	4,406	185,534	3,481	3,232	189,026	2,203	557	58,760
2002	17,985	4,363	187,409	3,457	3,264	192,910	2,204	566	59,330
2003	17,861	4,309	184,010	3,436	3,308	194,450	2,178	575	60,660
2004	17,762	4,252	181,230	3,409	3,325	195,240	2,328	586	63,590

SOURCE:- *Statistics of Education 2004*, tables 24 and 41.

Higher Education Statistics

The age-participation index (API) is the most quoted figure for the rise in student numbers. It expresses the number of under 21-year-old home-domiciled students entering higher education for the first time, as a percentage of the 18- to 19-year-old population.

Year of entry	API % (GB)	Total higher education students (UK)
1979	12	–
1980	13	–
1981	13	–
1982	13	–
1983	13	–
1984	14	–
1985	14	–
1986	14	–
1987	15	–
1988	15	–
1989	17	–
1990	19	–
1991	23	1,110
1992	28	1,226
1993	30	1,337
1994	32	1,467
1995	32	1,522
1996	33	1,566
1997	33	1,603
1998	31	1,623
1999	32	1,630
2000	33	1,654
2001	35	1,703

SOURCE:- *Department for Education and Skills.*

Transport

Transport by mode – as percentage of miles travelled

	Bus & coach	Car	Motorcycle	Cycle	All road	Rail	Air
1980	11	79	2	1	92	7	0.6
1990	7	85	1	1	94	6	0.7
2000	6	85	1	1	93	6	1.0
2003	6	85	1	1	93	6	1.2

SOURCE:- Transport Statistics; *Annual Abstract of Statistics* (table 15.4).

Current Vehicle Licences in Great Britain

	Cars	Motorcycles	Crown/exempt	Goods	Total
1980	16,233,000	1,372,000	412,000	480,000[a]	19,200,000
1985	18,258,000	1,148,000	695,000	486,000	21,157,000
1990	21,989,000	833,000	807,000	482,000	24,673,000
1995	22,722,000	594,000	1,169,000	421,000	25,369,000
2000	25,665,000	825,000	1,590,000	418,000	28,898,000
2003	27,715,000	1,005,000	1,887,000	426,000	31,207,000

[a] Estimate – until 1982 the goods category included light goods, and no figure compatible with subsequent classification was collected.

SOURCE:- *Annual Abstract of Statistics* (table 15.8).

Road Accident Fatalities
Great Britain

	Pedestrians	Cyclists	Motorcyclists[a]	Motorists[a]	Commercial[a,b]	Total
1980	1,941	302	1,163	2,278	326	6,010
1985	1,789	286	796	2,061	233	5,165
1990	1,676	256	659	2,371	215	5,217
1995	1,029	212	445	1,749	161	3,621
2000	857	125	605	1,665	136	3,409
2003	769	113	693	1,769	127	3,508

[a] Figure includes fatalities among passengers.
[b] Buses, coaches, heavy and light goods vehicles.

SOURCE:- *Annual Abstract of Statistics* (table 14.16).

Rail Systems
Passenger kilometres (millions)

	National rail	London Underground	Light rail[a]	Total
1980/1	30,300	4,249	n.a.	35,000
1985/6	29,700	5,971	n.a.	36,000
1990/1	33,200	6,164	323	39,727
1995/6	30,000	6,337	432	36,810
2000/1	39,218	7,470	771	47,505

[a] The largest components of this figure were the Tyne and Wear Metro, the Docklands Light Railway, and the Manchester Metrolink.

Air traffic to and from the UK
Aircraft flights and passengers carried

	Flights	*Passengers carried*
1980	506,900	42,644,600
1985	579,300	52,862,700
1990	819,200	77,408,200
1995	941,700	94,231,900
2000	1,235,800	138,493,100
2003	1,242,800	148,313,400

SOURCE:- *Annual Abstract of Statistics* (table 15.25).

Post and Telecommunications

	1st Class	*2nd Class*	*Letters posted (m)*	*Phones (m)*	*Mobiles (000s)*	*TV Licences*
1979	10p	8p	9,965	–	–	18,381
1980	12p	10p	10,207	13,937	–	18,285
1981	14p	11.5p	10,071	14,671	–	18,667
1982	15.5p	12.5p	9,985	15,159	–	18,554
1983	16p	12.5p	10,255	15,546	–	18,494
1984	17p	13p	10,665	16,044	–	18,632
1985	17p	12p	11,439	16,596	–	18,716
1986	18p	13p	11,721	17,120	–	18,705
1987	18p	13p	12,535	17,549	–	18,953
1988	19p	14p	13,568	18,106	–	19,354
1989	20p	15p	13,741	18,703	–	19,396
1990	22p	17p	15,293	19,246	–	19,645
1991	24p	18p	15,902	19,573	–	19,546
1992	24p	18p	16,038	19,729	–	19,631
1993	25p	19p	16,364	20,114	–	20,067
1994	25p	19p	16,651	–	–	20,413
1995	25p	19p	17,468	–	–	20,732
1996	26p	20p	18,322	–	–	21,105
1997	26p	19p	18,101	–	–	21,305
1998	26p	19p	18,389	23,361	9,023	21,723
1999	26p	19p	17,934	23,902	14,878	22,240
2000	27p	19p	18,738	24,498	27,185	22,625
2001	27p	19p	19,092	24,789	43,452	22,839
2002	27p	19p	–	24,922	46,283	23,500
2003	28p	20p	–	–	–	24,100

Employment

Major Employment Legislation

Employment Act, 1980, provided for payment of public funds towards the costs of ballots among Trade Union members over strike action.

Employment Act, 1982, provided for compensation from public funds for employees dismissed as a result of closed shop agreements.

Trade Union Act, 1984, made legal immunity conditional on the conduct of strike ballots and made the continued existence of political funds dependent on ten-yearly votes by the membership.

Wages Act, 1986. This reduced the powers and scope of wages councils by limiting them to determining a single minimum rate, and removing young people from their jurisdiction. Unauthorised deductions from wages became a civil matter rather than a criminal offence.

Sex Discrimination Act, 1986. This brought UK sex discrimination law into line with EU directives.

Employment Act, 1988. This made dismissal for non-membership of a union unfair dismissal in all circumstances. It made it illegal for trade unions to discipline members for crossing picket lines or refusing to strike, even if the strike had been approved by a ballot. It gave members of trade unions the right to prevent union funds from being used for unlawful purposes.

Employment Act, 1989. This removed restrictions on the hours and other employment terms of 16- and 17-year-olds. It abolished some restrictions on women's employment, such as the ban on working in mines. The Training Commission, which had replaced the Manpower Services Commission, was abolished.

Employment Act, 1990. This banned the pre-entry closed shop, and made it unlawful to refuse employment to someone for belonging or not belonging to a union. Trade unions lost their immunity from civil damages claims for all forms of secondary action.

Trade Union Reform and Employment Rights Act, 1993. This introduced restrictions on deduction of union subscriptions from wages, compelled unions to publish fuller accounts, tightened rules on strike ballots, abolished wages councils, and gave workers the right to join any union regardless of whether it was organised in their workplace.

Disability Discrimination Act, 1995. This substantially extended protection again discrimination for disabled people and imposed new responsibilities on employers and other bodies. It was enacted partly in response to European directives.

National Minimum Wage Act, 1998. Established a National Minimum Wage with a regulatory and enforcement framework, and gave statutory authority for the Low Pay Commission.

Employment Relations Act, 1999. Established procedures for statutory trade union recognition, a right to unpaid parental leave and a shorter, one-year qualifying period for unfair dismissal.

Employment Relations Act, 2004. Implemented European regulations on worker consultation and clarified the rules on collective bargaining set out in the previous act.

Major Employment Litigation

Thomas et al. v. Haringey [1979]. The Court of Appeal held that it was arguable that a local authority might be in breach of its duty to provide education when it failed to do so by reason of industrial action by school caretakers.

Messenger Newspaper Group Ltd v. NGA (1982) *(Industrial Relations Law Reports 1984, 397).* The Court of Appeal endorsed the powers of sequestrators seeking to secure control of union funds when the union had been fined for contempt for its actions in seeking to enforce a closed shop.

Mercury Communications Ltd v. Scott Garer (Industrial Cases Reports 1984, 74). The Court of Appeal ruled that it was possible under the *Employment Act 1982* to secure an interlocutory injunction against union actions that were not 'wholly or mainly' related to an industrial dispute.

Dimbleby & Sons Ltd. v. National Union of Journalists (Industrial Cases Reports 1984, 386). The House of Lords endorsed the granting of an interlocutory injunction against preventing a union from instructing its members to break contracts of employment in pursuits of a trade dispute that, under the *Employment Act 1980*, was excluded from protection.

Barretts and Baird (Wholesale) Ltd v. IPCS [1987] IRLR 3. Not only are union members liable in damages to their employer for breach of their employment contract, but the same breach of contract may give rise to further liabilities based on its 'unlawful' character.

Boxfoldia Ltd v. NGA [1988] ICR 752. Although members may authorise their union to decide on official industrial action, it does not follow that the union is authorised to act as their agent in terminating their employment contracts.

Associated British Ports v. TGWU [1989] IRLR 305, 318 CA. The Court issued an injunction against industrial action on the grounds that the union had no immunity against tort liability for inducing workers to breach their statutory duty with intent to injure. The judgment was subsequently reversed by the House of Lords on other grounds.

Dimskal Shipping Sa v. ITWF [1991] 3WLR 875 HL. Industrial action could be ruled unlawful secondary action even if it took place in another country (in this case Sweden) under whose law it was legal, according to the commercial law principle of 'economic duress'.

Associated Newspapers Ltd v. *Wilson* and *Associated British Ports* v. *Palmer and others [1995] IRLR 258*. The House of Lords held that it was not unlawful to refuse to pay financial benefits to those who refused to forsake collective bargaining and sign individual contracts.

Advisory Conciliation and Arbitration Service (ACAS) 1974–

The Conciliation and Arbitration Service was established within the Department of Employment in 1974. It was made an independent statutory body by the *Employment Protection Act, 1975*.

Chairman

1974	J. Mortimer
1981	(Sir) P. Lowry
1987	(Sir) D. Smith
1993	J. Hougham
2000	Rita Donaghy

Low Pay Commission 1997–

The Low Pay Commission (LPC) was given a statutory footing as a result of the *National Minimum Wage Act, 1998*, to advise the Government about the National Minimum Wage.

Chairman

1997	(Sir) G. Bain
2002	A. Turner

Disability Rights Commission 2000–

The Disability Rights Commission is an executive non-departmental public body established to advise the Government on issues of discrimination against disabled people, and to monitor the implementation of the *Disability Discrimination Act, 1995*.

Chairman

2000–	H. Massie

Earnings and Hours Worked

United Kingdom

| | Average weekly earnings (£) | | | | Average weekly hours | | | |
| | Manual workers | | Non-manual workers | | Manual workers | | Non-manual workers | |
Year	Men aged 21 & over	Women aged 18 & over	Men aged 21 & over	Women aged 18 & over	Men aged 21 & over	Women aged 18 & over	Men aged 21 & over	Women aged 18 & over
1979	93.0	55.2	113.0	66.0	46.2	39.6	38.8	36.7
1980	111.7	68.0	141.3	82.7	45.4	39.6	38.7	36.7
1981	121.9	74.5	163.1	96.7	44.2	39.4	38.4	36.5
1982	133.8	80.1	178.9	104.9	44.3	39.3	38.2	36.5
1983	143.6	87.9	94.9	115.1	43.9	39.3	38.4	36.5
1984	152.7	93.5	109.0	124.3	44.3	39.4	38.5	36.5
1985	163.6	101.3	225.0	133.8	44.5	39.5	38.6	36.6
1986	174.4	107.5	244.9	145.7	44.5	39.5	38.6	36.7
1987	185.5	115.3	265.9	157.2	44.6	39.7	38.7	36.8
1988	200.6	123.6	294.1	175.5	45.0	39.8	38.7	36.9
1989	217.8	134.9	323.6	195.0	45.3	39.9	38.8	36.9
1990	239.5	148.4	346.4	214.3	45.4	40.0	38.9	36.9
1991	253.1	159.2	375.7	236.8	44.4	39.7	38.7	36.8
1992	268.3	170.1	400.4	256.5	44.5	39.8	38.6	36.8
1993	274.3	177.1	418.2	268.7	44.3	39.8	38.6	36.9
1994	280.7	181.9	428.2	278.4	44.7	40.1	38.9	37.0
1995	291.3	188.1	443.3	288.1	45.2	40.2	39.0	37.0
1996	301.3	195.2	464.5	302.4	44.8	40.2	39.1	37.1
1997	314.3	201.1	483.5	317.8	45.1	40.2	39.1	37.1
1998	328.5	210.8	506.1	330.1	45.0	40.2	39.1	37.0
1999	335.0	221.9	525.5	346.9	44.4	39.9	39.0	37.0
2000	344.8	229.1	550.9	364.5	44.3	39.9	38.9	37.0
2001	359.9	241.8	582.4	388.8	44.3	39.9	39.0	37.1
2002	368.2	251.0	610.4	405.2	43.9	39.7	38.9	37.1

SOURCES:- *Department of Employment Gazette*; New Earnings Survey.

Labour Force

(000s; all over 16; figures for spring quarter each year)

	Males in employment	Males unemployed	Males inactive	Females in employment	Females unemployed	Females inactive
1979	14,824	774	4,087	9,541	666	11,259
1981	14,174	1,570	4,344	9,586	924	11,346
1983	13,645	1,825	4,862	9,543	1,040	11,573
1984	13,790	1,848	4,851	9,751	1,257	11,181
1985	13,931	1,798	4,908	9,958	1,181	11,177
1986	13,886	1,796	5,066	10,090	1,186	11,125

	Males in employment	Males unemployed	Males inactive	Females in employment	Females unemployed	Females inactive
1987	14,032	1,724	5,130	10,357	1,166	11,021
1988	14,492	1,401	5,087	10,730	984	10,906
1989	14,858	1,146	5,061	11,241	836	10,602
1990	14,946	1,085	5,103	11,372	785	10,556
1991	14,500	1,424	5,247	11,251	877	10,607
1992	14,132	1,856	5,631	11,497	939	10,933
1993	13,803	1,969	5,848	11,474	982	10,926
1994	13,889	1,805	5,926	11,542	943	10,920
1995	14,058	1,588	6,013	11,630	878	10,945
1996	14,110	1,519	6,088	11,825	819	10,873
1997	14,337	1,277	6,161	12,030	759	10,796
1998	14,479	1,066	6,286	12,121	706	10,825
1999	14,590	1,068	6,255	12,317	687	10,727
2000	14,773	972	6,273	12,495	661	10,675
2001	14,865	846	6,459	12,643	581	10,725
2002	14,886	909	6,526	12,773	615	10,673

Figures are for GB up to 1991 and for the UK from 1992 onwards.

SOURCE:- *Employment Gazette*; *Labour Market Trends* August 2003, table A1. From 1984 the ILO definition of unemployed is used.

Employees in Employment by Industry

	1980	1985	1990	1995	2000	2003
Agriculture, forestry, fishing	352	321	278	273	316	235
Mining, energy, utilities	716	582	441	237	200	202
Food, beverages, tobacco	705	575	524	472	498	469
Clothing, textiles	716	550	477	404	285	197
Paper, publishing, recording	538	477	481	463	464	439
Chemicals	420	339	324	254	238	225
Transport	1,036	889	924	920	1,008	1,033
Post and telecommunications	428	419	437	440	516	525
Financial services, IT, business services	1,669	2,039	2,701	3,455	4,496	4,645
Public administration	1,844	1,862	1,942	1,411	1,409	1,471
Education	1,586	1,577	1,735	1,826	2,120	2,218
Health and community services	2,500	2,790	3,114	3,632	3,991	4,147
Wood, rubber and plastics	554	473	546	318	321	298
Minerals and metals	642	430	388	707	660	578
Transport equipment	799	547	491	375	403	363
Construction	1,206	994	1,044	935	1,189	1,131
Wholesale and retail	3,281	3,186	3,472	4,052	4,404	4,478
Hotels and restaurants	959	1,027	1,256	1,431	1,668	1,799

The system of classification changed in 1992 and there are some discrepancies in what is included in each category between the 1990 figures and those for 1995.

SOURCES:- *Employment Gazette*; *Labour Market Trends* August 2003, table B12.

Trades Union Congresses 1979–

Date	Place	President	General Secretary	No. of Delegates	Members represented (000s)
3–7 Sep 79	Blackpool	T. Jackson	–	1,200	12,128
1–5 Sep 80	Brighton	T. Parry	–	1,203	12,173
7–11 Sep 81	Blackpool	A. Fisher	–	1,188	11,601
6–10 Sep 82	Brighton	A. Sapper	–	1,163	11,006
5–9 Sep 83	Blackpool	F. Chapple	–	1,155	10,810
3–7 Sep 84	Brighton	R. Buckton	N. Willis	1,121	10,082
2–6 Sep 85	Blackpool	J. Eccles	–	1,124	9,855
1–5 Sep 86	Brighton	K. Gill	–	1,091	9,586
7–11 Sep 87	Blackpool	F. Jarvis	–	1,065	9,243
5–9 Sep 88	Bournemouth	C. Jenkins	–	1,052	9,127
4–8 Sep 89	Blackpool	A. Christopher	–	1,006	8,652
3–7 Sep 90	Blackpool	Anne Maddocks	–	985	8,405
2–6 Sep 91	Glasgow	A. Smith	–	937	8,193
7–11 Sep 92	Blackpool	R. Bickerstaffe	–	892	7,762
6–10 Sep 93	Brighton	A. Tuffin	J. Monks	874	7,303
5–9 Sep 94	Blackpool	J. Knapp	–	878	7,298
4–8 Sep 95	Brighton	L. Mills	–	828	6,895
2–6 Sep 96	Blackpool	Margaret Prosser	–	821	6,790
1–5 Sep 97	Brighton	A. Dubbins	–	827	6,795
7–11 Sep 98	Blackpool	J. Edmonds	–	811	6,639
13–16 Sep 99	Brighton	Ld McKenzie	–	809	6,799
11–14 Sep 00	Glasgow	Rita Donaghy	–	772	6,746
10–11 Sep 01	Brighton	B. Morris	–	766	6,722
9–12 Sep 02	Blackpool	Sir T. Young	–	765	6,685
8–11 Sep 03	Brighton	N. de Gruchy	B. Barber	783	6,673
13–16 Sep 04	Brighton	R. Lyons	B. Barber	723	6,424
12–15 Sep 05	Brighton	Jeannie Drake	B. Barber	742	n/a

SOURCE:- *Trades Union Congress Reports, 1900–.*

The Largest Unions

Unions which at some time since 1979 have had over 200,000 members.

Amicus (2000) (Amalgamated Engineering and Electrical Union, 1851)

Amalgamated Society of Engineers (founded 1851) merged with other unions to form the Amalgamated Engineering Union (AEU) in 1920. In 1968 the AEU merged with the Amalgamated Union of Foundry Workers (AEF) which in 1970 merged with the Construction Engineering Workers and the Draughtsmen and Allied Technicians Association, taking the title the Amalgamated Union of Engineering Workers. Merged in 1992 with EETPU and became the Amalgamated Engineering and Electrical Union. Merged with MSF (Manufacturing, Science and Finance union – itself the product of the 1988 merger of ASTMS and TASS) in 2002. It also absorbed the printing union GPMU in 2004.

President		Gen. Sec.	
1967	H. Scanlon	1976	(Sir) J. Boyd
1978	T. Duffy	1982	G. Laird
1986	W. Jordan	1994	P. Gallagher
1995	D. Hall	1996	(Sir) K. Jackson
1996	*(office abolished)*	2002	D. Simpson

Manufacturing, Science, Finance (MSF) 1917 (1988)–2002

National Foreman's Association became Association of Supervisory Staff, Executives and Technicians (ASSET) in 1941. Became Association of Scientific, Technical and Managerial Staffs (ASTMS) in 1968 when it merged with the Association of Scientific Workers (founded in 1918 as National Union of Scientific Workers and became AScW in 1925). NFA joined TUC in 1919; AScW in 1942. Merged with TASS in 1988 to become MSF. Merged with AEEU in 2002.

Secretary	
1970	C. Jenkins
1988	{ C. Jenkins
	{ K. Gill
1989	K. Gill
1992	R. Lyons

Communication Workers Union (CWU) 1920 (1995)

Postal Telegraph Clerks' Association. UK Postal Clerks Association merged in 1914 to form Postal and Telegraph Clerks' Association. This merged in 1920 with Fawcett Association and other unions to form UPW. Name changed to Union of Communication Workers in 1980. (Legally banned from membership of TUC 1927–46.) In 1995 UCW merged with the National Communications Union (NCU – until 1975 the POEU), which represented telecommunications engineers, to form CWU.

Secretary	
1920	J. Bowen
1936	T. Hodgson
1944	C. Geddes
1957	R. Smith
1966	T. Jackson
1982	A. Tuffin
1993	A. Johnson
1995	{ A. Johnson
	{ T. Young
1997	{ D. Hodgson
	{ T. Young
1998	D. Hodgson
2001	B. Hayes

Confederation of Health Service Employees (COHSE) 1946–1992

Formed by a merger of various small hospital unions. Merged with NUPE and NALGO to form UNISON in 1992.

Secretary
1974   A. Spanswick
1983   D. Williams
1987   H. MacKenzie

Electrical, Electronics, Telecommunications and Plumbing Union (EETPU) 1889–1992

Originally Electrical Trades Union. In 1968 following mergers it became the Electrical, Electronic and Telecommunications Union – Plumbing Trades Union and then the Electrical, Electronics, Telecommunications and Plumbing Union. Expelled from TUC in 1988. Merged with AUEW 1992; EEPTU wing readmitted to TUC 1993.

President/General Secretary
1971   F. Chapple
1984   E. Hammond
1992   P. Gallagher

General Municipal Boilermakers and Allied Trades Union (GMB) 1924

National Union of General Workers (founded 1889 as the National Union of Gasworkers and General Labourers of GB and Ireland), National Amalgamated Union of Labour (founded 1889 as Tyneside and General Labourers' Union), and Municipal Employees' Association (founded 1894). Became National Union of General and Municipal Workers in 1924. Changed name to General and Municipal Workers Union for popular use in 1965. Merged with Amalgamated Society of Boilermakers, Shipwrights, Blacksmiths and structural workers to form GMB in 1982.

Secretary
1972   D. Basnett
1986   J. Edmonds
2003   P. Curran
2005   P. Kenny

Graphical, Paper and Media Union (GPMU) 1847 (1991) – 2004

Established by amalgamation of the National Union of Bookbinders and Machine Rulers and the National Union of Printing and Paper Workers as the National Union of Printing Bookbinding and Paper Workers (NUPBPW). In 1968 merged with the National Society of Operative Printers (NATSOPA) to form SOGAT. In 1971 the merger was dissolved but NUPBPW section kept name of SOGAT. Merged with National Graphical Association in 1991 to form GPMU. It merged with Amicus in 2004.

Secretary

1974	W. Keys
1985	Brenda Dean
1991	A. Dubbins

National Association of Schoolmasters/Union of Women Teachers (NASUWT) 1975–

Created in 1975, when the National Association of Schoolmasters and the Union of Women Teachers amalgamated.

General Secretary

1975	T. Casey
1983	F. Smithies
1990	N. de Gruchy
2002	E. O'Kane
2004	Christine Keates

National and Local Government Officers' Association (NALGO) 1905–93

National Association of Local Government Officers. 1930 amalgamated with National Poor Law Officers' Association and in 1963 with the British Gas Staffs Association. 1952 changed name to National and Local Government Officers' Association (joined TUC 1965). Merged with COHSE and NUPE to form UNISON in 1993.

General Secretary

1973	G. Drain
1983	J. Daly
1990	A. Jinkinson

National Union of Mineworkers (NUM) 1889 (1945)

Formed as the Miners' Federation of G.B., amalgamated with specialist unions, and renamed NUM in 1945.

President

1971	J. Gormley
1982	A. Scargill

National Union of Public Employees (NUPE) 1888 (1928)–1993

Formed as London County Council Protection Association; in 1894 became Municipal Employees Association; in 1920 the MEA and the National Union of Corporation Workers jointly affiliated to the TUC but in 1924 MEA was absorbed by NUGMW. The National Union of Corporation Workers became NUPE in 1928. Merged with COHSE and NALGO to form UNISON in 1993.

Secretary

1968	A. Fisher
1982	R. Bickerstaffe

National Union of Rail, Maritime, and Transport workers (RMT) 1913 (1989)

The National Union of Railwaymen was formed in 1913 from the merger of the Amalgamated Society of Railway Servants, the General Railway Workers' Union, and others. In 1989 the NUR merged with the National Union of Seamen and took its present title.

Secretary

1975	S. Weighell
1982	J. Knapp
2002	B. Crow

National Union of Teachers (NUT) 1870

Originally National Union of Elementary Teachers (till 1890). Affiliated to TUC in 1970.

Secretary

1975	F. Jarvis
1989	D. McAvoy
2004	S. Sinnott

Public and Commercial Services Union (PCS) 1902 (1998)

Assistant Clerks Association became Clerical Officers Association in 1919 and Civil Service Clerical Association in 1922. Changed name to CPSA in 1969 (not in TUC 1927–46). Merged with Public Services, Tax and Commerce Union (PTC) in 1998 to form PCS.

Secretary

1976	K. Thomas
1982	A. Kendall
1987	J. Ellis
1992	B. Reamsbottom
1998	{ B. Reamsbottom / J. Sheldon }
2001	B. Reamsbottom
2002	M. Serwotka

Transport and General Workers Union (TGWU) 1922–

Dock, Wharf, Riverside and General Workers' Union, National Union of Dock Labourers and other dockers' unions, United Vehicle Workers, National Union of Vehicle Workers and others. 1928 amalgamated with the Workers' Union.

Secretary

1977	M. Evans
1985	R. Todd
1992	B. Morris
2003	T. Woodley

Union of Construction, Allied Trades and Technicians (UCATT) 1860 (1971)–

Amalgamated Society of Carpenters and Joiners became, in 1921 after mergers, Amalgamated Society of Woodworkers (ASW). ASW merged in 1971 with the Amalgamated Union of Building Trade Workers (formed 1921), the Amalgamated Society of Painters and Decorators and the Association of Building Technicians.

Secretary
1978	L. Wood
1985	A. Williams
1991	G. Brumwell
2004	A. Ritchie

UNISON 1993

See above entries for COHSE, NALGO and NUPE.

General Secretary
1993	A. Jinkinson
1996	R. Bickerstaffe
2001	D. Prentis

Union of Shop, Distributive and Allied Workers (USDAW) 1921 (1946)

Cooperative Employees, and Warehouse and General Workers amalgamated in 1921 to form the National Union of Distributive and Allied Workers. 1946 fusion with National Amalgamated Union of Shop Assistants, Warehousemen and Clerks.

General Secretary
1979	W. Whately
1986	G. Davies
1997	B. Connor
2004	J. Hannett

SOURCE:- *Trades Union Congress Reports, 1979–.*

Membership of the Largest Unions

Membership (000s)

	1980	1985	1990	1995	2000	2003
Amicus (AEEU)	1,381	975	702	726	728	1,061
MSF	491	–	653	–	351	–
CWU	203	–	201	–	284	266
COHSE	213	–	203	–	–	–
EETPU	405	348	367	–	–	–
GMB	916	840	933	740	684	703
GPMU	206	–	166	–	200	102

	1980	1985	1990	1995	2000	2003
NASUWT	–	–	–	–	256	265
NALGO	782	752	744	1,355	–	–
NUM	257	135	53	11	5	4
NUPE	692	–	579	–	–	–
RMT (NUR)	170	130	118	59	55	70
NUT	249	–	169	–	286	331
PCS	–	–	–	–	268	324
TGWU	1,887	1,434	1,224	897	859	835
UCATT	348	–	207	–	115	102
UNISON	–	–	–	–	1,272	1,289
USDAW	450	385	362	283	310	321

SOURCE:- *Trades Union Congress Reports, 1980–; Reports of the Certification Officer.*

Unemployment, Industrial Disputes and Trade Union Statistics

	Unemployment		Industrial Disputes				No. of	No. of	No. of members
	Maximum (000s)	Minimum (000s)	Working days lost (000s)	No. of stoppages beginning in year	Total workers involved (000s)	Total no. of unions	union members (000s)	unions affiliated to TUC	of unions affiliated to TUC (000s)
1979	1,464 Jul	1,299 May	29,474	4,583	2,080	462	13,112	112	12,128
1980	2,244 Dec	1,471 Jan	11,964	830	1,330	453	13,289	109	12,173
1981	2,772 Oct	2,271 Jan	4,266	1,499	1,338	438	12,947	108	11,601
1982	3,097 Dec	2,770 Jun	5,313	2,101	1,528	414	12,106	105	11,006
1983	3,225 Jan	2,984 Jun	3,754	571	1,352	408	11,593	102	10,810
1984	3,284 Sep	3,030 Jun	27,135	1,221	1,464	394	11,236	98	10,082
1985	3,346 Sep	3,179 Jun	6,402	903	791	375	10,994	91	9,855
1986	3,408 Jan	3,216 Nov	1,920	1,074	720	370	10,821	88	9,586
1987	3,297 Jan	2,686 Nov	3,546	1,016	887	335	10,539	87	9,243
1988	2,722 Jan	2,047 Dec	3,702	781	790	330	10,475	83	9,127
1989	2,074 Jan	1,612 Nov	4,128	701	727	315	10,376	78	8,652
1990	1,850 Dec	1,556 Jun	1,903	630	298	309	10,158	78	8,405
1991	2,552 Dec	1,960 Jan	761	369	176	287	9,947	74	8,193
1992	2,983 Dec	2,674 Jan	528	240	148	275	9,585	72	7,762
1993	3,062 Jan	2,679 Nov	649	211	385	268	9,048	69	7,303
1994	2,887 Jan	2,417 Dec	278	203	107	254	8,700	68	7,298
1995	2,503 Jan	2,196 Nov	415	232	174	243	8,278	67	6,895
1996	2,311 Jan	2,196 Nov	1,303	230	364	261	7,982	73	6,790
1997	1,908 Jan	1,388 Nov	235	206	130	257	7,842	75	6,757
1998	1,479 Jan	1,272 Oct	282	159	93	252	7,801	74	6,639
1999	1,375 Jan	1,141 Dec	242	200	141	238	7,851	77	6,749
2000	1,236 Jan	1,001 Nov	499	207	183	237	7,898	76	6,746
2001	1,078 Jan	918 Oct	525	187	180	226	7,779	73	6,722
2002	1,024 Feb	905 Nov	1,323	141	918	216	7,751	70	6,590
2003	1,012 Feb	885 Nov	499	131	123	213	7,736	67	6,450
2004	957 Feb	803 Nov	905	125	172				
2005	885 Feb								

SOURCES:- *Annual Abstract of Statistics, Ministry of Labour Gazette, Employment Gazette, Labour Market Trends* and *Abstract of Labour Statistics; TUC Congress Reports.*

VIII
The Treasury and the Economy

Some Landmarks in the British Economy

12 Mar 79	European Monetary System starts
12 Jun 79	New Conservative Government's budget cuts income tax from 33% to 30% and raises VAT from 8% to 15%
24 Oct 79	Abolition of exchange controls
15 Nov 79	Minimum lending rate touches 17%
26 Mar 80	Announcement of Medium Term Financial Strategy (MTFS)
Jun 80	Britain becomes net exporter of oil
2 Jun 80	Agreement on reduction of Britain's EEC budget contribution
21 Nov 80	Youth Opportunities Programme doubled
Oct 80	£ reaches peak exchange with $ (2.39)
Jan 81	Bottom of worst post-war slump for Britain
20 Aug 81	Minimum lending rate abolished
27 Jul 82	Hire purchase controls abolished
9 Sep 82	Unemployment reaches 3 million
13 Mar 84	Beginning of miners' strike
26 Jun 84	Fontainebleau summit agrees permanent settlement of Britain's EEC contribution
28 Nov 84	Government sells 33% of British Telecom
3 Dec 84	Br Telecom Shares (sold in Nov) gain 45% premium in first stock exchange dealings
19 Dec 84	Hong Kong Agreement for 1997 handover
!8 Jan 85	FT Index breaks 1000 for the first time
4 Mar 85	End of year-long miners' strike (26.1m days lost)
7 Mar 85	£ touches bottom level of $1.05
10 Mar 86	Budget lowers basic income tax to 29%
27 Oct 86	'Big Bang' revolutionises stock exchange mechanics
17 Feb 86	Margaret Thatcher signs Single European Act
Jan 87	Guinness scandal leads to top City prosecutions
5 Feb 87	Wapping strike ends and transforms newspaper finances
17 Mar 87	Budget lowers basic income tax to 27%
19 Oct 87	'Black Monday' collapse in stock market
27 Nov 87	£ reaches $1.88, a five-year high

11 Mar 88	Budget reduces basic income tax to 25%; top rate to 40%
Sep 88	Worst ever trade deficit announced
29 Oct 89	Lawson resigns as Chancellor. Major succeeds
1 Apr 90	Start of poll tax
Apr 90	Unemployment begins strong upward rise
2 Aug 90	Invasion of Kuwait leads to rise in oil prices, which fall back sharply when Gulf War proves brief
8 Oct 90	United Kingdom joins Exchange Rate Mechanism at £1=2.95dm
1 Nov 90	Sir G. Howe resigns
28 Nov 90	J. Major becomes Prime Minister with N. Lamont as Chancellor
28 Feb 91	End of Gulf War
17 Mar 91	End of poll tax announced
11 Dec 91	Maastricht agreement signed with UK opt-outs
25 Dec 91	Yeltsin succeeds Gorbachev in Russia
10 Mar 92	Budget announces ending of April Budgets
9 Apr 92	Conservatives win General Election with low tax promises
17 Jun 92	Chancellor announces abolition of NEDC
16 Sep 92	'Black Wednesday': Britain leaves Exchange Rate Mechanism
12 Nov 92	Chancellor predicts a £37bn Public Sector Borrowing requirement for next year
16 Mar 93	Last Spring Budget imposes VAT on fuel
Apr 93	After 8 negative quarters recession officially ends
27 May 93	K. Clarke replaces N. Lamont as Chancellor
23 Jul 93	Maastricht Treaty finally approved by Parliament
29 Nov 93	House of Commons votes for Sunday shopping
30 Nov 93	First unified Budget involves expenditure cuts and higher taxes
15 Dec 93	GATT changes (Uruguay Round) approved by 117 countries
1 Apr 94	End of British Rail
5 May 94	Channel Tunnel opened
8 Jun 94	Dept of Employment figures show union penetration down to 31%
21 Jul 94	Blair takes over as Labour leader
6 Nov 94	Blair addresses CBI
28 Nov 94	Norway rejects EU membership
30 Nov 94	Budget cuts public expenditure
1 Jan 95	Austria, Finland and Sweden join EU
2 Feb 95	Bank rate up to 6.75%
26 Feb 95	Baring's Bank bankrupted by Far East speculation
26 Mar 95	Schengen agreement on open frontiers in much of EU
5 May 95	Clarke overrules Bank Governor on bank rate rise
30 Sep 95	Euro-Summit agrees 1999 date for European Monetary Union
16 Nov 95	Budget includes tax cuts
21 Mar 96	EU ban on British beef exports
20 Oct 96	Bank rate up to 6%
26 Nov 96	Budget takes 1p off income tax
18 Dec 96	Unemployment falls below 2m
20 Jan 97	Shadow Chancellor promises no Labour income tax increases
24 Feb 97	Halifax Building Society votes to become a Bank
1 May 97	Labour wins election. Brown becomes Chancellor
6 May 97	Control over interest rates transferred to Bank of England Monetary Policy Committee

2 Jun 97	Monetary Policy Committee named
12 Jun 97	Brown confirms Bank's responsibility for a 2.5% inflation target
1 Sep 97	Hong Kong Market slump foreshadows Far Eastern slump
20 Oct 97	Brown indicates likelihood of UK joining EMU
25 Nov 97	Last November Budget includes 1% income tax cut
16 Mar 98	EU ban on British beef exports partially lifted
16 May 98	G8 summit in Birmingham
11 Jun 98	Chancellor announces public-private partnership initiative with 51% of Air Traffic Control, the Tote, the Royal Mint and the Commonwealth Development Corporation made available for private ownership
14 Jul 98	Publication of Comprehensive Spending Review includes an extra £21bn for Health and £19bn for Education
1 Jan 99	EMU starts with 11 EU countries switching to euro currency
Apr 99	First quarter GDP figures reveal Britain has narrowly avoided recession
18 Jul 00	The Second Spending Review pledges 5.4% per annum real growth in education spending and 6.1% per year real growth in health spending over four years
Sep 00	FTSE 100 reaches all-time high of 6800
Sep 00	Blockades of fuel depots by lorry-drivers and farmers lead to Government concessions on fuel duties in November Pre-Budget report
Feb 01	Unemployment claimant count drops below 1 million
11 Sep 01	Terrorist attacks in US lead to collapse of world stock markets. FTSE 100 falls from 5250 in early Sep 2001 to 3300 in Mar 2003
15 Jul 02	Gordon Brown's third Spending Review pledges 6% per annum growth in education spending and 7.3% per annum growth in health spending
9 Jun 03	Chancellor Gordon Brown announces that five economic tests for entering the euro have not been met
10 Jul 03	Interest rates cut to 3.5%
12 Jul 04	Fourth Spending Review reaffirms continuing growth in spending on public services but puts more emphasis on efficiency savings and economies
27 Apr 05	Government announces Five Economic Tests to join the euro are most unlikely to be met

Sources of Government Economic Advice

The Treasury has provided governments with their main official guidance (see p. 138 for Permanent Secretaries). In addition, under the Cabinet Office or the Treasury, there have been the following official economic advisers.

Head of Government Economic Service (1964–)

1976	Sir A. Atkinson
1980	(Sir) T. Burns
1991	(Sir) A. Budd
1997	G. O'Donnell
2003	(Sir) N. Stern

Chief Economic Adviser to the Treasury (1999–2004)

1999   E. Balls

Outside the Civil Service there have been the following official bodies:

Bank of England (1696)

Governor

1971	G. Richardson (Ld)
1983	R. Leigh-Pemberton (Ld Kingsdown)
1993	(Sir) E. George
2003	M. King

Monetary Policy Committee of the Bank of England (1997)

Members

1997–2003	(Sir) E. George	1999–2002	S. Wadhwani
1997–	M. King	2000–03	C. Allsopp
1997–99	Sir A. Budd	2000–	C. Bean
1997–98	H. Davies	2000–	S. Nickell
1997–2000	W. Buiter	2001–	Kate Barker
1997–2000	C. Goodhart	2002–	Sir A.Large
1997–2001	DeAnne Julius	2002–	P. Tucker
1997–2002	D. Clementi	2002–	Marian Bell
1997–2002	I. Plenderleith	2003–	R. Lambert
1998–2000	J. Vickers	2003–	Rachel Lomax

SOURCE:- <www.bankofengland.co.uk>.

National Economic Development Council (1961–92)

Director-General of National Economic Development Office

1973	(Sir) R. McIntosh
1983	J. Cassels
1988	W. Eltis

Commission on Pay Comparability (1979–80)

Chairman

1979   H. Clegg

(See also Monopolies Commission, p. 221; Royal Commissions and Committees of Inquiry, pp. 156–60; Central Policy Review Staff, p. 134.)

Council of Economic Advisers (1997–)

Members

1997–	P. Gregg	2001–	S. Wood
1997–	C. Wales	2003–	M. Jacobs
1999–	Shriti Vadera	2004–05	E. Miliband
2000–	Maeve Sherlock		

Economic Interest Groups

Confederation of British Industry (1965)

Formed by a merger of the Federation of British Industries (FBI) (founded 1916), the National Association of British Manufacturers (1915) and the British Employers Confederation (1919).

President

1978	Sir J. Greenborough	1992	Sir M. Angus
1980	Sir R. Pennock	1994	Sir B. Nicholson
1982	Sir C. Fraser	1996	Sir C. Marshall
1984	Sir J. Cleminson	1998	Sir C. Thompson
1986	D. Nickson	2000	Sir I. Vallance
1988	Sir T. Holdsworth	2002	Sir J. Egan
1990	Sir B. Corby	2004	J. Sunderland

Director-General

1976	(Sir) J. Methven	1992	H. Davies
1980	Sir T. Beckett	1995	A. Turner
1987	(Sir) J. Banham	2000	D. Jones

Economic Pressure Groups

Adam Smith Institute (1977)
Aims of Industry (1942)
Association of British Chambers of Commerce (1860)
British Institute of Management (1947)
British Retail Consortium
Building Societies Association (1860)
Institute of Directors (1903)
National Farmers' Union (1908)
Trades Union Congress (1868) (see p. 181)
National Federation of Small Business
Low Pay Unit
Child Poverty Action Group

Consumer Organisations

Office of Fair Trading (1973–). Director General: 1973 J. Methven; 1976 (Sir) G. Borrie; 1995 J. Bridgeman; 2000–03 J. Vickers. Chairman: 2003 J. Vickers. Executive Director: 2003 Penny Boys

National Consumer Council (1975–). Director: 1975 A. Kershaw; 1975 J. Hosker; 1977 J. Mitchell; 1987 M. Healy; 1992 Ruth Evans; 1999–2002 Anna Bradley. Chief Exec.: 2003 E. Mayo.

Select Statistics

Retail Price Index (January 1987 = 100)

	Jan	Feb	Mar	Apr	May	Jun	Jul	Aug	Sep	Oct	Nov	Dec
1979	52.5	53.0	53.4	54.3	54.7	55.7	58.1	58.5	59.1	59.7	60.3	60.7
1980	62.2	63.1	63.9	66.1	66.7	67.4	67.9	68.1	68.5	68.9	69.5	69.9
1981	70.3	70.9	72.0	74.1	74.6	75.0	75.3	75.9	76.3	77.0	77.8	78.3
1982	78.7	78.8	79.4	81.0	81.6	81.9	81.9	81.9	81.9	82.3	82.7	82.5
1983	82.6	83.0	83.1	84.3	84.6	84.8	85.3	85.7	86.1	86.4	86.7	86.9
1984	86.8	87.2	87.5	88.6	89.0	89.2	89.1	89.9	90.1	90.7	91.0	90.9
1985	91.2	91.9	92.8	94.8	95.2	95.4	95.2	95.5	95.4	95.6	95.9	96.0
1986	96.2	96.6	96.7	97.7	97.8	97.8	97.5	97.8	98.3	98.5	99.3	99.6
1987	100.0	100.4	100.6	101.8	101.9	101.9	101.8	102.1	102.4	102.9	103.4	103.3
1988	103.3	103.7	104.1	105.8	106.2	106.6	106.7	107.9	108.4	109.5	110.0	110.3
1989	111.0	111.8	112.3	114.3	115.0	115.4	115.5	115.8	116.6	117.5	118.5	118.8
1990	119.5	120.2	121.4	125.1	126.2	126.7	126.8	128.1	129.3	130.3	130.0	129.9
1991	130.2	130.9	131.4	133.1	133.5	134.1	133.8	134.1	134.6	135.1	135.6	135.7
1992	135.6	136.3	136.7	138.8	139.3	139.3	138.8	138.9	139.4	139.9	139.7	139.2
1993	137.9	138.8	139.3	140.6	141.1	141.0	140.7	141.3	141.9	141.8	141.6	141.9
1994	141.3	142.1	142.5	144.2	144.7	144.7	144.0	144.7	145.0	145.2	145.3	146.0
1995	146.0	146.9	147.5	149.0	149.6	149.8	149.1	149.9	150.6	149.8	149.8	150.7
1996	150.2	150.9	151.5	152.6	152.9	153.0	152.4	153.1	153.8	153.8	153.9	154.4
1997	154.4	155.0	155.4	156.3	156.9	157.5	157.5	158.5	159.3	159.5	159.6	160.0
1998	159.5	160.3	160.8	162.6	163.5	163.4	163.0	163.7	164.4	164.5	164.5	164.4
1999	163.4	163.7	164.1	165.2	165.6	165.6	165.1	165.5	166.2	166.5	166.7	167.3
2000	166.6	167.5	168.4	170.1	170.7	171.1	170.5	170.5	171.7	171.6	172.1	172.2
2001	171.1	172.0	172.2	173.1	174.2	174.4	173.3	174.0	174.6	174.3	173.6	173.4
2002	173.3	173.8	174.5	175.7	176.2	176.2	175.9	176.4	177.6	177.9	178.2	178.5
2003	178.4	179.3	179.9	181.2	181.5	181.3	181.3	181.6	182.5	182.6	182.7	183.5
2004	183.1	183.8	184.6	185.7	186.5	186.8	186.8	187.4	188.1	188.6	189.0	189.9

SOURCE:- <www.statistics.gov.uk/STATBASE/expodata/files/6939125651.csv>.

Inflation rate
% change in Retail Price Index over preceding twelve months

	Annual % change	Jan	Feb	Mar	Apr	May	Jun	Jul	Aug	Sep	Oct	Nov	Dec
1979	13.4	9.3	9.6	9.8	10.1	10.3	11.4	15.6	15.8	16.5	17.2	17.4	17.2
1980	18.0	18.4	19.1	19.8	21.8	21.9	21.0	16.9	16.3	15.9	15.4	15.3	15.1
1981	11.9	13.0	12.5	12.6	12.0	11.7	11.3	10.9	11.5	11.4	11.7	12.0	12.0
1982	8.6	12.0	11.0	10.4	9.4	9.5	9.2	8.7	8.0	7.3	6.8	6.3	5.4
1983	4.6	4.9	5.3	4.6	4.0	3.7	3.7	4.2	4.6	5.1	5.0	4.8	5.3
1984	5.0	5.1	5.1	5.2	5.2	5.1	5.1	4.5	5.0	4.7	5.0	4.9	4.6
1985	6.1	5.0	5.4	6.1	6.9	7.0	7.0	6.9	6.2	5.9	5.4	5.5	5.7
1986	3.4	5.5	5.1	4.2	3.0	2.8	2.5	2.4	2.4	3.0	3.0	3.5	3.7
1987	4.2	3.9	3.9	4.0	4.2	4.1	4.2	4.4	4.4	4.2	4.5	4.1	3.7
1988	4.9	3.3	3.3	3.5	3.9	4.2	4.6	4.8	5.7	5.9	6.4	6.4	6.8
1989	7.8	7.5	7.8	7.9	8.0	8.3	8.3	8.2	7.3	7.6	7.3	7.7	7.7

	Annual % change	Jan	Feb	Mar	Apr	May	Jun	Jul	Aug	Sep	Oct	Nov	Dec
1990	9.5	7.7	7.5	8.1	9.4	9.7	9.8	9.8	10.6	10.9	10.9	9.7	9.3
1991	5.9	9.0	8.9	8.2	6.4	5.8	5.8	5.5	4.7	4.1	3.7	4.3	4.5
1992	3.7	4.1	4.1	4.0	4.3	4.3	3.9	3.7	3.6	3.6	3.6	3.0	2.6
1993	1.6	1.7	1.8	1.9	1.3	1.3	1.2	1.4	1.7	1.8	1.4	1.4	1.9
1994	2.4	2.5	2.4	2.3	2.6	2.6	2.6	2.3	2.4	2.2	2.4	2.6	2.9
1995	3.5	3.3	3.4	3.5	3.3	3.4	3.5	3.5	3.6	3.9	3.2	3.1	3.2
1996	2.4	2.9	2.7	2.7	2.4	2.2	2.1	2.2	2.1	2.1	2.7	2.7	2.5
1997	3.1	2.8	2.7	2.6	2.4	2.6	2.9	3.3	3.5	3.6	3.7	3.7	3.6
1998	3.4	3.3	3.4	3.5	4.0	4.2	3.7	3.5	3.3	3.2	3.1	3.0	2.8
1999	1.5	2.4	2.1	2.1	1.6	1.3	1.3	1.3	1.1	1.1	1.2	1.4	1.8
2000	3.0	2.0	2.3	2.6	3.0	3.1	3.3	3.3	3.0	3.3	3.1	3.2	2.9
2001	1.8	2.7	2.7	2.3	1.8	2.1	1.9	1.6	2.1	1.7	1.6	0.9	0.7
2002	1.7	1.3	1.0	1.3	1.5	1.1	1.0	1.5	1.4	1.7	2.1	2.6	2.9
2003	2.9	2.9	3.2	3.1	3.1	3.0	2.9	3.1	2.9	2.8	2.6	2.5	2.8
2004	3.0	2.6	2.5	2.6	2.5	2.8	3.0	3.0	3.2	3.1	3.3	3.4	3.5

SOURCE:- <www.statistics.gov.uk/>.

Gross Domestic Product, Taxes and Prices

	Standard rate of income tax at 1 Apr	Public sector net cash requirement (year ended 1 Apr)	Public sector debt as % of GDP	Gross domestic product at market prices (£m)	Real GDP per head (1970 = 100)	Purchasing power of £ (1987 = 100)
1979	33	–	–	197,355	122.4	–
1980	30	–	–	230,695	119.7	–
1981	30	–	–	253,000	117.9	–
1982	30	–	–	277,090	120.3	125
1983	30	–	–	302,774	124.5	120
1984	30	–	–	324,407	127.4	114
1985	30	–	–	354,952	131.5	108
1986	29	–	–	381,317	136.3	104
1987	27	–	–	419,631	142.1	100
1988	25	–	–	468,386	149.1	95
1989	25	–	–	514,168	151.7	88
1990	25	–	–	557,300	152.4	81
1991	25	–776	–	586,149	149.7	76
1992	25	13,856	–	610,854	149.5	74
1993	25	36,260	32.0	642,327	152.7	72
1994	25	46,131	37.2	681,327	159.3	71
1995	25	36,688	40.7	719,176	163.3	68
1996	24	31,485	42.7	763,290	167.0	67
1997	23	22,728	43.7	810,944	172.2	65
1998	23	1,112	41.5	859,436	176.6	63
1999	23	–6,979	39.1	903,865	179.6	62

	Standard rate of income tax at 1 Apr	Public sector net cash requirement (year ended 1 Apr)	Public sector debt as % of GDP	Gross domestic product at market prices (£m)	Real GDP per head (1970 = 100)	Purchasing power of £ (1987 = 100)
2000	22	–8,541	36.2	951,265	184.3	60
2001	22	–37,249	31.2	994,037	188.3	59
2002	22	3,318	30.2	1,043,945	–	58
2003	22	22,362	30.8	–	–	–

SOURCES:- *Annual Abstract of Statistics*; <www.statistics.gov.uk/>.

Production and Interest Rates

	Index of Production[a] (2000=100)	Car production (000s)	Coal production (million tonnes)	Steel production (million tonnes)	Agricultural output at basic prices (£m)	Balance of payments: current account (£m)
1979	76.6	1,070	121	21.13	–	–1,002
1980	71.6	924	128	11.08	–	1,740
1981	69.3	955	125	15.57	–	4,846
1982	70.7	888	122	13.71	–	2,233
1983	73.3	1,045	116	14.99	–	1,258
1984	73.3	909	50	15.12	–	–1,294
1985	77.3	1,048	91	15.72	–	–570
1986	79.2	1,019	105	14.73	–	–3,614
1987	82.4	1,143	102	17.41	–	–7,538
1988	86.4	1,227	102	18.95	–	–19,850
1989	88.2	1,299	99	18.74	–	–26,321
1990	87.9	1,296	92	17.84	–	–22,281
1991	85.0	1,237	93	16.47	–	–10,659
1992	85.2	1,292	84	16.21	15,545	–12,974
1993	87.1	1,376	68	16.62	16,001	–11,919
1994	91.8	1,467	49	17.28	16,605	–6,768
1995	93.4	1,532	52	17.60	17,813	–9,015
1996	94.7	1,686	49	17.99	17,422	–7,001
1997	96.0	1,698	47	18.50	15,468	–937
1998	97.0	1,748	40	17.32	14,109	–3,796
1999	98.1	1,787	36	16.28	13,659	–20,878
2000	100.0	1,641	31	15.15	12,822	–19,539
2001	98.4	1,492	32	13.54	13,428	–18,038
2002	95.7	1,630	30	11.67	13,448	–18,965
2003	95.0					

[a] The Index of Production (IoP) measures the volume of production of the manufacturing, mining and quarrying, and energy supply industries, which covered nearly 27 per cent of the UK economy in 1995. The index is measured at base year prices (currently 2000).

SOURCES:- *Annual Abstract of Statistics*; <www.statistics.gov.uk/statbase/Product.asp?vlnk=6230&More=N>.

Base Rates of Major Clearing Banks

1979	1 Jan	12.5		12 Apr	12.75–13		13 Nov	7
	14 Feb	13.5		19 Apr	12.5–12.75	1993	26 Jan	6
	6 Mar	13		12 Jun	12.5		23 Nov	5.5
	6 Apr	12		15 Jul	12	1994	8 Feb	5.25
	15 Jun	14		29 Jul	11.5		12 Sep	5.75
	16 Nov	17	1986	9 Jan	12.5		7 Dec	6.25
1980	4 Jul	16		19 Mar	11.5	1995	21 Feb	6.75
	24 Nov	14		8 Apr	11		13 Dec	6.5
1981	11 Mar	12		21 Apr	10.5	1996	18 Jan	6.25
	16 Sep	14		27 May	10		4 Feb	5.5
	1 Oct	16		10 Oct	11		8 Apr	5.25
	14 Oct	15.5	1987	10 Mar	10.5		8 Mar	6
	9 Nov	15		18 Mar	10		6 Jun	5.75
	3 Dec	14.5		28 Apr	9.5		30 Oct	6
1982	22 Jan	14		11 May	9	1997	6 May	6.25
	25 Feb	13.5		6 Aug	10		6 Jun	6.25–6.5
	12 Mar	13		23 Oct	9.5–10		9 Jun	6.5
	8 Jun	12.5		29 Oct	9.5		10 Jul	6.75
	13 Jul	12		4 Nov	9		7 Aug	7
	2 Aug	11.5		4 Dec	8.5		6 Nov	7.25
	18 Aug	11	1988	2 Feb	9	1998	4 Jun	7.5
	31 Aug	10.5		17 Mar	8.5		8 Oct	7.25
	7 Oct	10		11 Apr	8		5 Nov	6.75
	14 Oct	9.5		17 May	7.5		10 Dec	6.25
	4 Nov	9		2 Jun	8	1999	7 Jan	6
	26 Nov	10–10.25		6 Jun	8.5		4 Feb	5.5
1983	12 Jan	11		22 Jun	8.5–9		8 Apr	5.25
	15 Mar	10.5		28 Jun	9.5		10 Jun	5
	15 Apr	10		4 Jul	10		8 Sep	5–5.25
	15 Jun	9.5		18 Jul	10.5		10 Sep	5.25
	4 Oct	9		8 Aug	11		4 Nov	5.5
1984	7 Mar	8.75–9		25 Aug	12	2000	13 Jan	5.75
	15 Mar	8.5–8.75		25 Nov	13		10 Feb	6
	10 May	9–9.25	1989	24 May	14	2001	8 Feb	5.75
	27 Jun	9.25		5 Oct	15		5 Apr	5.5
	9 Jul	10	1990	8 Oct	14		10 May	5.25
	12 Jul	12	1991	13 Feb	13.5		2 Aug	5
	9 Aug	11.5		27 Feb	13		18 Sep	4.75
	10 Aug	11		22 Mar	12.5		4 Oct	4.5
	20 Aug	10.5		12 Apr	12		8 Nov	4
	7 Nov	10		24 May	11.5	2003	6 Feb	3.75
	20 Nov	9.75–10		12 Jul	11		10 Jul	3.5
	23 Nov	9.5–9.75		4 Sep	10.5		6 Nov	3.75
1985	11 Jan	10.5	1992	5 May	10	2004	5 Feb	4
	14 Jan	12		16 Sep	12		6 May	4.25
	28 Jan	14		17 Sep	10		10 Jun	4.5
	20 Mar	13.5		22 Sep	9		5 Aug	4.75
	29 Mar	3–13.5		16 Oct	8–9	2005	4 Aug	4.5
	2 Apr	13–13.25		19 Oct	8			

Where two figures are given it normally reflects the fact that some of the clearing banks have delayed falling into line with a rate cut or increase. Where the delay is only one day, only the date of the first change is given.

Government Borrowing and National Debt

Year	Public sector current spending £billion	Public sector current spending % GDP	Cyclically-adjusted Budget balances (% GDP) Public sector net borrowing	Cyclically-adjusted Budget balances (% GDP) Surplus on current budget	Gross nominal liabilities of the National Loans Fund (formerly known as National Debt) £ billion	Gross nominal liabilities of the National Loans Fund (formerly known as National Debt) % GDP	Money GDP (£ billion)
1979	66.3	38.4	4.9	–2.5	86.9	50.3	172.6
1980	79.4	38.2	4.0	–1.8	95.3	45.9	207.6
1981	96.6	40.8	3.4	–1.6	113.0	47.8	236.5
1982	110.6	42.6	–1.5	2.4	118.4	45.6	259.5
1983	120.9	42.7	–1.3	2.8	127.9	45.1	283.5
1984	130.4	42.3	0.1	1.7	142.9	46.3	308.3
1985	141.0	42.6	0.7	0.8	158.0	47.8	330.9
1986	148.7	41.0	0.4	0.9	171.4	47.2	362.8
1987	155.8	40.1	1.7	–1.0	185.8	47.9	388.1
1988	166.4	38.6	2.0	–1.3	197.4	45.8	431.2
1989	173.7	36.2	1.1	–0.7	197.3	41.1	479.9
1990	187.4	35.7	2.7	–1.5	192.9	36.7	525.1
1991	203.3	36.1	2.9	–1.4	198.7	35.3	563.7
1992	228.4	38.4	3.6	–1.8	214.8	36.1	594.9
1993	247.3	40.2	5.7	–3.7	249.1	40.5	615.1
1994	261.2	40.0	5.5	–3.9	307.3	47.0	652.9
1995	273.6	39.7	4.6	–3.2	349.5	50.6	689.7
1996	285.7	39.2	4.0	–2.6	391.2	53.6	728.7
1997	296.2	38.3	3.0	–2.3	419.8	54.2	773.4
1998	303.5	36.9	0.7	–0.1	419.3	50.9	822.8
1999	312.2	35.9	–0.1	0.8	419.2	48.2	868.4
2000	325.0	35.4	–1.3	1.8	426.2	46.3	919.1
2001	346.9	36.1	–0.9	1.4	426.0	44.2	961.9
2002	365.1	36.4	0.3	0.7	434.5	43.2	1004.1
2003	392.8	37.1	1.8	–0.7	448.0	42.4	1057.8
2004	425.5	38.1	2.2	–1.0			1115.9

The first four columns refer to financial year ended 31 March that year.

Balance of Trade

	Export of goods (£m)	Export of services (£m)	Import of goods (£m)	Import of services (£m)	Balance (£m)
1979	40,849	14,066	44,175	9,990	750
1980	47,493	15,114	46,164	11,285	5,158
1981	51,034	16,398	47,796	12,447	7,189
1982	55,657	17,051	53,778	13,853	5,077
1983	60,984	18,902	62,602	14,826	2,458
1984	70,565	21,094	75,974	16,603	–918
1985	78,291	23,783	81,707	17,016	3,351
1986	72,997	24,682	82,614	18,279	–3,214
1987	79,531	27,033	91,229	20,220	–4,885
1988	80,711	26,843	102,264	22,393	–17,103
1989	92,611	28,998	117,335	25,355	–21,081
1990	102,313	31,574	121,020	27,237	–14,370
1991	103,939	32,001	114,162	27,899	–6,121
1992	107,863	36,228	120,913	30,746	–7,568
1993	122,229	41,411	135,295	34,830	–6,485
1994	135,143	45,365	146,269	38,986	–4,747
1995	153,577	49,932	165,600	41,451	–3,542
1996	167,196	56,773	180,918	46,501	–3,450
1997	171,923	61,104	184,265	47,686	1,076
1998	164,056	66,278	185,869	52,969	–8,504
1999	166,166	72,628	195,217	59,494	–15,917
2000	187,936	79,071	220,912	65,645	–19,550
2001	190,055	82,314	230,703	69,098	–27,432
2002	186,517	87,203	233,192	71,626	–31,098
2003	188,602	91,112	236,018	75,510	–31,814

SOURCE:- <www.statistics.gov.uk/STATBASE/expodata/files/8487137181.csv>.

Central Government Revenue: Inland Revenue

									Amounts: £ million
Year	Income tax	Total	Corporation tax of which: ACT	Capital gains tax	IHT & CTT	Stamp duties	Oil tax	Other Inland Rev. taxes	Total Inland Rev.
1978–79	18,748	3,940	1,380	353	323	433	183	13	24,055
1979–80	20,599	4,646	1,831	431	401	620	1,435	26	28,201
1980–81	24,295	4,645	1,823	508	425	641	2,410	27	32,983
1981–82	28,720	4,930	1,993	526	480	797	2,390	2,418	40,282
1982–83	30,361	5,677	2,222	632	499	873	3,274	2,460	43,790
1983–84	31,108	6,184	2,118	671	599	1,138	6,017	68	45,796
1984–85	32,507	8,341	3,149	730	658	911	7,177	81	50,412
1985–86	35,353	10,708	3,808	908	881	1,226	6,375	62	55,520
1986–87	38,499	13,495	4,455	1,064	988	1,860	1,188	55	57,156
1987–88	41,402	15,734	4,947	1,379	1,078	2,440	2,296	28	64,357
1988–89	43,433	18,537	6,203	2,323	1,071	2,255	1,371	15	69,005
1989–90	48,801	21,495	7,267	1,854	1,233	2,117	1,050	10	76,559

Year	Income tax	Corporation tax Total	Corporation tax of which: ACT	Capital gains tax	IHT & CTT	Stamp duties	Oil tax	Other Inland Rev. taxes	Total Inland Rev.
1990–91	55,287	21,495	7,679	1,852	1,262	1,703	860	4	82,464
1991–92	57,493	18,263	7,936	1,140	1,299	1,697	–216	1	79,676
1992–93	56,797	15,783	8,738	982	1,211	1,265	69	1	76,108
1993–94	58,442	14,887	7,816	710	1,333	1,737	359	1	77,469
1994–95	63,100	19,390	8,085	926	1,411	1,798	712	1	87,336
1995–96	68,061	23,570	9,887	796	1,518	2,018	968	1	96,932
1996–97	69,071	27,578	11,887	1,131	1,558	2,467	1,729	–	103,745
1997–98	76,838	30,437	11,50	1,453	1,684	3,455	963	2,610	117,441
1998–99	86,507	30,032	11,00	2,002	1,786	4,623	502	2,614	128,067
1999–2000	93,910	34,322	1,737	2,122	2,047	6,898	853	–	140,152
2000–01	105,177	32,421	–449	3,236	2,221	8,165	1,517	–	152,737
2001–02	107,994	32,048	–	3,034	2,355	6,984	1,310	–	153,725
2002–03	109,507	29,320	–	1,596	2,354	7,549	958	–	151,284
2003–04	113,968	28,115	–	2,225	2,504	7,545	1,179	–	155,536
2004–05	123,700	32,400	–	2,000	2,900	8,800	1,500	–	171,200

Amounts: £ million

SOURCES:- *Annual Abstract of Statistics* and *Financial Statistics*; <www.hm-treasury.gov.uk/media/F6C/7E/public_fin_databank_211204.xls>.

Customs and Excise Duties, 1993– (£m)

Year	VAT	Fuel duty	Tobacco duty	Alcohol duty
1993–94	39,389	12,736	6,385	5,374
1994–95	41,817	14,253	7,388	5,560
1995–96	43,069	15,679	7,291	5,617
1996–97	46,657	17,174	8,039	5,631
1997–98	50,865	19,454	8,356	5,742
1998–99	52,311	21,553	8,207	5,966
1999–2000	56,779	22,553	5,684	6,429
2000–01	58,622	22,623	7,648	6,663
2001–02	61,043	21,916	7,755	6,955
2002–03	63,625	22,147	8,055	7,298
2003–04	69,275	22,786	8,093	7,565

SOURCE:- <www.uktradeinfo.com/index.cfm?task=factindex>.

Public Spending as a Percentage of GDP

Year	Current expenditure	Net investment	Total managed expenditure	Health	Education	Defence	Social Security
1978–79	42.7	2.4	45.3	–	–	–	–
1979–80	42.6	2.2	44.8	–	–	–	–
1980–81	45.5	1.8	47.3	–	–	–	–
1981–82	47.2	0.9	48.1	–	–	–	–

	Current expenditure	Net investment	Total managed expenditure	Health	Education	Defence	Social Security
1982–83	47.0	1.5	48.5	–	–	–	–
1983–84	46.3	1.8	48.3	–	–	–	–
1984–85	46.5	1.5	48.1	5.2	4.9	5.2	12.0
1985–86	44.3	1.2	45.5	5.0	4.6	5.0	11.9
1986–87	43.4	0.7	44.1	5.0	4.8	4.7	11.9
1987–88	41.4	0.7	42.1	4.9	4.7	4.3	11.2
1988–89	39.0	0.4	39.4	4.9	4.6	4.0	10.3
1989–90	38.5	1.2	39.7	4.8	4.6	3.9	10.0
1990–91	38.5	1.4	40.0	5.0	4.7	3.8	10.4
1991–92	40.5	1.8	42.3	5.4	4.9	3.8	11.7
1992–93	42.2	2.0	44.2	5.8	5.2	3.7	12.9
1993–94	42.0	1.6	43.6	5.7	5.1	3.5	13.2
1994–95	41.7	1.5	43.2	5.6	5.1	3.2	12.9
1995–96	41.2	1.4	42.6	5.6	4.9	3.0	12.7
1996–97	40.4	0.7	41.0	5.4	4.7	2.7	12.5
1997–98	38.7	0.6	39.2	5.3	4.5	2.5	11.8
1998–99	37.7	0.7	38.4	5.3	4.5	2.6	11.4
1999–2000	37.1	0.5	37.6	5.5	4.4	2.5	11.3
2000–01	37.8	0.6	38.4	5.6	4.6	2.6	11.3
2001–02	38.0	1.2	39.2	6.0	5.0	2.4	11.6
2002–03	38.4	1.4	39.8	6.3	5.1	2.5	11.7
2003–04	–	–	40.6	6.7	5.3	2.5	11.9

SOURCES: HM Treasury, *Public Finances Databank, April 2002*, London, 2002; <www.hm-treasury.gov.uk/Economic_Data_and_Tools/National_Statistics/natstat_index.cfm>.

UK Domestic Household Consumption Expenditure (£m)[a]

Year	Total	Food & drink	Alcohol & tobacco	Clothing & shoes	Housing	Transport	Recreation	Restaurants	Misc.
1979	115,586	20,988	6,659	9,475	17,394	17,091	11,293	12,017	8,681
1980	133,451	23,655	7,608	10,239	20,796	19,870	13,121	14,142	10,154
1981	147,502	24,946	8,637	10,520	25,040	21,852	14,325	15,429	11,331
1982	161,306	26,490	9,242	11,309	28,471	23,895	15,804	16,571	12,888
1983	177,501	28,061	9,925	12,536	31,076	27,154	17,327	18,731	14,618
1984	190,458	29,274	10,729	13,593	32,386	28,790	18,814	21,100	16,438
1985	208,536	30,657	11,485	15,366	35,661	31,881	20,650	23,191	18,379
1986	229,674	32,624	12,174	17,091	38,484	34,753	22,854	25,210	22,643
1987	251,825	34,482	12,649	18,300	40,876	38,997	25,864	27,225	27,054
1988	283,402	36,539	13,258	19,428	44,510	45,143	29,415	33,422	32,015
1989	310,607	39,305	13,755	20,228	48,715	49,634	33,146	37,200	36,747
1990	337,218	42,285	14,753	21,259	55,247	51,852	36,817	40,603	40,302
1991	358,802	44,576	16,204	22,485	63,318	52,170	38,300	42,077	42,492
1992	378,229	45,683	16,996	23,598	69,862	53,612	40,107	43,006	45,044
1993	400,827	47,171	17,697	24,887	73,890	56,671	42,677	46,170	48,813
1994	420,499	47,855	18,359	26,861	77,378	59,970	45,552	48,394	50,153

Year	Total	Food & drink	Alcohol & tobacco	Clothing & shoes	Housing	Transport	Recreation	Restaurants	Misc.
1995	442,914	49,790	18,776	28,030	81,412	62,733	51,075	50,383	52,329
1996	473,972	53,025	20,439	29,485	85,930	68,458	55,408	54,848	55,640
1997	502,908	53,832	21,553	30,901	90,214	75,458	59,971	57,266	59,171
1998	534,564	55,192	22,459	32,238	96,197	80,287	65,248	61,759	63,240
1999	565,062	57,025	24,458	33,275	101,211	84,193	69,732	64,413	68,432
2000	596,408	58,563	24,617	35,479	105,654	89,656	72,217	68,424	74,154
2001	626,059	59,974	25,158	37,042	113,467	92,560	76,005	71,493	79,204
2002	655,333	61,170	25,960	39,306	118,859	94,921	81,964	76,734	82,361
2003	681,057	63,082	27,342	41,192	125,459	97,988	83,713	81,188	84,719

[a] Estimates are given to the nearest £ million but cannot be regarded as accurate to this degree.

SOURCE:- *Economic Trends Annual Supplement.*

Concentration of Marketable Wealth Among Adult Population

Most wealthy percentages of population

Year	Percentages of wealth owned					
	1%	2%	5%	10%	25%	50%
1979	20	26	37	50	72	92
1980	19	25	36	50	73	91
1981	18	24	36	50	73	92
1982	18	24	36	49	72	91
1983	20	26	37	50	73	91
1984	18	24	35	48	71	91
1985	18	24	36	49	73	91
1986	18	24	36	50	73	90
1987	18	25	37	51	74	91
1988	17	23	36	49	71	92
1989	17	24	35	48	70	92
1990	18	24	35	47	71	93
1991	17	24	35	47	71	92
1992	18	25	38	50	73	93
1993	18	26	38	51	73	93
1994	19	27	39	52	74	93
1995	19	26	38	50	72	92
1996	20	27	40	52	74	93
1997	22	30	43	54	75	93
1998	22	28	40	52	72	91
1999	23	30	43	55	74	94
2000	23	31	44	56	75	95
2001[a]	22	29	42	54	72	94
2002[a]	23	30	43	56	74	94

[a] Provisional.

SOURCE:- *Inland Revenue Statistics.*

Shares of Total Income Tax Liability

Percentages

Quantile groups of taxpayers	Top 1%	Top 5%	Top 10%	Next 40%	Lower 50%	All taxpayers (=100%) £ billion
1990–91	15	32	42	43	15	60.2
1991–92	16	33	43	42	15	63.3
1992–93	16	33	44	43	13	60.7
1993–94	16	33	44	43	13	61.4
1994–95	17	34	45	42	13	66.3
1995–96	17	34	45	42	13	72.0
1996–97	20	37	48	40	12	73.7
1997–98	20	37	48	40	12	79.5
1998–99	21	39	49	39	12	88.0
1999–00	21	40	50	38	11	93.2
2000–01	22	41	52	37	11	105.5
2001–02	22	41	52	37	11	107.0
2002–03[a]	21	40	52	38	11	108.8
2003–04[b]	21	40	51	38	11	116.7
2004–05[b]	21	40	52	38	11	124.3

[a] This is the latest survey year.
[b] Projected estimates based upon the 2002–03 Survey of Personal Incomes, in line with December 2004 Pre-Budget Report. These projections are not within the scope of National Statistics.

This table gives an alternative presentation of how the total income tax burden is shared between different groups of taxpayers. Taxpayers in each year are ranked according to their tax liability and then grouped together (so in 2004–05 when there are 30 million taxpayers in total, the top 1% of taxpayers have some 21% of the total tax liability).

SOURCE:- *Inland Revenue Statistics.*

Consumer Credit

Hire Purchase and other instalment credit (Finance Houses, Durable Goods, Shops and Department Stores)–total outstanding business at end of period (£m).

	£m.		£m.		£m.
1979	6,901	1987	36,566	1995	68,203
1980	7,844	1988	42,839	1996	77,481
1981	13,403	1989	48,384	1997	88,081
1982	16,030	1990	52,522	1998	102,222
1983	18,933	1991	53,449	1999	116,155
1984	22,307	1992	52,593	2000	128,041
1985	26,112	1993	52,334	2001	141,719
1986	30,548	1994	58,056	2002	157,755

From 1981 figures include all consumer credit companies licensed to take deposits, both in monetary and retail sectors. The figures jump in 1983 with the inclusion of bank loans.

SOURCES:- *Annual Abstract of Statistics; Economic Trends.*

Budget Dates

1979	3 Apr	1988	15 Mar	1997	3 Jul
	12 Jun	1989	14 Mar	1998	17 Mar
1980	26 Mar	1990	20 Mar	1999	9 Mar
1981	10 Mar	1991	19 Mar	2000	21 Mar
1982	9 Mar	1992	10 Mar	2001	7 Mar
1983	15 Mar	1993	16 Mar	2002	17 Apr
1984	13 Mar	1993	30 Nov	2003	9 Apr
1985	19 Mar	1994	29 Nov	2004	17 Mar
1986	18 Mar	1995	28 Nov	2005	18 Mar
1987	17 Mar	1996	26 Nov		

Occasionally ad hoc statements by the Chancellor of the Exchequer on revised fiscal and economic arrangements have been referred to by the media as 'Budgets', although not so regarded by the Treasury. Such statements or 'mini-Budgets' occurred on 22 July 1974, 12 November 1974, 11 July 1975, 19 February 1976, 22 July 1976, 15 December 1976, 15 July 1977, 26 October 1977, 8 June 1978 and 15 November 1980.

In 1982 the forecast required under the *Industry Act, 1975* for decisions on public expenditure plans and proposed changes to National Insurance contributions were brought together in one 'Autumn Statement'. These took place on the following dates:

1982	8 Nov	1988	8 Nov
1983	17 Nov	1989	15 Nov
1984	11 Nov	1990	8 Nov
1985	12 Nov	1991	6 Nov
1986	6 Nov	1992	12 Nov
1987	3 Nov		

The Chancellor announced in his 1992 Budget that as from November 1993, the Budget and the Autumn Statement would be brought together and announced on the same day, in late November or early December. In the course of his 1997 Budget, the Chancellor announced that from 1998 the Budget would revert to the Spring, with a Pre-Budget Report published in November each year.

Pre-Budget Reports

1997	25 Nov	2001	27 Nov
1998	3 Nov	2002	27 Nov
1999	9 Nov	2003	10 Dec
2000	8 Nov	2004	2 Dec

In 1998 the Chancellor announced that in future all decisions about spending would be taken for three year periods, and announced to Parliament in a Comprehensive Spending Review; because the last year of the first review period overlapped with the first year of the second, these announcements would come every two years.

Spending Reviews

1998	14 Jul
2000	18 Jul
2002	15 Jul
2004	12 Jul

Privatisation 1979–97

In May 1979 the Conservatives came to power pledged to 'roll back the frontiers of the state', although the objective of systematically selling off state-owned assets was not at that stage clearly spelled out. Below is a list of the main privatisations since 1979, and the proceeds; it does not include sales by public corporations which retained the proceeds themselves, such as BR's sale of Sealink in 1984.

	Assets sold	*Net proceeds £m*
Nov 1979	5% of British Petroleum	276
Dec 1979	25% of ICL Computers	37
	Suez Finance Company shares	22
	Miscellaneous (mainly land and property)	42
Total revenue for 1979/80 from privatisation		**377**
Jun 1980	100% of Fairey (NEB subsidiary)	22
Jul 1980	50% of Ferranti (NEB subsidiary)	55
Feb 1981	49% of British Aerospace	43
	North Sea Oil licences	195
	Miscellaneous (mainly property assets)	90
Total revenue for 1980/81 from privatisation		**405**
Oct 1981	49% of Cable and Wireless	182
Feb 1982	100% of Amersham International	64
Feb 1982	100% of National Freight Corporation	5
Feb 1982	24% of British Sugar	44
	NEB subsidiaries	2
	New Towns	73

	Assets sold	Net proceeds £m
	Oil stockpiles	50
	Miscellaneous	74
Total revenue for 1981/82 from privatisation		**494**
Nov 1982	51% of Britoil (first cash call)	334
Feb 1983	52% of Associated British Ports	46
	Oil stockpiles	33
	Miscellaneous	42
Total revenue for 1982/83 from privatisation		**455**
Apr 1983	Britoil (second cash call)	293
Sep 1983	7% of British Petroleum	543
Dec 1983	25% of Cable and Wireless	263
Mar 1984	Scott Lithgow shipyard	12
	Miscellaneous	31
Total revenue for 1983/84 from privatisation		**1,139**
Apr 1984	48% of Associated British Ports	51
Jun 1984	Enterprise Oil	384
Nov 1984	British Telecom (first instalment)	1,358
	British Telecom (loan stock)	44
	NEB subsidiaries	168
	Forestry Commission land and miscellaneous	55
Total revenue for 1984/85 from privatisation		**2,050**
May 1985	British Aerospace	347
Jun 1985	British Telecom (second instalment)	1,246
Aug 1985	Britoil	426
Dec 1985	Cable and Wireless	577
	British Telecom (loan stock)	61
	NEB subsidiaries	30
	Land and buildings	18
Total revenue for 1985/86 from privatisation		**2,706**
Apr 1986	British Telecom (third instalment)	1,081
Dec 1986	British Gas (first instalment)	1,820
Feb 1987	British Airways (first instalment)	435
	British Gas (redemption of debt)	750
	British Telecom (loan stock)	53
	British Telecom (preference shares)	250
	NEB subsidiaries	34
	Wytch Farm	18
	Miscellaneous	16
Total revenue for 1986/87 from privatisation		**4,458**
Apr 1987	Royal Ordnance	186
May 1987	Rolls-Royce	1,029
Jun 1987	British Gas (second instalment)	1,758
Jul 1987	BAA	534
Aug 1987	British Airways (second instalment)	419
Aug 1987	Plant Breeding Institute	65

	Assets sold	Net proceeds £m
Oct 1987	British Petroleum (first instalment)	863
	British Telecom (loan stock)	23
	British Telecom (preference shares)	250
	Miscellaneous	12
Total revenue for 1987/88 from privatisation		**5,140**
Apr 1988	British Gas (third instalment)	1,555
May 1988	BAA	689
Aug 1988	British Petroleum (second instalment)	3,030
Dec 1988	British Steel	1,138
Mar 1989	General Practice Finance Corporation	67
(May 1987)	Rolls-Royce	3
	British Gas (redemption of debt)	250
	British Telecom (loan stock)	85
	British Telecom (preference shares)	250
	Miscellaneous	2
Total revenue for 1988/89 from privatisation		**7,069**
Aug 1988	Rover Group	150
Apr 1989	British Petroleum (third instalment)	1,363
Jun 1989	Short Brothers	30
Dec 1989	Water companies (first instalment)	423
	British Gas (mainly redemption of debt)	804
	British Steel	1,289
	British Telecom (loan stock)	92
	Harland and Wolff	8
	Water companies (debt redemption)	73
	Miscellaneous	−13
Total revenue for 1989/90 from privatisation		**4,226**
Jul 1990	British Gas (sale of shares)	150
Jul 1990	Water companies (second instalment)	1,487
Dec 1990	Electricity shares (England and Wales)	3,134
	British Gas (redemption of debt)	350
	British Telecom (loan stock)	100
	Wytch Farm	130
	Miscellaneous	−6
Total revenue for 1990/91 from privatisation		**5,346**
Jun 1991	Electricity shares (Scotland)	1,112
Jul 1991	Water companies (sale of shares)	1,483
Oct 1991	National Transcommunications	70
Dec 1991	British Telecom (first instalment)	1,666
Dec 1991	Insurance Services Group	12
Mar 1992	British Technology Group	24
	British Telecom (loan stock)	106
	Electricity shares (England and Wales)	2,329
	Redemption of Electricity debt	1,106
	Miscellaneous	15
Total revenue for 1991/92 from privatisation		**7,923**

	Assets sold	Net proceeds £m
	British Gas (redemption of debt)	350
Jun 1992	British Telecom (second instalment)	3,544
Aug 1992	Electricity shares (England and Wales)	1,465
	British Telecom (Loan stock)	113
	Electricity shares (Scotland)	907
	Redemption of Electricity debt	110
	Privatised companies' debt	1,337
	Northern Ireland Electricity	350
	Miscellaneous	–62
Total revenue for 1992/93 from privatisation		**8,189**
	British Telecom (third instalment)	3,773
	British Telecom (loan stock)	124
	Electricity shares (Scotland)	703
	Redemption of Electricity debt	154
	Northern Ireland Electricity	218
	Miscellaneous	–32
Total revenue for 1993/94 from privatisation		**5,453**
	British Coal	811
	British Telecom (third instalment)	1,519
	British Telecom (loan stock)	130
	Electricity shares (England and Wales)	1,724
	Redemption of Electricity debt	361
	Northern Ireland Electricity	187
	Privatised companies' debt	1,617
	Miscellaneous	21
Total revenue for 1994/95 from privatisation		**6,429**
	British Telecom (loan stock)	130
	Electricity shares (England and Wales)	1,029
	Privatised companies' debt	517
	Residual Share sales	750
Total revenue for 1995/96 from privatisation		**2,439**
	AEA Technology	215
	British Coal	111
	British Telecom (loan stock)	140
	Electricity shares (England and Wales)	796
	Nuclear industry (shares)	525
	Nuclear industry (redemption of debt)	160
	Privatised companies' debt	663
	Railtrack (shares)	910
	Railtrack (redemption of debt)	282
	Residual Share Sales	560
	Miscellaneous	138
Total revenue for 1996/97 from privatisation		**4,550**

SOURCES:- R. Vernon (ed.), *The Promise of Privatisation* (1988); J. Vickers and G. Yarrow, *Privatisation: an Economic analysis* (1988); also *Public Expenditure Statistical Analyses*, HM Treasury.

Nationalised Industries

British Airways, 1974–87

Responsible Minister	Chairman
1974 Sec. of State for Trade	1 Jul 79 Sir R. Stainton
1983 Sec. of State for Transport	3 Jan 81 J. (Ld) King

Established under the *Civil Aviation Act, 1971*, to take overall responsiblility for the activities of BEA and BOAC from 1 April 1972. Became fully operational from 1 April 1974. Became Limited Company in 1983. Sold by share issue in 1987.

British Airports Authority, 1966–87
(BAA plc, 1986–87)

Responsible Minister	Chairman
1974 Sec. of State for Trade	1 Mar 77 (Sir) N. Payne
1983 Sec. of State for Transport	

Established under the *Airports Authority Act, 1965*, to run Gatwick, Heathrow and Stansted, and since 1971 Edinburgh Turnhouse airports. Aberdeen and Glasgow were acquired in 1975. Became BAA plc under *Airports Act, 1986*. Sold by public share issue July 1987.

British Aerospace, 1977–81

Responsible Minister	Chairman
1977 Sec. of State for Industry	22 Mar 77 Ld Beswick
1983 Sec. of State for Trade and Industry	22 Mar 80 (Sir) A. Pearce

Established under the *Aircraft and Shipbuilding Act, 1977*, to promote the efficient and economical design, development, production, sale, repair and maintenance of civil and military aircraft, of guided weapons and of space vehicles. Became a public limited company under the *British Aerospace Act, 1980*. In 1981 51% of shares were sold to the private sector and employees. The remaining shares in government hands were sold in 1985.

Electricity Council, 1957–90

Responsible Minister	Chairman	
1974 Sec. of State for Energy	1 Apr 77	(Sir) F. Tombs
	1 Jan 81	(Sir) A. Bunch
	1 Apr 83	(Sir) P. Jones

Established under the *Electricity Act, 1957*, to co-ordinate development of the industry. Consists of 14 statutory corporations: the Electricity Council, the CEGB and 12 Area Electricity Boards. The Council was wound up in 1990, when the CEGB was broken up in anticipation of electricity privatisation.

Central Electricity Generating Board
(CEGB) 1957–90

Responsible Minister	*Chairman*	
1974 Sec. of State for Energy	9 May 77	G. England
	9 May 82	(*office vacant*)
	1 Jul 82	Sir W. (Ld) Marshall
	18 Dec 89	(*office vacant*)

Established under the *Electricity Act, 1957*, to own and operate the power stations and the National Grid, and to provide electricity in bulk to the 12 Area Boards. Under the *Electricity Act, 1989*, the CEGB was broken up into four companies – National Power, PowerGen, National Grid and Nuclear Electric, with effect from 1 April 1990.

North of Scotland Hydro-Electricity Board
(Scottish HydroElectric, 1990–91) 1943–90

Responsible Minister	*Chairman*	
1943 Secretary of State for Scotland	1 Jan 79	Ld Greenhill
	1 Jan 84	M. Joughin

Established under the *Hydro-Electric Development (Scotland) Act, 1943*, to supply electricity and to develop water power in the Highlands and Islands. In 1947 became responsible for all public generation and distribution of electricity in the North of Scotland. Under Electricity Act, 1989, name changed to Scottish HydroElectric, in April 1990, in preparation for privatisation which took place in June 1991.

South of Scotland Electricity Board
(Scottish Power, 1990–91) 1955–90

Responsible Minister	*Chairman*	
1955 Secretary of State for Scotland	1 Dec 54	(Sir) J. Pickles
	20 Feb 62	N. Elliot
	1 Apr 67	C. Allan
	1 Jan 74	F. Tombs
	1 Apr 77	D. Berridge
	22 Mar 82	(Sir) D. Miller

Established under the *Electricity Reorganisation (Scotland) Act, 1954*, to generate and distribute electricity throughout south of Scotland. Became Scottish Power in April 1990 under *Electricity Act, 1989*, and lost responsibility for nuclear power stations in Scotland. Sold by public share offer June 1991.

National Coal Board (NCB) 1946–87;
British Coal, 1987–97

Responsible Minister		*Chairman*	
1974	Sec. of State For Energy	3 Jul 71	(Sir) D. Ezra
1992	Pres. of Board of Trade	3 Jul 82	(Sir) N. Siddall
		1 Sep 83	I. MacGregor
		1 Sep 86	Sir R. Haslam
		1 Jan 91	N. Clarke
		1 Jul 97	P. Hutchinson

Established under the *Coal Industry Nationalisation Act, 1946*, to own and run the coal industry and certain ancillary activities. Changed name to British Coal under the *Coal Industry Act, 1987*. Most functions transferred to the Coal Authority under *Coal Industry Act, 1994*. On 31 December 97 the Corporation disposed of its remaining property and staff, although the shell company still exists.

Gas Council and Boards, 1948–73

Minister responsible		*Chairman*	
1970	Sec. of State for Trade and Industry	1 Jan 72	A. Hetherington

Established by the *Gas Act, 1948*, to co-ordinate 12 Area Gas Boards which were set up to manufacture and retail town gas. The Gas Council was responsible for the purchase and distribution of natural gas. Under the *Gas Act, 1972*, replaced by British Gas Corporation.

British Gas, 1973–86

Responsible Minister		*Chairman*	
1973	Sec. of State for Trade and Industry	1 Jan 73	(Sir) A. Hatherington
1974	Sec. of State for Energy	1 Jul 76	(Sir) D. Rooke

Established under the *Gas Act, 1972*, to take over responsibilities of Gas Council and Area Gas Boards. In 1984 British Gas's offshore oil interests were hived off to form Enterprise Oil. Became a public limited company under *Gas Act, 1986*, and sold by public share offer in December 1986.

United Kingdom Atomic Energy
Authority 1954– (UKAEA)

Responsible Minister		*Chairman*	
1974	Sec. of State for Energy	16 Oct 67	(Sir) J. Hill
1992	Pres. of Board of Trade	7 Jul 81	Sir W. Marshall
1997	Sec. of State for Trade and Industry	1 Oct 82	Sir P. Hirsch
		1 Oct 84	A. Allen
		1 Jan 87	J. Collier
		1 Jul 90	J. Maltby
		1 Jul 93	Sir A. Cleaver
		12 Mar 96	Sir K. Eaton
		1 Apr 02	D. Tunnicliffe
		1 May 04	Barbara Thomas Judge

Established under the *Atomic Energy Authority Act, 1954*, to be responsible for the development of nuclear energy and its applications. In May 1989 a commercial arm, AEA Technology, was established, which was privatised in 1996.

British National Oil Corporation (BNOC) 1976–82

Responsible Minister	Chairman
1976 Sec. of State for Energy	1 Jan 76 Ld Kearton

Established under the *Petroleum and Submarines Pipelines Act, 1975*, to search for and get, move, store and treat, buy, sell and deal in petroleum. In November 1982 the government sold its majority shareholding to the private sector.

British Nuclear Fuels, 1971–

Responsible Minister	Chairman	
1974 Sec. of State for Energy	1 Apr 71	(Sir) J. Hill
1992 Pres. of Board of Trade	1 Apr 83	C. Allday
1997 Sec. of State for Trade and Industry	1 Apr 86	(Sir) C. Harding
	1 Jul 92	J. Guinness
	1 Oct 99	H. Collum
	1 Jun 04	G. Campbell

Established under the *Atomic Energy Act, 1971*, from the former production group of the UK Atomic Energy Authority, taking over responsibility for the production, enrichment and reprocessing of nuclear fuel. Became a public limited company in 1984, with the Government the sole shareholder.

Nuclear Electric, 1990–96

Responsible Minister	Chairman
1990 Sec. of State for Energy	1 Jan 90 J. Collier
1992 Pres. of Board of Trade	

Established by the CEGB to take over the running of the nuclear power stations following the decision to exclude nuclear power stations from privatisation. In December 1995 Nuclear Electric became an operational subsidiary of a holding company, British Energy, which was floated on the stock exchange on 15 July 1996.

Scottish Nuclear, 1990–96

Responsible Minister	Chairman
1990 Sec. of State for Scotland	1 Apr 90 J. Hann

Took over the running of Scottish nuclear power stations from the South of Scotland Electricity Board as the electricity industry was prepared for privatisation under the *Electricity Act, 1989*. In December 1995 Scottish Nuclear became an operational subsidiary of a holding company, British Energy, which was floated on the stock exchange on 15 July 1996.

PowerGen, 1990–91

Responsible Minister	*Chairman*	
1990 Sec. of State for Energy	1 Apr 90	R. Malpas
	16 Nov 90	Sir G. Day

Formed when the CEGB was broken up prior to privatisation, with 39% of non-nuclear generating capacity. The Government sold 60% of the shares in February 1991.

National Power, 1990–91

Responsible Minister	*Chairman*	
1990 Sec. of State for Energy	1 Apr 90	Ld Marshall
	5 Jul 90	Sir T. Holdsworth

Formed when the CEGB was broken up prior to privatisation, with 61% of non-nuclear generating capacity. The Government sold 60% of the shares in February 1991.

Magnox Electric, 1996–98

Responsible Minister	*Chairman*	
1992 Pres. of Board of Trade	1 Apr 96	M. Baker

Magnox Electric was formed to run the Magnox power stations when the rest of Nuclear Electric was prepared for privatisation as part of British Energy. It was absorbed into BNFL in Jan 98.

London Regional Transport (LRT), 1984–2003

Responsible Minister	*Chairman*	
1984 Sec. of State for Transport	29 Jun 84	(Sir) K. Bright
	13 Mar 89	(Sir) W. Newton
	15 Sep 94	P. Ford
	23 Apr 98	B. Appleton
	1 Apr 99	Sir M. Bates
	8 May 01	B. Kiley
	17 Jul 01	Sir M. Bates

Established under the *London Regional Transport Act, 1984*, to take over responsibility for transport in London from the GLC. On 3 July 2000 it passed all its responsibilities apart from London Underground on to Transport for London. The Underground was taken over by Transport for London on 15 July 2003.

Transport for London (TfL), 2000–

Responsible Minister	*Chairman*	
2000 Mayor of London	1 Jul 00	K. Livingstone

Established under the *Greater London Authority Act, 1999*, to take over from London Regional Transport after establishment of the GLA and the London Mayor. TfL formally took control of London Underground on 15 July 2003.

British Railways Board (BR), 1963–98

Responsible Minister	*Chairman*	
1976 Sec. of State for Transport	12 Sep 76	(Sir) P. Parker
	12 Sep 83	(Sir) R. (Robert) Reid
	1 Apr 90	(Sir) R. (Bob) Reid
	1 Apr 95	J. Welsby

Established under the *Transport Act, 1962*, to take over the BTC's rail services. The *Railways Act, 1993*, laid down a framework for removing almost all operational functions to Railtrack, the train operating companies and the regulators. It continued to exist principally to manage a property portfolio. In January 1998 it became known for most purposes as Rail Property Ltd. The Government announced in July 1998 that the residual functions of the British Railways Board would be transferred to a Strategic Rail Authority.

British Transport Docks Board, 1963–84

Responsible Minister	*Chairman*	
1976 Sec. of State for Transport	1 May 71	Sir H. Browne
	1 May 82	K. Stuart

Established under the *Transport Act, 1962*, to administer publicly owned ports throughout the country. Under *Docks and Harbours Act, 1966*, became licensing authority for all but three ports. Sold off in 1983 and 1984 under the *Tranport Act, 1981*, to form Associated British Ports.

British Waterways Board, 1963–

Responsible Minister	*Chairman*	
1970 Sec. of State for Environment	1 Jul 68	Sir F. Price
2001 Sec. of State for Environment,	1 Jul 84	Sir L. Young
Food and Rural Affairs	1 Jul 87	A. Robertson *(acting)*
	22 Oct 87	D. Ingman
	1 Nov 93	*(office vacant)*
	1 Apr 94	B. Henderson
	14 Jul 99	G. Greener
	10 Jul 05	T. Hales

Established under the *Transport Act, 1962*, to take over inland waterways from the British Transport Commission. The *Transport Act, 1968*, extended its powers particularly in regard to recreation and amenities.

National Bus Company, 1968–91

Responsible Minister	*Chairman*	
1976 Sec. of State for Transport	1 Jan 79	Ld. Shepherd
	1 Jan 85	R. Brook
	8 Apr 86	R. Lund
	1 Apr 88	Sir P. Harrup

Established under the *Transport Act, 1968*, to take over responsibility for state-owned bus companies and bus manufacturing interests from the Transport Holding Company. Broken up and sold off following *Transport Act, 1985*. Formally wound up in April 1991.

National Freight Corporation, 1968–82

Responsible Minister	*Chairman*	
1976 Sec. of State For Transport	1 Jan 79	Sir R. Lawrence

Established under the *Transport Act, 1968*, to take over road haulage and shipping interests of the Transport Holding Company. Shipping interests terminated in 1971. Sold to the National Freight Consortium in 1982.

Scottish Transport Group, 1968–91

Responsible Minister	*Chairman*	
1968 Secretary of State for Scotland	1 Jan 78	A. Donnet (Ld)
	1 Jan 81	W. Stevenson
	1 Jan 87	I. Irwin

Established under the *Transport Act, 1968*, to control various transport activities in Scotland, including road passenger, insurance, tourism and shipping. Under the *Transport (Scotland) Act, 1989*, the Scottish Office announced a programme to dispose of STG's assets. This was largely complete by 1991, although the Group still formally exists.

British Steel Corporation, 1968–88

Responsible Minister	*Chairman*	
1974 Sec. of State for Industry	10 Sep 76	Sir C. Villiers
1983 Sec. of State for Trade and Industry	1 Jul 80	I. MacGregor
	1 Sep 83	(Sir) R. Haslam
	1 Apr 86	(Sir) R. Scholey

Established under the *Iron and Steel Act, 1967*, to take over the management of the major part of the steel industry. Sold by public share issue in December 1988 after becoming a public limited company under the terms of the *British Steel Act, 1988*.

Cable and Wireless Ltd, 1947–81

Responsible Minister	*Chairman*	
1974 Sec. of State for Industry	1 Nov 76	E. Short (Ld Glenamara)
1983 Sec. of State for Trade and Industry	15 Oct 80	(Sir) E. Sharp

Under the *Cable and Wireless Act, 1946*, the Government acquired all those shares of Cable and Wireless Ltd. not already in its possession. The company's UK assets were integrated into the Post Office and it continued to own and operate telecommunications services outside the UK. In 1981 the Government sold the majority of its shares; the remainder were sold in 1983 and 1985.

Post Office Corporation, 1970–2001
Consignia plc, 2001–02
Royal Mail Group, 2002–

Responsible Minister	*Chairman*	
1974 Sec. of State for Industry	31 Oct 77	Sir W. Barlow
1983 Sec. of State for Trade and Industry	1 Sep 80	Sir H. Chilver
	1 Oct 81	(Sir) R. Dearing
	1 Oct 87	Sir B. Nicholson
	1 Jan 93	(Sir) M. Heron
	16 Mar 98	N. Bain
	25 Mar 02	A. Leighton

Established under the *Post Office Act, 1969*, to take over from the office of the Postmaster General, responsibility for postal services, Giro and remittance services and telecommunications throughout the UK. In 1981 all telecommunications services were transferred to British Telecom.

British Telecom, 1981–84

Responsible Minister	*Chairman*	
1981 Sec. of State for Industry	27 Jul 81	Sir G. Jefferson
1983 Sec. of State for Trade and Industry		

Established under the *British Telecommunications Act, 1981*, to take over the telecommunication functions of the Post Office prior to privatisation. 50.2% of shares were sold in November 1984; the Government eventually sold its last 22% stake in the company in July 1993.

British Shipbuilders, 1977–90

Responsible Minister	*Chairman*	
1977 Sec. of State for Industry	1 Jul 77	Sir A. Griffin
1983 Sec. of State for Trade and Industry	1 Jul 80	(Sir) R. Atkinson
	1 Sep 83	G. Day
	1 May 86	P. Hares
	1 May 88	J. Lister
	4 Sep 89	C. Campbell

Established under the *Aircraft and Shipbuilding Industries Act, 1977*, to promote the efficient and economical design, development, production, sale, repair and maintenance of ships. Broken up from 1984. The last yard was sold in 1990, although the company was never formally wound up.

British Technology Group, 1981–92

Responsible Minister		*Chairman*	
1981	Sec. of State for Industry	20 Jul 81	Sir F. Wood
1983	Sec. of State for Trade and Industry	1 Nov 83	C. Barker

Established in 1981 as an umbrella organisation for the National Enterprise Board and the National Research Development Corporation, which retained separate legal identities until merged by the *British Technology Group Act, 1991*. It acted as a holding company for shares in high technology firms and had a brief to develop the potential of inventions made within the public sector. The group was sold to a consortium of investors in March 1992.

Rolls-Royce Ltd, 1971–87

Responsible Minister		*Chairman*	
1974	Sec. of State for Industry	5 Oct 72	Sir K. Keith *(Ld)*
1983	Sec. of State for Trade	22 Jan 80	Ld McFadzean
		31 Mar 83	Sir W. Duncan
		13 Nov 84	Sir A. Hall (acting)
		31 Jan 85	Sir F. Tombs

Established in February 1971 under the *Companies Act, 1960*, with the Government as the sole shareholder to ensure the continuance of those activities of Rolls-Royce Ltd which are essential to national defence and to air forces and airlines all over the world, Shares vested in NEB from 1 February 1976 to 12 August 1980. The Government sold its shares in 1987.

BL (British Leyland), 1975–86; Rover Group, 1986–88

Minister responsible		*Chairman*	
1975	Sec. of State for Industry	30 Oct 75	Sir R. Edwards
1983	Sec. of State for Trade and Industry	14 Apr 76	Sir R. Dobson
		1 Nov 77	(Sir) M. Edwardes
		8 Nov 82	Sir A. Bide
		1 May 86	(Sir) G. Day

Majority of shareholdings were purchased in 1975, using *Companies Act, 1960*, following financial problems. Shares vested in NEB from 30 October 1975 to 31 March 1981. Sold to British Aerospace, August 1988.

External Financing Requirements of Nationalised Industries
(excluding central government grants generally available to private sector)

Figures are billions of pounds. Year ending April.

Year	BA	Coal	Gas	BR	Shipb.	Steel	BT	Elec.	LRT	PO	Water	Total
1979	0.1	0.6	−0.4	0.6	0.1	0.8	−0.1	−0.1	–	–	0.3	2.3
1980	0.2	0.7	−0.4	0.7	0.2	0.6	0.3	0.3	–	–	0.3	3.0

Year	BA	Coal	Gas	BR	Shipb.	Steel	BT	Elec.	LRT	PO	Water	Total
1981	0.3	0.8	−0.4	0.8	0.2	1.1	−0.1	0.2	–	–	0.3	3.2
1982	0.2	1.2	–	1.0	0.1	0.8	0.2	−0.1	–	–	0.3	3.6
1983	–	1.0	−0.2	0.8	0.1	0.6	−0.3	−0.1	–	−0.1	0.3	2.1
1984	−0.2	1.2	–	0.8	0.3	0.3	−0.2	−0.3	–	−0.1	0.4	2.3
1985	−0.3	1.7	−0.2	1.0	0.2	0.5	−0.3	0.8	–	–	0.3	3.9
1986	−0.2	0.4	−0.2	0.9	–	0.4	–	−0.3	0.3	−0.1	0.2	1.7
1987	−0.1	0.9	−0.7	0.8	0.2	–	–	−1.2	0.3	−0.1	0.1	0.3
1988		0.9		0.5	0.1	−0.3		−1.1	0.2	−0.1	–	0.2
1989		0.8		0.4	0.1	−0.4		−1.7	0.2	−0.1	–	−0.5
1990		1.3		0.7				−1.4	0.3	–	–	1.0
1991		0.9		1.1				−0.3	0.5	–	–	2.3
1992		0.6		1.5				−0.1	0.6	−0.1		3.8
1993		0.8		2.1				−0.3	0.9	−0.1		4.4
1994		1.4		1.5					0.7	−0.2		3.6
1995		0.7		−0.4					0.8	−0.2		1.0
1996				−1.6					0.9	−0.2		−0.4
1997				−1.0						1.0	−0.3	−0.5
1998				0.1						0.7	−0.3	−0.7
1999										0.4	–	
2000										0.8	0.7	
2001										0.3	0.6	
2002										0.5	0.2	
2003										0.8	0.2	
2004										0.7	0.4	

Regulators of Privatised Industries

As utilities and public services were sold off into the private sector in the 1980s and 1990s, a number of regulating authorities were established with varying remits – all intended to protect the public interest.

Office of Gas Supply (OFGAS), 1986–99

Director General
1 Aug 86   (Sir) J. McKinnon
1 Nov 93   Clare Spottiswoode
1 Nov 98   C. McCarthy

Established under the *Gas Act, 1986.* In 1998 the Government announced its intention to merge the Gas and Electricity regulators in 1999.

Office of Electricity Regulation (OFFER), 1990–99

Director General of Electricity Supply
1 Sep 89   S. Littlechild
1 Jan 99   C. McCarthy

Established under the *Electricity Act, 1989.* In 1998 the Government announced its intention to merge the Gas and Electricity regulators in 1999.

Office of Gas and Electricity Markets
(OFGEM) 1999–

Chief Executive

1 Jan 99	C. McCarthy
1 Oct 03	A. Buchanan

Established under the *Competition Act, 1998,* and *Utilities Act, 2000* to take over the responsibilities of OFGAS and OFFER.

Office of Telecommunications (OFTEL),
1984–2003

Director General

1 Aug 84	(Sir) B. Carsberg
13 Jun 92	W. Wigglesworth
1 Apr 93	D. Cruikshank
1 Apr 98	D. Edmonds

Established under the *Telecommunications Act, 1984.*

Office of Communications (OFCOM), 2003–

Chief Executive

1 Mar 03	S. Carter

Established under the *Communications Act, 2003,* to take over the roles of OFTEL, the Independent Television Commission, the Radio Authority, Broadcasting Standards Commission and Radio Communications Agency.

Office of Water Services (OFWAT), 1989–

Director General

1 Aug 89	Sir I. Byatt
1 Aug 00	P. Fletcher

Established under the *Water Act, 1989.*

Office of the Rail Regulator (ORR), 1993–

Rail Regulator		*Chairman*		*Chief Executive*	
1 Dec 93	J. Swift	4 Jul 04	C. Bolt	4 Jul 04	Suzanne McCarthy
1 Dec 98	C. Bolt *(acting)*				
5 Jul 99–1 Jul 04	T. Winsor				

Established under the *Railways Act, 1993* to oversee the issue, modification and enforcement of licences to operate trains, networks, stations and light maintenance depots; the enforcement of domestic competition law in connection with the provision of railway services; the approval of agreements for access by operators of railway assets to track, stations and light maintenance depots; and consumer protection and promotion of passengers' interests.

Office of Passenger Rail Franchising (OPRAF), 1993–2001

Franchising Director

9 Nov 93	R. Salmon
1 Oct 96	J. O'Brien
1 May 99	M. Grant

Established under the *Railways Act, 1993*. It is responsible for letting the 25 passenger train franchises operating on the national railway network in Great Britain. It monitors and manages those franchises with a brief to protect passengers' interests, and encourage fresh investment in the railway.

Strategic Rail Authority (SRA), 2001–05

Chairman

1 Feb 01	Sir A. Morton
1 Dec 01	R. Bowker
1 Sep 04	D. Quarmby

Established under the *Transport Act, 2000*, to take over the functions of OPRAF. Following the Secretary of State for Transport's announcement in July 2004 about the future structure of the rail industry, the Strategic Rail Authority was expected to be wound up by the end of 2005.

Office of Electricity Regulation in Northern Ireland (OFFER-NI), 1992–96
Office for the Regulation of Electricity and Gas (OFREG), 1996–

Director General

1 Apr 92	G. Horton
1 Dec 95	D. McIldoon

Established under to regulate the provision of electricity in Northern Ireland in 1992. Took over responsibility for gas when it became available in Northern Ireland. D. McIlhoon formally appointed Director General of Gas Supply 10 June 1996.

Coal Authority, 1994–

Chairman

1 Oct 94	Sir D. White
1 Sep 99	J. Harris

Established under the *Coal Industry Act, 1994* to take over the residual functions of British Coal, including ownership of unmined reserves and settling subsidence claims not covered by coal mining companies.

Central Government Trading Bodies

Some central government trading bodies have raised revenue through the sales of goods and services, but have not been organised as public corporations:

Export Credit Guarantee Department 1975–
Forestry Commission 1918–
Her Majesty's Stationery Office (HMSO) 1786–[1]
Horserace Totalisator Board (Tote), 1963–
National Savings Bank 1969–
Land Authority for Wales 1975–99
Royal Mint 11th cent, reorganised 1870–[1]
Royal Ordnance Factories (sold to British Aerospace 1987)
Crown Estate 1762, reorganised 1961–
Land Registry 1862–[1]
National Audit Office 1983–

Other Quasi-governmental Organisations

The dividing line between nationalised industries and other quasi-autonomous national government organisations is by no means a clear one. Many of the organisations listed below enjoy similar legal status to the public corporations listed above – the main difference in many cases being one of size. Most official and academic studies indicate that there are between 250 and 350 central non-Departmental bodies of a permanent nature in the UK. The categories set out below do not purport to represent a comprehensive list, but do include some of the more notable examples.

1. *Those which act as agencies for the spending of government money*

    Regional Health Authorities
    University Grants Committee 1919–89
    Universities Funding Council 1989–93
    Polytechnics and Colleges Funding Council 1989–93
    Higher Education Funding Councils 1993–
    Manpower Services Commission 1974–88
    Sports Council (Sport England) 1972–
    Agricultural (and Food) Research Council 1934–94
    Biotechnology and Biological Sciences Research Council 1994–
    NHS Hospital Trusts 1991–
    Medical Research Council 1920–
    National Institute for (Health and) Clinical Excellence 1999–
    Natural Environment Research Council 1965–

---

[1] Now an agency under the Government's Next Steps programme.

Arts Council 1946–
National Film Finance Corporation 1949–84
National Research Development Corporation 1967–91 (*see above entry for British Technology Group*)
National Enterprise Board 1975–91 (*see above entry for British Technology Group*)
Housing Corporation 1964–
Social Science Research Council 1965–83
Economic and Social Research Council 1983–
British Council 1934–
British Film Commission 1992–
Legal Aid Board 1989–

2.　*Quasi-judicial and prosecuting bodies*

Monopolies and Mergers Commission 1973–99; Competition Commission 1999–
Price Commission 1973–79
Criminal Injuries Compensation Board 1964–
General and Special Commissioners of Income Tax
Parole Board 1967–
Mental Health Act Commission 1983–
Police Complaints Authority 1984–
Serious Fraud Office 1987–
Crown Prosecution Service 1986–

3.　*Bodies with statutory powers of regulation and licensing*

H.M. Land Registry 1925–[1]
Charity Commission 1853–
Independent Broadcasting Authority 1954–1990 (see p. 283)
Independent Television Commission 1991–2003
Radio Authority 1991–2003
Civil Aviation Authority 1971–
Office of Fair Trading 1973–
Commission for Local Authority Accounts in Scotland (Accounts Commission) 1975–
Audit Commission 1983–
Office of the Data Protection Registrar 1984–
Broadcasting Standards Council 1988–96
National Rivers Authority 1989–96
Environment Agency 1996–

[1] Now an agency under the Government's Next Steps programme.

4. *Statutory advisory or consultative bodies nominated wholly or in part by Ministers*

    Gaming Board for Great Britain 1968–
    Metrication Board 1969–80
    Consumer Councils of the Nationalised Industries
    Health and Safety Commission and Executive 1974–
    Law Commission 1965–
    Industrial Reorganisation Corporation 1966–70
    Countryside Commission (Agency) 1968–
    Equal Opportunities Commission 1975–
    Commission for Racial Equality 1977–
    Disability Rights Commission 2000–
    Advisory, Conciliation and Arbitration Service 1975–

5. *Executive agencies administering specific activities*

    National Dock Labour Board 1947–89
    Covent Garden Market Authority 1961–
    Northern Ireland Electricity 1973–92
    Northern Ireland Transport Holding Company 1968–
    National Ports Council 1964–81
    Regional Water Authorities (until 1991)

6. *Development agencies*

    New Town Development Corporations and Commission
    Scottish Development Agency 1975–91
    Scottish Enterprise 1991–
    Welsh Development Agency 1976–
    Highlands and Islands Development Board 1965–91
    Highlands and Islands Enterprise 1991–
    Colonial Development Corporation 1948–63
    Commonwealth Development Corporation 1963–
    Development Commission (for Rural England) 1909–88
    Rural Development Commission 1988–2000
    Urban Development Corporations

SOURCES:– For an analysis of the statutory provisions of the nationalised industries, see R. Pryke, *The Nationalised Industries: Policy and Performance since 1968* (1981); R. Vernon (ed.), *The Promise of Privatisation* (1988); J. Vickers and G. Yarrow, *Privatisation: An Economic Analysis* (1988); also *Public Expenditure Statistical Analyses*, HM Treasury.

IX
Devolution and Local Government

The British Isles

Scotland

Under the Treaty of Union, 1707, Scotland preserved her independent legal and judicial systems. Scotland developed arrangements for education and local government which were never assimilated to those of England and Wales. The established (Presbyterian) Church was also recognised by the Union settlement. After the abolition of the post of Secretary of State for Scotland in 1746, and between the date of the establishment of the Secretaryship for Scotland in 1885 (which became a full Secretaryship of State in 1926), a Scottish Development Agency, responsible to the Scottish Office, was set up in 1975. By 1977 most 'United Kingdom' Departments had regional offices in Scotland.

By 1983 the Scottish Office was organised into five Departments; the Department of Agriculture and Fisheries for Scotland, the Scottish Development Department, the Scottish Economic Planning Department, the Scottish Education Department, and the Scottish Home and Health Department. The office's headquarters in Edinburgh was complemented by a liaison office in Dover House, Whitehall. In 1995 the Departments were reorganised as Agriculture, Environment and Fisheries; Development; Education and Industry; Health; Home. From 1999 these departments came under the aegis of the devolved Scottish executive.

Scotland has always had its own separate legal and judicial systems, its bar, its established church, and its heraldic authority, Lord Lyon King-at-Arms. In 1979 the Select Committee on Scottish Affairs was reconstituted (see p. 97) and, except for 1987–92, lasted until 1999. After the passage of the *Scotland Act, 1978*, a referendum was held on 1 March 1979 to ascertain the electorate's views on the provisions for legislative devolution contained in the Act. In the referendum 1,230,937 voted 'Yes' and 1,153,502 voted 'No' but as the 'Yes' majority represented 32.9% of the registered electorate, failing to overcome the

40% provision of the enactment, an Order to Repeal the Scotland Act, 1978, was successfully moved on 20 June 1979, following the General Election of 3 May.

After its election in May 1997, the Labour Government moved quickly to fulfil its devolution promises. On 11 September 1997 on a 60.2% turnout the Scottish electorate voted 74.3% for the establishment of a Scottish Parliament and 63.5% for it to have limited taxing powers. The *Scotland Act, 1998*, gave the Scottish Parliament power in almost every field; but it reserved authority to the United Kingdom on a number of matters including the Constitution, social security, economic and monetary policy, aspects of trade and industry (including inward investment), consumer protection, employment (including minimum wage and equal opportunities), broadcasting, abortion, energy, defence and foreign affairs.

The Parliament is composed of 129 members, 73 elected first-past-the-post in the Westminster constituencies and 56 (seven in each of eight regions) under the additional member system of proportional representation. The first election took place on 6 May 1999 and the Parliament met in Edinburgh on 13 May. D. Dewar (Lab.) was chosen as the first First Minister of Scotland. J. Wallace (Lib. Dem.) was chosen as his Deputy. D. Dewar was sworn in by the Queen on 17 May 1999. The Queen opened the new Parliament on 1 July 1999.

Secretaries of State for Scotland

8 Apr 76	B. Millan	3 May 97	D. Dewar
5 May 79	G. Younger	17 May 99	J. Reid
11 Jan 86	M. Rifkind	24 May 01	Helen Liddell
20 Nov 90	I. Lang	29 May 02	A. Darling
5 Jul 95	M. Forsyth	*For junior ministers see pp. 5–15*	

The Scottish Executive *(assumed power on 1 July 1999)*

First Minister		*Deputy First Minister*	
1 Jul 99	D. Dewar (Lab.)	1 Jul 99	J. Wallace (Lib. Dem.)
27 Oct 00	H. McLeish (Lab.)	23 Jun 05	N. Stephen (Lib. Dem.)
21 Nov 01	J. McConnell (Lab.)		

Scottish Parliament Election, 6 May 1999

On 6 May 1999 the new Scottish Parliament was chosen. Each elector had two votes. 73 members were chosen directly, first-past-the-post, from the existing Westminster constituencies; 56 were elected on top-up lists from the eight Euro-constituencies.

	Con.	*Lab.*	*Lib. Dem.*	*SNP*	*Other*
Top-up seats	18	3	5	28	2
Direct seats	–	53	12	7	1
Total seats	18	56	17	35	3
Top-up vote	15.5%	34.0%	12.6%	276%	10.3%
Direct vote	15.6%	38.8%	14.2%	28.7%	2.1%

Turnout – Top-up 57.2%; Direct 58.9%.

Election 1 May 2003

	Con.	*Lab.*	*Lib. Dem.*	*SNP*	*Other*
Top-up seats	15	4	4	18	15
Direct seats	–	46	13	9	2
Total seats	18	50	17	27	17
Top-up vote	15.6%	29.4%	11.8%	23.7%	22.2
Direct vote	16.6%	34.5%	15.3%	20.9%	9.9

Turnout – Top-up 49.4%; Direct 49%.

Wales

From Plantagenet times the administration of Wales was London-centred. In 1979 a Select Committee on Welsh Affairs was appointed (see p. 97).

Welsh national or separatist feeling has often expressed itself in forces other than the movement for home rule or devolution. The most important aspects of this have been the campaigns on such matters as the Church, education, land, temperance reform and the Welsh language. The *Welsh Language Act, 1967*, paved the way for the removal of restrictions on the use of the Welsh language in official documents and in the administration of justice in Wales; the *Welsh Language Act, 1993*, extended the provisions of the 1967 Act. The *Education Reform Act, 1988* and the *Education Act, 1992* provided opportunities for the development of a Welsh ethos in education (Curriculum Cymreig) and the use of Welsh in the 15–18 age group was estimated at 25% in 1999.

In 1901, 50% of the population spoke Welsh; in 1931 the figure was 37%; in 1951, 29%; in 1961, 26%; in 1971, 21%; in 1981, 19%; and in 1991, 19%. A Welsh language television channel was established in 1982.

In 1978 the *Wales Act* provided for the establishment of a devolved Welsh Assembly in Cardiff, subject to a referendum. In the referendum on 1 March 1979, 243,048 (11.9% or 20.2% of valid votes) voted 'Yes'; 956,330 (46.9% or 79.8% of valid votes) voted 'No' and 41.2% did not vote; the highest 'Yes' vote (34.5%) was in Gwynedd and the lowest (12.1%) was in Gwent.

Following its election victory in May 1997, the Labour Party moved swiftly to implement its promise of a Welsh Assembly. In a Referendum on 18 September 1997, on a 50.1% turnout Wales voted by 50.3% to 49.7% in favour of a Welsh Assembly. The *Government of Wales Act 1998* provided for a National Assembly (Cynulliad) for Wales. The Assembly has limited political functions and, unlike the Scottish Parliament has no tax-raising powers. It is composed of 60 members, 40 elected first-past-the-post in the Westminster constituencies and 20 (four in each of five regions) under the additional member system of proportional representation. The first election took place on 6 May 1999 and the Assembly met on 13 May in Cardiff.

At first there was a minority Labour Government but in February 2000 after the resignation of A. Michael an understanding between Labour and the Liberal Democrats was arrived at. In October 2000 this turned into a formal coalition which continued until the 2003 election when Labour secured an effective majority of one seat which lasted until the defection of a Labour member in April 2005.

Secretary of State for Wales

5 Mar 74	J. Morris	27 Oct 98	A. Michael
7 May 79	N. Edwards	28 Jul 99	P. Murphy
3 Jun 87	P. Walker	24 Oct 02	P. Hain
4 May 90	D. Hunt	*For junior ministers see pp. 6–16*	
27 May 93	J. Redwood	*First Secretary of Wales*	
5 Jul 05	W. Hague	11 May 99	A. Michael
3 May 97	R. Davies	15 Feb 00	R. Morgan

Welsh Assembly Election, 6 May 1999

On 6 May 1999 the new Welsh Assembly was chosen. Each elector had two votes. Forty members were chosen directly, first-past-the-post, from the existing Westminster constituencies; 20 were elected on top-up lists from the eight Euro-constituencies.

	Con.	*Lab.*	*Lib. Dem.*	*PC*	*Other*
Top-up seats	8	1	3	8	–
Direct seats	1	27	3	9	–
Total seats	9	28	6	17	3
Top-up vote	16.5%	35.5%	12.5%	30.6%	4.9%
Direct vote	15.8%	37.6%	13.5%	28.4%	4.7%

Turnout – Top-up 46.1%; Direct 46.3%.

1 May 2003

	Con.	*Lab.*	*Lib. Dem.*	*PC*	*Other*
Top-up seats	10	30	3	7	–
Direct seats	1	–	3	5	1
Total seats	11	30	6	12	1
Top-up vote	19.2%	36.6%	12.7%	19.7%	11.9%
Direct vote	19.9%	40.0%	14.1%	21.2%	4.7%

Turnout – Top-up 38%; Direct 38.3%.

SOURCES: J. Davies, *A History of Wales* (1993); B. Taylor and K. Thompson, *Scotland and Wales: Nations Again?* (1999); G. Day and D. Thomas (1990 onwards).

Northern Ireland 1972–

After sectarian troubles and terrorist activities which from 1969 onwards cost several hundred lives and led to the sending of substantial British military forces, the British Government on 30 March 1972 passed the *Northern Ireland (Temporary Provisions) Act.* This Act suspended Stormont and transferred all the functions of the Government and Parliament of Northern Ireland to a new Secretary of State for Northern Ireland, acting by Order-in-Council, for one year (extended annually until 1998).

Secretary of State for Northern Ireland

24 Mar 72	W. Whitelaw	24 Jul 89	P. Brooke
2 Dec 73	F. Pym	11 Apr 92	Sir P. Mayhew
5 Mar 74	M. Rees	2 May 97	Mo Mowlam
10 Sep 76	R. Mason	11 Oct 99	P. Mandelson
5 May 79	H. Atkins	24 Jan 01	J. Reid
14 Sep 81	J. Prior	24 Oct 02	P. Murphy
11 Sep 84	D. Hurd	6 May 05	P. Hain
3 Sep 85	T. King	*For junior ministers see pp. 5–15*	

The *Northern Ireland Act, 1982*, again attempted to restore devolved institutions to the province. On 25 Oct 1979, the Secretary of State, H. Atkins had announced that the new Conservative Government favoured devolution in Northern Ireland. In November 1979 a White Paper was published, *The Government of Northern Ireland: A Working Paper for a Conference* (Cmnd. 7763), setting out principles to be observed in the transfer of power, and issues for discussion at a round-table conference. The conference held between January and March 1980 failed to reach agreement. A further White Paper, *The Government of Northern Ireland – Proposals for Further Dicussion* (Cmnd. 7950), published in July 1980, put forward further proposals for discussion.

In February 1982, J. Prior, the new Secretary of State, held further discussions with the Northern Ireland parties, and in April 1982, a third White Paper, *Northern Ireland – A Framework for Devolution* (Cmnd. 8451), was published, proposing a scheme of 'Rolling devolution' given legislative effect by the *Northern Ireland Act* which was placed on the statute book on 23 July 1982. This provided for the election of a Northern Ireland Assembly whose functions would initially be limited to scrutiny, deliberation and advice, pending cross-community agreement on the transfer of certain legislative powers.

The election for the Assembly was held on 20 October 1982, and of the 78 seats, 26 went to the Official Unionists, 21 to the Democratic Unionists, 14 to the SDLP, 10 to Alliance, 5 to Sinn Fein, 1 to a Popular Unionist and 1 to an Independent Unionist. However, Sinn Fein and the SDLP refused to take their seats in the Assembly, while on 21 November 1983 most of the Official Unionists withdrew after some murders in Armagh.

The SDLP took part in a New Ireland forum with the leaders of the three main parties in Ireland – Fine Gael, Fianna Fail and the Labour Party – which met for the first time on 30 May 1983 in Dublin, and produced a report on 2 May 1984 advocating fresh approaches.

On 15 November 1985 an Anglo-Irish Agreement was signed at Hillsborough. Article 1 restated the British Government's commitment to N. Ireland remaining part of the United Kingdom as long as that was the wish of the majority of the population. Article 2 provided for regular inter-governmental conferences. The 15 Unionist M.P.s resigned their seats in protest against the Agreement; 14 of them were returned in the subsequent by-elections.

On 26 March 1991 the UK Government announced a basis ('the three strands') on which peace talks should proceed. After some meetings the initiative came to a halt in July 1991. Renewed talks in March to November 1992 again ended in failure. In the following year there were increased contacts between the London and Dublin governments which resulted in the Downing Street Declaration of 15 December 1993 offering talks about reform to all parties that would renounce violence.

A cease-fire was announced by the IRA on 31 August 1994 and by the Loyalist paramilitary organisations on 13 October 1994. An international body on the decommissioning of paramilitary weapons was appointed by the Government under the former US Senator, George Mitchell; it published its report on 20 January 1996, setting out principles of non-violence under which settlement talks could begin. However, the IRA ended its cease-fire on 9 February 1996 with a bomb at Canary Wharf. On 30 May 1996 elections took place for a Northern Ireland Forum, from those participating in multi-party talks were to be drawn. On 16 May 1997 the newly elected Labour Government approved contacts between officials and Sinn Fein. The IRA renewed its cease-fire on 20 July 1997 and on 9 September 1997 the IRA accepted the Mitchell principles for the talks.

The talks culminated in the 'Good Friday Agreement' of 10 April 1998 supported by almost all parties except I. Paisley's Democratic Unionist Party. The Agreement stated that the status of Northern Ireland could only be changed with the consent of its people and committed the Irish Government to formally withdrawing its Constitutional claim to sovereignty over the whole of the Island. It provided for a 108-seat parliament to be elected by proportional representation. Executive functions were to be taken over by ministers and committees, allocated according to party strength. A North–South Ministerial Council was to develop co-operation between Belfast and Dublin. Prisoners were in time to be released and paramilitary weapons decommissioned.

On 22 May 1998 the Agreement was endorsed by 71% of the electorate on an 80% turnout. On 25 June 1998 Assembly elections took place.

Northern Ireland Assembly Elections

		DUP	UUP	UKUP	Allce	SDLP	SF	Other
1998	Votes	18.1%	21.3%	4.5%	6.6%	22.0%	17.6%	9.9%
	Seats	24	28	5	6	24	18	7
2003	Votes	25.6%	23.5%	0.7%	–3.7%	17.0%	22.7%	6.8%
	Seats	30	27	1	6	18	24	24

Arguments over decommissioning delayed the establishment of the new Executive; the Assembly met for the first time on 1 July 1998 but devolved powers did not finally take effect until 2 December 1999, with D. Trimble as First Minister. It was suspended from 11 February 2000 to 30 May 2000 over decommissioning of IRA weapons and then again on 14 October 2002 after reports about IRA intelligence-gathering.

(See pp. 263–4 for Army activities)

SOURCES:- P. Bew et al., *Northern Ireland 1921–1996* (1996); P. Buckland, *A History of Northern Ireland* (1981); W. D. Flackes and S. Elliott (eds) *Northern Ireland: A Political Directory 1968–93* (1994); J. McGarry and B. O'Leary (eds) *The Future of Northern Ireland* (1990) and *The Politics of Antagonism* (1993); M. Cunningham, *The Constitution of Northern Ireland* (1989); D. Keogh and M. Haltzel (eds) *Northern Ireland and the Politics of Reconciliation* (1993); J. Whyte, *Interpreting Northern Ireland* (1990); D. McKittrick, *The Search for Peace in Northern Ireland* (1994).

The Channel Islands

The Channel Islands which were originally part of the Duchy of Normandy have been associated with England since 1066. They have their own legislative assemblies, systems of local administration, fiscal systems, and courts of law. The Islanders have general responsibility for the regulation of their local affairs subject to the prerogative of the Crown over appointment to the chief posts in the local administrations and the necessity of Royal Assent to legislative measures passed by the insular assemblies. Most of the laws by which they are governed emanate from their representative assemblies and although they cannot be regarded as local authorities most of their public services are provided by these assemblies in the same way as local government services are provided and administered in Great Britain.

The Channel lslands are divided into two Bailiwicks, one comprising Jersey and the other, Alderney, Sark, and Guernsey with its dependants, Herm and Jethou. Each Bailiwick has a Lieutenant-Governor appointed by the Crown for a period of five years, through whom all official communications between the UK Government and the Islands pass, and in whom certain executive functions are vested. A Bailiff, also appointed by the Crown, presides over the local legislatures, the States, and over the sittings of the Royal Court. The Islands have their own Courts of Law, but there remains leave to appeal to the Judicial Committee of the Privy Council.

The Island Assemblies may initiate legislation but they must then petition the Sovereign in Council to give these measures force of law. Acts of the UK Parliament do not apply to the Channel Islands unless by express provision or necessary application. As a general rule Parliament refrains from legislating on matters with which these assemblies can deal unless for some special reason a UK act must be preferred to local legislation.

The public revenues of the Islands are raised by duties on imported goods, by income taxes and other taxes. Proposals made by the States for raising revenue require authorisation by Order in Council but responsibility for determining how the revenue shall be spent is, in practice, left to the States. Immunity from taxation for Crown purposes has been a privilege of the Islanders since the time of Edward VI.

SOURCE:- *Report of the Commission on the Constitution* (Cmnd. 5460–1/1973).

Jersey

Lieutenant-Governor		*Bailiff*	
1979	Sir P. Whiteley	1973	(Sir) F. Ereaut
1985	Sir W. Pillar	1988	(Sir) P. Crill
1990	Sir J. Sutton	1995	(Sir) P. Bailhache
1995	Sir M. Wilkes		
2001	Sir J. Cheshire		

Guernsey

Lieutenant-Governor		*Bailiff*	
1974	Sir J. Martin	1973	(Sir) J. Loveridge
1980	Sir P. Le Cheminant	1994	(Sir) C. Frossard
1985	Sir A. Boswell	2000	(Sir) G. Dorey
1990	Sir M. Wilkins	1999	Sir de V. Carey
1994	Sir J. Coward		
2000	Sir J. Foley		

The Isle of Man

This island was successively under the rule of Norway, of Scotland, of the Stanley family and of the Dukes of Atholl before it became a Crown Dependency in 1765. For over 1,000 years the internal affairs of the island have been regulated by the Tynwald, which has evolved from the Lord of Man's Council composed of his chief officials and other persons of importance and the House of Keys. The latter comprises 24 representatives elected by all over the age of 18 who have resided in the island for six months. The consent of both the Legislative Council and the Keys is requisite for any Act of Tynwald except when in two successive sessions of a Parliament the Keys pass the same Bill, or an essentially similar one, which is once rejected by the Council. In that case the Bill is deemed to have been passed by the Council. All legislation by Tynwald depends for its validity on confirmation by Royal Assent granted by the Lieutenant Governor or, in certain rare cases, in the form of orders made by the Queen in Council.

Most of the public services are provided by Tynwald and administered by Boards of Tynwald, but the Lieutenant Governor is still the executive authority for certain services, including the administration of justice. In 1866, Tynwald was granted certain financial powers which had been removed from it in 1765. This process continued through the following decades until, by Tynwald's *Isle of Man Contribution Act of 1958* the Treasury's control over the Island's finance was removed enabling the Tynwald to regulate its own finances and Customs, although under the Act, the Island continues to make an annual contribution to the Exchequer for defence and common services. There is a statutory body of members of Tynwald known as the Executive Council the duty of which is to consider and advise the Lieutenant Governor upon all matters of principle and policy and legislation.

SOURCES:- *Report of the Commission on the Constitution* (Cmnd. 5460–1/1973); D. Kermode, *Devolution at Work: A Case Study of the Isle of Man* (1979).

Lieutenant-Governor

1973	Sir J. Paul	1990	Sir L. Jones
1980	Sir N. Cecil	1995	Sir T. Daunt
1985	(Sir) L. New	2000	I. MacFadyen

Devolution: Main Landmarks

1 Mar 79	Scotland votes 'Yes' in Referendum (33% to 31% with 36% not voting); Wales votes 'No' (12% to 47% with 41% not voting)
28 Jun 79	Parliament passes resolution nullifying *Scotland Act, 1978*
5 Jul 79	Parliament passes resolution nullifying *Wales Act, 1978*
5 Apr 82	Government outlines new Northern Ireland proposals in *Northern Ireland – A Framework far Devolution* (Cmnd. 8451)

26 Oct 82	Northern Ireland Assembly elected
2 May 84	Irish forum proposals published in Dublin
Nov 86	Anglo-Irish Agreement
30 Mar 89	First meeting of Scottish Convention, an interparty discussion forum, boycotted by the Conservatives and the Nationalists
10 Dec 93	Downing St Declaration on Northern Ireland
May 94	Reorganisation of Welsh local government
May 94	Reorganisation on Scottish local government
1 May 97	Labour win General Election with a commitment to Scottish and Welsh devolution
11 Sep 97	Scottish Referendum
18 Sep 97	Welsh Referendum
Apr 98	Good Friday Agreement
22 May 98	Good Friday Agreement endorsed by Referendum
1 Apr 98	*Government of Wales Act* gets Royal Assent
19 Nov 98	*Scotland Act* gets Royal Assent
6 May 99	First Election to Scottish Parliament
6 May 99	First Election to Welsh Assembly
22 May 99	D. Dewar becomes First Minister of Scotland
1 Jul 99	Welsh Assembly installed
2 Dec 99	Devolved powers for Northern Ireland Assembly take effect
11 Feb 00	NI Assembly suspended over decommissioning
30 May 00	NI Assembly restored
14 Oct 02	NI Assembly suspended again, over IRA intelligence-gathering
1 May 03	Second Elections to Scottish Parliament see Labour–Lib. Dem. coalition returned with reduced majority, with strong gains by minor parties. Labour secures bare majority in Welsh Assembly
26 Nov 03	Second election to NI Assembly sees DUP overtake UUP and Sinn Fein overtake SDLP. Assembly remains suspended
5 Nov 04	The only English region to hold a referendum on an elected regional assembly, the North-East, votes decisively against – 77.9% to 22.1%, on a 47.7% turnout by all-postal ballot

SOURCES:- K. Wright, *The People Say Yes: The Making of Scotland's Parliament* (1997); V. Bogdanor, *Devolution in the United Kingdom* (1999); see also the White Papers listed in the chronology above.

Local Government

Structure

London

From 1965 to 1986 London was governed by the Greater London Council (GLC), with powers over housing, economic development, transport, strategic planning and emergency services; the 32 London boroughs; and the Inner London Education Authority (ILEA), overseeing education in the inner boroughs. The GLC was abolished in 1986, and ILEA in 1990; their powers were given to the individual boroughs, with residual authority over London-wide issues resting with the Government Office for London. In 2000 the Greater London Authority (a Mayor and 25-member Assembly) took over most strategic functions from the Government Office for London.

Metropolitan areas

From 1974 to 1986 the six other major metropolitan areas of England were ruled by a two-tier system of metropolitan counties (West Midlands, Greater Manchester, Merseyside, West Yorkshire, South Yorkshire and Tyne & Wear) under which were 36 metropolitan district councils. In 1986 the metropolitan counties were abolished, and the metropolitan districts became unitary authorities.

The rest of England and Wales

From 1974 to 1995 the rest of England and Wales was ruled by a two-tier system of 47 county councils and 333 district councils. In 1995 Welsh County Councils were abolished and Wales was divided into 22 unitary authorities.

Between 1995 and 1997, 45 English districts were converted into single-purpose unitary authorities but all the 35 English counties (except the Isle of Wight) shared power with the 337 non-metropolitan districts.

Scotland

From 1975 to 1996 Scotland was divided into two tiers – nine regional councils and 53 district councils – plus three unitary island councils. In 1996 the Regional Councils were abolished, and the districts reorganised into 29 unitary authorities plus the three island councils.

Major Legislation Affecting Local Government

Local Government, Planning Act, 1980. This complex and diverse Act relaxed certain Ministerial controls on authorities and required them to publish reports and information about the performance of their functions (as prescribed by the Secretary of State). It brought the operations of direct labour organisations under control – to secure more regulated working, separate accounting, open tendering, and prescribed rates of return. It extended arrangements for the payment of rates by instalments and added rate rebates for the disabled. It provided for registers of underused land owned by public authorities in designated areas. The Act also provided for a new control system for local authority capital expenditure – giving expenditure allocations a switching of resources between authorities and between financial years. A new system for the distribution of rate support grant – with a single block grant in place of the previous 'needs' and 'resources' elements – was a major change.

Local Government Finance Act, 1982. This provided for the abolition of supplementary rates and precepts and required them to be levied for complete financial years. By amendment of the 1980 Act it provided expressly for adjustments in block grant payable to an authority to be made by reference to central government guidance. This was designed to encourage reductions in expenditure on account of general economic conditions. The Act also established the Audit

Commission for Local Authorities in England and Wales – which will appoint the auditors (whether from the private sector or from the Commission). The Commission is also responsible for studies of the economy, efficiency and effectiveness of local services (and the impact on them of statutory provisions and Ministerial initiatives). It is appointed by the Secretary of State, who may direct it in the discharge of its functions.

Local Authority (Expenditure Powers) Act, 1983. This was intended to facilitate the aid which local authorities could give to industry – in particular to top up expenditure by the 'free two pence' powers in s. 137 of the *Local Government Act 1972.*

Rates Act, 1984. This allowed for rate limitation – 'rate capping' – by a selection scheme or by one of general limitation. It also required authorities to consult industrial and commercial ratepayers before reaching decisions on expenditure and its financing and to provide additional information to ratepayers.

Local Government Act, 1985. This abolished the Greater London Council and the six Metropolitan County Councils and distributed their functions and responsibilities among their component boroughs, some joint authorities and Whitehall.

Local Government Finance Act, 1988. This replaced the domestic rates with a community charge (or 'poll tax'). Non-domestic rates were nationalised and the systems of grant reformed. Changes were to take effect in 1990.

Education Reform Act, 1988. This transferred control of polytechnics from local to central government as well as allowing schools to opt out of local authority control and the national curriculum.

Local Government Act, 1989. This required local authorities to expose their provision of services to compulsory competitive tender.

Local Government Act, 1992. This abolished the poll tax and replaced it with a 'council tax'. It provided for a structural reorganisation of local government in Scotland, Wales and the non-metropolitan areas of England.

Local Government (Scotland) Act, 1994. This replaced the nine Regional Council and 53 districts in Mainland Scotland with 29 Unitary Authorities.

Local Government (Wales) Act, 1994. This replaced the 12 Counties and 37 Districts in Wales with 22 Unitary Authorities.

Greater London Authority (Referendums) Act 1998. This provided for a referendum on the principle of a Greater London Authority with an Assembly and a directly elected Mayor.

Local Government Act, 2000. This laid down a new structure of local administration with the council led by an executive subject to scrutiny by other councillors.

Local Government Act, 2003. This drastically reorganised the rules for local government finance and accounting.

Regional Assemblies (Preparations) Act, 2003. This gave the powers for regions to hold referendums on the establishment of elected regional assemblies.

Local Authority Interest Groups

The interests of the local authorities have been represented by two main kinds of groups. First, there are the associations of each tier of local authorities. Most powerful amongst these have been the Association of Metropolitan Authorities, the Association of County Councils, and the Association of District Councils, all established in 1974. In 1997 these organisations merged into a single Local Government Association; there is a separate Convention of Scottish Local Government Authorities. In addition, there are associations representing each of the professions in local government services, notably the Chartered Institute of Public Finance and Accountancy. All kinds of municipal employees were represented by the National and Local Government Officers Association (1905), the National Union of Public Employees (1886) and other unions. In 1993, NALGO and NUPE combined to form UNISON.

Commission for Local Administration in England
Chairman

1974	Lady Serota
1982	(Sir) D. Yardley
1994	E. Osmotherly
2001	T. Redmond

Commission for Local Administration in Wales
Chairman

1974	D. Jones-Williams
1979	A. Jones
1991	E. Moseley
2003	A. Peat

Commission for Local Administration in Scotland (since 2002, Scottish Public Services Ombudsman)

Chairman

1975	R. Moore	1994	F. Marks
1978	J. Russell	2000	I. Smith
1982	E. Gillett	2002	Alice Brown
1986	R. Peggie		

New Towns Commission
Chairman

1961	Sir D. Anderson		1978	C. Macpherson
1964	Sir M. Wells		1982	Sir N. Shields
1971	(Sir) D. Pilcher		1998	Sir A. Cockshaw

In May 1999 the New Towns Commission merged with the corporate functions of the Urban Regeneration Agency (URA) to create English Partnerships, now the government's national regeneration agency.

English Partnerships
Chairman

1999	Sir A. Cockshaw
2002	Margaret Ford

Local Government Elections

Party Control in Major Cities

Belfast
1976– No clear majority.

Birmingham
1976–79 Conservative. 1979–80 No clear majority. 1980–82 Labour. 1982–84 Conservative. 1984–2004 Labour. 2004– No clear majority.

Bradford
1974–80 Conservative. 1980–82 Labour. 1982–86 No clear majority. 1986–88 Labour. 1988–90 Conservative. 1990–2002 Labour. 2002– No clear majority.

Bristol
1972–83 Labour. 1983–86 No clear majority. 1986–2003 Labour. 2003– No clear majority.

Cardiff
1976–79 Conservative. 1973–83 Labour. 1983–87 Conservative. 1987–91 No clear majority. 1991–2004 Labour. 2004– No clear majority.

Coventry
1975–79 Conservative. 1979–2002 Labour. 2004– Conservative.

Edinburgh
1977–84 Conservative. 1984–92 Labour. 1992–95 No clear majority. 1995– Labour.

Glasgow
1977–80 No clear majority. 1980– Labour.

Leeds
1976–79 Conservative. 1979–80 No clear majority. 1980–2004 Labour. 2004– No clear majority.

Leicester
1976–79 Conservative. 1979–2003 Labour. 2003– No clear majority.

Liverpool
1974–83 No clear majority (Liberal largest party 1974–76; Labour 1976–83). 1983–92 Labour. 1992–98 No clear majority. 1998– Liberal Democrat.

Manchester
1971– Labour.

Newcastle
1974–2004 Labour. 2004– Liberal Democrat.

Nottingham
1976–79 Conservative. 1979–87 Labour. 1987–89 Conservative. 1989–91 No clear majority. 1991– Labour.

Plymouth
1966–91 Conservative. 1991–2000 Labour. 2000–03 Conservative. 2003 Labour.

Portsmouth
1965–90 Conservative. 1990–95 No clear majority. 1995–2000 Labour. 2000– No clear majority.

Sheffield
1969–99 Labour. 1999–2000 Liberal Democrat. 2003–03 No clear majority. 2003–Labour.

Southampton
1976–84 Conservative. 1984–87 Labour. 1987–88 No clear majority. 1988–2000 Labour. 2000– No clear majority.

Stoke on Trent
1971–2003 Labour. 2003–04 No overall control. 2004– Labour.

Sunderland
1972– Labour.

Wolverhampton
1978–79 No clear control. 1979–87 Labour. 1987–88 No clear majority. 1988–92 Labour. 1992–94 No clear majority. 1994– Labour.

Local Government Elections, 1973–
Metropolitan Counties 1973–81[a]

| | Party control | | | | Seats | | | |
	Con.	Lab.	Lib.	No clear control	Con.	Lab.	Lib./Al.	Other
12 Apr 73	–	6	–	–	141	402	49	9
5 May 77	4	2	–	–	360	213	19	8
7 May 81	–	6	–	–	122	425	50	3

[a] Not including GLC.

Other Counties (England and Wales 1973–93; England only thereafter)

| | Party control | | | | Seats | | | | |
	Con.	Lab.	Lib.	No clear control	Con.	Lab.	Lib./Al.	Other	Nat./Ind.
3 May 73	18	11		18	1,484	1,397	210	513	18
5 May 77	36	3	–	8	2,524	641	71	445	37
7 May 81	19	14	–	13	1,560	1,376	340	371	23
2 May 85	10	9	12	7	1,370	1,269	640	360	21
4 May 89	17	13	1	7	1,456	1,297	458	273	25
6 May 93	1	14	12	9	966	1,389	867	237	41
1 May 97	9	8	2	15	873	745	495	90	–
4 May 01	16	7	–	11	1,016	749	409	81	–
5 May 05	23	6	3	2	1,147	575	470	77	–

Metropolitan Districts

| | Party control | | | | Seats | | | | |
	Con.	Lab.	Lib.	No clear control	Con.	Lab.	Lib./Al.	Other	Nat./Ind.
3 May 79[a,b]	11	18	–	7	986	1,317	116	87	–
1 May 80	6	27	–	3	770	1,548	133	75	–
6 May 81	7	24	–	5	751	1,457	222	42	–
5 May 83	7	24	–	5	745	1,481	213	39	–
3 May 84	5	25	–	6	690	1,523	228	40	–
1 May 86	1	27	–	8	560	1,663	228	30	–
7 May 87	1	27	–	8	552	1,632	271	26	–
5 May 88	2	28	–	6	537	1,656	268	20	–
3 May 90	2	31	–	3	505	1,721	238	17	–
2 May 91	1	32	–	3	460	1,748	244	29	–
7 May 92	1	24	–	11	556	1,612	273	40	–
6 May 94	1	23	–	12	519	1,581	338	43	–
5 May 95	–	30	–	6	382	1,738	324	37	–
3 May 96	–	32	–	4	196	1,877	355	53	–
7 May 98	–	31	1	4	230	1,815	382	54	–
6 May 99	–	29	3	4	295	1,682	449	55	–
5 May 00	2	26	8	5	413	1,503	501	61	–
3 May 02	1	25	2	8	431	1,486	497	64	–
2 May 03	1	21	2	12	471	1,419	517	71	–
6 May 04	4	16	3	17	547	1,182	595	121	–

[a] From 1975 onwards one-third of Metropolitan District councillors came up for re-election in each year, except those in which there are no county elections. The seats are the totals for both continuing and newly elected councillors.
[b] The 1979 elections took place simultaneously with the General Election.

Other Districts including Unitary Authorities (England)

	Con.	Lab.	Lib.	No clear control
6 May 76	176	29	–	91
4 May 78[a]	176	30	–	90
3 May 79[b]	166	49	–	81
1 May 80	148	53	3	82
6 May 82	139	59	2	96
5 May 83	145	55	3	93
3 May 84	140	53	3	100
8 May 86	123	64	5	104
7 May 87	123	56	9	108
5 May 88	128	58	8	102
3 May 90	116	65	5	110
2 May 91	72	78	20	126
7 May 92	76	74	21	125
6 May 94	65	70	30	125
5 May 95	8	111	45	124
3 May 96	9	117	50	111
7 May 98	12	112	37	123
6 May 99	62	89	21	112
5 May 00	77	76	19	102
3 May 02	83	67	22	100
2 May 03	111	39	26	100
6 May 04	12	35	24	971

[a] Forty-four of the 316 non-metropolitan districts in England opted that after 1976 one-third of their councillors would retire at a time. 1978 saw the first such elections.
[b] The 1979 elections took place simultaneously with the General Election.

Other districts: Wales 1973–91[a]

	Con.	Lab.	Lib.	No clear control
7 Jun 73	1	19	–	17
6 May 76	4	9	–	24
3 May 79	2	16	–	17
5 May 83	3	14	–	20
7 May 87	2	18	–	17
2 May 91	–	20	–	17

[a] A few Welsh authorities before 1995 had annual elections which are not reported here.

Welsh Unitary Authorities 1995–[a]

	Party control				Seats			
	Con.	Lab.	Lib.	No clear control	Con.	Lab.	Lib./Al.	other	Nat./ind.
5 May 95	–	14	–	8	42	726	79	113	312
6 May 99	–	8	–	14	74	562	95	242	295
6 May 04	1	8	–	13	109	479	148	173	355

[a] A few Welsh authorities before 1995 had annual elections which are not reported here.

Scottish Regions 1974–94

	Party control				Seats			
	Con.	Lab.	Lib.	No clear control	Con.	Lab.	Lib./Al.	Other	Nat./ind.
9 May 74	1	2	–	6	115	171	11	18	19
2 May 78	2	4	–	3	135	174	7	96	17
6 May 82	2	3	–	4	119	186	25	88	23
8 May 86	–	4	–	5	65	223	40	81	36
3 May 90	–	4	–	5	52	233	40	78	42
6 May 94	–	4	–	5	31	220	62	73	67

Scottish Districts 1974–92

	Party control				Seats			
	Con.	Lab.	Lib.	No clear control	Con.	Lab.	Lib./Al.	Other	Nat./ind.
9 May 74	5	17	–	31	241	428	17	335	62
3 May 77	8	5	–	40	277	299	31	335	70
1 May 80	6	24	–	23	229	494	40	307	54
3 May 84	4	25	1	23	189	545	78	278	59
5 May 88	3	24	2	24	162	553	84	242	113
7 May 92	4	19	2	28	204	468	94	392	150

Scottish Unitary Authorities 1995–

	Party control				Seats			
	Con.	Lab.	Lib.	No clear control	Con.	Lab.	Lib./Al.	Other	Nat./ind.
4 Apr 95	–	20	–	12	82	613	123	181	160
6 May 99	–	15	–	17	108	550	156	205	203
2 May 03	–	13	–	19	124	506	175	182	733

Metropolitan Counties 1973–81

	Councillors				% of vote			
	Con.	*Lab.*	*Lib.*	*Other*	*Con.*	*Lab.*	*Lib.*	*Other*
5 May 1977								
Greater Manchester	82	23	–	–	56.6	34.6	7.5	1.9
Merseyside	67	26	6	–	47.7	32.0	19.1	1.2
South Yorkshire	31	62	2	–	39.7	44.7	6.3	9.4
Tyne & Wear	44	54	4	–	49.4	40.7	6.4	3.4
West Midlands	82	18	3	–	56.5	31.7	4.1	6.1
West Yorkshire	54	30	4	–	50.3	35.4	10.3	4.1
Greater London	64	28	–	–	52.6	32.9	7.8	6.3
May 1981								
Greater Manchester	19	78	9	–	30.6	49.8	18.0	1–7
Merseyside	27	56	15	–	29.3	45.6	24.2	1.0
South Yorkshire	14	82	3	1	25.8	58.2	12.8	3.2
Tyne & Wear	23	72	7	2	29.4	55.9	12.2	2.5
West Midlands	25	74	5	–	36.0	50.3	9.8	3.9
West Yorkshire	14	63	11	–	30.2	47.5	21.0	1.3
Greater London	41	50	1	–	39.4	41.4	15.0	4.2

Greater London Council, 1964–81

	Councillors		
	Con.	*Lab.*	*Lib.*
1977	64	28	–
1981	41	50	–
1986[a]			

[a] From 1964 to 1986 the Inner London Education Authority (ILEA), covering the former LCC area, was a special committee of the GLC, made up of all its members in the Inner London Area. Following the abolition of the GLC, ILEA members were directly elected on 8 May 1986; Labour won 45 seats, the Conservatives 11 and the Alliance 2. ILEA was abolished on 1 April 1990.

Control and Representation in London Boroughs, 1978–

	Control				Councillors			
	Con.	*Lab.*	*Lib.*	*No clear control*	*Con.*	*Lab.*	*Lab./All.*	*Other*
1978	17	14	–	1	960	882	30	36
1982	17	12	–	3	984	781	124	25
1986	11	15	–	4	685	957	249	23

	Control				Councillors			
	Con.	*Lab.*	*Lib.*	*No clear control*	*Con.*	*Lab.*	*Lab./All.*	*Other*
1990	12	14	3	3	731	925	229	29
1994	5	17	3	7	518	1045	323	31
1998	4	18	2	8	538	1050	301	28
2002	8	15	3	6	655	865	307	34

London Government

On 7 May 1998, on a 34% turnout, electors in the Greater London Area voted 72%–28% in favour of the Government's proposals for a Greater London Authority with a directly elected Mayor. The first London Mayoral election was held in May 2000, using the Alternative Vote electoral system; the independent candidate K. Livingstone was elected. He was re-elected in May 2004, this time standing as the official Labour candidate. On each occasion elections were held on the same day for the London Assembly, with 14 constituency members and 11 top-up members. No party has held a majority in the London Assembly.

5 May 2000

First-preference vote

K. Livingstone (Ind.)	667,877 (38.1%)
S. Norris (Con.)	464,434 (26.5%)
F. Dobson (Lab.)	223,884 (12.8%)
Susan Kramer (Lib. Dem.)	203,452 (11.6%)
Others	154,515 (8.9%)

6 May 2004

First-preference vote

K. Livingstone (Lab.)	685,541 (36.8%)
S. Norris (Con.)	542,423 (29.1%)
S. Hughes (Lib. Dem.)	284,736 (15.3%)
F. Maloney (UKIP)	115,665 (6.2%)
Others	235,397 (12.6%)

London Assembly Elections

	Con.	*Lab.*	*Lib. Dem.*	*Green*	*UKIP*	*Total*
May 2000						
Top-up seats	1	3	4	3	0	11
Constituency seats	8	6	0	0	0	14
Total seats	9	9	4	3	0	25
10 June 2004						
Top-up seats	0	2	5	2	2	11
Constituency seats	9	5	0	0	0	14
Total seats	9	7	5	2	2	25

National vote share in local elections

Since 1979 experts at Plymouth University have calculated how votes cast in the annual local elections equate to national vote share. This is not the same as the share of total votes cast, since it is adjusted to allow for the pattern of areas which are holding elections (for example, allowance has to be made for years when Scotland has no elections).

GB Nat Equiv Vote %	Con.	Lab.	Lib. Dem.	Other
1979[a]	45	38	14	3
1980	40	42	13	5
1981	38	41	17	4
1982	40	29	27	4
1983	39	36	20	5
1984	38	37	21	4
1985	32	39	26	3
1986	34	37	26	3
1987	38	32	27	3
1988	39	38	18	5
1989	36	42	19	3
1990	33	44	17	6
1991	35	38	22	5
1992	46	30	20	4
1993	31	39	25	5
1994	28	40	27	5
1995	25	47	23	5
1996	29	43	24	4
1997[1]	31	44	17	8
1998	33	37	25	5
1999	34	36	25	5
2000	38	30	26	6
2001[a]	33	42	19	6
2001 local est.	31	39	25	5
2002	34	33	25	8
2003	35	30	27	8
2004	37	26	27	10
2005[a]	33	36	23	8
2005 local est.	31	34	27	8

[a] When General Elections and local Elections have been held on the same day, the General Election result is given, except in 2001 and 2005 when a separate estimate of the vote share in local elections is given.

SOURCES:- J. Stewart and G. Stoker, *The Future of Local Government* (1989); T. Travers, *The Politics of Local Government Finance* (1987); T. Byrne, *Local Government* (5th. edn 1990); D. Wilson and C. Game, *Local Government in the United Kingdom* (1998); D. Butler et al., *Failure in British Government: The Politics of the Poll Tax* (1994); C. Rallings and M. Thrasher, *The Local Elections Handbook* (annually from 1985); C. Rallings and M. Thrasher (eds), *Local Elections in Britain: A Statistical Digest* (1993) gives summary election results for all local authorities in Great Britain 1973–92; C. Rallings and M. Thrasher, *Local Elections in Britain* (1998).

X

International Affairs

Major Treaties and Documents Subscribed to by Britain since 1979

(For a more detailed chronology of EU developments see pp. 248–9)

21 Dec 79	Lancaster House agreement between Britain and the leaders of the main parties in Zimbabwe-Rhodesia
19 Dec 84	Hong Kong treaty between Britain and China signed in Peking
28 Feb 86	Single European Act
7 Feb 92	Maastricht Treaty on European Union (ratified 2 August 1993)
14 Jun 92	Rio Treaty – the United Nations Framework Convention on Climate Change
14 Jun 94	Sulphur Emissions Protocol
15 Apr 94	Agreement establishing World Trade Organisation (GATT Uruguay Round)
24 Sep 96	Comprehensive Nuclear Test Ban Treaty (ratified 6 April 1998)
2 Apr 97	Amsterdam Treaty on European Union
1 Dec 97	Landmines Treaty banning the production and use of landmines (ratified 31 July 98)
11 Dec 97	Kyoto Protocol tightened the requirements on reduction of carbon and sulphur emissions laid down at Rio
16 Dec 97	NATO expansion protocol
10 Apr 98	British Irish Agreement on Northern Ireland (Good Friday Agreement)
19 Nov 99	Agreement on Adaptation of the Treaty on Conventional Armed Forces – reduced the upper limit on European conventional armed forces
26 Feb 01	Nice Treaty on the European Union
14 Nov 01	Doha Declaration on the use of free trade to promote world development
29 Oct 04	Treaty establishing a Constitution for Europe signed in Rome

International Organisations

Britain is a member of numerous international organisations, including many agencies of the United Nations. Below is therefore not a comprehensive list. In each case Britain was a founder member.

World Bank and International Monetary Fund, 1945–

These two institutions were established as a result of the 1944 Bretton Woods Agreement. The IMF is responsible for ensuring the stability of the international monetary and financial system – the system of international payments and exchange rates. The Fund has a remit to promote economic stability and prevent crises, to help resolve crises when they do occur, and to promote growth and alleviate poverty – through surveillance, technical assistance and lending. The World Bank is primarily concerned with loans to developing countries. The two institutions are closely allied and have adjacent offices in Washington DC.

United Nations (UN), 1946–

Britain was one of the original signatories of the Charter of the United Nations. Since 1946 the British Government has had a permanent representative at the United Nations in New York. In addition, a Minister of State at the Foreign Office has usually been given special responsibility for United Nations affairs.

North Atlantic Treaty Organisation (NATO), 1949–

NATO was established in 1949 bringing together countries of western Europe with the United States and Canada in a mutual defence pact. Its military organisation is based in Brussels.

General Agreement on Tariffs and Trade (GATT), 1948–94

The General Agreement on Tariffs and Trade was the forum for deciding trade rules for most of the latter part of the twentieth century – although it was originally a provisional framework put in place after the failure to establish an International Trade Organisation.

World Trade Organisation (WTO), 1995–

The World Trade Organisation was established as a result of the Uruguay Round of world trade negotiations (1986–94) to replace GATT. It is based in Geneva.

G8 (G7), 1975–

The first summit of the world's six largest economies took place in 1975 at Rambouillet in France, prompted by concerns over the economic problems that faced the world at that time. Canada joined the group in 1976, at the Puerto Rico Summit hosted by the United States. The European Community, now the European Union, was given observer status the following year at the London Summit. It became known as the G7, and the G8 when Russia became a full member in 1997. The annual summit has evolved from an ad hoc forum dealing essentially with macroeconomic matters to a regular gathering with a broad-based agenda which addresses a wide range of international economic, political, and social issues. The 'leaders only' format, with foreign and finance ministers meeting separately in advance, was introduced in Birmingham, in 1998.

15–17 Nov 75	Rambouillet	6–8 Jul 92	Munich
27–28 Jun 76	Puerto Rico	7–9 Jul 93	Tokyo
6–8 May 77	London	8–10 Jul 94	Naples
16–17 Jul 78	Bonn	15–17 Jun 95	Halifax (Canada)
28–29 Jun 79	Tokyo	27–29 Jun 96	Lyons
22–23 Jun 80	Venice	20–22 Jun 97	Denver
19–21 Jul 81	Ottawa	15–17 May 98	Birmingham
4–6 Jun 82	Versailles	18–20 Jun 99	Cologne
28–30 May 83	Williamsburg (USA)	21–23 Jul 00	Okinawa
7–9 Jun 84	London	20–22 Jul 01	Genoa
2–4 May 85	Bonn	26–27 Jun 02	Kananaskis
4–6 May 86	Tokyo		(Canada)
8–10 Jun 87	Venice	1–3 Jun 03	Evian
19–21 Jun 88	Toronto	8–10 Jun 04	Sea Island, Georgia
14–16 Jul 89	Paris		(USA)
9–11 Jul 90	Houston	6–8 Jul 05	Gleneagles
15–17 Jul 91	London		

British Ambassadors to Leading Powers, 1979–

France

8 Dec 75	Sir N. Henderson	29 Jun 93	Sir C. Mallaby
20 Apr 79	Sir R. Hibbert	10 Jul 96	Sir M. Jay
4 Mar 82	Sir J. Fretwell	6 Dec 01	Sir J. Holmes
22 Jun 87	Sir E. Fergusson		

Germany

30 Sep 75	Sir O. Wright	17 Jan 93	(Sir) N. Broomfield
17 Mar 81	Sir J. Taylor	1 Mar 97	Sir C. Meyer
1 Sep 84	Sir J. Bullard	1 Jan 98	(Sir) P. Lever
20 Mar 88	Sir C. Mallaby	13 May 03	Sir P. Torry

Italy

14 Oct 76	Sir A. Campbell	5 Jul 92	Sir P. Fairweather
12 Jul 79	Sir R. Arculus	10 Jul 96	(Sir) T. Richardson
1 Mar 83	Ld Bridges	4 May 00	(Sir) J. Shepherd
3 Dec 87	Sir D. Thomas	1 Apr 03	Sir I. Roberts
14 Nov 89	Sir S. Egerton		

Russia (USSR)

1 Apr 78	(Sir) C. Keeble	3 Jun 92	Sir B. Fall
16 Sep 82	Sir I. Sutherland	12 Jul 95	Sir A. Wood
18 Jul 85	Sir B. Cartledge	12 Jan 00	Sir R. Lyne
23 May 88	Sir R. Braithwaite	3 Jun 04	A. Brenton

Turkey

15 Jun 77	Sir D. Dodson	23 Oct 92	J. Goulden
30 Jan 80	Sir P. Laurence	23 Mar 95	Sir K. Prendergast
28 Feb 83	(Sir) M. Russell	28 Mar 97	(Sir) D. Logan
1 Nov 86	(Sir) T. Dault	20 Dec 01	(Sir) P. Westmacott

USA

21 Jul 77	P. Jay
9 Jul 79	Sir N. Henderson
2 Sep 82	Sir O. Wright
28 Aug 86	Sir A. Acland
20 Aug 91	Sir R. Renwick
15 Aug 95	Sir J. Kerr
31 Oct 97	Sir C. Meyer
27 Jun 03	Sir D. Manning

North Atlantic Council

1975	Sir J. Killick
18 Sep 79	Sir C. Rose
15 Feb 82	Sir J. Graham
30 Aug 86	(Sir) M. Alexander
25 Jan 91	(Sir) J. Weston
1 Apr 95	(Sir) J. Goulden
14 Dec 00	(Sir) D. Manning
26 Oct 01	E. Jones Parry
25 Jun 03	P. Ricketts

European Communities/Union

18 Oct 71	(Sir) M. Palliser
1 Jul 75	Sir D. Maitland
5 May 79	(Sir) M. Butler
14 Oct 85	(Sir) D. Alexander
2 Sep 90	(Sir) J. Kerr
28 Aug 95	(Sir) S. Wall
17 Nov 00	(Sir) N. Sheinwald
8 May 03	J. Grant

United Nations

25 Mar 74	I. Richard
9 Sep 79	Sir A. Parsons
17 Aug 82	Sir J. Thomson
29 May 87	Sir C. Tickell
7 Sep 90	Sir D. Hannay
15 Jul 95	Sir J. Weston
8 Aug 98	Sir J. Greenstock
1 Jul 03	E. Jones Parry

European Union

The European Union (Communities), 1973–

The EEC was established on 1 January 1958 (under the Treaty of Rome 25 March 1957) with France, Germany, Italy, Belgium, Holland and Luxembourg as members. Britain, Denmark and Ireland joined on 1 January 1973. Greece joined on 6 January 1982. Spain and Portugal joined on 1 January 1986. Austria, Finland and Sweden joined on 1 January 1995, bringing the total membership to 15. On 1 May 2004 ten more countries joined – the Czech Republic, Estonia, Cyprus, Latvia, Lithuania, Hungary, Malta, Poland, Slovenia and Slovakia – taking the total to 25 countries. Since 1993, when the Maastricht Treaty came into effect, the Community has formally been known as the European Union.

The European Commission (until 1 November 2004 composed of two commissioners from each of the larger nations and one each from the smaller ones; from that date reduced to one commissioner per country) initiates all EU laws and is responsible for ensuring that they are put into operation. The laws themselves are primarily made by the Council of Ministers on which the national Minister responsible for the subject under discussion sits. Decisions are sometimes taken unanimously but in certain areas can be made by a weighted majority. Since the Single European Act and the Treaties of Maastricht, Amsterdam and Nice the European Parliament has had an increased share of law-making power in certain areas. The European Court of Justice has the final say on any dispute relating to the implementation of EU laws. Committees and Subcommittees of the House of Commons and House of Lords scrutinise the work of the European institutions.

The fundamental policies of the European Union stemming from the Treaty of Rome have been the creation of a customs union and its transformation into a single market, the common external trade policy, and the common agricultural policy. However, an increasing number of other policy areas have been developed at European level including regional and social funds, environmental policy, scientific research and development programmes and the move to create economic and monetary union in Europe. The Maastricht Treaty added two other areas of activity to run alongside the main work carried out under the Treaty of Rome. These are a common foreign and security policy and co-operation in justice and law enforcement.

A Chronology of Events since 1979

7 Jun 79	60 Con.; 17 Lab.; 4 Other UK members elected to European Parliament
2 Dec 79	Dublin summit: Mrs Thatcher asks for budgetary abatement
14 Dec 79	European Parliament rejects the Community budget for spending too much on agriculture and not enough on the Regional and Social funds
18 May 80	EC states impose economic sanctions against Iran in support of the United States
30 May 80	Agreement is reached among EC foreign ministers in dispute over Britain's budget contribution (Britain gets two-third rebate for three years). The Commission is asked to report on long-term reform (the Mandate)
6 Jan 81	Greece enters the Community. New Commission takes office under Gaston Thorn
27 Nov 81	London summit of EC leaders fails to reach agreement on the Commission's Mandate report. Britain's hopes of getting a long-term solution to her budget problems fade
2 Apr 82	Argentina invades the Falklands. The EEC states swiftly back Britain in a programme of economic sanctions against Argentina

18 May 82	The British veto over farm price increases is overruled in the Agriculture Council, but France states that Luxembourg Compromise still stands
24 Dec 82	European Parliament rejects supplementary budgets containing British and West German rebates
9 Jun 83	Mrs Thatcher's Government returned with an increased majority
3 Oct 83	Labour makes withdrawal 'an option' rather than a certainty should Labour Government be returned
20 Dec 83	The European Parliament freezes British and West German rebates again after the failure of the Athens summit to come to a long-term solution to the budget problem
14 Jun 84	Second direct elections to the European Parliament. Conservatives lose 15 seats: Con. 45, Lab. 32, SNP 1
14 Jun 84	Commission publishes Cockfield White Paper on completing Single Market by 31 December 1992
29 Jun 84	At Milan Summit UK, Danish and Portugese veto overridden on calling an inter-governmental conference to reform treaties
26 Jun 84	British Budget settlement agreed at Fontainebleau
6 Jan 85	New Commission takes office under Jacques Delors
3 Dec 85	Luxembourg summit agrees Single European Act
1 Jan 86	Spain and Portugal join Community
11 Jun 87	Mrs Thatcher wins third UK election
1 Jul 87	Single European Act comes into force
20 Sep 88	Mrs Thatcher criticises further European integration in Bruges speech
6 Jan 89	Second Delors Commission takes office
15 Jun 89	Third direct elections to the European Parliament. Conservatives lose 13 seats: Con. 32, Lab. 45, SNP 1
9 Nov 89	Fall of Berlin Wall
8 Dec 89	Intergovernmental Conference convened for December 1991. Eleven states adopt Social Charter
3 Oct 90	German Unification takes place.
8 Oct 90	Britain joins Exchange Rate Mechanism at 2.955 dm to £
28 Oct 90	Rome Summit leaves Mrs Thatcher isolated on monetary union, provoking Sir G. Howe to resign from UK cabinet
28 Nov 90	J. Major replaces Margaret Thatcher as PM
10 Dec 91	Maastricht Summit endorses IGC proposals
9 Apr 92	Conservatives win fourth successive UK election
2 Jun 92	Danish referendum narrowly rejects Maastricht Treaty
16 Sep 92	'Black Wednesday'. UK takes sterling from Exchange Rate Mechanism
20 Sep 92	French referendum narrowly endorses Maastricht Treaty
4 Nov 92	Commons vote 319–316 for further consideration of Maastricht Bill
6 Jan 93	Third Delors Commission takes office
17 May 93	Second Danish referendum endorses Maastricht Treaty
22 Jul 93	UK Government position on Social Chapter rejected by Commons, 324–316; wins vote of confidence next day 339–299
1 Nov 93	Maastricht Treaty comes into force
29 Mar 94	UK Cabinet accepts Ioannina compromise on blocking votes

9 Jun 94	Fourth direct elections to the European Parliament. Con. MEPs cut from 32 to 18. Lab. get 62 Lib. Dems 2 and SNP 2.
25 Jun 94	UK vetoes Dehaene as Commission President
15 Jul 94	Santer chosen as Commission President
28 Nov 94	Norwegian referendum rejects EU membership
1 Jan 95	Austria, Finland and Sweden join EU
18 Jan 95	Euro-Parliament confirms Santer 418–103
26 Mar 95	Seven States accept Schengen Agreement on open borders
26 May 96	UK Government threatens non-cooperation after EU failure to lift ban on British beef
22 Jun 96	Compromise on beef agreed at Florence Summit
16 Jul 96	Council invites Czechoslovakia, Estonia, Hungary, Poland and Slovenia to apply for membership
1 May 97	All British parties fight general election with a commitment to a Referendum before joining monetary union. Labour wins landslide victory
Jun 97	UK signs Social Protocol endorsing Social Chapter
20 Oct 97	Brown indicates no constitutional objection to joining EMU
13 Dec 98	Luxembourg Summit lifts ban on UK beef exports
Dec 98	*European Elections Act* provides for PR
1 Jan 99	EMU starts for 11 countries
	The European Convention of Human Rights incorporated into UK law
14 Jan 99	Santer Commission narrowly survives censure over allegations of fraud and mismanagement
15 Mar 99	Santer Commission resigns en masse
1 May 99	Amsterdam Treaty enters into force
5 May 99	Prodi approved to replace Santer as President of Commission
10 Jun 99	Fifth direct elections to European Parliament. MEPs: 36 Con.; 29 Lab.; 10 Lib. Dem.; Others 12.
1 Aug 99	Lifting of the ban on British beef exports
15 Jan 00	Opening of Intergovernmental Conference on enlargement of EU
7 Dec 00	Charter of Fundamental Rights of the EU proclaimed in Nice
1 Jan 02	Notes and coins enter circulation in twelve euro-zone countries
28 Feb 02	Opening of Convention on the Future of Europe
31 May 02	European Union ratifies Kyoto Protocol
9 Oct 02	Commission agrees the accession of ten new member countries
16 Apr 03	Treaty of accession for the ten new members is signed
4 Oct 03	Opening of Intergovernmental Conference in Rome on new EU constitution
19 Apr 04	Tony Blair announces Britain will hold referendum on any future European Constitution
10 Jun 04	Sixth direct elections to European Parliament. MEPs: 27 Con.; 19 Lab.; 12 Lib. Dem.; 12 UKIP; 2 Green; 6 others
18 Jun 04	Heads of Government at European Council in Brussels agree new constitution, subject to ratification by national Parliaments and referendums
22 Nov 04	Portuguese Prime Minister Jose Baroso succeeds Prodi as President of Commission

Summits, 1979–

Since 1975 there has always been at least one 'European Council' during each member state's six-month Presidency of the Council of Ministers. The following summits have taken place since 1979.

12–13 Mar 79	Paris	24–25 Jun 94	Corfu
21–22 Jun 79	Strasbourg	15 Jul 94	Brussels
29–30 Nov 79	Dublin	9–10 Dec 94	Essen
27–28 Apr 80	Luxembourg	26–27 Jun 95	Cannes
12–13 Jun 80	Venice	22–23 Sep 95	Majorca
1–2 Dec 80	Luxembourg	15–16 Dec 95	Madrid
23–24 Mar 81	Maastricht	29 Mar 96	Turin
29–30 Jun 81	Luxembourg	21–22 Jun 96	Florence
26–27 Nov 81	London[1]	5 Oct 96	Dublin
29–30 Mar 82	Brussels	13–14 Dec 96	Dublin
28–29 Jun 82	Brussels	16–17 Jun 97	Amsterdam
3–4 Dec 82	Copenhagen	20–21 Nov 97	Luxembourg
21–23 Mar 83	Brussels	12–13 Dec 97	Luxembourg
17–19 Jun 83	Stuttgart	12 Mar 98	London[1]
4–6 Dec 83	Athens	26 May 98	Brussels[2]
19–20 Mar 84	Brussels	16–17 Jun 98	Cardiff[1]
14–17 Jun 84	Fontainebleau	11–12 Dec 98	Vienna
3–4 Dec 84	Dublin	3–4 Jun 99	Cologne
29–30 Mar 85	Brussels	15–16 Oct 99	Tampera
28–29 Jun 85	Milan	10–11 Dec 99	Helsinki
2–3 Dec 85	Luxembourg	23–24 Mar 00	Lisbon[2]
26–27 Jun 86	The Hague	19–20 Jun 00	Santa Maria de Feira
5–6 Dec 86	London[1]	7–9 Dec 00	Nice
23–24 Jun 87	Brussels	23–24 Mar 01	Stockholm
4–5 Dec 87	Copenhagen	15–16 Jun 01	Gothenburg
27–28 Jun 88	Hanover	21 Sep 01	Brussels[2]
2–3 Dec 88	Rhodes	14–15 Dec 01	Laeken
26–27 Jun 89	Madrid	15–16 Mar 02	Barcelona
8–9 Dec 89	Strasbourg	21–22 Jun 02	Seville
28 Apr 90	Dublin I	24–25 Oct 02	Brussels[2]
25–26 Jun 90	Dublin II	12–13 Dec 02	Copenhagen
27–28 Oct 90	Rome I	17 Feb 03	Brussels[2]
14–15 Dec 90	Rome II	20–21 Mar 03	Brussels
28–29 Jun 91	Luxembourg	20–21 Jun 03	Thessaloniki
9–10 Dec 91	Maastricht	16–17 Oct 03	Brussels[2]
26–27 Jun 92	Lisbon	12–13 Dec 03	Brussels
16 Oct 92	Birmingham[1]	17–18 Jun 04	Brussels
11–12 Dec 92	Edinburgh[1]	16–17 Dec 04	Brussels
20–22 Jun 93	Copenhagen	16–17 Jun 05	Brussels
29 Oct 93	Brussels	15–16 Dec 05	Brussels
10–11 Dec 93	Brussels		

[1] Under British Presidency.
[2] Special European Council.

Net UK Payments to European Community Institutions (£m)

	Gross	Abatement	Refund	Receipts	Net Contribution
1973	181	0	0	76	105
1974	179	0	0	149	30
1975	341	0	0	396	−55
1976	463	0	0	295	168
1977	737	0	0	368	369
1978	1,348	0	0	526	822
1979	1,606	0	0	658	948
1980	1,767	0	98	964	705
1981	2,174	0	693	1,084	397
1982	2,862	0	1,019	1,240	603
1983	2,976	0	807	1,521	648
1984	3,201	0	528	2,017	656
1985	3,555	166	61	1,483	1,845
1986	4,493	1,701	0	2,216	576
1987	5,203	1,153	0	1,569	1,705
1988	4,507	1,595	0	1,569	1,343
1989	5,587	1,156	0	2,116	2,315
1990	6,355	1,697	0	2,184	2,474
1991	5,805	2,497	0	2,766	542
1992	6,737	1,881	0	2,823	2,033
1993	7,982	2,540	0	3,291	2,151
1994	7,188	1,726	0	3,254	2,208
1995	8,890	1,208	0	3,665	4,017
1996	9,131	2,411	0	4,368	2,352
1997	7,813	1,733	0	4,738	1,342
1998	10,090	1,378	0	4,115	4,597
1999	10,287	3,171	0	3,479	3,638
2000	10,517	2,085	0	4,241	4,192
2001	9,379	4,560	0	3,430	1,389
2002	9,438	3,099	0	3,201	3,138
2003	10,966	3,559	0	3,725	3,682
2004	11,687	2,756	0	4,766	4,165

SOURCE:- Treasury paper *European Community Finances*, April 2004, Cm 6134.

European Parliament, 1973–

Under the Treaty of Rome, each member country's Parliament nominated delegates from its own members to serve in a European Parliament which met monthly in Strasbourg or Luxembourg. Its main functions have been advisory and supervisory. It has to be consulted on the Community Budget and it can, by a two-thirds majority, dismiss the Commissioners en bloc. After the enlargement of the Community in 1973 it had 198 members. The UK was entitled to send 36 members but, in the absence of Labour representation, it at first sent only

22 (18 Conservative, 2 Liberal, 1 Scottish National Party and 1 Independent). After the 1975 Referendum a Labour delegation was selected and until 1979 there were 18 Labour, 16 Conservative, 1 Liberal and 1 Scottish National representative (26 were M.P.s and 10 peers).

On 7–10 June 1979, 15–18 June 1984 and 15–18 June 89, Community-wide elections took place for a directly elected Parliament which expanded by stages from 410 members to 518 members.

The 1986 Single European Act first granted the Parliament a positive, if limited, role in the European Commission's legislative process.

Following the implementation of the Maastricht Treaty in 1993, the Parliament gained important new legislative powers (co-decision). The Parliament also gained the power to vote in – and vote out – the Commission.

In 1991 it was decided to expand the Parliament to 567 members. The UK delegation rose from 81 to 87 at the 9–12 June 1994 elections. Following the 1995 enlargement the Parliament was expanded to 826 members and this number was elected on 10–13 June 1999.

From 1979 to 1994 British MEPs were elected from single-member constituencies (Northern Ireland returned three members using the Single Transferable Vote system). Following the *European Election Act 1999*, a system of regional list proportional representation was adopted, with the nine regions of England returning between four and eleven members each, Scotland eight and Wales five. Elections were held on this basis on 10–13 June 1999. With the expansion of the European Union in 2004 to incorporate ten new countries, the parliamentary delegations from existing members were reduced. The UK allocation fell from 87 to 78 – seven from Scotland, four from Wales, three from Northern Ireland and the remaining 64 from the ten English regions (ranging from three in the North-East to ten in the South-East, in proportion to population). These elections were held on 10–13 June 2004.

Leaders of the British Party Delegations

Conservative		Labour				
Jan 73	(Sir) P. Kirk	Jul 75	M. Stewart	Jan 00	S. Murphy	
Feb 77	G. Rippon	Nov 76	J. Prescott	Sep 02	G. Titley	
Jun 79	(Sir) J. Scott-Hopkins	Jun 79	Barbara Castle	*Liberal Democrat*		
Jun 82	Sir H. (Ld) Plumb	Jun 85	A. Lomas	Jun 99	Diana Wallace	
Apr 87	(Sir) C. Prout	Jun 87	D. Martin	Jun 04	C. Davies	
Jun 94	Ld Plumb	Jun 88	B. Seal			
Jan 97	T. Spencer	Jun 90	G. Ford			
Sep 97	E. McMillan-Scott	Jun 93	Pauline Green			
Dec 01	J. Evans	Jun 94	W. David			
Dec 04	T. Kirkhope	Jul 98	A. Donnelly			

SOURCES:- M. Westlake, *Britain's Emerging Euro-Elite (1994)*; <www.conservatives.com>; <www.eplp.org.uk>.

Referendum on EEC Membership

(Thursday 5 June 1975)

'Do you think that the United Kingdom should stay in the European Community (the Common Market)?'

	Total electorate[b]	Total votes[a]	% turnout[b]	% 'Yes'	Highest 'Yes'	Lowest 'Yes'
England	33,339,959	21,722,222	64.6	68.7	76.3	62.9
Wales	2,015,766	1,345,545	66.7	64.8	74.3	56.9
Scotland	3,698,462	2,286,676	61.7	58.4	72.3	29.5
N. Ireland[a]	1,032,490	498,751		47.4	52.1	52.1
UK[b]	40,086,677	29,453,194	64.5	64.5	76.3	29.5

[a] The votes were counted on a county basis except in Northern Ireland which was treated as a single unit. In 66 of the 68 counties there was a 'Yes' majority. (Shetland voted 56.3% 'No' and Western Isles 70.5% 'No'.)

[b] Service votes are only in the total votes and in the 'Yes' percentages.

(For 1979 referendums in Scotland and Wales see pp. 223–6)

Direct Elections to European Parliament

	%		% votes				Seats			
	Turnout	Con.	Lab.	Lib.	Nat.	Oth.	Con.	Lab.	Lib.	Nat.
1979 Thu 7 Jun										
England	31.3	53.4	32.6	13.2	–	0.8	54	12	–	–
Wales	34.4	36.6	41.5	9.6	11.7	0.6	1	3	–	–
Scotland	33.7	33.7	33.0	13.9	9.4	–	5	2	–	1
GB	32.1	50.6	33.1	13.1	2.5	0.7	60	17	–	1
N. Ireland[a]	55.7	–	–	0.2	99.8	–	–	–	–	3
UK	32.7	48.4	31.6	12.6	2.5	4.9	60	17	–	3

Electorate 41,152,763 Votes cast 13,446,083

	%		% votes				Seats			
	Turnout	Con.	Lab.	Lib.	Nat.	Oth.	Con.	Lab.	Lib.	Nat.
1984 Thu 7 Jun										
England	31.6	43.1	35.0	20.4	–	1.5	42	24	–	–
Wales	39.7	25.4	44.5	17.4	12.2	0.5	1	3	–	
Scotland	33.0	25.7	40.7	15.6	17.8	0.2	2	5	–	1
GB	31.8	40.8	36.5	19.5	2.5	0.8	45	32	–	1
N. Ireland[a]	63.5	–	–	–	100.0	–	–	–	–	3
UK	32.6	39.9	36.0	19.1	2.4	5.6	45	32	–	4

Electorate 42,493,274 Votes cast 13,998,274

	Turnout	% Con.	Lab.	% votes Lib.	Nat.	Oth.	Seats Con.	Lab.	Lib.	Nat.	UKIP	Green

1989 Thu 15 Jun

	Turnout	Con.	Lab.	Lib.	Nat.	Oth.	Con.	Lab.	Lib.	Nat.		
England	35.8	37.2	39.2	6.7	–	16.9	32	34	–	–		
Wales	41.1	23.1	49.7	3.2	12.2	13.0	–	4	–	–		
Scotland	40.8	20.5	40.8	4.4	26.9	7.3	–	7	–	1		
GB	35.9	34.7	40.1	6.4	–	19.0	32	45	–	1		
N. Ireland[a]	48.4	–	–	–	100.0	–	–	–	–	3		
UK	36.8	33.5	38.7	6.2	3.2	18.4	32	45	–	–4		

Electorate 43,037,821 Votes cast 15,893,403

1994 Thu 9 Jun

	Turnout	Con.	Lab.	Lib.	Nat.	Oth.	Con.	Lab.	Lib.	Nat.		
England	35.5	30.5	43.5	18.4	–	7.6	18	51	2	–		
Wales	38.2	14.6	55.9	8.7	17.1	3.7	–	5	–	–		
Scotland	43.1	14.5	42.5	7.2	32.6	1.6	–	6	–	2		
GB	36.2	27.9	44.2	16.7	4.3	6.9	18	62	2	2		
N. Ireland[a]	48.7	–	–	–	100.0	–	–	–	–	3		
UK	36.8	26.9	42.6	16.1	4.1	10.2	18	62	–	5		

Electorate 43,037,821 Votes cast 15,749,417

1999 Thu 10 Jun

	Turnout	Con.	Lab.	Lib.	Nat.	Oth.	Con.	Lab.	Lib.	Nat.	UKIP	Green
England	23.0	38.5	21.5	13.3	–	16.7	33	24	9	–	3	2
Wales	28.3	22.8	31.9	8.2	29.6	7.5	1	2	–	2	–	–
Scotland	24.8	19.8	28.7	9.8	27.2	14.5	2	3	1	2	–	–
GB	23.1	35.8	28.0	12.7	4.6	18.9	36	29	10	4	3	2
N. Ireland[a]	57.7	–	–	–	100.0	–	–	–	–	3	–	–
UK	24.1	34.8	27.0	12.1	4.3	21.8	36	29	10	7	3	2

Electorate 44,495,741 Votes cast 10,681,080

2004 Thu 10 Jun

	Turnout	% Con.	Lab.	% votes LD.	Nat.	UKIP	Oth.	Seats Con.	Lab.	Lib.	Nat.	UKIP	Green
England	38.7	27.9	21.7	15.3	–	17.2	17.9	24	15	11	–	12	2
Wales	41.4	19.4	32.5	10.5	17.4	10.5	9.7	1	2	–	1	–	–
Scotland	30.9	17.8	26.4	13.1	19.7	6.7	16.3	2	2	1	2	–	–
GB	38.2	26.7	22.6	14.9	2.4	16.1	17.2	27	19	12	3	12	2
N. Ireland[a]	51.7	–	–	–	–	100.0	–	–	–	–	–	3	
UK	38.5	25.9	21.9	14.4	2.3	15.6	19.9	27	19	12	3	12	2

Electorate 44,191,160 Votes cast 17,007,882

[a] N. Ireland used the Single Transferable Vote system of proportional representation.

European Court of Justice, 1973–

This was established under the Treaty of Rome to adjudicate on disputes arising out of the application of the Community treaties. Its regulations are enforceable on all member countries. After 1973 it had nine judges and four advocates-general. With the accession of Spain, Portugal and Greece the Court grew to 12 judges, and there were subsequent expansions to 15 in 1995 and 25 in 2004. It has become increasingly important as the powers of the Union have widened. It has ruled against Britain on numerous occasions, some of which are listed on pp. 151–2.

British Members of European Commission

1 Jan 73	Sir C. Soames	1 Jan 89	B. Millan
1 Jan 73	G. Thomson	1 Jan 93	Sir L. Brittan
1 Jan 77	R. Jenkins (President)	1 Jan 93	B. Millan
1 Jan 77	C. Tugendhat	1 Jan 95	N. Kinnock
1 Jan 81	C. Tugendhat	Sep 99	N. Kinnock *(Interim)*
1 Jan 81	I. Richard	Sep 99	C. Patten *(Interim)*
1 Jan 85	Ld Cockfield	1 Jan 00	N. Kinnock
1 Jan 85	S. Clinton Davies	1 Jan 00	C. Patten
1 Jan 89	Sir L. Brittan	22 Nov 04	P. Mandelson

Ministers with Special EEC Responsibilities

(Ministers of State at the Foreign Office)

Feb 77–May 79	F. Judd	Jul 94–May 97	D. Davis
May 79–Jun 83	D. Hurd	May 97–Jul 98	D. Henderson
Jun 83–Jan 86	M. Rifkind	Jul 98–Jun 99	Joyce Quin
Jan 86–Jul 89	Lynda Chalker	Jun 99–Oct 99	G. Hoon
Jul 89–Jul 90	F. Maude	Oct 99–Jun 01	K. Vaz
Jul 90–May 93	T. Garel-Jones	Jun 01–Oct 02	P. Hain
May 93–Jul 94	D. Heathcoat-Amory	Oct 02–May 05	D. MacShane
		May 05–	D. Alexander

British Member of the European Court

1 Jan 73	Ld Mackenzie-Stuart
1 Jan 88	Sir G. Slynn
1 Jan 92	(Sir) D. Edward
8 Jan 04	Sir K. Schiemann

SOURCES:- D. Butler and D. Marquand, *European Elections and British Politics* (1980); D. Butler and P. Jowett, *Party Strategies in Britain: A Study of the 1984 European Elections* (1985); D. Butler and M. Westlake, *British Politics and European Elections 1994* (1995); T. Bainbridge and A. Teasdale, *The Penguin Companion to European Union* (2nd edn 1998); S. George, *An Awkward Partner* (3rd edn 1998); H. Young, *This Blessed Plot: Britain and Europe* (1988). See also *The Times Guides to the European Parliament* (1979, 1984, 1989, 1994, 1999 and 2004).

Non-EU European Organisations with British Membership

Western European Union (WEU), 1947–

The UK, France, the Netherlands, Belgium and Luxembourg signed a 50-year treaty in Brussels, 17 March 1948, for collaboration in economic, cultural and social matters and for collective self-defence. Western Union's defence functions were formally transferred to NATO 20 December 1950. In 1954 Italy and West Germany were invited to join and WEU was formally inaugurated 6 May 1955. Its social and cultural functions were transferred to the Council of Europe 1 July 1960 but the WEU Council continued to hold regular consultative meetings.

Council of Europe, 1949–

Following the 1948 Congress of Europe at The Hague, the Council of Europe came into being in May 1949. Its founder members were Belgium, Denmark, France, Ireland, Italy, Luxembourg, the Netherlands, Norway, Sweden and the UK. Turkey and Greece joined later in 1949, Iceland in 1950, West Germany in 1951, Austria in 1956, Cyprus in 1961, Switzerland in 1963 and Malta in 1965. It is run by a Committee of Ministers and Consultative Assembly (630 members, 18 from UK in 2005). The Council of Europe aims to foster European co-operation in every field and about 80 Conventions have been concluded, ranging from extradition rules to equivalence of degrees. One of its main achievements was the European Convention on Human Rights signed in 1950 (with violations examinable by the European Court of Human Rights set up in 1959).

European Court of Human Rights, 1959–

Britain has been involved in a number of cases brought under the European Convention of Human Rights, established by the Council of Europe in 1950 and agreed to by Britain although not incorporated into British law until the *Human Rights Act, 1998*, which came into effect on 2 October 2000. In the following cases some or all of the complainant's argument has been found proved against the British authorities.

21 Feb 75	Golder (Prisoner: Access to a solicitor)
18 Jan 78	Ireland (Internment and interrogation in N. Ireland)
25 Apr 78	Tyrell (Isle of Man: corporal punishment)
26 Apr 79	*Sunday Times* (Press freedom: Contempt of Court in Thalidomide case)
13 Aug 81	Young, James and Webster (Closed shop)
22 Oct 81	Dudgeon (Homosexuality in N. Ireland)
5 Nov 81	X (Review of mental patient's detention)
25 Feb 82	Campbell and Cosans (Corporal punishment in schools)
25 Mar 83	Silver et al. (Censorship of prisoners' correspondence)
28 Jun 84	Campbell and Fell (Prison visitors: conduct of disciplinary proceedings)
2 Aug 84	Malone (Telephone tapping)
28 May 85	Abdulaziz, Cabales, & Balkanadali (Sex discrimination in immigration law)

24 Nov 86	Gillow (Residence rules in Guernsey)
2 Mar 87	Weeks (Re-detention of prisoner released on licence)
8 Jul 87	O., H., W., B., & R. (Access to children in local authority care)
27 Apr 88	Boyle and Rice (Prisoners' letters and visits)
29 Nov 88	Brogan et al. (Length of detention under terrorism law)
7 Jul 89	Gaskin (Access to personal records)
7 Jul 89	Soering (Extradition to USA on murder charge)
28 Mar 90	Granger (Legal aid for prisoner's appeal)
30 Aug 90	Fox, Campbell & Hartley (Detention in N. Ireland)
30 Aug 90	McCallum (Prisoner's letters)
25 Oct 90	Thynne, Wilson & Gunnell (Discretionary life sentences)
26 Nov 91	*Observer* et al., *Guardian* et al. (Spycatcher)
26 Nov 91	*Sunday Times* (No. 2) (Spycatcher)
25 Mar 92	Campbell (Censorship of prisoner's correspondence with solicitor)
26 Oct 93	Darnell (Medical discipline – length of proceedings)
24 Feb 95	McMichael (Access to documents in adoption case)
13 Jul 95	Tolstoy Miloslavsky (Guarantee of plaintiffs' costs)
27 Sep 95	McCann (Costs of Gibraltar IRA shooting case)
23 Oct 95	Boner (Unfair denial of legal aid)
21 Feb 96	Singh (Release on parole; access to lawyer)
10 Jun 96	Benham (Fair trial of poll tax non-payer)
15 Nov 96	Chahal (Unfair attempt at extradition to India)
17 Dec 96	Saunders (Use of unfairly obtained evidence)
2 May 97	'D' (Enforcement of extradition)
25 Jun 97	Halford (Telephone tapping by police in sex discrimination dispute)
19 Feb 98	Bowman (Non-candidate's right to spend money in an election)
1 Jul 98	Tinnelly et al. (Access to documents in NI contracts case)
23 Nov 98	McLeod (Disproportionate force by police in repossession case)
23 Sep 98	'A' (Corporal punishment of boy by stepfather)
23 Sep 98	Steel et al. (Police detention of animal rights protesters)
20 Oct 98	McConnell (Guernsey: Member of the Executive is not an independent judge)
18 Feb 99	Matthews (Gibraltarians right to vote in European elections)
18 Feb 99	Hood Army (Procedures in trying an alleged deserter)
18 Feb 99	Cable et al. (Conduct of Court Martial)
22 Jul 99	Scarth (Entitlement to a public hearing in an arbitration case)
27 Sep 99	Smith and Ford (Right of homosexuals to serve in armed forces)
27 Sep 99	Lustig-Prean and Beckett (Right of homosexuals to serve in armed forces)
12 Oct 99	Perks et al. (Arrest for non-payment of poll tax)
25 Nov 99	Hashman and Harrup (Binding over of hunt saboteurs)
16 Dec 99	T. and V. (Fair trial of a child)
17 Dec 99	Taylor (Equal age for granting fuel allowances)
12 May 00	Khan (Use of intercepted pager messages in evidence)
19 Sep 00	I.J.L., G.M.R. and A.K.P (Use of evidence in Guinness trial)
19 Jun 01	Atlan (Non-disclosure of prosecution evidence)
10 Jul 01	Price (Treatment of disabled prisoner)
24 Jul 01	Hirst (Delay in parole hearing of discretionary life prisoner)
25 Sep 01	PG and JH (Use of covert listening devices)

16 Oct 01	O'Hara and Brennan (Questioning of suspects in Northern Ireland)
30 Oct 01	Devlin (Denial of employment on security grounds)
26 Feb 02	Morris (Conduct of courts martial)
14 Mar 02	Paul and Audrey Edwards (Failure to protect prisoner from cellmate)
19 Mar 02	Devenney (Unfair dismissal on security grounds in Belfast)
28 May 02	Stafford (Tariff for mandatory life sentence)
28 May 02	Kingsley (Gaming board procedures)
28 May 02	McShane (Inadequate investigation into killing by army in Belfast)
4 Jun 02	William Faulkner (Interference with prisoner's correspondence)
11 Jun 02	Willis (Male entitlement to widow's benefits)
2 Jul 02	Wilson, and the National Union of Journalists, Palmer, Wyeth and the National Union of Rail Maritime and Transport Workers and Doolan and Others (Financial inducements to surrender union representation)
11 Jul 02	I. (Legal treatment of transsexuals)
11 Jul 02	Christine Goodwin (Legal treatment of transsexuals)
16 Jul 02	Armstrong (Admissibility of covert recordings)
16 Jul 02	P., C. and S. (Procedures in adoption and care proceedings)
26 Sep 02	Benjamin and Wilson (Minister's powers on release of life prisoners)
8 Oct 02	Beckles (Right to silence in police station)
10 Oct 02	D.P. and J.C. (Failure of local authority to prevent child abuse)
22 Oct 02	Perkins and R. (Homosexuals in armed forces)
22 Oct 02	Beck, Copp and Bazeley (Homosexuals in armed forces)
22 Oct 02	Taylor-Sabori (Use of intercepted pager messages in evidence)
5 Nov 02	Allen (Use of evidence from cellmate informer)
26 Nov 02	E. et al. (Failure of local authority to prevent child abuse)
10 Dec 02	Waite (Lack of hearing to determine recall of released life prisoner)
17 Dec 02	Mitchell and Holloway (Delay in resolving civil dispute)
28 Jan 03	Peck (Lack of remedy for person filmed on CCTV)
20 Feb 03	Hutchison Reid (Procedure for adjudicating on release of mental patient)
29 Apr 03	McGlinchey (Lack of effective remedy)
27 May 03	Hewitson (Bugging to obtain evidence)
12 Jun 03	Chalkley (Bugging to obtain evidence)
12 Jun 03	Easterbrook (Tariff set by Home Secretary)
24 Jun 03	Stretch (Inability to renew building lease)
24 Jun 03	Dowsett (Non-disclosure of evidence)
1 Jul 03	Finucane (Inadequate investigation into circumstances of death)
8 Jul 03	Hatton et al. (Right to effective remedy in English law)
17 July 03	Mellors (Delay in appeal hearing)
17 July 03	Perry (Covert videotaping of suspect for identification purposes)
22 July 03	Edwards and Lewis (Non-disclosure of prosecution evidence)
7 Oct 03	Von Bulow (Tariff for mandatory life sentence)
9 Oct 03	Ezeh and Connors (Legal representation in prison disciplinary hearings)
16 Oct 03	Wynne (Tariff for mandatory life sentence)
25 Nov 03	Lewis (Police bugging a drug suspect's home)
16 Dec 03	Grieves (Conduct of court martial)

In all but one of the cases found against it the British Government took measures to comply with the Convention. The exception was the Brogan case in 1988, when the Government derogated from the Convention but in 1999 the relevant Clause in the *Anti-Terrorism Act* was repealed.

SOURCES:- HC Research Paper 97/137; HC Deb 11 Jul 83 col. 256w.; ONS database; Cm. 3700/1997.

Commonwealth

The Commonwealth evolved from a loose association of white dominions within the former British Empire to a formal structure bringing together 1.7 billion people in 53 sovereign states. It has had a permanent secretariat at Lancaster House in London since 1965. In 1991 the Commonwealth Heads of Government Meeting adopted the Harare Declaration committing members to human rights, democracy, and resisting racism. This was refined by the Millbrook Commonwealth Action Programme of 1995.

Commonwealth Heads of Government Meetings, 1979–

1–10 Aug 79	Lusaka	24–27 Oct 97	Edinburgh
30 Sep 81–7 Oct 81	Melbourne	12–15 Nov 99	Durban
23–29 Nov 83	New Delhi	2–5 Mar 02	Coolum (Australia)
16–22 Oct 85	Nassau	5–8 Dec 03	Abuja
13–17 Oct 87	Vancouver	25–28 Nov 05	Valletta
18–24 Oct 89	Kuala Lumpur	*Secretary-General*	
16–22 Oct 91	Harare	Jul 75	(Sir) S. Ramphal (Guyana)
21–25 Oct 93	Nicosia	Jul 90	E. Anyaoku (Nigeria)
10–13 Nov 95	Auckland	Apr 00	D. McKinnon (New Zealand)

Independent Self-Governing Members of the Commonwealth

United Kingdom		1947–72, 1989	Pakistan *(Republic 1956)*
1856	New Zealand	1948	Ceylon (Sri Lanka 1972)
1867	Canada[1]		*(Republic 1972)*
1901	Australia[1]	1953–63	Federation of Rhodesia
1909–61, 1994–	South Africa[1]		and Nyasaland[4]
1907–33	Newfoundland[1,2]	1957	Ghana *(Republic 1960)*
1922–49	Ireland (Eire)	1957	Malaya (Malaysia 1963)
1947	India[3] *(Republic 1950)*		

[1] These were recognised as having 'Dominion Status' 1907.

[2] From 1933 to 1949 Newfoundland was governed by a UK Commission of Government. In 1949 Newfoundland joined Canada as the tenth Province.

[3] Indian representatives were invited to attend Imperial Conferences and Prime Ministers' Meetings 1917–47.

[4] Although the Central African Federation, set up in 1953, and composed of N. Rhodesia, S. Rhodesia and Nyasaland, was not a fully independent member of the Commonwealth, her Prime Ministers were invited to Prime Ministers' Meetings 1955–62 and the Prime Minister of Rhodesia was invited 1962–65.

(Elective Monarchy)		1968	Swaziland *(Indigenous*
1958–62[5]	West Indies Federation		*Monarchy)*
1960–95, 1999–		1968	Nauru *(Republic 1968)*
	Nigeria *(Republic 1963)*	1968	Mauritius *(Republic 1992)*
1961	Cyprus *(Republic 1960)*	1970–87, 1997–	
1961–1997[6]	Sierra Leone		Fiji *(Republic 1987)*
	(Republic 1971)	1970	Tonga *(Indigenous Monarchy)*
1961	Tanganyika (Tanzania 1965)	1970	Western Samoa *(Indigenous*
	(Republic 1962)		*Monarchy)*
1962	Jamaica	1972	Bangladesh *(Republic 1972)*
1962	Trinidad and Tobago	1973	Bahamas
	(Republic 1976)	1974	Grenada
1962	Uganda *(Republic 1963)*	1975	Papua-New Guinea
1963–64	Zanzibar (See Tamzania)	1976	Seychelles *(Republic 1976)*
1963	Kenya *(Republic 1964)*	1978	Dominica
1964	Zambia *(Republic 1964)*	1978	Solomon Islands
1964	Malta *(Republic 1974)*	1978	Tuvalu
1963	Kenya *(Republic 1964)*	1979	St Lucia
1964	Zambia *(Republic 1964)*	1980	Vanuatu *(Republic 1980)*
1964	Malta *(Republic 1974)*	1979	Kiribati *(Republic 1979)*
1964	Malawi *(Republic 1966)*	1979	St Vincent and the Grenadines
1965	The Gambia *(Republic 1970)*	1980	Vanuatu *(Republic 1980)*
1965	Singapore *(Republic 1965)*	1980	Zimbabwe *(Republic 1980)*
1966	Botswana *(Republic 1966)*	1981	Antigua and Barbuda
1966	Lesotho	1981	Belize
	(Indigenous Monarchy)	1982	Maldive Islands
1966	Guyana *(Republic 1970)*		*(Republic 1982)*[7]
1966	Barbados	1983	St Christopher and Nevis
1966	Botswana	1984	Brunei
	(Republic 1966)		*(Indigenous Monarchy)*
1966	Guyana *(Republic 1970)*	1990	Namibia *(Republic 1990)*
1966	Lesotho	1995	Mozambique *(Independent*
	(Indigenous Monarchy)		*Republic)*
1966	Barbados	1995	Cameroon *(Independent*
1968	Nauru *(Republic 1968)*		*Republic)*

[5] Barbados, Jamaica, Trinidad, Tobago, the Leeward and Windward Islands all formed the West Indies Federation between 1958 and 1962.
[6] Following a coup, Sierra Leone's membership was suspended in 1997.
[7] Special Membership.

British Colonies and Dependencies

Anguilla (1625). Colony. Part of St Kitts and Nevis until it became a separate dependency 1980. Governor: 1985 A. Baillie 1990 B. Canty 1992 A. Shave 1995 A. Hoole 1997 R. Harris 2000 P. Johnstone 2004 A. Huckle.

Ascension (1815). Dependency of Colony of St Helena since 1922.

Bermuda (1684). Colony. Governor: 1977 Sir P. Ramsbotham 1981 Sir R. Posnett 1983 Ld Dunrossil 1988 Sir D. Langley 1992 Ld Waddington 1997 T. Masefield 2002 Sir J. Vereker.

British Antarctic Territory (1982). Territory.

British Indian Ocean Territory (1965). Territory. The Chagos Archipelago and Aldabra, Farquhar and Desroches Islands were formed into a single British Dependency in 1965.

British Virgin Islands (1672). Colony. Governor: 1978 J. Davidson 1982 D. Barwick 1987 M. Herdman 1992 P. Penfold 1995 D. Mackilligin 1998 F. Savage 2000 T. Macan.

Cayman Islands (1670). Separate dependency under British rule following Jamaican Independence 1962. Governor: 1974 T. Russell 1982 P. Lloyd 1987 A. Scott 1992 M. Gore 1995 J. Owen 1999 P. Smith 2002 B. Dinwiddy.

Falkland Islands (1833). Colony. Invaded by Argentina, then recaptured 1982. Governor: 1976 J. Parker 1980 (Sir) R. Hunt (Civil Commissioner 1982–85) 1986 G. Jewkes 1989 W. Fullerton 1993 D. Tatham 1996 R. Ralph 1999 D. Lamont 2002 H. Pearce.

Gibraltar (1713). Colony. Largely self-governing since 1968. Governor: 1978 Sir W. Jackson 1982 Sir D. Williams 1985 Sir P. Terry 1989 Sir D. Reffell 1993 Sir J. Chapple 1995 Sir H. White 1997 Sir R. Luce 2000 (Sir) D. Durie 2003 Sir F. Richards.

Hong Kong (1843). Colony. Kowloon ceded to Britain in 1860. New Territories leased to Britain for 99 years in 1898. 1997 reversion of whole colony to China agreed 1984. Reverted 1997. Governor: 1971 M. Maclehose 1982 Sir E. Youde (*1986 vacant*) 1987 Sir D. Wilson 1992–97 C. Patten.

Montserrat (1632). Colony. Partially evacuated due to volcanic activity 1995. Governor 1977 W. Jones 1980 D. Dale 1985 A. Watson 1987 C. Turner 1990 D. Taylor 1993 F. Savage 1997 A. Abbott 2001 A. Longrigg 2004 Deborah Barnes-Jones.

New Hebrides (1906). Administered as Anglo-French condominium. Independence granted as Republic of Vanuatu 1980.

Pitcairn Island (1898). Colony. First settled 1790. Administered via the British High Commission in New Zealand.

Rhodesia (1889). Formerly Southern Rhodesia – originally a chartered company. Part of Federation of Rhodesia and Nyasaland 1953–63. Resumed status as a self-governing colony with name of Rhodesia 1964. Unilateral declaration of independence 1965. Returned to British rule as Zimbabwe-Rhodesia 1979. Granted independence as Zimbabwe 1980. Governor 1979–80: Ld Soames.

St Helena (1673). Colony since 1834. Ascension 1922 and Tristan da Cunha 1938 are its dependencies. Governor: 1976 G. Guy 1981 J. Massingham 1984 F. Baker 1988 R. Stimson 1991 A. Hoole 1995 D. Smallman 1999 D. Hollamby 2003 M. Clancy.

Tristan da Cunha (1815). Dependency of Colony of St Helena 1938. (Evacuated 1961–63).

Turks and Caicos Islands (1766). Separate dependency under British rule following Jamaican Independence 1962. Governor: 1978 J. Strong 1982 C. Turner 1987 M. Bradley 1993 M. Bourke 1996 J. Kelly 2000 M. Jones 2002 J. Poston.

Defence

Royal Navy
First Sea Lord

1977	Sir T. Lewin
1979	Sir H. Leach
1982	Sir J. Fieldhouse
1985	Sir W. Staveley
1989	Sir J. Oswald
1993	Sir B. Bathurst
1995	Sir J. Slater
1998	Sir M. Boyce
2001	Sir N. Essenhigh
2002	Sir A. West

Army
Chief of General Staff

1976	Sir R. Gibbs
1979	Sir E. Bramall
1982	Sir J. Stanier
1985	Sir N. Bagnall
1988	Sir J. Chapple
1992	Sir P. Inge
1994	Sir C. Guthrie
1997	Sir R. Wheeler
2000	Sir M. Walker
2003	Sir M. Jackson

Royal Air Force
Chief of Air Staff

1977	Sir M. Beetham
1982	Sir K. Williamson
1985	Sir D. Craig
1988	Sir P. Harding
1992	Sir M. Graydon
1997	Sir R. Johns
2000	Sir P. Squire
2003	Sir J. Stirrup

Defence Staff
Chief of Defence Staff

1977	Sir E. Ashmore
1979	Sir T. Lewin
1982	Sir E. Bramall
1985	Sir J. Fieldhouse
1988	Sir D. Craig
1991	Sir R. Vincent
1993	Sir P. Harding
1994	Sir P. Inge
1997	Sir C. Guthrie
2001	Sir M. Boyce
2003	Sir M. Walker

Military strength[a] (as at 1 April; spending in year beginning April that year)

	Army[b]	Navy[c] ('000s)	Air Force	Infantry battalions	Surface ships	Strike Air Squadrons	Spending (£m)
1980	159	72	90	56	53	15	11,182
1985	162	70	93	56	50	11	17,943
1990	153	63	90	55	47	11	22,298
1995	112	48	71	41	40	6	21,517
2000	104	39	51	40	38	5	22,105
2004	104	37	49	40	35	5	26,171

[a] Trained personnel only.
[b] Includes Gurkhas.
[c] Includes Royal Marines.

Major Military Operations

Northern Ireland, 1969–97

On 14 August 1969 the Government of Northern Ireland informed the UK Government that as a result of the severe rioting in Londonderry it had no alternative but to ask for the assistance of the troops at present stationed in Northern Ireland to prevent a breakdown in law and order. British troops moved into Londonderry that day, and into Belfast on 15 August 1969. On 19 August 1969 GOC Northern Ireland assumed overall responsibility for security in the Province. The Provisional IRA declared a cease-fire on 31 August 1994. They resumed their activity on 9 February 1996. A second IRA cease-fire came into effect on 20 July 1997.

Costs and Casualties

| | Regular Army | | UDR/RIR[b] | | RUC | | Civil |
	Strength[a]	Deaths	Strength	Deaths	Strength	Deaths	deaths
1969	7,495	0	–	–	3,044	1	11
1970	7,170	0	4,008	0	3,808	2	21
1971	13,762	43	6,786	5	4,086	11	104
1972	16,661	103	9,074	24	4,257	17	305
1973	15,342	58	7,982	8	4,391	13	158
1974	14,067	28	7,795	7	4,565	15	151
1975	13,913	14	7,861	6	4,902	11	205
1976	13,672	14	7,769	15	5,253	23	222
1977	13,632	15	7,843	14	5,692	14	55
1978	13,600	14	7,862	7	6,110	10	40
1979	13,000	38	7,623	10	6,642	14	37
1980	11,900	8	7,373	8	6,935	9	41
1981	11,600	10	7,479	13	7,334	21	36
1982	10,900	21	7,111	7	7,718	12	45
1983	10,200	5	6,925	10	8,003	19	44
1984	10,000	9	6,468	10	8,127	9	36
1985	9,700	2	6,494	4	8,259	23	25
1986	10,500	4	6,408	8	8,234	12	37
1987	11,400	3	6,531	8	8,236	16	66
1988	11,200	21	6,393	12	8,227	6	54
1989	11,200	12	6,230	2	8,259	9	39
1990	11,500	7	6,043	8	8,243	12	49
1991	11,200	6	6,276	8	8,217	6	75
1992	12,600	5	6,000	2	8,478	3	76
1993	12,500	6	5,600	2	8,464	6	70
1994	11,600	1	5,398	2	8,493	3	56
1995	9,900	0	5,255	0	8,415	1	8
1996	10,500	1	4,966	1	8,423	0	14
1997	8,500	1	4,792	1	8,485	4	17

[a] Figure for Regular Army strength is at 31 December up until 1982; 1 July thereafter. It does not include any UDR or Royal Irish Regiment personnel.
[b] The Ulster Defence Regiment was formed on 1 April 1970. The figures include permanent, part-time, male and female members. On 1 July 1992 the UDR merged with the Royal Irish Rangers to form the Royal Irish Regiment. The figures from 1994 onwards are the regular strength at 1 April.

SOURCES:- Ministry of Defence and Northern Ireland Office.

Falklands, 1982

On 2 April 1982 Argentine forces landed on the Falklands and took over the Islands and South Georgia. An expeditionary force was despatched and on 25 April South Georgia was recaptured. British forces landed on West Falkland on 20 May and by 14 July Port Stanley was recaptured and all the Argentine forces surrendered. The British forces under Rear-Admiral J. Woodward lost six ships and 20 aircraft. The total casualties were 254 killed and 777 wounded. The cost of the operation from April to June was estimated at £35 million.

The First Gulf War, 1990–91

On 2 August 1990, Iraqi Armed Forces invaded and occupied Kuwait. The same day the Security Council of the United Nations passed Resolution 660 demanding unconditional Iraqi withdrawal. US, British and other forces were deployed in Saudi Arabia and the Persian Gulf. On 29 November 1990 the UN Security Council authorised the use of 'all necessary means' to free Kuwait if the Iraqis failed to withdraw by 15 January 1991 (Resolution 678). On 16 January 1991 American, British and other allied planes began an aerial bombardment of Iraq. On 24 Feburary 1991 Allied ground forces crossed the Iraqi and Kuwaiti borders from Saudi Arabia. On 26 Feburary 1991 Kuwait City fell to Allied troops and on 28 Feburary 1991 Allied and Iraqi forces agreed a cease-fire. British forces under Lt. Gen. Sir P. de la Billiere lost 24 killed and 43 wounded. The total cost was estimated at £2,094 million, although contributions from allies who took no military part in operations amounted to £2,023 million.

Bosnia, 1992–

A civil war afflicted this province of the former Yugoslavia from April 1992 until the Dayton peace accord of 21 November 1995. British peace-keeping troops were first deployed in Bosnia-Herzegovina in September 1992 with a limited mandate to escort UN food convoys. Under the Dayton agreement a NATO-led international force known as IFOR was established, succeeded in 1996 by SFOR. In 2004 the UK still contributed some 1,900 personnel to SFOR operations. SFOR's mandate includes armed forces reform, the arrest of individuals indicted for war crimes, tackling organised crime, corruption and extremism, assisting in the return of displaced persons and supporting the UN's High Representative, Lord Ashdown.

Kosovo, 1999–

In the winter of 1998–99 public opinion in Western countries became increasingly concerned by news reports of atrocities committed by Serbian soldiers and police in the southern Serbian province of Kosovo, where ethnic Albanians comprised 85% of the population, and where the Kosovo Liberation Army was fighting for greater autonomy. On 19 March 1999 talks broke down between the Serbian government, the European Union, Russia and the USA at Rambouillet in France. On 24 March 1999 NATO forces began bombing operations in Kosovo and the rest of Serbia and Montenegro. The vast majority of sorties were flown by US aircraft, but British planes were also involved; none were lost. Bombing raids continued daily until 10 June 1999 when Serbian leader Slobodan Milosevic agreed to a UN Security Council Resolution which dictated terms for Serbian military withdrawal from Kosovo. Over the next few days a NATO force (K-FOR) occupied the whole of Kosovo, under the command of a British General, Sir M. Jackson. Some 3,000 UK troops were still deployed in Kosovo in 2005.

Sierra Leone, 2000–01

British forces played a leading role in the restoration the elected President Kabbah of Sierra Leone. The rebels agreed to disarm in November 2000. There was little actual fighting, although one British soldier was killed in an operation to free some British soldiers held hostage by a rebel group. In 2001, a series of British Short Term Training Teams completed a programme of basic infantry training for some 10,000 Sierra Leonean soldiers, although a token military presence remains.

Afghanistan, 2001–02

Following the terrorist attacks in the United States on 11 September 2001, British forces took part in a US led operation to remove the Taliban regime in Afghanistan which was blamed for sheltering the Al-Qaeda terrorist organisation. The British contribution to the initial military operation in Afghanistan included Tomahawk missiles launched from submarines and air-to-air refuelling and air reconnaissance undertaken by aircraft of the RAF. Royal Marine Commandos were deployed on the ground in Afghanistan to assist US and other nations' forces. The United Kingdom also acted as the initial lead nation for the International Security Assistance Force (ISAF), which was formed as a result of a United Nations Security Council Resolution and deployed in January 2002 for a period of three months. This was subsequently extended until June 2003 when responsibility for ISAF was handed over to Turkey.

The Second Gulf War, 2003

On 8 November 2002 the United Nations Security Council unanimously passed Resolution 1441 warning Iraq of 'serious consequences' if it failed to comply with UN inspection of its programmes for weapons of mass destruction. Inspectors were sent in, and reported that there was evidence of subterfuge by Iraq, although they produced little solid evidence of current nuclear, chemical or biological capability. The United States and Britain judged that Iraq was failing to comply, and on 17 March 2003 announced the end of the UN process.

The UN inspectors left Iraq the following day. On 20 March 2003 bombing operations began, and the same day US and British forces crossed the border from Kuwait into Iraq. On 9 April Iraqi civilians assisted by US soldiers tore down a statue of Saddam Hussein in the centre of Baghdad – symbolising the fall of the city. On 1 May 2003 President Bush announced the end of major combat operations. A total of 46,000 UK personnel under Air Marshal B. Burridge were deployed in the operation – just under 10% of the coalition total – and British aircraft flew 2,519 sorties out of a total of 41,400. Up to 1 May 2003, 33 British military personnel lost their lives in the operation. British troops continued to be stationed in the Basra area in southern Iraq after the conflict; in early 2005 the British deployment stood at around 9,000 and the total British death toll had risen to 95. The cost of military involvement in Iraq to the UK taxpayer was £847 million in the 2002–03 fiscal year and £1,188 million in the 2003–04 fiscal year (*Operations in Iraq: Lessons for the Future*, Ministry of Defence, December 2003).

SOURCES:- *Whitaker's Almanack*; First Report on the Defence Estimates by House of Commons Select Committee on Defence, 1992.478.

XI
The Media

The Press

National Daily Newspapers

The policies of national newspapers between 1979 and 2005 have inevitably fluctuated. Policy should be taken only as a general indication of the nature of the paper. In very few cases have newspapers been the official organ of a political party.

Daily Express, 1900

Proprietors: Trafalgar House property group (Chairman: V. (Ld) Matthews). In 1985 Express Newspapers were taken over by United Newspapers (Chairman: D. (Ld) Stephens). In 1996 United Newspapers merged with MAI under Ld Hollick to form United News and Media. Acquired by Northern and Shell (R. Desmond) in 2000.

Policy: Independent conservative. Switched to support Labour after 1996, but returned to an independent conservative policy after 2001.

Editors: D. Jameson, 1977. A. Firth, 1980. C. Ward, 1981. Sir L. Lamb, 1983. (Sir) N. Lloyd, 1986. R. Addis, 1995. Rosie Boycott, 1998. C. Williams, 2001. P. Hill, 2003.

Daily Mail, 1896

Proprietors: Associated Newspapers Ltd (Chairman 3rd (1971), 4th (1998) Lds Rothermere).

Policy: Independent. Right-wing Conservative.

Editors: (Sir) D. English, 1971. P. Dacre, 1992.

Daily Mirror, 1903

Proprietors: Reed International 1970 (Chairman: (Sir) D. Ryder. (Sir) A. Jarratt, 1974). Control of Mirror Group Newspapers acquired by Maxwell Foundation 1984 (Chairman R. Maxwell; I. Maxwell 1991). Control acquired by creditor banks, 1992 under Chief Executive: D. Montgomery. Consortium sold to Trinity plc 1999 (Sir V. Blank), which changed its name to Trinity Mirror.

Policy: Independent. Since 1940s Labour-supporting.

Editors: M. Molloy, 1975. R. Stott, 1985. R. Greenslade, 1990. R. Stott, 1991. D. Banks, 1992. C. Myler, 1994. P. Morgan, 1995. R. Wallace, 2004.

Daily Star, 1978

Proprietors: Beaverbrook Newspapers (Chairman: V. Matthews). At first printed in Manchester and distributed only in North. Acquired by United Newspapers (Ld Stevens) in 1985. In 1996 United Newspapers merged with MAI under Ld Hollick to form United News and Media. Acquired by Northern and Shell (R. Desmond) in 2000.

Policy: Independent.

Editors: P. Grimsditch, 1978. L. Turner, 1982. M. Gabbert, 1987. B. Hitchen, 1987. P. Walker, 1994. P. Hill, 1998. Dawn Neesom, 2003.

Daily Telegraph, 1855

Proprietors: The Berry family from 1928. M. Berry (Ld Hartwell) became Editor-in-Chief in 1968. Acquired by Hollinger Group (C. Black), 1987. C. Black removed from control of Hollinger, 2004.

Policy: Conservative.

Editors: W. Deedes, 1974. M. Hastings, 1986. C. Moore, 1996. M. Newland, 2003.

Financial Times, 1888

Proprietors: Controlling interest held by Pearson plc since 1957.

Policy: Finance, independent.

Editors: F. Fisher, 1973. (Sir) G. Owen, 1981. R. Lambert, 1991. A. Gowers, 2001.

Independent, 1986

Proprietors: Newspaper Publishing Co. Ltd. From 2000 the dominant shareholder was Independent News and Media (Chairman: (Sir) T. O'Reilly).

Policy: Independent.

Editors: A. Whittam-Smith, 1986. I. Hargreaves, 1994. A. Marr, 1996. Rosie Boycott, 1998. A. Marr, 1998. S. Kelner, 1998.

Guardian, 1821

Proprietors: The Manchester Guardian & Evening News Ltd. *Manchester Guardian* until 1959. The Scott Trust.

Policy: Independent liberal.

Editors: P. Preston 1975. A. Rusbridger, 1995.

Morning Star, 1966
Proprietors: Morning Star Co-operative Society. Successor to the *Daily Worker*.
    Policy: Communist.
    Editors: G. Matthews, 1966. T. Chater, 1974. J.Haylett, 1995.

(Post), 1988 (10 Nov–17 Dec only)
Proprietors: Messenger Group Newspapers (E. Shah).
    Policy: Independent.
    Editor: L. Turner.

Sun, 1964
Proprietors: Since 1969 News International Ltd (R. Murdoch).
    Policy: Conservative until 1996. Then Labour.
    Editors: (Sir) L. Lamb, 1975. K. McKenzie, 1981. S. Higgins, 1994. D. Yelland, 1998. Rebekah Wade, 2002.

The Times, 1785[1]
Proprietors: From 1966 owned by the Thomson Organisation. Acquired by News International, 1981 (Chairman: R. Murdoch).
    Policy: Independent conservative. Supported Labour in 2001.
    Editors: W. Rees-Mogg, 1967. H. Evans, 1981. C. Douglas-Home, 1983. C. Wilson, 1985. S. Jenkins, 1990. P. Stothard, 1992. R. Thomson, 2003.

(Today), 1986–95
Proprietors: Messenger Group (E. Shah). Bought by Lonrho, 1986. Bought by News International (Chairman: R. Murdoch) 1987.
    Policy: Independent.
    Editors: B. MacArthur, 1986. D. Montgomery, 1987. M. Dunn, 1991. R. Stott, 1993–95.

National Sunday Newspapers
(excluding all those not published in London)

The Business, 1996
Proprietors: Press Holdings Ltd (the Barclay brothers).
    Policy: Independent.
    Editor: A. Neil, 1996.

Daily Star Sunday, 2002
Proprietors: Northern and Shell (R. Desmond).
    Policy: Independent.
    Editor: H. Whittow, 2002.

---

[1] *The Times* suspended publication from 1 December 1978 to 12 November 1979.

Independent on Sunday, 1990

Proprietors: Newspaper Publishing Co. Ltd. From 2000 the dominant shareholder was Independent News and Media (Chairman: (Sir) T. O'Reilly).

    Policy: Independent.

    Editors: A.Whittam Smith, 1990. I. Jack, 1992. P. Wilby, 1995. Rosie Boycott, 1996. K. Fletcher, 1998. T. Davies, 1999.

Mail on Sunday, 1982

Proprietors: Associated Newspapers Ltd (Chairman: 3rd Ld Rothermere; 4th Ld Rothermere 1998).

    Policy: Independent Conservative.

    Editors: B. Shrimsley, 1982. Sir D. English, 1982. S. Steven, 1982. J. Holborow, 1992. P. Wright, 1998.

News of the World, 1843

Proprietors: News International Ltd (R. Murdoch) since 1969.

    Policy: Independent conservative.

    Editors: B. Shrimsley, 1975. K. Donlan, 1980. B. Askew, 1981. D. Jameson, 1981. N. Lloyd, 1984. D. Montgomery, 1985. Wendy Henry, 1987. Patsy Chapman, 1988. P. Morgan, 1994. P. Hall, 1995. A. Coulson, 2003.

Observer, 1791

Proprietors: Atlantic Richfield, 1976. Sold to Lonrho, 1980 (Chairman: R. Rowland). Taken over by Guardian and Evening News Group, 1993.

    Policy: Independent liberal.

    Editors: D. Trelford, 1976. J. Fenby, 1993. A. Jaspan, 1995. W. Hutton, 1996. R. Alton, 1998.

People, 1881

Proprietors: Reed International 1970 (Chairman: (Sir) D. Ryder. A. Jarratt, 1974). Control acquired by R. Maxwell, 1984. I. Maxwell, 1991. Control acquired by creditor banks, 1992. Consortium sold to Trinity plc 1999 (Sir V. Blank), which changed its name to Trinity Mirror.

    Policy: Independent.

    Editors: G. Pinnington, 1972. R. Stott, 1984. E. Burrington, 1985. J. Blake, 1988. Wendy Henry, 1989. R. Stott, 1990. W. Haggerty, 1991. Bridget Rowe, 1992. L. Gould, 1996. B. Parsons, 1997. N. Wallis, 1998. M. Thomas, 2003.

(Sunday Correspondent), 1989–90.

Proprietors: Sunday Publishing Co. plc.

    Policy: Independent.

    Editors: P. Cole, 1989. J. Bryant 1990.

Sunday Express, 1918

Proprietors: Taken over by Trafalgar House property group, 1977. Chairman: V. (Ld) Matthews. Acquired by United Newspapers, 1985 (Chairman D. (Ld) Stevens). In 1996 United Newspapers merged with MAI under Ld Hollick to form United News and Media. Acquired by Northern and Shell (R. Desmond) in 2000.

   Policy: Independent conservative.

   Editors: J. Douglas, 1920. J. Gordon, 1928. (Sir) J. Junor, 1954. R. Esser, 1986. R. Morgan, 1989. Eve Pollard, 1991. B. Hitchen, 1994. R. Addis, 1995. Amanda Platell, 1998. M. Pilgrim, 1999. M. Townsend, 2001.

Sunday Mirror, 1963

Proprietors: Control acquired by Reed International 1970 (Chairman: (Sir) D. Ryder. 1974, A. Jarratt). Bought by R. Maxwell, 1984. I. Maxwell, 1991. Control acquired by creditor banks, 1992. Consortium sold to Trinity plc 1999 (Sir V. Blank), which changed its name to Trinity Mirror.

   Policy: Independent.

   Editors: M. Christiansen, 1963. R. Edwards, 1972. M. Molloy, 1986. Eve Pollard, 1988. Bridget Rowe, 1991. C. Myler, 1992. Tessa Hilton, 1994. P. Connew, 1996. J. Cassidy, 1996. Amanda Platell, 1996. Bridget Rowe, 1997. B. Parsons, 1998. C. Myler, 1998. Tina Weaver, 2001. M. Thomas, 2003.

Sunday Telegraph, 1961

Proprietors: The Sunday Telegraph Ltd (M. Berry (Ld Hartwell)). Bought by Hollinger plc (C. (Ld) Black) 1987. Ld Black ousted from board 2004.

   Policy: Independent conservative.

   Editors: J. Thompson, 1976. P. Worsthorne, 1986. T. Grove, 1989. C. Moore, 1992. D. Lawson, 1995. Sarah Sands, 2005.

Sunday Times, 1822

Proprietors: Bought by R. Thomson in 1959 (Thomson Allied Newspapers). Times Newspapers Ltd, formed in 1967 to run *The Times* and *Sunday Times*. Control acquired by News International, 1981 (Chairman: R. Murdoch).

   Policy: Independent conservative.

   Editors: H. Evans, 1967. F. Giles, 1981. A. Neil, 1983. J. Witherow, 1994.

(Sunday Today), 1986–7

Proprietors: Messenger Group Newspapers (E. Shah). Control acquired by Lonrho, 1986. Bought by News International (Chairman R. Murdoch) 1987.

   Policy: Independent.

   Editor: B. MacArthur.

London Evening Newspapers

(Evening News), 1881–1980, 1987 (March–October only)

Proprietors: Associated Newspapers Ltd, 1905. Merged with *Evening Standard*, 1980. Briefly relaunched by Associated Newspapers in 1987.

   Policy: Conservative.

   Editors: L. Kirby, 1974–80. J. Lees, 1987.

Evening (New) Standard, 1827

Proprietors: From 1977 Trafalgar House property group (Chairman: V. Matthews). Sold to Associated Newspapers, 1980 (Chairman: Ld Rothermere) and merged with *Evening News* as *(New) Standard*. Reverted to name *Evening Standard* in 1987.

   Policy: Independent conservative.

   Editors: C. Wintour, 1978. L. Kirkby, 1980. J. Lees, 1986. P. Dacre, 1991. S. Steven, 1992. (Sir) M. Hastings, 1996. Veronica Wadley, 2002.

(London Daily News), 1987 (February–July only)

Proprietors: Mirror Group Newspapers (Chairman: R. Maxwell).
Policy: Independent Labour-leaning.
Editor: M. Linklater.

Partisan Tendencies and Circulations of National Daily Newspapers in British General Elections, 1979–2005

	Circulation (millions) and Party support						
	1979	*1983*	*1987*	*1992*	*1997*	*2001*	*2005*
D. Express	2.5	1.9	1.7	1.5	1.2	0.9	0.9
	Con.	Con.	Con.	Con.	Con.	Lab.	Con.
D. Mail	2.0	1.8	1.8	1.7	2.1	2.3	2.3
	Con.	Con.	Con.	Con.	Con.	Con.	Con.
D. Mirror	3.8	3.3	3.1	2.9	2.8	2.1	1.6
	Lab.	Lab.	Lab.	Lab.	Lab.	Lab.	Lab.
D. Telegraph	1.4	1.3	1.1	1.0	1.1	1.0	0.9
	Con.	Con.	Con.	Con.	Con.	Con.	Con.
Guardian	0.3	0.4	0.5	0.4	0.4	0.4	0.3
	Lab./	All./	Lab.	Lab./	Lab./	Lab./	Lab.
	Lib.	Con.		Lib. D.	Lib. D.	Lib. D.	–
Independent	–	–	0.3	0.4	0.3	0.2	0.2
	–	–	None	None	Lab.	Lab./L.D.	Lib.Dem.
Sun	3.9	4.2	4.0	3.6	3.9	3.3	3.1
	Con.	Con.	Con.	Con.	Lab.	Lab.	Lab.
The Times	–	0.3	0.4	0.4	0.8	0.7	0.7
		Con.	Con.	Con.	Con.	Lab.	Lab.
Today	–	–	0.3	0.5	–	–	–
			–/Coal.	Con.	–	–	–
Daily Star	n.a.	1.3	1.3	0.8	0.7	0.6	0.7

Partisanship in Elections

	1979	1983	1987	1992	1997	2001	2005
Circulation	13,789	14,527	14,824	13,546	13,180	11,586	10,774
Total Con.	9,731	11,260	10,914	8,728	4,461	3,326	4,030
Circulation	(71%)	(78%)	(74%)	(64%)	(34%)	(29%)	(37%)
Con. vote	13,698	13,012	13,763	14,093	9,601	8,358	8,733
	(44%)	(42%)	(42%)	(42%)	(31%)	(32%)	(33%)
Total Lab.	4,058	3,267	3,924	3,332	7,947	8,260	5,813
Circulation	(29%)	(22%)	(26%)	(25%)	(60%)	(71%)	(54%)
Lab. vote	11,532	8,457	10,030	11,560	13,518	10,725	(9,562)
	(37%)	(28%)	(31%)	(34%)	(44%)	(41%)	(36%)
Total Lib. (D).	–	417	307	429	–	197	226
Circulation	–	(3%)	(2%)	(3%)	–	(2%)	(2%)
Lib. (D) Vote	4,314	7,781	7,341	5,999	5,243	4,813	5,982
	(14%)	(25%)	(23%)	(18%)	(17%)	(18%)	(23%)

SOURCE:- (of circulation figures) Audit Bureau of Circulation. Circulation figures are for the period of the year in which the election was held.

Circulations of National Newspapers, 1980–

National Daily Newspapers
(to nearest 000)

	1980	1990	2000[a]	2004[b]	2005[b]
D. Express	2,325	1,585	973	957	884
D. Mail	1,985	1,708	2,372	2,485	2,278
D. Mirror	3,651	3,083	2,241	1,919	1,602
D. Star	1,033	833	626	902	735
D. Telegraph	1,456	1,076	974	915	863
Guardian	375	424	379	383	327
Independent	–	411	189	249	226
Sun	3,837	3,855	3,587	3,411	3,098
The Times	316	420	678	661	654

[a] Figure for July 2000.
[b] Figure for January 2004.
SOURCE:- Audit Bureau of Circulation.

Circulation of National Sunday Newspapers, 1980–

(000s)

	1980	1990	2000[a]	2004[b]	2005[b]
Independent on Sunday	–	352	204	206	176
News of the World	4,472	5,056	4,014	3,845	3,417
Observer	1,018	551	386	460	405
Mail on Sunday	–	1,903	2,267	2,364	2,336
People	3,856	2,566	1,475	1,056	870

	1980	1990	2000[a]	2004[b]	2005[b]
Sunday Express	3,100	1,664	894	930	866
Sunday Mirror	3,856	2,894	1,881	1,674	1,441
Sunday Telegraph	1,032	594	767	696	660
Sunday Times	1,419	1,165	1,280	1,370	1,197

[a] Figure for July.
[b] Figure for April.

SOURCE:- Audit Bureau of Circulation.

Provincial Morning Daily Newspapers, 1900–

Sporting newspapers and publications such as the *Hull Shipping Gazette* and the *Hartlepool Daily Shipping List* have been omitted. Bold type indicates newspapers still being published on 1 January 2005.

ABERDEEN – *Aberdeen Daily Journal* (1746). Merged with *Aberdeen Free Press* Nov 1922 and became **Aberdeen Press and Journal**.

BELFAST – **Belfast News-Letter** (1737).

Irish News (and Belfast Morning News) (1881).

BIRMINGHAM – **Birmingham Post** (1857).

BRISTOL – **Western Daily Press** (1858).

CARDIFF – **Western Mail** (1869).

DARLINGTON – **Northern Echo** (1870).

DUNDEE – **Courier and Advertiser** (1861).

EDINBURGH – **Scotsman** (1817).

GLASGOW – **Glasgow) Herald** (1783).

Daily Record (1895).

IPSWICH – **East Anglian Daily Times** (1874).

LEAMINGTON – *Leamington, Warwick, Kenilworth and District Morning News* (1896). Ceased publication 1991.

LEEDS – **Yorkshire Post** (1754).

LIVERPOOL – **Liverpool Daily Post** (1855).

Journal of Commerce (1861).

NEWCASTLE – **Journal** (1832).

NORWICH – **Eastern Daily Press** (1870).

PLYMOUTH – **Western Morning News** (1860).

SHEFFIELD – *Sheffield Morning Telegraph* (1855). Closed 1987.

SOURCE:- *Willing's Press Guide; Writers' and Artists' Yearbook.*

Main Political Weeklies

The Economist, 1843

Proprietors: The Economist Newspaper Limited.

Policy: Independent.

Editors: A. Knight, 1974. R. Pennant-Rea, 1986. B. Emmott, 1993.

New Statesman, 1913

Proprietors: Statesman Publishing Company (largest shareholder: G. Robinson). Merged with *New Society* in 1988.

  Policy: Independent radical.

  Editors: B. Page, 1978, H. Stephenson, 1982. J. Lloyd, 1986. S. Weir, 1988. S. Platt, 1991. I. Hargreaves, 1996. P. Wilby, 1998, J. Kampfner, 2005.

The Spectator, 1828

Proprietors: The Spectator Limited since 1898. J. St. L. Strachey, 1898. (Sir) E. Wrench, 1925. I. Gilmour, 1954. H. Creighton, 1967. H. Keswick, 1975. A. Clough, 1981.

  Policy: Independent conservative.

  Editors: A. Chancellor, 1975. C. Moore, 1984. D. Lawson, 1989. F. Johnson, 1995. B. Johnson, 1999.

Tribune, 1937

Proprietors: Tribune Publications, Ltd.

  Policy: Left-wing.

  Editors: R. Clements, 1959. C. Mullin, 1982. N. Williamson, 1984. P. Kelly, 1986. P. Anderson, 1990. M. Seddon, 1993. C. McLaughlin, 2004.

The Press Council, 1953–90

Chairman

1978	(Sir) P. Neill
1983	Sir Z. Cowen
1989	L. Blom-Cooper

The General Council of the Press was formed in 1953 in response to a recommendation of the Royal Commission on the Press (Cmd. 7700). It consisted of 15 editorial representatives and ten managerial representatives. Its objects were to preserve the freedom of the press, to review any developments likely to restrict the supply of information of public interest and importance, to encourage training of journalists and technical research and to study developments in the press tending towards greater concentration or monopoly.

In 1963 it was reorganised to bring in lay members and the title was changed to the Press Council. The objects of the Council were extended to include considering complaints about the conduct of the press or the conduct of persons and organisations towards the press, and publishing relevant statistical material.

In 1977 the Press Council accepted the recommendation of the Royal Commission on the Press that in addition to its independent lay Chairman, it should consist of equal numbers of press and lay members. From 1978 to 1990, the composition was 12 representatives from newspaper and magazine management, four from the National Union of Journalists, two from the Institute of Journalists, 18 lay representatives, eight non-voting consultative members and a lay Chairman. Lay members were appointed by an independent body, the Press Council Appointments Commission. The NUJ representatives withdrew from the Council in 1980, and only returned in May 1990, seven months before the Council was wound up.

Press Complaints Commission, 1991–

Chairman

1991	Ld McGregor of Durris
1995	Ld Wakeham
2003	Sir C. Meyer

The Press Complaints Commission began work on 1 January 1991. Its establishment followed the publication of the Report of the Calcutt Committee in June 1990. That had recommended the setting up of such a Commission in place of the Press Council, which it regarded as 'ineffective as an adjudicating body'. The central planks of the self-regulatory system were an independent Board of Finance to fund its activities, a Code Committee to produce and keep up to date a Code of Practice, and the Commission itself. By the start of 1991, a committee of national and regional editors under Patsy Chapman, then editor of the *News of the World*, had produced a 16-clause Code of Practice for the Commission to uphold. All publishers and editors committed themselves publicly to their own Code and to ensuring secure and adequate funding of the Commission to uphold it. The Commission itself was established on the lines suggested in the Calcutt Report – and consisted of national, regional and periodical editors alongside a group of lay members. In 1995 the Government endorsed self regulation of the press under the Press Complaints Commission in its White Paper *Privacy and Media Intrusion*.

SOURCES:- *Willing's Press Guide, 1900–*; Press Council Annual Reports, *The Press and the People*.

Broadcasting

The British Broadcasting Corporation

The British Broadcasting Company Ltd was formed by some 200 manufacturers and shareholders on 18 October 1922, registered on 15 December 1922, and received its licence on 18 January 1923. A system of paid licences for owners of radio receivers was started in 1922. This was followed by the establishment of the British Broadcasting Corporation under Royal Charter (20 December 1926), which came into operation on 1 January 27. It was to be a public service body 'acting in the national interest' and financed by licence fees paid by all owners of radio receivers. Under the royal charter the BBC was granted a licence for ten years and was to be directed by a board of governors nominated by the government. The charter was renewed and modified 1 January 1937, 1 January 1947, 1 July 1952, 30 July 1964. It was extended until 31 July 1979 in 1976 (Cmnd. 6581). In July 1979 it was extended for a further period until 31 July 1981, when it was replaced by a new charter (Cmnd. 8313) to last until 31 December 1996. On 6 July 1994 the National Heritage Secretary P. Brooke announced in the White Paper *The Future of the BBC – Serving the Nation, Competing Worldwide* (Cm. 2621) that the Charter would be renewed for another ten years until 2006, and that the licence fee would remain the basis of BBC funding for at least the next five years. In October 1998 the Secretary of State for Culture, Media and Sport C. Smith announced a review of the role and funding of the BBC, but confirmed that the licence fee would continue until 2006. The review chaired by city economist G. Davies (later appointed Chairman of the BBC Governors) entitled *The Future Funding of the BBC*, which reported in July 1999, concluding that the licence fee should remain the main funding mechanism for the foreseeable future. Tessa Jowell took over as Secretary of State for Culture, Media and Sport in June 2001. On 11 December 2003 she launched a public consultation entitled the *Review of the BBC's Royal Charter*.

British Broadcasting Corporation, 1927–, Board of Governors

Chairmen

1 Jan 73	Sir M. Swann
1 Aug 80	G. Howard (Ld)
1 Aug 83	S. Young
29 Aug 86	*(vacant)*
6 Nov 86	M. Hussey
1 Apr 96	Sir C. Bland
1 Oct 01	G. Davies
28 Jan 04	*(vacant)*
2 Apr 04	M. Grade

Vice-Chairmen

26 Jun 75	M. Bonham Carter
1 Aug 81	Sir W. Rees-Mogg
1 Aug 86	Ld Barnett
1 Aug 93	Ld Cocks
1 Aug 98	Baroness Young of Old Scone
1 Jan 01	G. Davies
1 Jan 02	Ld Ryder
1 Aug 04	A. Salz

Governors

1972–79	R. Fuller
1972–80	G. Howard
1974–81	Stella Clarke
1976–81	P. Chappell
1976–82	Ld Allen
1977–82	Lady Serota
1978–85	Sir J. Johnston
1979–84	C. Longuet-Higgins
1981–83	P. Moons
1981–83	S. Young
1981–88	Jocelyn Barrow
1982–87	Daphne Park
1982–87	Sir J. Boyd
1983–88	M. McAlpine
1984–89	Lady Parkes
1985–87	E of Harewood
1985–90	Sir C. Keeble
1988–93	J. Roberts
1988–98	B. Jordan
1988–93	(Lady) P. D. James
1988–93	K. Oates
1990–95	Jane Glover
1990–95	Shawhar Sadeque
1990–98	Ld N. Gordon-Lennox
1993–98	Margaret Spurr
1994–99	Janet Cohen
1995–2000	Sir D. Scholey
1995–2003	(Sir) R. Eyre
1995–2000	A. White
1998–2004	Dame P. Neville-Jones
1998–	R. Sondhi
1998–2002	(Sir) T. Young
1999–2002	Heather Rabbatts
2000–2004	D. Gleeson
2002–	Angela Sarkis
2002–	Dame R. Deech
2003–	Deborah Bull
2004–	R. Tait

Governors appointed to represent national interests

N. Ireland

1978	Lady Faulkner
1985	J. Kincade
1991	Sir K. Bloomfield
1999	F. Monds

Scotland

1979	(Sir) R. Young
1984	W. Peat
1989	Sir G. Hills
1994	N. Drummond
1999	Sir R. Smith
2005	J. Peat

Wales

1979	A. Roberts
1986	J. Parry
1992	G. Jones
1996	R. Jones
2002	M. Jones

Director-General

1 Oct 77	(Sir) I. Trethowan
1 Aug 82	A. Milne
29 Jan 87	*(vacant)*
26 Feb 87	(Sir) M. Checkland
23 Dec 92	(Sir) J. Birt
1 Jan 00	G. Dyke
28 Jan 04	*(vacant)*
22 Jun 04	M. Thompson

BBC Radio

The BBC originally offered one basic radio service, known as the National Programme, together with variant Regional Services. In 1939 these services were all replaced by a single Home Service; the Forces Programme, providing a lighter alternative, began in 1940. In 1945 Regional Home Services, as variants of the Home Service, were restarted, and the Light Programme replaced the Forces Programme. In 1946 the Third Programme was introduced to provide a second alternative service. Very high frequency (VHF) transmissions began in 1955, in order to improve the quality and coverage of the existing services. In 1964 the Music Programme was added, using the Third Programme wavelengths in the daytime, and in 1967 a fourth network came into being to provide a pop music service replacing the offshore 'pirate' stations; this was called Radio 1, and the existing national services were renamed Radio 2 (Light Programme), Radio 3 (Third and Music Programmes) and Radio 4 (Home Service).

In 1970 the radio networks were reorganised as 'generic' services following publication of the BBC's proposals in Broadcasting in the Seventies, and the English regional radio services were then gradually wound down, though the regional centres continued to provide programmes for the networks. The regional radio broadcasts in the three National Regions started to develop as autonomous services with the opening of Radio Ulster in 1975. In 1978 there was a major reorganisation of the radio frequencies used for the national networks, and Radio 4 became available throughout the United Kingdom on the long-wave band. This enabled the national services – Radio Scotland, Radio Wales, Radio Cymru (Welsh language, on VHF only) and Radio Ulster – to become fully independent of Radio 4. Regular network services of sports programming were carried on Radio 2 and, for cricket, on Radio 3. Radios 3 and 4 carried Open University programmes on their VHF-FM bands and Radio 4 also carried Schools and Continuing Education output. In 1978 also the BBC began regular broadcasting on radio of recorded material from Parliamentary proceedings (see pp. 78–9). On 27 August 1990 a fifth network, Radio 5, began broadcasting using medium wave frequencies to carry youth and education programmes, and take over sports broadcasting from Radio 2. In March 1994 Radio 5 was relaunched as Radio 5 Live, a news and sport network. Test Match Special was broadcast on Radio 4's long wave frequency. In 2002 the BBC launched a number of additional national radio stations available via digital audio broadcasting (DAB), digital satellite and the internet – 1 Extra (black music), 6 Music (rock and indie music), BBC 7 (arts), Asian Network and 5 Live Sports Extra.

BBC Local Radio

The BBC first began a limited experiment in Local Radio in 1967. The following stations broadcast in England and the Channel Islands.

Radio Berkshire	1992	Radio Lincolnshire	1980
Radio Bristol	1970	BBC London 94.9 (formerly	
Radio Cambridgeshire	1982	GLR, formerly Radio London)	1970
Radio Cleveland (formerly		Radio Merseyside	1967
Radio Teesside)	1970	Radio Newcastle	1971
Radio Cornwall	1983	Radio Norfolk	1980
Radio Cumbria (formerly		Radio Northampton	1982
Radio Carlisle)	1975	Radio Nottingham	1968
CWR (Coventry &		Radio Oxford	1970
Warwickshire Radio)	1990–95	Radio Sheffield	1967
Radio Derby	1971	Radio Shropshire	1985
Radio Devon	1983	Radio Solent	1970
Dorset FM	1993–96	Somerset Sound	1988
Radio Durham	1968–72	Southern Counties Radio	
Radio Essex	1986	(formerly Radio Surrey and	
Radio Furness	1982	Radio Sussex)	1994
Radio Gloucestershire	1988	Radio Stoke	1968
GMR (formerly Radio Manchester)	1970	Radio Suffolk	1990
Radio Guernsey	1982	Radio Surrey	1991–94
Radio Hereford & Worcester	1989	Radio Sussex (formerly	
Radio Humberside	1971	Radio Brighton)	1968–94
Radio Jersey	1982	Three Counties Radio	
Radio Kent (formerly		(formerly Radio Bedfordshire)	1985
Radio Medway)	1970	Radio WM (formerly	
Radio Lancashire (formerly Radio		Radio Birmingham)	1970
Blackburn)	1971	Wiltshire Sound	1989
Radio Leeds	1968	Radio York	1983
Radio Leicester	1967		

BBC Television

On 2 November 1936 the first scheduled public service television was started from Alexandra Palace. The service was suspended from September 1939 until

June 1946. The first stations outside London, in the Midlands and the North, began transmitting in 1949 and 1951 respectively. By 1966, with more than 100 transmitting stations, BBC Television was within the range of more than 99% of the population of the United Kingdom. In April 1964 a second BBC channel was opened in the London area. In 1967 it began broadcasting in colour; by this time it was available to more than two-thirds of the population of the UK. In 1969 colour transmissions were started on BBC1. BBC1 began breakfast-time broadcasting in 1983. In November 1997 BBC News 24 was launched – a news service initially available only on cable. In September 1998 BBC Parliament, providing live coverage of parliamentary proceedings, went on air (it succeeded a previous private venture, the Parliament channel). Also in September 1998, the BBC launched BBC Choice, an entertainment channel available only on digital broadcasting systems; it was relaunched as BBC3 in 2003, following approval from the Department of Culture, Media and Sport. In 1999 the BBC launched BBC Knowledge, relaunched as BBC4 in 2002. All of these were funded by the licence fee.

World Service television (BBC World) began broadcasting in March 1991, using local transmitters and satellites to reach a large audience initially principally in south and south-east Asia. It is intended to be self-financing through advertising, although it has consistently made a loss. The BBC has become increasingly involved through its commercial arm BBC Worldwide in channels financed by advertising and subscription and aimed primarily at overseas audiences: BBC Prime (an entertainment channel) went on air in 1996, and BBC America in March 1998. In 1997 six channels for the domestic UK market were launched as a joint venture with the American cable television channel Flextech; their content relied heavily on the BBC's back catalogue of programmes.

Broadcast Receiving Licences and BBC Expenditure

Since 1922 the BBC's domestic services have been financed mainly by the issue of licences. World Service radio is funded by grant-in-aid from the Foreign and Commonwealth Office, and some other services, including the BBC World television service, rely on commercial revenue.

The cost of the licence

Year	Sound/black & white	Colour
1979	£12	£34
1981	£15	£46
1985	£18	£58
1988	£21	£62.50
1989	£22	£66
1990	£24	£71

Year	Sound/black & white	Colour
1991	£25.50	£77
1992	£26.50	£80
1993	£27.50	£83
1994	£28	£84.50
1995	£28.50	£86.50
1996	£30	£89.50
1997	£30.50	£91.50
1998	£32.50	£97.50
1999	£33.50	£101
2000	£34.50	£104
2001	£36.50	£109
2002	£37.50	£112
2003	£38.50	£116
2004	£40.50	£121

	Total licences issued 000s	Sound & monochrome TV 000s	Colour TV 000s	Expenditure on revenue account (£000s)	
				Home	External
1980	18,285	5,383	12,902	363,400	40,100
1985	18,716	2,896	15,820	808,700	83,900
1990	19,645	1,681	17,964	1,261,900	132,500
1995	21,700	600	20,500	1,756,500	189,900
2000	23,300	200	22,400	2,328,800	194,900
2004	24,500	100	20,400	2,993,600	233,900

The difference between the total and other licences column is explained by the issue of concessionary licences for the elderly and the blind.

SOURCES:- *BBC Annual Report & Accounts; Annual Abstract of Statistics.*

Independent Broadcasting

The Independent Broadcasting Authority (IBA) replaced the Independent Television Authority in 1973, reflecting the introduction of Independent Local Radio, and the Independent Television Commission (ITC) in 1991, when the Radio Authority was established. The ITC licensed and regulated all commercial television services, terrestrial, cable and satellite, teletext, television advertising and sponsorship, and programme output. In 2003 the Office of Communications (Ofcom) took over all the functions of the ITC, Radio Authority, and Oftel. The following Acts have been passed significantly affecting Independent Broadcasting:

Independent Broadcasting Authority Act, 1979. This Act gave the IBA responsibility for establishing transmitters for a fourth television channel.

Broadcasting Act, 1980. This Act extended the life of the IBA until 1996. It laid down the operating condition of the fourth television channel, which was to be separately established in Wales by the Welsh fourth Channel Authority, and also established a Broadcasting Complaints Commission.

Broadcasting Act, 1981. This consolidated the *Independent Broadcasting Authority Acts, 1973, 1974, and 1978,* and the *Broadcasting Act, 1980.*

Cable and Broadcasting Act, 1984. This made provision for the establishment of a Cable Authority to provide cable programmes and amended the *Broadcasting Act, 1981,* to provide for the establishment of a Satellite Broadcasting Board.

Broadcasting Act, 1987. This extended the period of the contracts between the IBA and the ITV companies, now expiring on 31 December 1992, to give more time for the consideration of a new licensing system.

Broadcasting Act, 1990. This replaced the Independent Broadcasting Authority and the Cable Authority with the Independent Television Commission and the Radio Authority, and laid down new procedures for licensing and regulating commercially funded television services. The most important consequence was that subject to meeting a quality threshold, regional TV licences would be awarded to the highest bidder.

Broadcasting Act, 1996. This amended and replaced certain elements of the 1990 Act, and established a regime for the introduction of digital terrestrial television. It also liberalised rules on media ownership, and merged the Broadcasting Standards Council with the Broadcasting Complaints Commission.

Office of Communications Act, 2002. This established the Office of Communications to replace the ITC, Radio Authority, and Broadcasting Standards Commission.

Communications Act, 2003. This gave Ofcom statutory powers over content and regulation, and relaxed the regime for mergers and foreign takeovers of broadcasting companies.

Independent Broadcasting Authorities

Independent Broadcasting Authority, 1972–90

	Chairman		Director-General
1 Apr 75	Lady Plowden	15 Oct 70	(Sir) B. Young
1 Jan 81	Ld Thomson of Monifieth	31 Oct 82	J. Whitney
1 Jan 89	(Sir) G. Russell	1 Apr 89	Shirley Littler (Lady)

Independent Television Commission, 1991–2003

	Chairman		Chief Executive
1 Jan 91	Sir G. Russell	1 Jan 91	D. Glencross
1 Jan 97	Sir R. Biggam	5 Mar 95	P. Rogers
		1 Sep 00	Patricia Hodgson

Radio Authority, 1991–2003

Chairman		*Chief Executive*	
1 Jan 91	Ld Chalfont	1 Jan 91	P. Baldwin
1 Jan 95	Sir P. Gibbings	1 Jul 95	T. Stoller
1 Jul 03	D. Witherow	1 Jul 03	D. Vick

Office of Communications (Ofcom), 2003–

Chairman

29 Dec 03   D. Currie

Chief Executive

29 Dec 03   S. Carter

Channel 3 – ITV Programme Contracting Companies

The following programme companies have held ITV franchises in the UK in the period since 1979. A reallocation of contracts was announced on 28 December 1980, and took effect in January 1982. The *Broadcasting Act, 1990*, laid down a new procedure under which the newly established Independent Television Commission awarded licences to the highest bidder, subject to programme proposals meeting a quality threshold, and the proposals being considered financially sustainable. In 1992 Yorkshire Television merged with Tyne Tees, although they retained separate identities on air. In November 1993 the Government announced a limited relaxation of the ITV ownership rules, enabling one ITV company to hold two large regional licences, except in London. A number of proposed mergers were subsequently announced, leading to the concentration of most of ITV under Carlton and Granada. In 2002 these two companies announced the intention to merge, and following a competition inquiry the merger went through on 2 February 2004. The deal was largely brokered by M. Green, who was ousted in a shareholder revolt on 21 October 2003, to be succeeded as Chairman of ITV by C. Allen. ITV plc held 12 of the 15 licences – the exceptions being owned by SMG (Scottish and Grampian), Ulster TV and Channel.

On air *Off air*	*Company*	*Franchise Areas*
17 Feb 56–31 Dec 81	Associated (ATV)	Midlands (weekday)
3 May 56–	Granada	N.W. England (weekday)
31 Aug 57–	Scottish (STV)	Central Scotland
30 Aug 58–31 Dec 81	Southern	South of England
15 Jan 59–	Tyne-Tees	N.E. England
27 Oct 59–	Anglia	East of England
31 Oct 59–	Ulster	Northern Ireland
29 Apr 61–11 Aug 81	Westward	S.W. England
1 Sep 61–	Border	The Borders
30 Sep 61–	Grampian	N.E. of Scotland
1 Sep 62–	Channel	Channel Islands
4 Mar 68–	Harlech (HTV)	Wales & W. England

On air	Off air	Company	Franchise Areas
29 Jul 68–		Yorkshire	Yorkshire
30 Jul 68–31 Dec 92		Thames	London (weekday)
2 Aug 68–		London Weekend (LWT)	London (weekend)
12 Aug 81–31 Dec 92		TSW	S.W. England
1 Jan 81–31 Dec 92		TVS	South of England
1 Jan 81–		Central	Midlands
1 Feb 83–31 Dec 92		TV-am	(breakfast)
1 Jan 93–		Carlton	London (weekday)
1 Jan 93–		GMTV	(breakfast)
1 Jan 93–		Meridian	South of England
1 Jan 93–		Westcountry	S.W. England

The ITV Network Centre

Founded in 1993, following the *1990 Broadcasting Act*, the Network Centre is an organisation responsible for commissioning new programmes for the network, either from independent production companies or from ITV companies. As well as commissioning all networked programmes, the Centre is also responsible for preparing the network's programme schedule, although ultimate control over scheduling rests with the companies themselves. In 2004 it became the operational centre of ITV plc. The programme budget in 2004 for ITV1 was £849 million. ITV plc is also responsible for ITV2 (launched December 1998), ITV3 (November 2004) and the ITV News Channel (August 2000).

Chief Executive
Jul 92–Oct 95   A. Quinn

Network Director
Oct 92–Jun 97   M. Plantin

Chief Executive
Oct 97–Jan 00   R. Eyre
May 01–May 02   S. Prebble

Chief Executive, ITV plc
Feb 04–   C. Allen

Director of Programmes
Sep 97–Dec 02   D. Liddiment
Feb 03–   N. Pickard

Note: Due to restructuring, M. Plantin took control of the centre on A. Quinn's retirement in 1995. R. Eyre took full control on M. Plantin's departure.

Channel Four

The fourth television channel in the UK is provided by Channel Four Television Corporation in England, Scotland and Northern Ireland, and in Wales by S4C.

The Channel 4 Television Company was established as a subsidiary of the IBA under the *Broadcasting Act, 1980*. It went on air on 2 November 1982. It became an independent corporation as a result of the *Broadcasting Act, 1990*, selling its own advertising airtime from 1 January 1993.

Chairman		*Director/Chief Exec*	
1981	E. Dell	1981	J. Isaacs
1987	Sir R. Attenborough	1989	M. Grade
1992	Sir M. Bishop	1997	M. Jackson
1997	V. Treves	2002	M. Thompson
2004	L. Johnson	2004	A. Duncan

S4C

The S4C Authority, Sianel Pedwar Cymru, the regulatory body for the fourth channel in Wales, was also established under the *Broadcasting Act, 1980*. S4C began transmission on 1 November 1982.

Chairman	
1981	Sir G. Daniel
1986	J. Davies
1992	I. P. Edwards
1998	Mrs E. Stephens

Channel 5

The licence to provide the fifth channel was awarded to Channel 5 Broadcasting in October 1995. Like the Channel 3 licences, it was awarded by competitive tender for a ten-year term from the start of the service which commenced on 30 March 1997. Before the commencement of the service, Channel 5 Broadcasting was required to make arrangements to retune domestic video equipment to eliminate interference where those devices were affected by its transmissions. Around 6 million homes were affected. Channel 5 is regulated by the ITC.

Chairman		*Chief Executive*	
1997	G. Dyke	1997	D. Elstein
1999	R. Sautter	2000	Dawn Airey
2003	T. Betts	2003	Jane Lighting

Finances of Independent Broadcasting, 1979–90
(£ 000s)

Year	ITV revenue	ILR revenue	ITA/IBA/ITC	Govt. Levy
1979	346,796	44,587	22,317	70,018
1980	529,311	44,858	24,443	45,380
1981	611,223	50,824	30,243	55,495
1982	697,170	60,748	36,441	59,110
1983	824,417	70,800	53,769	38,673
1984	912,265	75,700	58,253	28,321
1985	982,603	72,100	62,595	41,409

Year	ITV revenue	ILR revenue	ITA/IBA/ITC	Govt. Levy
1986	1,183,000	79,006	65,331	22,090
1987	1,325,871	99,400	68,052	76,225
1988	1,508,400	125,000	71,531	87,553
1989	1,613,537	145,000	74,919	100,139
1990	1,613,672	143,400	74,759	108,298

SOURCE:- B. MacDonald, *Broadcasting in the United Kingdom – A Guide to Information Sources* (2nd edn, 1993).

Finances of Independent Television, 1991–2000
Net Advertising Revenue (£m)

	ITV	C4	S4C	TVam/GMTV	Total	Levy/Tender payment
1991	1,344	250	3.5	74	1,672	114
1992	1,411	242	3	75	1,731	69
1993	1,400	328	4	64	1,796	369
1994	1,501	391	6	74	1,972	381
1995	1,585	446	8	80	2,119	397
1996	1,658	489	8	77	2,256	412
1997	1,682	510	9	71	2,272	423
1998	1,764	553	9	65	2,777	462
1999	1,874	590	9	70	2,889	398
2000	1,912	604	9	58	2,566	n/a

Sponsorship of terrestrial television rose from £9 million in 1992 to £31 million in 1997.

Note: Exchequer levy ceased in 1992. Tender payments, which are the price paid to the Treasury for Channel 3, Channel 5, teletext and cable licences, are made up of two parts: percentage of qualifying revenue, set by the ITC, and the cash bid each company made for their licence, index linked and payable annually. When Ofcom replaced the ITC it ceased publishing this data in this form.

SOURCE:- *ITC Annual Report and Accounts, 1992–2000*.

Cable Television

There were experiments with cable television as early as the 1950s, with localised relay operators offered wired television in areas of poor reception. In 1972 community cable television services were established in Greenwich, Bristol, Swindon, Sheffield and Wellingborough, but most turned out not to be financially viable. In 1983 a Government White Paper took up the recommendations of the Hunt Committee and proposed granting interim licences for new cable services providing new programming material, financed by private enterprise. This was the basis of the *Cable and Broadcasting Act, 1984*, which established the Cable Authority as the regulatory body. Under the *Broadcasting Act, 1990*, the ITC took over these functions with effect from 1 January 91. There are restrictions on ownership of cable operators which bar existing terrestrial TV companies or political or religious organisations from gaining control.

Cable Authority, 1984–90

Chairman		*Director-General*	
1984	R. Burton	1984	J. Davey

Multichannel Television

The origins of direct broadcasting by satellite can be traced back to the first live television transmissions by the Telstar satellite on 11 July 1962. But the development of a service direct into people's homes was hampered by the limitations of the technology and the large capital cost. The legislative framework for digital television was set out in the *Broadcasting Act 1996*, enabling the ITC to license and regulate commercial digital services. Digital signals allow far more information to be transmitted, meaning better reception, more channels, easier encryption, and the potential for interactive services such as home shopping and home banking. Analogue television will eventually be phased out, although no date has been set for discontinuing it.

Chronology of development of multichannel and digital broadcasting

Nov 82	Home Office accepts Part Report's findings on satellite system technology.
Jul 84	BBC and ITV companies are joined by other companies in 'Club of 21' to plan for DBS services.
Jun 85	Satellite Broadcasting Board tells Government the consortium cannot proceed, due to prohibitive cost of using British-made satellite stipulated by Government.
Apr 86	IBA advertises for 15 year contract for DBS on system of contractor's choice.
Dec 86	British Satellite Broadcasting wins contract, proposing to transmit from the Marcopolo high-power satellite using the latest D-MAC transmission technology and 'squarial' home dish aerials. Major shareholders include Anglia, Granada and Pearson.
Jun 88	R. Murdoch announces plans for Sky Television on Astra satellite.
Feb 89	Sky Television begins transmission.
Apr 90	BSB begins DBS transmissions.
Nov 90	BSB and Sky announce merger to form British Sky Broadcasting (BSkyB).
May 92	BSkyB buys exclusive rights to live FA Premier League football coverage.
Oct 98	BSkyB launches UK's first digital TV service and attracts 100,000 customers in its first month. Digital terrestrial TV broadcasts start.
Nov 98	British Digital Broadcasting launches its pay TV service under the ON digital brand name (subsequently changed to ITV Digital).
Sep 01	BSkyB reaches 5 million digital subscribers and switches off its analogue service.
May 02	ITV Digital closes down.
Oct 02	Freeview launched, offering free digital terrestrial programmes via a set-top box.

Channel Share of Viewing

(based on all transmission hours for all areas receiving TV)

	BBC1	BBC2	ITV	C4	C5	Others
1979	46	11	43	–	–	–
1980	46	11	43	–	–	–
1981	39	11	50	–	–	–
1982	38	12	50	–	–	–
1983	37	11	48	4	–	–
1984	36	19	48	5	–	–
1985	35	11	47	7	–	–
1986	36	11	45	8	–	–
1987	37	12	43	8	–	–
1988	38	11	42	9	–	–
1989	39	11	42	9	–	–
1990	38	10	43	9	–	–
1991	35	10	42	10	–	4
1992	34	10	41	11	–	5
1993	33	10	40	11	–	6
1994	32	11	37	11	–	9
1995	32	11	37	11	–	9
1996	33	12	35	11	–	10
1997	31	12	33	11	2	12
1998	30	11	32	10	4	13
1999	28	11	31	10	5	14
2000	27	11	29	11	6	17
2001	27	11	27	10	6	20
2002	26	11	24	10	6	22
2003	26	11	24	10	7	24
2004	25	10	23	10	7	26

SOURCES:- JICTAR (to 1980); BARB (from July 1981).

Penetration of Multichannel and Digital Television

(figures for January) (000s of homes)

	Satellite	DTT	Cable	Total
1992	1,893		409	2,302
1993	2,387		625	3,012
1994	2,754		744	3,498
1995	3,060		973	4.033
1996	3,542		1,399	4,941
1997	3,804		1,845	5,649
1998	4,117		2,471	6,588
1999	4,414		2,911	7,126
2000	4,196		3,352	7,618

	Satellite	DTT	Cable	Total
2001	5,450		3,490	9,010
2002	5,732	794	3,794	10,320
2003	6,497	873	3,440	10,600
2004	7,016	2,075	3,277	12,036

SOURCE:- BARB.

Independent Local Radio

Under the *Sound Broadcasting Act, 1972*, the IBA (from 1991 the Radio Authority) were given the responsibility for issuing licences to independent local radio stations. They also regulated programme and advertising output. The first stations to go on air were Capital Radio and LBC in London in October 1973. The first outside London was Radio Clyde in Glasgow in December 1973.

1988	First commercial station 'splits' frequencies (broadcasting different stations on FM and AM frequencies). First to do it permanently was CountySound.
1989	'Incremental' commercial radio stations launched in London, Birmingham, Manchester, Bristol and Bradford as alternative services. While the term 'incremental' is now no longer used, these stations were mainly aimed at ethnic minorities in particular areas – broadcasting black dance music, or asian music to widen listener choice.
1990	Independent Broadcasting Authority (the commercial radio and television authority) splits into the Independent Television Commission and the Radio Authority, with the Broadcasting Act allowing more deregulation in the industry.
1992	Launch of Classic FM, first national commercial radio station, on 7 September. The first commercial station to play anything other than 24-hour pop music, the rapid growth of advertising on commercial radio is attributed to Classic FM.
1992	Launch of RAJAR, a body jointly funded by commercial radio and the BBC, giving industry-approved listening figures for all subscribing UK radio services.
1993	Launch of Virgin 1215, now Virgin Radio, on 30 April.
1994	Radio 1 leaves AM frequencies for new commercial station.
1995	Talk Radio UK begins broadcasting on 14 February (now 'TalkSport').
1997	Radio Authority launches Sallies, small scale local licences for smaller communities.
2002	Launch of Digital Audio Broadcasting (DAB) radio leads to rapid increase in number of radio stations: over 700 by early 2005.
2003	Radio Authority replaced by Ofcom.

Broadcasting Complaints Commission, 1981–96

This was established under the *Broadcasting Act, 1980* (amended by the Broadcasting Act, 1981 and the *Cable and Broadcasting Act, 1984*, and replaced by the *Broadcasting Act, 1990*) to consider and adjudicate on complaints of unfair treatment or invasion of privacy by BBC, ITC or Radio Authority licensed services. Its findings are published in the *Radio Times*, *TV Times*. etc. where appropriate, or broadcast on air.

Chairman

1981	Lady Pike
1985	Sir T. Skyrme
1987	Lady Anglesey
1992	Brigid Wells
1992	P. Pilkington
1996	Jane Leighton

Broadcasting Standards Council, 1988–96

This was established by the Home Secretary in 1988, and put on a statutory footing by the *Broadcasting Act, 1990*, to consider standards in portrayal of sex and violence, and matters of taste and decency on TV, radio and video.

Chairman

1988	Sir W. Rees-Mogg
1993	Lady Howe

Broadcasting Standards Commission, 1997–2003

This was established by the *Broadcasting Act, 1996*, to take over the work of the Broadcasting Complaints Commission and the Broadcasting Standards Council. It was replaced by Ofcom on 29 December 2003.

Chairman

1997	Lady Howe
1999	Ld Holme
2001	Ld Dubs

The Internet as a News Provider

From the early 1990s the internet played an increasingly important part as a provider of news in the UK. All the major broadcasters and newspapers entered the market with news services on the internet. The number of page impressions – the industry standard measure of usage – has risen every year, with spectacular peaks of usage coinciding with major news events (elections, September 11, military conflicts, the Indian Ocean tsunami). A study in 2003 by KPMG on behalf of the Department of Culture, Media and Sport, relying on figures collated by Nielsen Netratings for the first quarter of 2003 (including the Iraq war), revealed the following:

	Reach (%)	Total page views (million)	Page views per person	Visits per person	Minutes use	Share of time online (%)
News on BBCi	50.7	139.2	38.5	4.71	0:29:42	50.2
Guardian Unlimited	22.3	26.6	16.7	2.71	0:11:02	8.2
Freeserve News	17.1	6.5	5.4	2.53	0:05:53	3.3
CNN.com	12.3	10.7	12.2	2.62	0:08:24	3.4
Electronic Telegraph	10.1	18.5	25.6	4.14	0:24:18	8.2
Sky News UK	7.8	8.2	14.7	2.35	0:07:49	2.0
Times Online	7.5	9.4	17.7	2.48	0:12:34	3.1
Annova	7.0	6.3	12.6	2.45	0:08:48	2.1
Yahoo! News	7.0	7.6	15.2	4.87	0:15:24	3.6
MSN News	6.8	2.8	5.7	3.22	0:04:13	1.0
MSNBC	5.9	1.9	4.5	1.69	0:03:17	0.6
The Sun	5.3	12.9	34.2	4.76	0:17:59	3.2
Google News	5.1	2.0	5.6	1.82	0:02:14	0.4
FT.com	4.4	9.2	29.5	3.77	0:21:43	3.2
Guardian (Observer)	4.1	0.9	3.1	1.40	0:02:53	0.4
Genre sample total (39 sites)	7,137,000	290.2	40.7	5.38	0:29:58	100.0%

SOURCE:- Nielson//NetRatings Custom Analysis (UK Home Panel, quarter to March 2003).

Inquiries into Broadcasting

Chairman	Set up	Reported	Cd. No.	Cost
Ld Hunt of Tanworth	Apr 82	Oct 82	8679	£47,388
Sir A. Part	Jul 82	Nov 82	8751	£34,625
A. Peacock	May 85	Jul 86	9824	£268,761
J. Sadler	Feb 89	Mar 91	1436	£215,000

SOURCES:- A. Davidson, *Under the Hammer: The Inside Story of the 1991 ITV Franchise Battle* (1992); B. MacDonald, *Broadcasting in the United Kingdom: A Guide to Information Sources* (1993); N. B. Sendall, *Independent Television in Britain* (vols 1 & 2, 1982 & 1983); J. Potter, *Independent Television in Britain* (vols 3 & 4, 1989 & 1990); P. Bonner with L. Aston, *Independent Television in Britain* (vol 5, 1998).

XII
Political Allusions

The student of political history becomes familiar with allusive references to places, events, scandals, phrases and quotations. This chapter attempts to collect the most outstanding of these allusions.

Political Place-Names

At one time or another in the past 25 years the following place-names were sufficiently famous to be alluded to without further explanation. Any such list must necessarily be very selective. No foreign names are included here even though that means omitting the Falklands and the Gulf. No venues of party conferences are included, even though that means omitting Brighton (Conservatives in 1984) or Blackpool (Labour in 1994). No constituency names are included as such, even though that means omitting some which are indelibly associated with individuals like Finchley (Margaret Thatcher's seat 1959–92) or others where sensational elections had a lasting national impact, like Crosby (by-election won by Shirley Williams in 1981).

Aldermaston, Berkshire. Site of Atomic Weapons Research Establishment. Site of the Campaign for Nuclear Disarmament's protests during the 1980s.

Balmoral Castle, Aberdeenshire. Summer home of the Sovereign since 1852.

Brixton, London, SW2. Scene of anti-police riots in April and July 1981.

Buckingham Palace. Bought by George III in 1761. Official residence of the Sovereign since 1837.

Carlton Club. London meeting place of Conservatives.

Carmelite House, EC4. Headquarters of the *Daily Mail* until 1988.

Catherine Place. London home of T. Garel-Jones, and meeting place of ministers on 20 November 1990.

Chequers, Buckinghamshire. Country house given to the nation by Lord Lee of Fareham in 1917 and used as country residence for Prime Ministers from 1921.

Chevening, Kent. Country House bequeathed to the nation by Earl Stanhope. Now allocated by the Prime Minister to a Cabinet colleague. Site of Budget preparations in the 1980s and 1990s.

Coldharbour Lane, Brixton, London. Childhood home of J. Major, featured in 1991 party conference speech and in party election broadcast in 1992.

Congress House, Gt Russell St, WC1. Headquarters of Trades Union Congress 1960–.

Cowley St, London, SW1. Headquarters of the Social Democratic Party, 1981–88, and of the (Social and) Liberal Democrats 1988–.

Dorneywood, Buckinghamshire. Country house bequeathed to the nation in 1954 by Ld Courtauld-Thomson as an official residence for any minister designated by the Prime Minister.

Downing St, SW1. Number 10 is the Prime Minister's official residence. Number 11 is the official residence of the Chancellor of the Exchequer. Number 12 houses the offices of the Government Whips.

Ettrick Bridge, Roxburgh. Constituency home of Sir D. Steel since 1966. Scene of meeting of Alliance leaders, 29 May 1983.

Fleet St, EC4. Location of *Daily Telegraph* and *Daily Express* until the late 1980s. Generic name for the London press.

Grand Hotel, Brighton. Scene of bombing on 11 October 1984 of Conservative Conference Headquarters.

Granita, London N1. Restaurant where T. Blair and G. Brown met in May 1994 to discuss who should stand for the leadership of the Labour Party.

Greenham Common, Berkshire. Air base at which Cruise missiles were first sited (November 1983). Women protesters camped outside it from September 1981 until 1991.

Holy Loch, Argyll. Site of US atomic submarine base 1962–92.

Holyrood, Edinburgh. Site of the Scottish Parliament, 2004–.

Islington. London borough where T. Blair and other New Labour figures lived 1994–97.

Limehouse, E14. Home of D. Owen 1965– and scene of meeting on 25 January 1981, which produced 'The Limehouse Declaration' which anticipated the formation of the Social Democratic Party.

Maze, The, County Antrim (formerly Long Kesh). Prison where many convicted terrorists were held from 1968 onwards. Scene of hunger strike in which ten Republican prisoners died in 1981.

Millbank. The BBC moved their Westminster operations to Number 4 Millbank in 1990, and were soon followed by ITN and Sky News. The Labour Party's media and electioneering operation was in the Millbank Tower from 1995 to 2002.

Molesworth, Cambridgeshire. Air base. Scene of demonstrations against Cruise missiles 1985–93.

Old Queen St, SW1. Headquarters of Labour Party 2002–05.

Portland Place, W1. Headquarters of the British Broadcasting Corporation 1932–.

St James Palace, W1. Royal Palace. Foreign Ambassadors continue to be accredited to the Court of St James.

St Paul's, Bristol. Scene of anti-police riot, April 1980.

Sandringham House, Norfolk. Royal residence since 1861.

Smith Square, SW1. Location of the Labour Party Headquarters (Transport House) 1928–80; of the Conservative Party Headquarters 1958–2004 and of the Liberal Party Headquarters 1965–68.

Southall. West London suburb with large population of Asian origin. Scene of violent disturbances in anti-National Front riot, 23 April 1979.

Stormont, Belfast. Site of Parliament and Government of Northern Ireland.

Threadneedle St, EC2. Site of the Bank of England.

Toxteth, Liverpool 8. Scene of rioting, July 1981.

Victoria St, SW1. Location of the Conservative Party Headquarters (Number 25) 2004–, and Headquarters of the Labour Party Campaign Headquarters (Number 55), 2005.

Walworth Rd, London, SE17. 150 Walworth Rd was the headquarters of the Labour Party 1980–97.

Wapping, East London. Site of headquarters of News International, where *The Times*, the *Sunday Times*, the *Sun* and the *News of the World* have been produced and printed since 1986.

Westminster, London. Parliament meets in the Palace of Westminster and Westminster has become a generic name for parliamentary activity.

Whitehall, London. Many Government departments are situated in Whitehall and it has become a generic name for civil service activity.

Windsor Castle, Berkshire. Official royal residence since the eleventh century.

Political Quotations

From time to time an isolated phrase becomes an established part of the language of political debate. Such phrases are frequently misquoted and their origins are often obscure. Here are a few which seem to have had an especial resonance. The list is far from comprehensive; it merely attempts to record the original source for some well-used quotations.

Labour isn't working.

Slogan on Conservative poster designed by Saatchi and Saatchi, showing dole queue in August 1978 and widely used in the 1979 election.

Crisis? What Crisis? (Journalist: 'What ... of the mounting chaos in the country at the moment?' Callaghan: 'I don't think that other people in the world would share the view that there is mounting chaos.')

Sun headline, 11 January 1979, referring to J. CALLAGHAN at London airport on return home from Guadaloupe summit during widespread strikes, 10 January 1979.

The Labour Way is the Better Way.

Title of Labour election manifesto published April 1979.

I don't see how we can talk with Mrs Thatcher ... I will say to the lads, come on, get your *snouts in the trough.*

S. WEIGHELL, speaking in London, 10 April 1979, echoing his speech at the Labour Party Conference, Blackpool, 6 October 1978, 'If you want it to go out ... that you now believe in the philosophy of the pig trough those with the biggest snouts get the largest share, I reject it.'

There is no alternative.

A phrase widely attributed to Margaret THATCHER in 1979 and 1980.

We are fed up with *fudging and mudging,* with mush and slush.

D. OWEN, at Labour Party Conference, Blackpool, 2 October 1980.

The Lady's not for turning.

Margaret THATCHER, Conservative Party Conference, Brighton, 10 October 1980.

Breaking the mould of British politics.

Phrase widely used after 1981 about the goals of the Alliance. Its origin seems to lie in R. JENKINS, *What Matters Now* (1972), quoting Andrew Marvell on Cromwell 'Casting Kingdoms of Old/Into another mould.'

Go back to your constituencies and *prepare for Government.*

D. STEEL addressing Liberal Party Conference in Llandudno, 18 September 1981.

He [his unemployed father in the 1930s] didn't riot. *He got on his bike* and looked for work.

N. TEBBIT, Conservative Party Conference, Blackpool, 15 October 1981.

'GOTCHA.'

Sun headline on 4 May 1982 on the sinking of the Argentine cruiser Belgrano.

Let me make one thing absolutely clear. *The NHS is safe with us.*

Margaret THATCHER, addressing Conservative Party Conference, Brighton, 8 October 1982.

Heckler: 'At least Mrs Thatcher has got *guts.'* N. Kinnock: 'And it's a pity that people had to leave theirs on the ground at *Goose Green* in order to prove it.'

N. KINNOCK during TV South's election programme *The South Decides*, 5 June 1983.

The enemy within is just as dangerous to our liberty ... It is battle that we must win.

Margaret THATCHER referring to A. SCARGILL and the Miners' Strike, article in *Daily Express*, 20 July 1984.

We must try to starve the terrorist and the hijacker of *the oxygen of publicity on which they depend.*

Margaret THATCHER, quoted in *Financial Times*, 16 July 1985.

I'll tell you what happens with impossible promises. You start with implausible resolutions, which are then pickled into a rigid dogma or code. And you end up with the *grotesque chaos of Labour Council –* a Labour Council *– hiring taxis to scuttle round a city handing out redundancy notices* to its own workers.

N. KINNOCK, addressing Labour Party Conference in Bournemouth, 1 October 1985 (these words are from the advance text).

As one person said, it is perhaps being *economical with the truth.*

Sir R. ARMSTRONG, Permanent Secretary to the Cabinet, under cross examination in an Australian Court over the British

Government's attempt to prevent publication of the book *Spycatcher*, 18 November 1986. The phrase can be traced back to Mark Twain and Edmund Burke.

Why am I the first Kinnock *for a thousand generations* to be able to get to university?

N. KINNOCK, speech 15 May 1987.

I think we've been through a period where too many people have been given to understand that if they have a problem, it's the government's job to cope with it ... They're casting their problem on society. And, you know, *there is no such thing as society*. There are individual men and women, and there are families, and no government can do anything except through people, and people must look to themselves first.

Margaret THATCHER, article in *Woman's Own*, 31 October 1987.

Nigel was Chancellor. Nigel's position was *unassailable*, unassailable.

Margaret THATCHER, in an interview with B. Walden on ITV three days after N. Lawson's resignation, 29 October 1989

I have a young family and for the next few years I should like to devote more time to them while they are still so young.

N. FOWLER in his letter of resignation to the Prime Minister, 3 January 1990.

I am naturally very sorry to see you go, but understand your reasons for doing so, particularly your wish to be able to *spend more time with your family.*

Margaret THATCHER replying to N. FOWLER's resignation letter, 3 January 1990.

The President of the Commission, M. Delors, said at this conference the other day that he wanted the European Parliament to be the democratic body of the Community, he wanted the Commission to be the Executive, and he wanted the Council of Ministers to be the Senate. *No. No. No.*

Margaret THATCHER speaking in the House of Commons on her return from the Rome summit, 30 October 1990.

The time has come for others to consider their own response to the *tragic conflict of loyalties* with which I have myself wrestled for perhaps too long.

Sir G. HOWE in his resignation speech, House of Commons, 13 November 1990.

Britain has done itself no good by the distinction drawn between the skill of blue collar and white collar workers ... In the next ten years we will have to continue to make changes which will make the whole of this country a *genuinely classless society*.

J. MAJOR writing in *Today*, 24 November 1990.

I want to see us build *a country that is at ease with itself*, a country that is confident and a country that is able and willing to build a better quality of life for all its citizens.

J. MAJOR speaking in Downing Street on becoming Prime Minister, 28 November 1990.

Rising unemployment and the recession have been the price we've had to pay to get inflation down. But that is *a price well worth paying*.

N. LAMONT, House of Commons, 16 May 1991.

The *green shoots of economic spring* are appearing once again.

N. LAMONT speaking at the Conservative Party Conference, 9 October 1991.

Labour's Double Whammy.

Slogan attacking Labour tax plans coined by Conservative Central Office and used on pre-election publicity material, February 1992.

I think what is important is if we can get the government to understand the notion of *tough on crime, tough on the causes of crime*. If we can get them to agree to that then we've got a chance.

T. BLAIR, in an interview on *The World This Weekend*, BBC Radio, 21 February 1993.

Je ne regrette rien.

N. LAMONT speaking at a press conference during the Newbury by-election campaign, 12 May 1993.

Fifty years from now Britain will still be the country of long shadows on county grounds, *warm beer*, invincible green suburbs, dog lovers and pools fillers and – as George Orwell said – 'old maids bicycling to holy communion through the morning mist' and – if we get our way – Shakespeare still be read even in school.

J. MAJOR, Speech to Conservative Group for Europe, 22 April 1993.

I can bring other people into the Cabinet, that is right, but where do you think most of the poison has come from? It is coming

J. MAJOR, referring to Eurosceptic critics in Cabinet in off-the-record remarks to M. Brunson of ITN, 23 July 1993.

from the dispossessed and the never-possessed. You and I can both think of ex-ministers who are going around causing all sorts of trouble. Would you like three more of the *bastards* out there?

The old values – neighbourliness, decency, courtesy – they're still alive, they're still the best of Britain ... It is time to return to those core values, time to get back to basics, to self-discipline and respect for the law, to consideration for others, to accepting responsibility for yourself and your family and not shuffling off on other people and the State.

J. MAJOR, Conservative Party Conference, Blackpool, 8 October 1993.

Under my leadership, I will *never* allow this country to *be isolated* or left behind *in Europe.*

T. BLAIR, Labour Party Conference, Blackpool, 4 October 1994.

Our party: New Labour. Our mission: New Britain. *New Labour New Britain.*

T. BLAIR, Labour Party Conference, Blackpool, 4 October 1994.

Our new economic approach does not simply require us to adapt to changes in the practical world but is also rooted in changes in the world of economic ideas. Ideas which stress the growing importance of international co-operation and new theories of economic sovereignty across a wide range of areas – macroeconomics, trade, the environment, the growth of *post neo-classical endogenous growth theory* and the symbiotic relationships between growth and investment in people and infrastructure ...

G. BROWN, in a speech attributed to his adviser E. BALLS discussing how improved public services could boost growth, at a conference on global economics at the National Film Theatre, 27 September 1994.

If is falls to me to start a fight to cut out the cancer of bent and twisted journalism in our country *with the simple sword of truth and the trusty shield of British fair play,* so be it.

J. AITKEN, launching a libel action against the *Guardian* newspaper, 10 April 1995. He subsequently lost the action and was jailed for perjury.

On message.

Phrase attributed by journalists to Labour Party media officials at the party conference in Brighton, October 1995.

Ask me my three main priorities for government and I will tell you; *education, education and education.*

T. BLAIR, Conference Speech, Blackpool, 1 October 1996.

Tell the kids to get *their scooters off my lawn.*

Words attributed to K. CLARKE at lunch with BBC political correspondents, 4 December 1996, referring to press officials at Conservative Central Office allegedly trying to control his public statements. It was an echo of H. WILSON'S remark to H. Scanlon, 1 June 1969.

New Labour, New Danger.

Conservative poster advertisement during the 1997 election also known as 'demon eyes'.

We have been *elected as New Labour and we will govern as new Labour.*

T. BLAIR victory speech, Royal Festival Hall, 2 May 1997.

There is *something of the night* in his personality.

Remark attributed to Ann WIDDECOMBE referring to M. HOWARD, first quoted in the *Sunday Times*, 11 May 1997.

I think most people who have dealt with me, think *I'm a pretty straight sort of guy* and I am.

T. BLAIR interview on BBC's *On The Record*, 16 November 1997, during the controversy over a donation to the Labour Party by Formula One boss Bernie Ecclestone.

Psychologically flawed.

Phrase attributed to aides of the Prime Minister describing the Chancellor G. BROWN. The Prime Minister's Press Secretary A. CAMPBELL subsequently denied ever using the phrase. First appeared in Sunday newspapers, 18 January 1998.

But ours is *prudence for a purpose* – to meet the people's priorities.

G. BROWN, Budget speech, 17 March 1998.

A day like today is not a day for soundbites, really. But *I feel the hand of history upon our shoulders.* I really do.

T. BLAIR speaking in Belfast before the talks which produced the Good Friday Agreement, 8 April 1998.

I bear the *scars on my back* after two years in government.

T. BLAIR talking about public sector reform during a speech to venture capitalists, 6 July 1999.

The day of the *bog-standard comprehensive* is over.

Quote attributed to A. CAMPBELL speaking as Prime Minister's Official Spokesman about the launch of the Government's Education Green Paper, 12 February 2001.

It is now *a very good day to get out anything we want to bury*. Councillors' expenses?

In a memo written by Jo MOORE at 2.55pm on 11 September 2001, as Special Adviser to Stephen Byers, then Secretary of State for Transport, Local Government & the Regions. Widely quoted as 'a good day to bury bad news'.

The document discloses that his military planning allows for some of the WMD to be *ready within 45 minutes* of an order to use them.

T. BLAIR, foreword to UK Government dossier on Iraq's weapons of mass destruction, 24 September 2002.

Do not underestimate the determination of a *quiet man*.

I. DUNCAN SMITH speech to Conservative Party Conference, 10 October 2002.

I warn the Minister that we are worried about the Government's undermining of British public opinion with such appalling, reprehensible and cack-handed initiatives as the *dodgy dossier* that No. 10 published last week.

B. JENKIN speaking in the House of Commons, 11 February 2003; the *Guardian* had revealed that the Government dossier on Iraq had been plagiarised from the internet.

Downing Street, our source says, ordered a week before publication, ordered it to be *sexed up*, to be made more exciting and ordered more facts to be discovered.

A. GILLIGAN in an interview with J. Humphrys on the *Today* Programme at 6.07am on 29 May 2003 regarding the Government's dossier on Iraq's weapons.

This *grammar school boy* will take no lessons from that public school boy on the importance of children from less privileged backgrounds gaining access to university.

M. HOWARD responding to an attack by T. BLAIR on Conservative plans for higher education at Prime Minister's Questions, 3 December 2003.

There is nothing you could ever say to me now that I could ever believe.	Attributed to G. BROWN speaking to T. BLAIR in Septemper 2004, quoted in *Brown's Britain* by R. PESTON, published 9 January 2005.
Are you thinking what we're thinking?	Conservative Party election slogan, May 2005.

Political Scandals

The following list is not comprehensive but indicates most of the more celebrated examples. A few others are implicit in the list of ministerial resignations
on pp. 27–8.

1976–79	Thorpe (Liberal Leader ultimately acquitted of conspiracy to murder)
1979	Blunt (Spy scandal)
1983	Parkinson (Sex scandal)
1986	Westland (Helicopter takeover)
1992	Mellor (Ministerial indiscretion)
1992	Matrix-Churchill (Arms for Iraq)
1993	Mates (involvement with Asil Nadir scandal)
1994	'Back to Basics' (a succession of six private scandals affecting Ministers and Conservative MPs)
1995–97	Cash for Questions (allegations that a number of Conservative MPs had accepted improper payments)
1997	Ecclestone (allegations that a £1 million donation by Bernie Ecclestone led to Formula One's exemption from a tobacco advertising ban)
1998	Mandelson (resigned from the Cabinet on 23 December 2001 after it emerged he had borrowed £373,000 from the then Paymaster General Geoffrey Robinson to purchase a house in Notting Hill)
1999	Aitken (served seven months in jail after lying in court during his libel case against the *Guardian* and Granada television)
2001	Hinduja (Mandelson resigned from the Government for a second time after admitting making misleading statements about Mr Hinduja's passport application)
2001	Jo Moore (Special adviser who referred to September 11 as 'a very good day to get out anything we want to bury')
2002	Mittal (Blair wrote a letter supporting a bid by Lakshmi Mittal's company to take over Romania's state steel industry after Mr Mittal donated £125,000 to the Labour Party)
2002	Cheriegate (Cherie Blair faced criticism after Peter Foster, partner of Carole Caplin her fitness guru, helped in the purchase of flats in Bristol)
2003	Kelly (Government weapons scientist who took his own life after he was revealed as the source of a story that the government had 'sexed-up' a dossier on Iraq's weapons of mass destruction)
2004	Betsygate (Iain Duncan Smith accused of employing his wife as diary secretary without enough work for her to do)

Major Civil Disturbances and Demonstrations (in Great Britain)

23 Apr 79	Southall (confrontation between police and anti-National Front demonstrators)
2 Apr 80	St Paul's, Bristol (anti-police riots)
11–13 Apr 81	Brixton (anti-police riot with racial overtones; more trouble July 1981)
5–6 Jul 81	Toxteth (major riot)
1981–91	Greenham Common (women's protests against nuclear weapons)
Mar 84–Mar 85	Miners' strike (many confrontations between police and pickets)
6 Oct 85	Broadwater Farm, North London (riot)
Jan 86–Feb 87	Wapping (confrontation between police and pickets)
Mar 90	London and many other places (anti-poll tax demonstrations and riots)
1 Apr 90	Strangeways Prison, Manchester (prisoners' riot)
21 Oct 92	London (march against pit closures)
10 Jul 97	London (countryside march)
1 Mar 98	London (countryside march)
1 May 00	London (anti-capitalist riots)
Sep 00	Across Britain (fuel protests)
Jun/Jul 01	Bradford, Oldham, Burnley (race riots)
22 Sep 02	London (countryside march)
16 Feb 03	London and other cities (anti-war marches)

Political Assassinations (Members of the House of Lords or House of Commons)

5 Apr 1979	A. Neave (IRA bomb in his car at the House of Commons)
27 Aug 1979	Earl Mountbatten (killed by bomb on holiday in the Irish Republic)
10 Oct 1984	Sir A. Berry (IRA bomb at Conservative Conference)
30 Jul 1990	I. Gow (IRA bomb at his Sussex home)

Bibliographical Note

This book does not attempt to provide an extensive bibliography of works on British politics since 1979. We list below some attempts at comprehensive listings in various periods or fields. The main sources of factual data used in compiling this book are mentioned separately in the appropriate sections. There are, however, some works of reference of such major importance and reliability that it seems useful to collect them together here as a help or reminder to those involved in research.

This book originated before the advent of microfiches, CD-Roms and the internet. Much of the original material could only be found between hard covers. Most data in these pages is now available in machine-readable form. As the 1990s advanced, more and more newspaper and government publications appeared on the internet, together with search engines that have greatly facilitated the recovery of information. *The Times* and the *Independent* are each available from 1988 onwards on CD-Rom and from the mid-1990s on the internet, and all other serious journals have followed them; some find the electronic *Telegraph* and *Guardian* to be particularly user-friendly. Computerised library catalogues enable scholars to pursue research through increasingly sophisticated subject indexes. At the conclusion of this note a list of some of the most useful internet sites available in 2005 is provided.

Many of the most useful sources of reference are Stationery Office publications. Summaries, guides and short-cuts to these are provided in the *Stationery Office: Catalogue of Government Publications* (annually), and the Sectional *Lists of Government Publications*, published by the Stationery Office for individual departments. An HMSO *Guide to Official Statistics* has been published biennially since 1976. Chadwyck-Healey have published on CD-Rom and microfiche all government papers since 1986, together with a comprehensive catalogue.

For reference to day-to-day political events the *Official Index to the Times (1906–)* is the most complete guide. *Keesing's Contemporary Archives* (1931–86), *Keesing's Record of World Events* (1987–) and *Keesings Record of UK Events* (1988–97) give a concise summary of news reported in the national press. Brief chronologies of the year's major events (including some very minor ones) are printed in the *Annual Register of World Events*, which also covers them in greater detail in the main text of the book. The Foreign Office have published an annual *Survey of World Affairs* since 1967. Fuller chronologies and narratives are available in the annual volumes *Contemporary Britain* published by the Institute of Contemporary British History since 1990. Briefer summaries of the year's events are to be found in *Whitaker's Almanack*.

For biographical details of leading figures in British politics see the *Dictionary of National Biography* (totally revised in 2004) and the *Concise Dictionary of National Biography*. There is also *Who Was Who* (1971–80, 1981–90 and 1991–95), and for those still alive, *Who's Who*. Appointments are recorded in many official sources. The major annual publications are: the *Imperial Calendar* and *Civil Service List* (replaced in 1973 by two works, *Civil Service Year Book* and *Diplomatic List*), *HM Ministers and Senior Staff in Public Departments* and now published annually, and the *London Gazette*, where appointments are announced officially, which appears about once a fortnight. Since 1978 the House of Commons has published a *Weekly Information Bulletin*. Official appointments are also recorded in the annual Lists of the Foreign Office, the Colonial Office, and the Commonwealth Relations Office, the Army, Navy and Air Force Lists, the Law Lists, and the Annual Estimates of the civil, revenue and service departments.

There are handbooks on Parliament, giving the names of M.P.s, details of procedure and officials: *Dod's Parliamentary Companion* and *Vacher's Parliamentary Companion*. After every General Election *The Times* has published *The Times Guide to the House of Commons*. There is also C. Rallings and M. Thrasher's *British Electoral Facts 1832–1999* (2000).

The annual almanacks provide an extremely useful source of information. Amongst these the most notable are *Whitaker's Almanack*, *The Statesman's Year-Book*, the *Yearbook of International Organisations*, the *United Nations Yearbook* and *Britain: An Official Handbook* (published with varying titles by the Central Office of Information). Another valuable source is *Councils, Committees, and Boards* (10th edn 1998).

The major sources for British statistics are quoted in notes to the tables throughout the book. The most readily available is the official *Annual Abstract of Statistics*. This appears both annually, and in a form covering ten-year periods since 1945. The *Monthly Digest of Statistics* is also very helpful. The Censuses of Population, Industry and Production, though infrequent, provide the firmest figures in their area – much of the information in annual publications is only estimated. The reports of the major revenue departments, the Commissioners for Customs and Excise, the Commissioners for Inland Revenue, and the Registrars-General for England and Wales and for Scotland, are major sources of statistical information; so are the reports of the other Government Departments, and especially the *Gazette* produced until 1995 by the Ministry of Labour and its successor ministries it was succeeded by *Labour Market Trends* in 1995. There is also the annual *Abstract of Labour Statistics*. Other major sources of information are the monthly *Financial Statistics*, the London and Cambridge Economic Service published about three times a year in *The Times' Review of Industry*, B. R. Mitchell and P. Deane's *British Historical Statistics* (2nd edn 1988). Statistical time-series are available in the annual Blue Books on *National Income and Expenditure* (1969–). Much statistical information is presented in A. H. Halsey's *Twentieth Century British Social Trends* (2000). There is also the annual *Social Trends*.

Bibliographical references can be checked through the *British National Bibliography* and the *Cumulative Book Index*; there is also the *London Bibliography of the Social Sciences* (published from 1931 to 1989 and then absorbed into the *International Bibliography of the Social Sciences*, published annually since 1953). For information on many aspects of British politics the *Encyclopaedia Britannica* or *Chambers' Encyclopaedia* may give a lead. Weekly journals, especially *The Economist* (which is indexed), may provide much additional information. Apart from *The Times*, the national dailies were not indexed for the pre-electronic age, which makes reference a slow process. But some newspaper libraries have their own index system and may be of help.

The learned journals with most material on British politics are the *Political Quarterly* (1930–); *Parliamentary Affairs* (1947–); *Public Administration* (1923–85) and *Public Policy and Administration* (1986–); *Political Studies* (1953–); *British Journal of Political Science* (1971–); *The Table* (Journal of the Commonwealth Parliamentary Association, 1931); *Government and Opposition* (1965–); the *Journal of Contemporary History* (1966–); *Contemporary British History* (1986–) and *Twentieth Century British History* (1990–). *International Political Science Abstracts*, published annually since 1951, gives a classified abstract of journal articles, and so does the *British Humanities Index* (1962–). The most comprehensive work is P. Catterall's *British History 1945–87: An Annotated Bibliography* (1994).

Internet Addresses

This list is far from exhaustive, but most of the sites below have links to other relevant sites. One problem with information available on the internet is that sites are continually appearing or disappearing, whilst the addresses of others are liable to alter. All of the internet addresses that follow are correct as of 22 July 2005.

Newspapers

Electronic *Telegraph*: <www.telegraph.co.uk>
Daily Telegraph Opinion: <www.dailytelegraph.co.uk>
The Economist: <www.economist.com>
The *Express*: <www.express.co.uk>
The *Guardian* and the *Observer*: <www.guardian.co.uk>
Financial Times: <www.ft.com>
The *Independent*: <www.independent.co.uk>
The *Mirror*: <www.mirror.co.uk>
The Times and the *Sunday Times*: <www.timesonline.co.uk>

Television

BBC: <www.bbc.co.uk>
BBC News Online: <http://news.bbc.co.uk>
ITN: <www.itn.co.uk>
ITV: <www.itv.com>
Channel 4: <www.channel4.com>
Channel 5: <www.five.tv>
SKY News: <www.sky.com/skynews/home>
CNN: <www.cnn.com>

Political Parties

Conservative Party: <www.conservative-party.org.uk>
Labour Party: <www.labour.org.uk>
Liberal Democrats: <www.libdems.org.uk>
The Green Party: <http://greenparty.org.uk>
Plaid Cymru: <www.plaidcymru.org>
Scottish Conservatives: <www.scottishtories.org.uk>
Scottish Labour Party: <www.scottishlabour.org.uk>
Scottish Liberal Democrats: <www.scotlibdems.org.uk>
Scottish Nationalists: <www.snp.org>
DUP: <www.dup.org.uk>
SDLP: <www.sdlp.ie>
Sinn Fein: <www.sinnfein.ie>
UUP: <www.uup.org>

Government Departments and Agencies

Number 10 Downing Street: <www.number-10.gov.uk>
Benefits (DWP site): <www.dwp.gov.uk/lifeevent/benefits>
The Cabinet Office: <www.cabinet-office.gov.uk>
Child Support Agency: <www.csa.gov.uk>
Crown Prosecution Service: <www.cps.gov.uk>
Dept for Constitutional Affairs: <www.dca.gov.uk>
Dept for Culture, Media and Sport: <www.culture.gov.uk>
Dept for Education and Skills: <www.dfes.gov.uk>
Dept for Environment, Food and the Rural Affairs: <www.defra.gov.uk>
Dept of Health: <www.dh.gov.uk>
Dept for International Development: <www.dfid.gov.uk>
Dept of Trade and Industry: <www.dti.gov.uk>
Dept for Transport: <www.dft.gov.uk>
Dept for Work and Pensions: <www.dwp.gov.uk>
Foreign and Commonwealth Office: <www.fco.gov.uk>
Freedom of Information: <www.foi.gov.uk>

Greenwich 2000, Millennium Dome: <www.greenwich2000.com/millennium/experience/>

HM Revenue and Customs: <www.hmrc.gov.uk/>

HM Treasury: <www.hm-treasury.gov.uk>

The Home Office: <www.homeoffice.gov.uk>

Ministry of Agriculture, Fisheries and Food: see DEFRA

Ministry of Defence: <www.mod.uk>

National Insurance Contributions (Inland Revenue): see HM Revenue and Customs

Office of the Deputy Prime Minister: <www.odpm.gov.uk>

The Northern Ireland Office: <www.nio.gov.uk>

The Scottish Executive: <www.scotland.gov.uk/Home>

The Women's Unit: <www.womenandequalityunit.gov.uk/>

General Information

Directgov – Website of the UK Government: <www.direct.gov.uk>

Official Catalogue of UK pulications since 1980 <http://ukop.co .uk>

Parliament: <www.parliament.uk>

> *Hansard* – House of Commons: <www.parliament.the-stationery-office.co.uk/pa/cm/cmpubns.htm>
>
> *Hansard* – House of Lords: <www.publications.parliament.uk/pa/ld/ldhansrd.htm>
>
> House of Commons Research Papers: <www.parliament.uk/parliamentary_publications_and_archives/research_papers.cfm>

Bills Before Parliament: <www.parliament.the-stationery-office.co.uk/pa/pabills.htm>

Electoral Commission: <www.electoralcommission.org.uk>

Dictionary of National Biography: <www.oxforddnb.com>

Hansard Society: <www.hansard-society.org.uk>

Parliamentary and Health Service Ombudsman: <www.ombudsman.org.uk>

Senior Judicial List (via Dept for Constitutional Affairs website): <www.dca.gov.uk/judicial/senjudfr.htm>

Government Information Service – now links to Directgov: <www.direct.gov.uk/Homepage/fs/en>

Central Office of Information: <www.coi.gov.uk>

Statistics (Statbase) – now integrated in to main ONS site – use search facility

Office of National Statistics: <www.statistics.gov.uk/>

The National Audit Office: <www.nao.org.uk/>

The Stationery Office: <www.tso.co.uk>

UK Official Documents: <www.official-documents.co.uk>

Office of Public Sector Information: <www.opsi.gov.uk/>

Local Government Information Unit: <www.lgiu.gov.uk>

Scottish Parliament: <www.scottish.parliament.uk>
National Assembly for Wales: <www.wales.gov.uk/index.htm>
Social Science Information Gateway: <www.sosig.ac.uk/>
British Election Manifestos since 1945: <www.psr.keele.ac.uk/area/uk/man.htm>
International Bibliography of the Social Sciences: <www.bids.ac.uk>
Institute of Historical Research: <www.history.ac.uk/>
Public Record Office: <www.pro.gov.uk>
Directory of UK Government on the Web: <www.tagish.co.uk/links/>

International Organisations

Main Europe Portal: <www.europe.eu.int>
European Court of Human Rights: <www.echr.coe.int/echr>
European Court of Human Rights Judgments: <www.echr.coe.int/ECHR/
    EN/Header/Case+Law/Case+law+information/Lists+of+judgments/>
European Parliament: <www.europarl.eu.int>
NATO: <www.nato.int>
United Nations: <www.un.org>
World Bank: <www.worldbank.org>

Index